Organized Crime

Organized Crime

From Trafficking
to Terrorism

Volume Two

Frank G. Shanty,

Editor

Patit Paban Mishra,
Contributing Editor

A B C · C L I O

Santa Barbara, California   Denver, Colorado   Oxford, England

Library of Congress Cataloging-in-Publication Data

Organized crime : from trafficking to terrorism / Frank G. Shanty, editor, Patit Paban Mishra, contributing editor.
      p. cm.
   Includes bibliographical references and index.
   ISBN-13: 978-1-57607-337-7 (hard copy : alk. paper)
   ISBN-13: 978-1-59884-102-2 (ebook)
  1. Organized crime.   2. Terrorism.   I. Shanty, Frank, 1950–   II. Mishra, Patit Paban.
HV6441.O745 2007
364.1'06—dc22

                                                                        2007017471

07   06   05   04   03   10 9 8 7 6 5 4 3 2 1

This book is also available on the World Wide Web as an eBook. Visit http://www.abc-clio.com for details.

ABC-CLIO, Inc.
130 Cremona Drive, P.O. Box 1911
Santa Barbara, California 93116-1911

This book is printed on acid-free paper. ∞
Manufactured in the United States of America

Contents

Contents

Tables referenced in a document can be accessed by viewing the original source document.

Primary Source Documents

Introduction

This volume provides a compilation of national and international laws and treaties that have been adopted in an attempt to control, if not curtail, the nefarious activities of organized criminal groups and terrorist organizations. In the post-9/11 world, with so much attention being directed to a possible nexus between criminals and terrorists, the documents presented in this volume focus on terrorism as well as global organized crime.

Criminal activity is as old as human civilization. To some degree it is extant in all historical periods, and thus it would be difficult to find a crime-free society or nation. In modern times or, more specifically, in the contemporary period, crime has played a pervasive role. With sophisticated communication systems and ample resources, crime with its continually expanding global reach poses a danger to human society and threatens national as well as international security. Compared to earlier periods, crime has become more organized and spans national borders.

Structured criminal groups are engaging in a wide range of unlawful activities. These activities are not confined by borders, ethical considerations, or the impact on innocent persons. The sole motive of these groups is to achieve the nefarious goal of becoming rich by any means or, in the case of certain terrorist groups, to achieve specific political aims. Apart from getting a helping hand from state-of-the-art technology, organized criminal groups are aided by corrupt officials, inadequate legislation, bank secrecy, economic and political instability, drug addiction, the lure of becoming rich, etc. In the post–Cold War period, the end of communism in the Soviet Union and in Eastern Europe along with the emergence of weak democracies has resulted in a proliferation of criminal groups. Crimes such as narcotics trafficking, money laundering, terrorist financing, human trafficking, extortion, kidnapping, and cyber crimes have become globalized. Modern channels of communication (satellite and cellular phones and e-mails) have become the preferred method of communication between members of various criminal entities. Doing business in a clandestine way, these criminal operators are engaged in legitimate business enterprises such as real estate, construction work, dock loading, licensed gambling, financial organizations, and trash dumping. These legitimate ventures often serve as fronts to hide illegal activities and profits.

Drug production and trafficking and the abuse of these agents are global phenomena. The illegal drug trade involves the cultivation, production, and distribution of such substances as cannabis, heroin, and cocaine. The two most important areas for the cultivation of raw opium are the Golden Triangle of Laos, Myanmar, and Thailand and the Golden Crescent region of Afghanistan, Pakistan, and Iran. Drug abuse affects persons of all ages, classes, and ethnic groups. The consequences are generations of addicted individuals, increased rates of crime, and a significant rise in the number of people contracting the AIDS virus. Drug-related problems bring misery and hardship to millions of families and threaten the collective security of nations. The criminal groups engaged in the trafficking and distribution of illegal drugs generate billions of dollars in profits. Afghanistan, Myanmar, and Laos are major producers of illicit opium and heroin. Colombia is the largest supplier of illicit coca in the world. Apart from these drugs, there are also amphetamine-type stimulants, with clandestine laboratories operated by different crime groups. The menace from opiates and other illegal drugs could be attested by the fact that about 5 percent of the world's population consumes these illicit products. Additionally, numerous studies have confirmed that the global trade in these substances spawns domestic and international instability by sustaining regional insurgencies and conflict.

Open or porous borders, poverty, wars, ethnic conflicts, and gender discrimination are factors behind human trafficking. Organized crime groups have established a profitable business in this arena. Human trafficking generates billions of dollars annually. Trafficking in women and children for sex and forced labor is one of the most heinous crimes. The victim leads a life of misery that involves forced drug use, rape, starvation, and seclusion. Almost every country in the world is affected by human trafficking, and the majority of the victims are from Asia. A thriving sex industry exists in many parts of the world. The largest source for prostitution comes from the former Soviet Union and East European countries. The major traffickers are gangs emanating from China, Mexico, Russia, and Italy who possess local networks so as to provide victims with false documentation, transport, and safe harbor.

Organized criminals need to hide their illegal profits so that the money can be used without any hindrance by government regulatory bodies and law enforcement. Through multiple transactions, money laundering transforms finances for criminal entrepreneurs. Illegal financial transactions total an estimated $300–500 billion per year. Inadequate legal provisions, bank secrecy, and lax financial regulations make it easier for money launderers to achieve their ends. The international nature of illegal financial transactions has an adverse impact on the economy and society of a nation. The criminals use currency exchange and stock brokering organizations, shell corporations, and trading companies to launder their illegal profits. Money laundering to finance terrorist activities is another operation with devastating effects. While organized criminals are motivated primarily by financial gain, terrorists seek political influence and generally publicize their cause. In many instances, terrorist groups seek out unlawful enterprises to generate capital to sustain their activities and organizations. Terrorist funding also comes from individual contributors and social, cultural, and religious organizations.

In the interdependent world of today, organized crime has posed a great danger to international financial markets. Apart from creating economic problems in a country, legitimate domestic and foreign businesses also suffer a great deal. Organized crime also hampers the normal political functioning of the state. Global organized crime can have a corrupting and damaging effect on state political institutions. The smuggling of nuclear materials has not occurred on a large scale, but a number of instances have occurred. Therefore, the potential for these weapons falling into the hands of criminals and terrorists cannot be ruled out. National and international regulatory bodies have responded to the nature and seriousness of organized crime. Anticrime legislation with stringent measures has been passed in national legislatures to combat organized criminal activity. Additionally, there are amendments to existing statutes so as to tackle the problem in a more effective way. There is also increasing cooperation among national, regional, and international associations. The United Nations, through it various agencies, is involved in checking the activities of organized crime.

This volume provides scholars, the academic community, and the general reader with a compendium of international documents that address this very serious threat to global peace and security.

1.
African Union Convention on Preventing and Combating Corruption

The African Union took a measured step against corruption in its meeting held in Maputo on 11 July 2003. The preamble called for a better life for the African people, the strengthening of democratic institutions, and good governance. The member states would eradicate corruption and other related offenses in the public as well as the private sector. Legislative measures would be enacted in respective countries in order to criminalize corruption-related offenses such as extortion, bribery, and illicit enrichment. Article 22 called for the establishment of the Advisory Board on Corruption within the African Union.

Source
African Union, http://www.africa-union.org/root/au/ Documents/Treaties/Text/Convention%20on% 20Combating%20Corruption.pdf.

Preamble
The Member States of the African Union:

Considering that the Constitutive Act of the African Union recognizes that freedom, equality, justice, peace and dignity are essential objectives for the achievement of the legitimate aspiration of the African peoples;

Further Considering that Article 3 of the said Constitutive Act enjoins Member States to coordinate and intensify their cooperation, unity, cohesion and efforts to achieve a better life for the peoples of Africa;

Cognizant of the fact that the Constitutive Act of the African Union, inter alia, calls for the need to promote and protect human and peoples' rights, consolidate democratic institutions and foster a culture of democracy and ensure good governance and the rule of law;

Aware of the need to respect human dignity and to foster the promotion of economic, social, and political rights in conformity with the provisions of the African Charter on Human and People's Rights and other relevant human rights instruments;

Bearing in mind the 1990 Declaration on the Fundamental Changes Taking Place in the World and their Implications for Africa; the 1994 Cairo Agenda for Action Relaunching Africa's Socioeconomic Transformation; and the Plan of Action Against Impunity adopted by the Nineteenth Ordinary Session of the African Commission on Human and Peoples Rights in 1996 as subsequently endorsed by the Sixty fourth Ordinary Session of the Council of Ministers held in Yaounde, Cameroon in 1996 which, among others, underlined the need to observe principles of good governance, the primacy of law, human rights, democratization and popular participation by the African peoples in the processes of governance.

Concerned about the negative effects of corruption and impunity on the political, economic, social and cultural stability of African States and its devastating effects on the economic and social development of the African peoples;

Acknowledging that corruption undermines accountability and transparency in the management of public affairs as well as socio-economic development on the continent;

Recognizing the need to address the root causes of corruption on the continent;

Convinced of the need to formulate and pursue, as a matter of priority, a common penal policy aimed at protecting the society against corruption, including the adoption of appropriate legislative and adequate preventive measures;

Determined to build partnerships between governments and all segments of civil society, in particular, women, youth, media and the private sector in order to fight the scourge of corruption;

Recalling resolution AHG-Dec 126(**XXXIV**) adopted by the Thirty-fourth Ordinary Session of the Assembly of Heads of State and Government in June 1998 in Ouagadougou, Burkina Faso, requesting the Secretary General to convene, in cooperation with the African Commission on Human and Peoples' Rights, a high level meeting of experts to consider ways and means of removing obstacles to the enjoyment of economic, social and cultural rights, including the fight against corruption and impunity and propose appropriate legislative and other measures;

Further Recalling the decision of the 37th ordinary session of the Assembly of Heads of State and Government of the OAU held in Lusaka, Zambia, in July 2001 as well as the Declaration adopted by the first session of the Assembly of the Union held in Durban, South Africa in July 2002, relating to the New Partnership for Africa's Development (NEPAD) which calls for the setting up of a coordinated mechanism to combat corruption effectively.

Have agreed as follows:

Article 1

Definitions
1. For the purposes of this Convention;

"Chairperson of the Commission" means Chairperson of the Commission of the African Union;

"Confiscation" means any penalty or measure resulting in a final deprivation of property, proceeds or instrumentalities ordered by a court of law following proceedings in relation to a criminal offence or offences connected with or related to corruption;

"Corruption" means the acts and practices including related offences proscribed in this Convention;

"Court of Law" means a court duly established by a domestic law;

"Executive Council" means the Executive Council of the African Union;

"Illicit enrichment" means the significant increase in the assets of a public official or any other person which he or she cannot reasonably explain in relation to his or her income.

"Private Sector" means the sector of a national economy under private ownership in which the allocation of productive resources is controlled by market forces, rather than public authorities and other sectors of the economy not under the public sector or government;

"Proceeds of Corruption" means assets of any kind corporeal or incorporeal, movable or immovable, tangible or intangible and any document or legal instrument evidencing title to or interests in such assets acquired as a result of an act of corruption;

"Public official" means any official or employee of the State or its agencies including those who have been selected, appointed or elected to perform activities or functions in the name of the State or in the service of the State at any level of its hierarchy;

"Requested State Party" means a State Party requested to extradite or to provide assistance under this Convention;

"Requesting State Party" means a State Party making a request for extradition or assistance in terms of this Convention;

"State Party" means any Member State of the African Union which has ratified or acceded to this Convention and has deposited its instruments of

ratification or accession with the Chairperson of the Commission of the African Union.

2. In this Convention, the singular shall include the plural and vice versa.

Article 2

Objectives

The objectives of this Convention are to:

1. Promote and strengthen the development in Africa by each State Party, of mechanisms required to prevent, detect, punish and eradicate corruption and related offences in the public and private sectors.
2. Promote, facilitate and regulate cooperation among the State Parties to ensure the effectiveness of measures and actions to prevent, detect, punish and eradicate corruption and related offences in Africa.
3. Coordinate and harmonize the policies and legislation between State Parties for the purposes of prevention, detection, punishment and eradication of corruption on the continent.
4. Promote socio-economic development by removing obstacles to the enjoyment of economic, social and cultural rights as well as civil and political rights.
5. Establish the necessary conditions to foster transparency and accountability in the management of public affairs.

Article 3

Principles

The State Parties to this Convention undertake to abide by the following principles:

1. Respect for democratic principles and institutions, popular participation, the rule of law and good governance.
2. Respect for human and peoples' rights in accordance with the African Charter on Human and Peoples Rights and other relevant human rights instruments.
3. Transparency and accountability in the management of public affairs.
4. Promotion of social justice to ensure balanced socio-economic development.
5. Condemnation and rejection of acts of corruption, related offences and impunity.

Article 4

Scope of Application

1. This Convention is applicable to the following acts of corruption and related offences:

   (a) the solicitation or acceptance, directly or indirectly, by a public official or any other person, of any goods of monetary value, or other benefit, such as a gift, favour, promise or advantage for himself or herself or for another person or entity, in exchange for any act or omission in the performance of his or her public functions;

   (b) the offering or granting, directly or indirectly, to a public official or any other person, of any goods of monetary value, or other benefit, such as a gift, favour, promise or advantage for himself or herself or for another person or entity, in exchange for any act or omission in the performance of his or her public functions;

   (c) any act or omission in the discharge of his or her duties by a public official or any other person for the purpose of illicitly obtaining benefits for himself or herself or for a third party;

   (d) the diversion by a public official or any other person, for purposes unrelated to those for which they were intended, for his or her own benefit or that of a third party, of any property belonging to the State or its agencies, to an independent agency, or to an individual, that such official has received by virtue of his or her position;

   (e) the offering or giving, promising, solicitation or acceptance, directly or indirectly, of any undue advantage to or by any person who directs or works for, in any capacity, a private sector entity, for himself or herself or for anyone else, for him or her to act, or refrain from acting, in breach of his or her duties;

(f) the offering, giving, solicitation or acceptance directly or indirectly, or promising of any undue advantage to or by any person who asserts or confirms that he or she is able to exert any improper influence over the decision making of any person performing functions in the public or private sector in consideration thereof, whether the undue advantage is for himself or herself or for anyone else, as well as the request, receipt or the acceptance of the offer or the promise of such an advantage, in consideration of that influence, whether or not the influence is exerted or whether or not the supposed influence leads to the intended result;

(g) illicit enrichment;

(h) the use or concealment of proceeds derived from any of the acts referred to in this Article; and

(i) participation as a principal, co-principal, agent, instigator, accomplice or accessory after the fact, or on any other manner in the commission or attempted commission of, in any collaboration or conspiracy to commit, any of the acts referred to in this article.

2. This Convention shall also be applicable by mutual agreement between or among two or more State Parties with respect to any other act or practice of corruption and related offences not described in this Convention.

Article 5

Legislative and Other Measures

For the purposes set forth in Article 2 of this Convention, State Parties undertake to:

1. Adopt legislative and other measures that are required to establish as offences, the acts mentioned in Article 4 paragraph 1 of the present Convention.

2. Strengthen national control measures to ensure that the setting up and operations of foreign companies in the territory of a State Party shall be subject to the respect of the national legislation in force.

3. Establish, maintain and strengthen independent national anticorruption authorities or agencies.

4. Adopt legislative and other measures to create, maintain and strengthen internal accounting, auditing and follow-up systems, in particular, in the public income, custom and tax receipts, expenditures and procedures for hiring, procurement and management of public goods and services.

5. Adopt legislative and other measures to protect informants and witnesses in corruption and related offences, including protection of their identities.

6. Adopt measures that ensure citizens report instances of corruption without fear of consequent reprisals.

7. Adopt national legislative measures in order to punish those who make false and malicious reports against innocent persons in corruption and related offences.

8. Adopt and strengthen mechanisms for promoting the education of populations to respect the public good and public interest, and awareness in the fight against corruption and related offences, including school educational programmes and sensitization of the media, and the promotion of an enabling environment for the respect of ethics.

Article 6

Laundering of the Proceeds of Corruption

States Parties shall adopt such legislative and other measures as may be necessary to establish as criminal offences:

a) The conversion, transfer or disposal of property, knowing that such property is the proceeds of corruption or related offences for the purpose of concealing or disguising the illicit origin of the property or of helping any person who is involved in the commission of the offence to evade the legal consequences of his or her action.

b) The concealment or disguise of the true nature, source, location, disposition, movement or ownership of or rights with respect to property which is the proceeds of corruption or related offences;

c) The acquisition, possession or use of property with the knowledge at the time of receipt, that such property is the proceeds of corruption or related offences;

Article 7

Fight against Corruption and Related Offences in the Public Service

In order to combat corruption and related offences in the public service, State Parties commit themselves to:

1. Require all or designated public officials to declare their assets at the time of assumption of office during and after their term of office in the public service.
2. Create an internal committee or a similar body mandated to establish a code of conduct and to monitor its implementation, and sensitize and train public officials on matters of ethics.
3. Develop disciplinary measures and investigation procedures in corruption and related offences with a view to keeping up with technology and increase the efficiency of those responsible in this regard.
4. Ensure transparency, equity and efficiency in the management of tendering and hiring procedures in the public service.
5. Subject to the provisions of domestic legislation, any immunity granted to public officials shall not be an obstacle to the investigation of allegations against and the prosecution of such officials.

Article 8

Illicit Enrichment

1. Subject to the provisions of their domestic law, State Parties undertake to adopt necessary measures to establish under their laws an offence of illicit enrichment.

2. For State Parties that have established illicit enrichment as an offence under their domestic law, such offence shall be considered an act of corruption or a related offence for the purposes of this Convention.

3. Any State Party that has not established illicit enrichment as an offence shall, in so far as its laws permit, provide assistance and cooperation to the requesting State with respect to the offence as provided in this Convention.

Article 9

Access to Information

Each State Party shall adopt such legislative and other measures to give effect to the right of access to any information that is required to assist in the fight against corruption and related offences.

Article 10

Funding of Political Parties

Each State Party shall adopt legislative and other measures to:

(a) Proscribe the use of funds acquired through illegal and corrupt practices to finance political parties; and

(b) Incorporate the principle of transparency into funding of political parties.

Article 11

Private Sector

State Parties undertake to:

1. Adopt legislative and other measures to prevent and combat acts of corruption and related offences committed in and by agents of the private sector.
2. Establish mechanisms to encourage participation by the private sector in the fight against unfair competition, respect of the tender procedures and property rights.
3. Adopt such other measures as may be necessary to prevent companies from paying bribes to win tenders.

Article 12

Civil Society and Media
State Parties undertake to:

1. Be fully engaged in the fight against corruption and related offences and the popularisation of this Convention with the full participation of the Media and Civil Society at large;
2. Create an enabling environment that will enable civil society and the media to hold governments to the highest levels of transparency and accountability in the management of public affairs;
3. Ensure and provide for the participation of Civil Society in the monitoring process and consult Civil Society in the implementation of this Convention;
4. Ensure that the Media is given access to information in cases of corruption and related offences on condition that the dissemination of such information does not adversely affect the investigation process and the right to a fair trial.

Article 13

Jurisdiction
1. Each State Party has jurisdiction over acts of corruption and related offences when:

   (a) the breach is committed wholly or partially inside its territory;
   (b) the offence is committed by one of its nationals outside its territory or by a person who resides in its territory; and
   (c) the alleged criminal is present in its territory and it does not extradite such person to another country.
   (d) when the offence, although committed outside its jurisdiction, affects, in the view of the State concerned, its vital interests or the deleterious or harmful consequences or effects of such offences impact on the State Party.

2. This Convention does not exclude any criminal jurisdiction exercised by a State Party in accordance with its domestic law.

3. Notwithstanding the provision of paragraph I of this Article, a person shall not be tried twice for the same offence.

Article 14

Minimum Guarantees of a Fair Trial
Subject to domestic law, any person alleged to have committed acts of corruption and related offences shall receive a fair trial in criminal proceedings in accordance with the minimum guarantees contained in the African Charter on Human and Peoples' Rights and any other relevant international human rights instrument recognized by the concerned States Parties.

Article 15

Extradition
1. This Article shall apply to the offences established by the State Parties in accordance with this Convention.

2. Offences falling within the jurisdiction of this Convention shall be deemed to be included in the internal laws of State Parties as crimes requiring extradition. State Parties shall include such offences as extraditable offences in extradition treaties existing between or among them.

3. If a State Party that makes extradition conditional on the existence of a treaty receives a request for extradition from a State Party with which it does not have such treaty, it shall consider this Convention as a legal basis for all offences covered by this Convention.

4. A State Party that does not make extradition conditional on the existence of a treaty shall recognize offences to which this Convention applies as extraditable offences among themselves.

5. Each State Party undertakes to extradite any person charged with or convicted of offences of corruption and related offences, carried out on the

territory of another State Party and whose extradition is requested by that State Party, in conformity with their domestic law, any applicable extradition treaties, or extradition agreements or arrangements existing between or among the State Parties.

6. Where a State Party in whose territory any person charged with or convicted of offences is present and has refused to extradite that person on the basis that it has jurisdiction over offences, the Requested State Party shall be obliged to submit the case without undue delay to its competent authorities for the purpose of prosecution, unless otherwise agreed with the Requesting State Party, and shall report the final outcome to the Requesting State Party.

7. Subject to the provisions of its domestic law and any applicable extradition treaties, a Requested State Party may, upon being satisfied that the circumstances so warrant and are urgent and at the request of the Requesting State Party, take into custody a person whose extradition is sought and who is present in its territory, or take other appropriate measures to ensure that the person is present at the extradition proceedings.

Article 16

Confiscation and Seizure of the Proceeds and Instrumentalities of Corruption
1. Each State Party shall adopt such legislative measures as may be necessary to enable:

(a) its competent authorities to search, identify, trace, administer and freeze or seize the instrumentalities and proceeds of corruption pending a final judgement;

(b) confiscation of proceeds or property, the value of which corresponds to that of such proceeds, derived, from offences established in accordance with this convention;

(c) repatriation of proceeds of corruption.

2. The Requested State Party shall, in so far as its law permits and at the request of the Requesting State Party, seize and remit any object:

(a) which may be required as evidence of the offence in question; or

(b) which has been acquired as a result of the offence for which extradition is requested and which, at the time of arrest is found in possession of the persons claimed or is discovered subsequently.

3. The objects referred to in clause 2 of this Article may, if the Requesting State so requests, be handed over to that State even if the extradition is refused or cannot be carried out due to death, disappearance or escape of the person sought.

4. When the said object is liable for seizure or confiscation in the territory of the Requested State Party the latter may, in connection with pending or ongoing criminal proceedings, temporarily retain it or hand it over to the Requesting State Party, on condition that it is returned to the Requested State Party.

Article 17

Bank Secrecy
1. Each State Party shall adopt such measures necessary to empower its courts or other competent authorities to order the confiscation or seizure of banking, financial or commercial documents with a view to implementing this Convention.

2. The Requesting State shall not use any information received that is protected by bank secrecy for any purpose other than the proceedings for which that information was requested, unless with the consent of the Requested State Party.

3. State Parties shall not invoke banking secrecy to justify their refusal to cooperate with regard to acts of corruption and related offences by virtue of this Convention.

4. State Parties commit themselves to enter into bilateral agreements to waive banking secrecy on doubtful accounts and allow competent authorities the right to obtain from banks and financial institutions, under judicial cover, any evidence in their possession.

Article 18

Cooperation and Mutual Legal Assistance
1. In accordance with their domestic laws and applicable treaties, State Parties shall provide each other with the greatest possible technical cooperation and assistance in dealing immediately with requests from authorities that are empowered by virtue of their national laws to prevent, detect, investigate and punish acts of corruption and related offences.

2. If two or several State Parties have established relations on the basis of uniform legislation or a particular regime, they may have the option to regulate such mutual relations without prejudice to the provisions of this Convention.

3. State Parties shall co-operate among themselves in conducting and exchanging studies and researches on how to combat corruption and related offences and to exchange expertise relating to preventing and combating corruption and related offences.

4. State Parties shall co-operate among themselves, where possible, in providing any available technical assistance in drawing up programmes, codes of ethics or organizing, where necessary and for the benefit of their personnel, joint training courses involving one or several states in the area of combating corruption and related offences.

5. The provisions of this Article shall not affect the obligations under any other bilateral or multilateral treaty which governs, in whole or in part, mutual legal assistance in criminal matters.

6. Nothing in this Article shall prevent State Parties from according one another more favourable forms of mutual legal assistance allowed under their respective domestic law.

Article 19

International Cooperation
In the spirit of international cooperation, State Parties shall:

1. Collaborate with countries of origin of multi-nationals to criminalise and punish the practice of secret commissions and other forms of corrupt practices during international trade transactions.
2. Foster regional, continental and international cooperation to prevent corrupt practices in international trade transactions.
3. Encourage all countries to take legislative measures to prevent corrupt public officials from enjoying ill-acquired assets by freezing their foreign accounts and facilitating the repatriation of stolen or illegally acquired monies to the countries of origin.
4. Work closely with international, regional and sub regional financial organizations to eradicate corruption in development aid and cooperation programmes by defining strict regulations for eligibility and good governance of candidates within the general framework of their development policy.
5. Cooperate in conformity with relevant international instruments on international cooperation on criminal matters for purposes of investigations and procedures in offences within the jurisdiction of this Convention.

Article 20

National Authorities
1. For the purposes of cooperation and mutual legal assistance provided under this Convention, each State Party shall communicate to the Chairperson of the Commission at the time of signing or depositing its instrument of ratification,

the designation of a national authority or agency in application of offences established under Article 4 (1) of this Convention.

2. The national authorities or agencies shall be responsible for making and receiving the requests for assistance and cooperation referred to in this Convention.

3. The national authorities or agencies shall communicate with each other directly for the purposes of this Convention.

4. The national authorities or agencies shall be allowed the necessary independence and autonomy, to be able to carry out their duties effectively.

5. State Parties undertake to adopt necessary measures to ensure that national authorities or agencies are specialized in combating corruption and related offences by, among others, ensuring that the staff are trained and motivated to effectively carry out their duties.

Article 21

Relationship with Other Agreements
Subject to the provisions of Article 4 paragraph 2, this Convention shall in respect to those State Parties to which it applies, supersede the provisions of any treaty or bilateral agreement governing corruption and related offences between any two or more State Parties.

2.
Council of Europe Additional Protocol to the Criminal Law Convention on Corruption

The Council of Europe Additional Protocol to the Criminal Law Convention on Corruption entered into force on 1 February 2005. This protocol augments the Criminal Law Convention on Corruption by including the active and passive bribery of domestic and foreign arbitrators and jurors as criminal offenses.

Source
Council of Europe, http://www.justice.gov.sk/dwn/r6/05/dbpk_tp_dpa.rtf.

The member States of the Council of Europe and the other States signatory hereto,

Considering that it is desirable to supplement the Criminal Law Convention on Corruption (ETS No. 173, hereafter "the Convention") in order to prevent and fight against corruption;

Considering also that the present Protocol will allow the broader implementation of the 1996 Programme of Action against Corruption,

Have agreed as follows:

Chapter I—Use of Terms

Article 1—Use of Terms
For the purpose of this Protocol:

1. The term *"arbitrator"* shall be understood by reference to the national law of the States Parties to this Protocol, but shall in any case include a person who by virtue of an arbitration agreement is called upon to render a legally binding decision in a dispute submitted to him/her by the parties to the agreement.
2. The term *"arbitration agreement"* means an agreement recognised by the national law whereby the parties agree to submit a dispute for a decision by an arbitrator.
3. The term *"juror"* shall be understood by reference to the national law of the States Parties to this Protocol but shall in any case include a lay person acting as a member of a collegial body which has the responsibility of deciding on the guilt of an accused person in the framework of a trial.
4. In the case of proceedings involving a foreign arbitrator or juror, the prosecuting State may apply the

definition of arbitrator or juror only in so far as that definition is compatible with its national law.

Chapter II—Measures to Be Taken at National Level

Article 2—Active Bribery of Domestic Arbitrators
Each Party shall adopt such legislative and other measures as may be necessary to establish as criminal offences under its domestic law, when committed intentionally, the promising, offering or giving by any person, directly or indirectly, of any undue advantage to an arbitrator exercising his/her functions under the national law on arbitration of the Party, for himself or herself or for anyone else, for him or for her to act or refrain from acting in the exercise of his or her functions.

Article 3—Passive Bribery of Domestic Arbitrators
Each Party shall adopt such legislative and other measures as may be necessary to establish as criminal offences under its domestic law, when committed intentionally, the request or receipt by an arbitrator exercising his/her functions under the national law on arbitration of the Party, directly or indirectly, of any undue advantage for himself or herself or for anyone else, or the acceptance of an offer or promise of such an advantage, to act or refrain from acting in the exercise of his or her functions.

Article 4—Bribery of Foreign Arbitrators
Each Party shall adopt such legislative and other measures as may be necessary to establish as criminal offences under its domestic law the conduct referred to in Articles 2 and 3, when involving an arbitrator exercising his/her functions under the national law on arbitration of any other State.

Article 5—Bribery of Domestic Jurors
Each Party shall adopt such legislative and other measures as may be necessary to establish as criminal offences under its domestic law the conduct referred to in Articles 2 and 3, when

involving any person acting as a juror within its judicial system.

Article 6—Bribery of Foreign Jurors
Each Party shall adopt such legislative and other measures as may be necessary to establish as criminal offences under its domestic law the conduct referred to in Articles 2 and 3, when involving any person acting as a juror within the judicial system of any other State.

Chapter III—Monitoring of Implementation and Final Provisions

Article 7—Monitoring of Implementation
The Group of States against Corruption (GRECO) shall monitor the implementation of this Protocol by the Parties.

Article 8—Relationship to the Convention
1. As between the States Parties the provisions of Articles 2 to 6 of this Protocol shall be regarded as additional articles to the Convention.

2. The provisions of the Convention shall apply to the extent that they are compatible with the provisions of this Protocol.

Article 9—Declarations and Reservations
1. If a Party has made a declaration in accordance with Article 36 of the Convention, it may make a similar declaration relating to Articles 4 and 6 of this Protocol at the time of signature or when depositing its instrument of ratification, acceptance, approval or accession.

2. If a Party has made a reservation in accordance with Article 37, paragraph 1, of the Convention restricting the application of the passive bribery offences defined in Article 5 of the Convention, it may make a similar reservation concerning Articles 4 and 6 of this Protocol at the time of signature or when depositing its instrument of ratification, acceptance, approval or accession. Any other reservation made by a Party, in accordance with

Article 37 of the Convention shall be applicable also to this Protocol, unless that Party otherwise declares at the time of signature or when depositing its instrument of ratification, acceptance, approval or accession.

3. No other reservation may be made.

3.
Council of Europe Criminal Law Convention on Corruption

The Council of Europe Criminal Law Convention on Corruption entered into force on 1 July 2002. The Criminal Law Convention on Corruption is a comprehensive document that covers active and passive bribery of public, private, and state officials, both domestic and foreign. The convention also addresses influence trading, money laundering, and accounting offenses that are tied to and covered by Articles 2 through 12 of this instrument. Article 19 refers to "proportionate and dissuasive sanctions and measures, including . . . deprivation of liberty." This document also includes provisions for protection of witnesses, "gathering of evidence," and the "confiscation of proceeds." International cooperation among the parties is also addressed.

Source
Council of Europe, http://conventions.coe.int/Treaty/en/Treaties/Html/173.htm.

Preamble
The member States of the Council of Europe and the other States signatory hereto,

Considering that the aim of the Council of Europe is to achieve a greater unity between its members;

Recognising the value of fostering co-operation with the other States signatories to this Convention;

Convinced of the need to pursue, as a matter of priority, a common criminal policy aimed at the protection of society against corruption, including the adoption of appropriate legislation and preventive measures;

Emphasising that corruption threatens the rule of law, democracy and human rights, undermines good governance, fairness and social justice, distorts competition, hinders economic development and endangers the stability of democratic institutions and the moral foundations of society;

Believing that an effective fight against corruption requires increased, rapid and well-functioning international co-operation in criminal matters;

Welcoming recent developments which further advance international understanding and co-operation in combating corruption, including actions of the United Nations, the World Bank, the International Monetary Fund, the World Trade Organisation, the Organisation of American States, the OECD and the European Union;

Having regard to the Programme of Action against Corruption adopted by the Committee of Ministers of the Council of Europe in November 1996 following the recommendations of the 19th Conference of European Ministers of Justice (Valletta, 1994);

Recalling in this respect the importance of the participation of non-member States in the Council of Europe's activities against corruption and welcoming their valuable contribution to the implementation of the Programme of Action against Corruption;

Further recalling that Resolution No. 1 adopted by the European Ministers of Justice at their 21st Conference (Prague, 1997) recommended the speedy implementation of the Programme of Action against Corruption, and called, in particular, for the early adoption of a criminal law convention providing for the co-ordinated incrimination of corruption offences, enhanced co-operation for the prosecution of such offences as well as an effective follow-up mechanism open to member States and non-member States on an equal footing;

Bearing in mind that the Heads of State and Government of the Council of Europe decided, on the occasion of their Second Summit held in Strasbourg on 10 and 11 October 1997, to seek common responses to the challenges posed by the growth in corruption and adopted an Action Plan which, in order to promote co-operation in the fight against corruption, including its links with organised crime and money laundering, instructed the Committee of Ministers, *inter alia,* to secure the rapid completion of international legal instruments pursuant to the Programme of Action against Corruption;

Considering moreover that Resolution (97) 24 on the 20 Guiding Principles for the Fight against Corruption, adopted on 6 November 1997 by the Committee of Ministers at its 101st Session, stresses the need rapidly to complete the elaboration of international legal instruments pursuant to the Programme of Action against Corruption;

In view of the adoption by the Committee of Ministers, at its 102nd Session on 4 May 1998, of Resolution (98) 7 authorising the partial and enlarged agreement establishing the "Group of States against Corruption—GRECO", which aims at improving the capacity of its members to fight corruption by following up compliance with their undertakings in this field,

Have agreed as follows:

Chapter I—Use of Terms

Article 1—Use of Terms
For the purposes of this Convention:

a. *"public official"* shall be understood by reference to the definition of "official", "public officer", "mayor", "minister" or "judge" in the national law of the State in which the person in question performs that function and as applied in its criminal law;
b. the term *"judge"* referred to in sub-paragraph a above shall include prosecutors and holders of judicial offices;
c. in the case of proceedings involving a public official of another State, the prosecuting State may apply the definition of public official only insofar as that definition is compatible with its national law;
d. *"legal person"* shall mean any entity having such status under the applicable national law, except for States or other public bodies in the exercise of State authority and for public international organisations.

Chapter II—Measures to Be Taken at National Level

Article 2—Active Bribery of Domestic Public Officials
Each Party shall adopt such legislative and other measures as may be necessary to establish as criminal offences under its domestic law, when committed intentionally, the promising, offering or giving by any person, directly or indirectly, of any undue advantage to any of its public officials, for himself or herself or for anyone else, for him or her to act or refrain from acting in the exercise of his or her functions.

Article 3—Passive Bribery of Domestic Public Officials
Each Party shall adopt such legislative and other measures as may be necessary to establish as criminal offences under its domestic law, when committed intentionally, the request or receipt by any of its public officials, directly or indirectly, of any undue advantage, for himself or herself or for anyone else, or the acceptance of an offer or a

promise of such an advantage, to act or refrain from acting in the exercise of his or her functions.

Article 4—Bribery of Members of Domestic Public Assemblies
Each Party shall adopt such legislative and other measures as may be necessary to establish as criminal offences under its domestic law the conduct referred to in Articles 2 and 3, when involving any person who is a member of any domestic public assembly exercising legislative or administrative powers.

Article 5—Bribery of Foreign Public Officials
Each Party shall adopt such legislative and other measures as may be necessary to establish as criminal offences under its domestic law the conduct referred to in Articles 2 and 3, when involving a public official of any other State.

Article 6—Bribery of Members of Foreign Public Assemblies
Each Party shall adopt such legislative and other measures as may be necessary to establish as criminal offences under its domestic law the conduct referred to in Articles 2 and 3, when involving any person who is a member of any public assembly exercising legislative or administrative powers in any other State.

Article 7—Active Bribery in the Private Sector
Each Party shall adopt such legislative and other measures as may be necessary to establish as criminal offences under its domestic law, when committed intentionally in the course of business activity, the promising, offering or giving, directly or indirectly, of any undue advantage to any persons who direct or work for, in any capacity, private sector entities, for themselves or for anyone else, for them to act, or refrain from acting, in breach of their duties.

Article 8—Passive Bribery in the Private Sector
Each Party shall adopt such legislative and other measures as may be necessary to establish as criminal offences under its domestic law, when committed intentionally, in the course of business activity, the request or receipt, directly or indirectly, by any persons who direct or work for, in any capacity, private sector entities, of any undue advantage or the promise thereof for themselves or for anyone else, or the acceptance of an offer or a promise of such an advantage, to act or refrain from acting in breach of their duties.

Article 9—Bribery of Officials of International Organisations
Each Party shall adopt such legislative and other measures as may be necessary to establish as criminal offences under its domestic law the conduct referred to in Articles 2 and 3, when involving any official or other contracted employee, within the meaning of the staff regulations, of any public international or supranational organisation or body of which the Party is a member, and any person, whether seconded or not, carrying out functions corresponding to those performed by such officials or agents.

Article 10—Bribery of Members of International Parliamentary Assemblies
Each Party shall adopt such legislative and other measures as may be necessary to establish as criminal offences under its domestic law the conduct referred to in Article 4 when involving any members of parliamentary assemblies of international or supranational organisations of which the Party is a member.

Article 11—Bribery of Judges and Officials of International Courts
Each Party shall adopt such legislative and other measures as may be necessary to establish as criminal offences under its domestic law the conduct referred to in Articles 2 and 3 involving any holders of judicial office or officials of any international court whose jurisdiction is accepted by the Party.

Article 12—Trading in Influence

Each Party shall adopt such legislative and other measures as may be necessary to establish as criminal offences under its domestic law, when committed intentionally, the promising, giving or offering, directly or indirectly, of any undue advantage to anyone who asserts or confirms that he or she is able to exert an improper influence over the decision-making of any person referred to in Articles 2, 4 to 6 and 9 to 11 in consideration thereof, whether the undue advantage is for himself or herself or for anyone else, as well as the request, receipt or the acceptance of the offer or the promise of such an advantage, in consideration of that influence, whether or not the influence is exerted or whether or not the supposed influence leads to the intended result.

Article 13—Money Laundering of Proceeds from Corruption Offences

Each Party shall adopt such legislative and other measures as may be necessary to establish as criminal offences under its domestic law the conduct referred to in the Council of Europe Convention on Laundering, Search, Seizure and Confiscation of the Products from Crime (ETS No. 141), Article 6, paragraphs 1 and 2, under the conditions referred to therein, when the predicate offence consists of any of the criminal offences established in accordance with Articles 2 to 12 of this Convention, to the extent that the Party has not made a reservation or a declaration with respect to these offences or does not consider such offences as serious ones for the purpose of their money laundering legislation.

Article 14—Account Offences

Each Party shall adopt such legislative and other measures as may be necessary to establish as offences liable to criminal or other sanctions under its domestic law the following acts or omissions, when committed intentionally, in order to commit, conceal or disguise the offences referred to in Articles 2 to 12, to the extent the Party has not made a reservation or a declaration:

a. creating or using an invoice or any other accounting document or record containing false or incomplete information;
b. unlawfully omitting to make a record of a payment.

Article 15—Participatory Acts

Each Party shall adopt such legislative and other measures as may be necessary to establish as criminal offences under its domestic law aiding or abetting the commission of any of the criminal offences established in accordance with this Convention.

Article 16—Immunity

The provisions of this Convention shall be without prejudice to the provisions of any Treaty, Protocol or Statute, as well as their implementing texts, as regards the withdrawal of immunity.

Article 17—Jurisdiction

1. Each Party shall adopt such legislative and other measures as may be necessary to establish jurisdiction over a criminal offence established in accordance with Articles 2 to 14 of this Convention where:

a. the offence is committed in whole or in part in its territory;
b. the offender is one of its nationals, one of its public officials, or a member of one of its domestic public assemblies;
c. the offence involves one of its public officials or members of its domestic public assemblies or any person referred to in Articles 9 to 11 who is at the same time one of its nationals.

2. Each State may, at the time of signature or when depositing its instrument of ratification, acceptance, approval or accession, by a declaration addressed to the Secretary General of the Council of Europe, declare that it reserves the right not to apply or to apply only in specific cases or conditions the jurisdiction rules laid down in paragraphs 1 b and c of this article or any part thereof.

3. If a Party has made use of the reservation possibility provided for in paragraph 2 of this article, it shall adopt such measures as may be necessary to establish jurisdiction over a criminal offence established in accordance with this Convention, in cases where an alleged offender is present in its territory and it does not extradite him to another Party, solely on the basis of his nationality, after a request for extradition.

4. This Convention does not exclude any criminal jurisdiction exercised by a Party in accordance with national law.

Article 18—Corporate Liability
1. Each Party shall adopt such legislative and other measures as may be necessary to ensure that legal persons can be held liable for the criminal offences of active bribery, trading in influence and money laundering established in accordance with this Convention, committed for their benefit by any natural person, acting either individually or as part of an organ of the legal person, who has a leading position within the legal person, based on:

  —a power of representation of the legal person; or
  —an authority to take decisions on behalf of the legal person; or
  —an authority to exercise control within the legal person;

as well as for involvement of such a natural person as accessory or instigator in the above-mentioned offences.

2. Apart from the cases already provided for in paragraph 1, each Party shall take the necessary measures to ensure that a legal person can be held liable where the lack of supervision or control by a natural person referred to in paragraph 1 has made possible the commission of the criminal offences mentioned in paragraph 1 for the benefit of that legal person by a natural person under its authority.

3. Liability of a legal person under paragraphs 1 and 2 shall not exclude criminal proceedings against natural persons who are perpetrators, instigators of, or accessories to, the criminal offences mentioned in paragraph 1.

Article 19—Sanctions and Measures
1. Having regard to the serious nature of the criminal offences established in accordance with this Convention, each Party shall provide, in respect of those criminal offences established in accordance with Articles 2 to 14, effective, proportionate and dissuasive sanctions and measures, including, when committed by natural persons, penalties involving deprivation of liberty which can give rise to extradition.

2. Each Party shall ensure that legal persons held liable in accordance with Article 18, paragraphs 1 and 2, shall be subject to effective, proportionate and dissuasive criminal or non-criminal sanctions, including monetary sanctions.

3. Each Party shall adopt such legislative and other measures as may be necessary to enable it to confiscate or otherwise deprive the instrumentalities and proceeds of criminal offences established in accordance with this Convention, or property the value of which corresponds to such proceeds.

Article 20—Specialised Authorities
Each Party shall adopt such measures as may be necessary to ensure that persons or entities are specialised in the fight against corruption. They shall have the necessary independence in accordance with the fundamental principles of the legal system of the Party, in order for them to be able to carry out their functions effectively and free from any undue pressure. The Party shall ensure that the staff of such entities has adequate training and financial resources for their tasks.

Article 21—Co-operation with and between National Authorities
Each Party shall adopt such measures as may be necessary to ensure that public authorities, as well

as any public official, co-operate, in accordance with national law, with those of its authorities responsible for investigating and prosecuting criminal offences:

    a. by informing the latter authorities, on their own initiative, where there are reasonable grounds to believe that any of the criminal offences established in accordance with Articles 2 to 14 has been committed, or

    b. by providing, upon request, to the latter authorities all necessary information.

Article 22—Protection of Collaborators of Justice and Witnesses
Each Party shall adopt such measures as may be necessary to provide effective and appropriate protection for:

    a. those who report the criminal offences established in accordance with Articles 2 to 14 or otherwise co-operate with the investigating or prosecuting authorities;

    b. witnesses who give testimony concerning these offences.

Article 23—Measures to Facilitate the Gathering of Evidence and the Confiscation of Proceeds
1. Each Party shall adopt such legislative and other measures as may be necessary, including those permitting the use of special investigative techniques, in accordance with national law, to enable it to facilitate the gathering of evidence related to criminal offences established in accordance with Articles 2 to 14 of this Convention and to identify, trace, freeze and seize instrumentalities and proceeds of corruption, or property the value of which corresponds to such proceeds, liable to measures set out in accordance with paragraph 3 of Article 19 of this Convention.

2. Each Party shall adopt such legislative and other measures as may be necessary to empower its courts or other competent authorities to order that bank, financial or commercial records be made available or be seized in order to carry out the actions referred to in paragraph 1 of this article.

3. Bank secrecy shall not be an obstacle to measures provided for in paragraphs 1 and 2 of this article.

Chapter III—Monitoring of Implementation

Article 24—Monitoring
The Group of States against Corruption (GRECO) shall monitor the implementation of this Convention by the Parties.

Chapter IV—International Co-operation

Article 25—General Principles and Measures for International Co-operation
1. The Parties shall co-operate with each other, in accordance with the provisions of relevant international instruments on international co-operation in criminal matters, or arrangements agreed on the basis of uniform or reciprocal legislation, and in accordance with their national law, to the widest extent possible for the purposes of investigations and proceedings concerning criminal offences established in accordance with this Convention.

2. Where no international instrument or arrangement referred to in paragraph 1 is in force between Parties, Articles 26 to 31 of this chapter shall apply.

3. Articles 26 to 31 of this chapter shall also apply where they are more favourable than those of the international instruments or arrangements referred to in paragraph 1.

Article 26—Mutual Assistance
1. The Parties shall afford one another the widest measure of mutual assistance by promptly processing requests from authorities that, in conformity with their domestic laws, have the

power to investigate or prosecute criminal offences established in accordance with this Convention.

2. Mutual legal assistance under paragraph 1 of this article may be refused if the requested Party believes that compliance with the request would undermine its fundamental interests, national sovereignty, national security or *public order.*

3. Parties shall not invoke bank secrecy as a ground to refuse any co-operation under this chapter. Where its domestic law so requires, a Party may require that a request for co-operation which would involve the lifting of bank secrecy be authorised by either a judge or another judicial authority, including public prosecutors, any of these authorities acting in relation to criminal offences.

Article 27—Extradition

1. The criminal offences established in accordance with this Convention shall be deemed to be included as extraditable offences in any extradition treaty existing between or among the Parties. The Parties undertake to include such offences as extraditable offences in any extradition treaty to be concluded between or among them.

2. If a Party that makes extradition conditional on the existence of a treaty receives a request for extradition from another Party with which it does not have an extradition treaty, it may consider this Convention as the legal basis for extradition with respect to any criminal offence established in accordance with this Convention.

3. Parties that do not make extradition conditional on the existence of a treaty shall recognise criminal offences established in accordance with this Convention as extraditable offences between themselves.

4. Extradition shall be subject to the conditions provided for by the law of the requested Party or by applicable extradition treaties, including the grounds on which the requested Party may refuse extradition.

5. If extradition for a criminal offence established in accordance with this Convention is refused solely on the basis of the nationality of the person sought, or because the requested Party deems that it has jurisdiction over the offence, the requested Party shall submit the case to its competent authorities for the purpose of prosecution unless otherwise agreed with the requesting Party, and shall report the final outcome to the requesting Party in due course.

Article 28—Spontaneous Information

Without prejudice to its own investigations or proceedings, a Party may without prior request forward to another Party information on facts when it considers that the disclosure of such information might assist the receiving Party in initiating or carrying out investigations or proceedings concerning criminal offences established in accordance with this Convention or might lead to a request by that Party under this chapter.

Article 29—Central Authority

1. The Parties shall designate a central authority or, if appropriate, several central authorities, which shall be responsible for sending and answering requests made under this chapter, the execution of such requests or the transmission of them to the authorities competent for their execution.

2. Each Party shall, at the time of signature or when depositing its instrument of ratification, acceptance, approval or accession, communicate to the Secretary General of the Council of Europe the names and addresses of the authorities designated in pursuance of paragraph 1 of this article.

Article 30—Direct Communication

1. The central authorities shall communicate directly with one another.

2. In the event of urgency, requests for mutual assistance or communications related thereto may be sent directly by the judicial authorities, including public prosecutors, of the requesting Party to such authorities of the requested Party. In such cases a copy shall be sent at the same time to the central authority of the requested Party through the central authority of the requesting Party.

3. Any request or communication under paragraphs 1 and 2 of this article may be made through the International Criminal Police Organisation (Interpol).

4. Where a request is made pursuant to paragraph 2 of this article and the authority is not competent to deal with the request, it shall refer the request to the competent national authority and inform directly the requesting Party that it has done so.

5. Requests or communications under paragraph 2 of this article, which do not involve coercive action, may be directly transmitted by the competent authorities of the requesting Party to the competent authorities of the requested Party.

6. Each State may, at the time of signature or when depositing its instrument of ratification, acceptance, approval or accession, inform the Secretary General of the Council of Europe that, for reasons of efficiency, requests made under this chapter are to be addressed to its central authority.

Article 31—Information
The requested Party shall promptly inform the requesting Party of the action taken on a request under this chapter and the final result of that action. The requested Party shall also promptly inform the requesting Party of any circumstances which render impossible the carrying out of the action sought or are likely to delay it significantly.

4.
Inter-American Convention against Corruption

The Inter-American Convention against Corruption, adopted at the third plenary session held on 29 March 1996, calls on states to criminalize acts of corruption, specifically the bribery of domestic and foreign government officials and illicit enrichment. Article VI addresses the specific acts of corruption and applies these acts to "solicitation" as well as "acceptance" on the part of the official whether "directly or indirectly." Bribes can take many forms (e.g., money, gifts, favors, or promises). Additionally, states are required to enact legislation to criminalize acts of corruption as specified in this instrument. In an effort to eliminate acts of corruption, the convention calls on all parties to cooperate with each other in matters relating to extradition, bank secrecy laws, and technical assistance.

Source
Organization of American States, Office of International Law, http://www.oas.org/juridico/english/Treaties/b-58.html.

Preamble
THE MEMBER STATES OF THE ORGANIZATION OF AMERICAN STATES,

CONVINCED that corruption undermines the legitimacy of public institutions and strikes at society, moral order and justice, as well as at the comprehensive development of peoples;

CONSIDERING that representative democracy, an essential condition for stability, peace and development of the region, requires, by its nature, the combating of every form of corruption in the performance of public functions, as well as acts of corruption specifically related to such performance;

PERSUADED that fighting corruption strengthens democratic institutions and prevents distortions in the economy, improprieties in public administration and damage to a society's moral fiber;

RECOGNIZING that corruption is often a tool used by organized crime for the accomplishment of its purposes;

CONVINCED of the importance of making people in the countries of the region aware of this problem and its gravity, and of the need to strengthen participation by civil society in preventing and fighting corruption;

RECOGNIZING that, in some cases, corruption has international dimensions, which requires coordinated action by States to fight it effectively;

CONVINCED of the need for prompt adoption of an international instrument to promote and facilitate international cooperation in fighting corruption and, especially, in taking appropriate action against persons who commit acts of corruption in the performance of public functions, or acts specifically related to such performance, as well as appropriate measures with respect to the proceeds of such acts;

DEEPLY CONCERNED by the steadily increasing links between corruption and the proceeds generated by illicit narcotics trafficking which undermine and threaten legitimate commercial and financial activities, and society, at all levels;

BEARING IN MIND the responsibility of States to hold corrupt persons accountable in order to combat corruption and to cooperate with one another for their efforts in this area to be effective; and

DETERMINED to make every effort to prevent, detect, punish and eradicate corruption in the performance of public functions and acts of corruption specifically related to such performance,

HAVE AGREED

to adopt the following

Inter-American Convention against Corruption

Article I

Definitions
For the purposes of this Convention:

"Public function" means any temporary or permanent, paid or honorary activity, performed by a natural person in the name of the State or in the service of the State or its institutions, at any level of its hierarchy.

"Public official", "government official", or "public servant" means any official or employee of the State or its agencies, including those who have been selected, appointed, or elected to perform activities or functions in the name of the State or in the service of the State, at any level of its hierarchy.

"Property" means assets of any kind, whether movable or immovable, tangible or intangible, and any document or legal instrument demonstrating, purporting to demonstrate, or relating to ownership or other rights pertaining to such assets.

Article II

Purposes
The purposes of this Convention are:

1. To promote and strengthen the development by each of the States Parties of the mechanisms needed to prevent, detect, punish and eradicate corruption; and
2. To promote, facilitate and regulate cooperation among the States Parties to ensure the effectiveness of measures and actions to prevent, detect, punish and eradicate corruption in the perfor-

mance of public functions and acts of corruption specifically related to such performance.

Article III

Preventive Measures
For the purposes set forth in Article II of this Convention, the States Parties agree to consider the applicability of measures within their own institutional systems to create, maintain and strengthen:

1. Standards of conduct for the correct, honorable, and proper fulfillment of public functions. These standards shall be intended to prevent conflicts of interest and mandate the proper conservation and use of resources entrusted to government officials in the performance of their functions. These standards shall also establish measures and systems requiring government officials to report to appropriate authorities acts of corruption in the performance of public functions. Such measures should help preserve the public's confidence in the integrity of public servants and government processes.

2. Mechanisms to enforce these standards of conduct.

3. Instruction to government personnel to ensure proper understanding of their responsibilities and the ethical rules governing their activities.

4. Systems for registering the income, assets and liabilities of persons who perform public functions in certain posts as specified by law and, where appropriate, for making such registrations public.

5. Systems of government hiring and procurement of goods and services that assure the openness, equity and efficiency of such systems.

6. Government revenue collection and control systems that deter corruption.

7. Laws that deny favorable tax treatment for any individual or corporation for expenditures made in violation of the anticorruption laws of the States Parties.

8. Systems for protecting public servants and private citizens who, in good faith, report acts of corruption, including protection of their identities, in accordance with their Constitutions and the basic principles of their domestic legal systems.

9. Oversight bodies with a view to implementing modern mechanisms for preventing, detecting, punishing and eradicating corrupt acts.

10. Deterrents to the bribery of domestic and foreign government officials, such as mechanisms to ensure that publicly held companies and other types of associations maintain books and records which, in reasonable detail, accurately reflect the acquisition and disposition of assets, and have sufficient internal accounting controls to enable their officers to detect corrupt acts.

11. Mechanisms to encourage participation by civil society and nongovernmental organizations in efforts to prevent corruption.

12. The study of further preventive measures that take into account the relationship between equitable compensation and probity in public service.

Article IV

Scope
This Convention is applicable provided that the alleged act of corruption has been committed or has effects in a State Party.

Article V

Jurisdiction
1. Each State Party shall adopt such measures as may be necessary to establish its jurisdiction over the offenses it has established in accordance with this Convention when the offense in question is committed in its territory.

2. Each State Party may adopt such measures as may be necessary to establish its jurisdiction over the offenses it has established in accordance with this Convention when the offense is committed by one of its nationals or by a person who habitually resides in its territory.

3. Each State Party shall adopt such measures as may be necessary to establish its jurisdiction over the offenses it has established in accordance with this Convention when the alleged criminal is present in its territory and it does not extradite such person to another country on the ground of the nationality of the alleged criminal.

4. This Convention does not preclude the application of any other rule of criminal jurisdiction established by a State Party under its domestic law.

Article VI

Acts of Corruption
1. This Convention is applicable to the following acts of corruption:

    a. The solicitation or acceptance, directly or indirectly, by a government official or a person who performs public functions, of any article of monetary value, or other benefit, such as a gift, favor, promise or advantage for himself or for another person or entity, in exchange for any act or omission in the performance of his public functions;

    b. The offering or granting, directly or indirectly, to a government official or a person who performs public functions, of any article of monetary value, or other benefit, such as a gift, favor, promise or advantage for himself or for another person or entity, in exchange for any act or omission in the performance of his public functions;

    c. Any act or omission in the discharge of his duties by a government official or a person who performs public functions for the purpose of illicitly obtaining benefits for himself or for a third party;

    d. The fraudulent use or concealment of property derived from any of the acts referred to in this article; and

    e. Participation as a principal, coprincipal, instigator, accomplice or accessory after the fact, or in any other manner, in the commission or attempted commission of, or in any collaboration or conspiracy to commit, any of the acts referred to in this article.

2. This Convention shall also be applicable by mutual agreement between or among two or more States Parties with respect to any other act of corruption not described herein.

Article VII

Domestic Law
The States Parties that have not yet done so shall adopt the necessary legislative or other measures to establish as criminal offenses under their domestic law the acts of corruption described in Article VI(1) and to facilitate cooperation among themselves pursuant to this Convention.

Article VIII

Transnational Bribery
Subject to its Constitution and the fundamental principles of its legal system, each State Party shall prohibit and punish the offering or granting, directly or indirectly, by its nationals, persons having their habitual residence in its territory, and businesses domiciled there, to a government official of another State, of any article of monetary value, or other benefit, such as a gift, favor, promise or advantage, in connection with any economic or commercial transaction in exchange for any act or omission in the performance of that official's public functions.

Among those States Parties that have established transnational bribery as an offense, such offense shall be considered an act of corruption for the purposes of this Convention.

Any State Party that has not established transnational bribery as an offense shall, insofar as its laws permit, provide assistance and cooperation with respect to this offense as provided in this Convention.

Article IX

Illicit Enrichment

Subject to its Constitution and the fundamental principles of its legal system, each State Party that has not yet done so shall take the necessary measures to establish under its laws as an offense a significant increase in the assets of a government official that he cannot reasonably explain in relation to his lawful earnings during the performance of his functions.

Among those States Parties that have established illicit enrichment as an offense, such offense shall be considered an act of corruption for the purposes of this Convention.

Any State Party that has not established illicit enrichment as an offense shall, insofar as its laws permit, provide assistance and cooperation with respect to this offense as provided in this Convention.

Article X

Notification

When a State Party adopts the legislation referred to in paragraph 1 of articles VIII and IX, it shall notify the Secretary General of the Organization of American States, who shall in turn notify the other States Parties. For the purposes of this Convention, the crimes of transnational bribery and illicit enrichment shall be considered acts of corruption for that State Party thirty days following the date of such notification.

Article XI

Progressive Development

1. In order to foster the development and harmonization of their domestic legislation and the attainment of the purposes of this Convention, the States Parties view as desirable, and undertake to consider, establishing as offenses under their laws the following acts:

a. The improper use by a government official or a person who performs public functions, for his own benefit or that of a third party, of any kind of classified or confidential information which that official or person who performs public functions has obtained because of, or in the performance of, his functions;

b. The improper use by a government official or a person who performs public functions, for his own benefit or that of a third party, of any kind of property belonging to the State or to any firm or institution in which the State has a proprietary interest, to which that official or person who performs public functions has access because of, or in the performance of, his functions;

c. Any act or omission by any person who, personally or through a third party, or acting as an intermediary, seeks to obtain a decision from a public authority whereby he illicitly obtains for himself or for another person any benefit or gain, whether or not such act or omission harms State property; and

d. The diversion by a government official, for purposes unrelated to those for which they were intended, for his own benefit or that of a third party, of any movable or immovable property, monies or securities belonging to the State, to an independent agency, or to an individual, that such official has received by virtue of his position for purposes of administration, custody or for other reasons.

2. Among those States Parties that have established these offenses, such offenses shall be considered acts of corruption for the purposes of this Convention.

3. Any State Party that has not established these offenses shall, insofar as its laws permit, provide assistance and cooperation with respect to these offenses as provided in this Convention.

Article XII

Effect on State Property
For application of this Convention, it shall not be necessary that the acts of corruption harm State property.

Article XIII

Extradition
1. This article shall apply to the offenses established by the States Parties in accordance with this Convention.

2. Each of the offenses to which this article applies shall be deemed to be included as an extraditable offense in any extradition treaty existing between or among the States Parties. The States Parties undertake to include such offenses as extraditable offenses in every extradition treaty to be concluded between or among them.

3. If a State Party that makes extradition conditional on the existence of a treaty receives a request for extradition from another State Party with which it does not have an extradition treaty, it may consider this Convention as the legal basis for extradition with respect to any offense to which this article applies.

4. States Parties that do not make extradition conditional on the existence of a treaty shall recognize offenses to which this article applies as extraditable offenses between themselves.

5. Extradition shall be subject to the conditions provided for by the law of the Requested State or by applicable extradition treaties, including the grounds on which the Requested State may refuse extradition.

6. If extradition for an offense to which this article applies is refused solely on the basis of the nationality of the person sought, or because the Requested State deems that it has jurisdiction over the offense, the Requested State shall submit the case to its competent authorities for the purpose of prosecution unless otherwise agreed with the Requesting State, and shall report the final outcome to the Requesting State in due course.

7. Subject to the provisions of its domestic law and its extradition treaties, the Requested State may, upon being satisfied that the circumstances so warrant and are urgent, and at the request of the Requesting State, take into custody a person whose extradition is sought and who is present in its territory, or take other appropriate measures to ensure his presence at extradition proceedings.

Article XIV

Assistance and Cooperation
1. In accordance with their domestic laws and applicable treaties, the States Parties shall afford one another the widest measure of mutual assistance by processing requests from authorities that, in conformity with their domestic laws, have the power to investigate or prosecute the acts of corruption described in this Convention, to obtain evidence and take other necessary action to facilitate legal proceedings and measures regarding the investigation or prosecution of acts of corruption.

2. The States Parties shall also provide each other with the widest measure of mutual technical cooperation on the most effective ways and means of preventing, detecting, investigating and punishing acts of corruption. To that end, they shall foster exchanges of experiences by way of agreements and meetings between competent bodies and institutions, and shall pay special attention to methods and procedures of citizen participation in the fight against corruption.

Article XV

Measures regarding Property
1. In accordance with their applicable domestic laws and relevant treaties or other agreements that may be in force between or among them, the States Parties shall provide each other the broadest possible measure of assistance in the identification, tracing, freezing, seizure and forfeiture of property or proceeds obtained, derived from or used in the commission of offenses established in accordance with this Convention.

2. A State Party that enforces its own or another State Party's forfeiture judgment against property or proceeds described in paragraph 1 of this article shall dispose of the property or proceeds in accordance with its laws. To the extent permitted by a State Party's laws and upon such terms as it deems appropriate, it may transfer all or part of such property or proceeds to another State Party that assisted in the underlying investigation or proceedings.

Article XVI

Bank Secrecy
1. The Requested State shall not invoke bank secrecy as a basis for refusal to provide the assistance sought by the Requesting State. The Requested State shall apply this article in accordance with its domestic law, its procedural provisions, or bilateral or multilateral agreements with the Requesting State.

2. The Requesting State shall be obligated not to use any information received that is protected by bank secrecy for any purpose other than the proceeding for which that information was requested, unless authorized by the Requested State.

Article XVII

Nature of the Act
For the purposes of articles XIII, XIV, XV and XVI of this Convention, the fact that the property obtained or derived from an act of corruption was intended for political purposes, or that it is alleged that an act of corruption was committed for political motives or purposes, shall not suffice in and of itself to qualify the act as a political offense or as a common offense related to a political offense.

Article XVIII

Central Authorities
1. For the purposes of international assistance and cooperation provided under this Convention, each State Party may designate a central authority or may rely upon such central authorities as are provided for in any relevant treaties or other agreements.

2. The central authorities shall be responsible for making and receiving the requests for assistance and cooperation referred to in this Convention.

3. The central authorities shall communicate with each other directly for the purposes of this Convention.

Article XIX

Temporal Application
Subject to the constitutional principles and the domestic laws of each State and existing treaties between the States Parties, the fact that the alleged act of corruption was committed before this Convention entered into force shall not preclude procedural cooperation in criminal matters between the States Parties. This provision shall in no case affect the principle of non-retroactivity in criminal law, nor shall application of this provision interrupt existing statutes of limitations relating to

crimes committed prior to the date of the entry into force of this Convention.

Article XX

Other Agreements or Practices
No provision of this Convention shall be construed as preventing the States Parties from engaging in mutual cooperation within the framework of other international agreements, bilateral or multilateral, currently in force or concluded in the future, or pursuant to any other applicable arrangement or practice.

Article XXI

Signature
This Convention is open for signature by the Member States of the Organization of American States.

Article XXII

Ratification
This Convention is subject to ratification. The instruments of ratification shall be deposited with the General Secretariat of the Organization of American States.

Article XXIII

Accession
This Convention shall remain open for accession by any other State. The instruments of accession shall be deposited with the General Secretariat of the Organization of American States.

Article XXIV

Reservations
The States Parties may, at the time of adoption, signature, ratification, or accession, make reservations to this Convention, provided that each reservation concerns one or more specific

provisions and is not incompatible with the object and purpose of the Convention.

Article XXV

Entry into Force
This Convention shall enter into force on the thirtieth day following the date of deposit of the second instrument of ratification. For each State ratifying or acceding to the Convention after the deposit of the second instrument of ratification, the Convention shall enter into force on the thirtieth day after deposit by such State of its instrument of ratification or accession.

Article XXVI

Denunciation
This Convention shall remain in force indefinitely, but any of the States Parties may denounce it. The instrument of denunciation shall be deposited with the General Secretariat of the Organization of American States. One year from the date of deposit of the instrument of denunciation, the Convention shall cease to be in force for the denouncing State, but shall remain in force for the other States Parties.

Article XXVII

Additional Protocols
Any State Party may submit for the consideration of other States Parties meeting at a General Assembly of the Organization of American States draft additional protocols to this Convention to contribute to the attainment of the purposes set forth in Article II thereof.

Each additional protocol shall establish the terms for its entry into force and shall apply only to those States that become Parties to it.

Article XXVIII

Deposit of Original Instrument
The original instrument of this Convention, the English, French, Portuguese, and Spanish texts of which are equally authentic, shall be deposited with the General Secretariat of the Organization of American States, which shall forward an authenticated copy of its text to the Secretariat of the United Nations for registration and publication in accordance with Article 102 of the United Nations Charter. The General Secretariat of the Organization of American States shall notify its Member States and the States that have acceded to the Convention of signatures, of the deposit of instruments of ratification, accession, or denunciation, and of reservations, if any.

5.
Principles to Combat Corruption in African Countries

Corruption in government and the private sector is an international problem that requires strategies that focus on prevention, the enactment and enforcement of laws, and education. The twenty-five points cited below are an attempt by the Global Coalition for Africa to address this growing threat to national, regional, and international security.

Source
Respondanet, http://www.respondanet.com/english/anti_corruption/publications/documents/africa.htm.

We, Ministers and representatives of Government, the list of which is annexed hereto, having met under the auspices of the Global Coalition for Africa in Washington DC on February 23, 1999,

Concerned about the devastating effects of corruption on the social, economic and political foundations of nations, and on their economic and social development and efforts to eradicate poverty;

Desirous of launching a concerted and collaborative effort to combat corrupt practices and thereby contribute to the global fight against corruption;

Acknowledging that anti-corruption efforts, to be successful, require political will at the highest level and committed leadership at all levels, and must involve civil society;

Determined to eliminate corruption through effective preventive and deterrent measures including strict enforcement of legislation, rules and regulations;

Aware that good governance, accountability and transparency are necessary to counter corruption;

Mindful of the UN General Assembly resolution on actions against corruption and other collective regional efforts to combat corruption such as those by the Organization for Economic Cooperation and Development (OECD) and the Organization of American States (OAS);

Now therefore do agree that Governments should:

1. Demonstrate the leadership and political will to combat and eradicate corruption in all sectors of government and society by improving governance and economic management, by striving to create a climate that promotes transparency, accountability and integrity in public as well as private endeavors, and by restoring popular confidence in the government.
2. Establish budgetary and financial transparency and strong financial management systems.
3. Eliminate unnecessary government regulations that negatively affect economic activity; and establish simple, readily available regulatory procedures with clear criteria and deadlines.
4. Enact and enforce criminal laws which will deal effectively with corruption offenses by imposing severe penalties on individuals convicted of corruption or corrupt practices, and on business

entities found to be involved in such practices. Enact and enforce criminal and civil laws that provide for the recovery, seizure, forfeiture or confiscation of property and other assets acquired through corruption.

5. Eliminate conflicts of interest by adopting and enforcing effective national laws, guidelines, ethical regulations or codes of conduct for public officials, which include rules on conflict of interest and requirements for the regular disclosure of financial interests, assets, liabilities, gifts and other transactions.

6. Undertake necessary administrative reforms to restore the morale and integrity of the public service, for example by ensuring merit-based recruitment and promotion policies and procedures and providing adequate benefits, including remuneration and pension schemes.

7. Promote transparency in procedures for public procurement and the sale or licensing of economic rights and interests by eliminating bureaucratic red tape, by providing for open and competitive bidding for government contracts, by the prohibition of bribery, and by adopting procedures for resolving challenges to the award of contracts or the sale or licensing of economic rights.

8. Adopt revenue collection systems that eliminate opportunities for tax evasion, and reform regulatory processes that facilitate customs duties evasion, especially in regard to international business transactions.

9. Require companies and organizations to maintain adequate and accurate financial books and records, and to adhere to internationally accepted standards of accounting.

10. Establish and enforce self-regulating codes of conduct for different professions, including those in the private sector.

11. Promote standards for corporate governance and the protection of shareholder rights.

12. Prohibit individuals found guilty of corruption from bidding on public contracts or otherwise doing business with governments. Publish details of companies that are found to have, or whose subsidiaries, agents or representatives are found to have, engaged in corrupt practices, and bar them from bidding on public contracts or otherwise doing business with the government for a period of time specified in national legislation.

13. Ensure that anti-corruption agencies are autonomous, independent, governed by a clear body of law, and effectively empowered to initiate and pursue investigations of corruption, and provide for the prosecution of offenders in accordance with investigations and due process.

14. Establish other accountability and oversight mechanisms, including as appropriate inspector general and audit offices.

15. Adopt legislative mechanisms and procedures for the public to submit complaints of corruption and corrupt practices, including the protection of witnesses and whistle blowers.

16. Facilitate the involvement and participation of civil society, on a continuous basis, in the formulation, execution and monitoring of anti-corruption reform programs.

17. Restore and maintain the independence of the judiciary and ensure adherence to high standards of integrity, honesty and commitment in the dispensation of justice through, among other things, adopting a judicial code of conduct.

18. Guarantee the public's right to information about corruption and corrupt activities through protection of the freedom of the press and effective parliamentary oversight and scrutiny.

19. Adopt cooperative arrangements at the regional and/or sub-regional level which provide for the mutual exchange of ideas, information, best practices, intelligence and experiences for the purpose of minimizing risks of cross-border corruption including international business transactions.

20. Facilitate the cooperative investigation of cases involving corruption by rendering mutual legal assistance in obtaining evidence, documents, articles, records and witness statements.

21. Provide assistance in the investigation, recovery, seizure, freezing, forfeiture and confiscation of property in respect of the proceeds of corruption

as well as the reciprocal enforcement of forfeiture and other such orders.

22. Apply reciprocal obligations for the extradition of
those accused or convicted of corruption
offenses.

23. Take preventive measures, including the short-
term harmonization of relevant laws, regulations
and procedures, for example those relating to
taxes, customs tariffs and duties, and public procurement.

24. Establish government-to-government mechanisms to monitor implementation of these principles, including a mutual reporting and evaluation
process.

25. Consider the elaboration and adoption of an
African convention for combating corruption
based on the foregoing principles, and encourage
the establishment of a global anti-corruption convention.

6.
United Nations Convention against Corruption

The United Nations Convention against Corruption
is a stand-alone document. Its focus is on public- and
private-sector corruption, and it addresses measures
to "promote effective practices aimed at the prevention of corruption." Some of these measures, enumerated in Chapter 2, provide guidance to states in
matters relative to hiring practices, remuneration,
training in appropriate "standards of conduct," financial disclosures, and the establishment of administrative protocols that specifically address matters relating
to "conflict of issues." Additionally, the convention
calls on all states to adopt legislation that criminalize
offenses such as the act of bribery or the acceptance
of such by national or international public officials.
This convention also addresses bribery-related
offenses that occur in the private sector and the laundering of money, as in the proceeds of crime. The convention calls on all states to cooperate with each other
and the international community both in the prevention of and the ongoing fight against corruption.

Source
United Nations, Office on Drugs and Crime, http://www
.unodc.org/unodc/crime_convention_corruption.html.

Preamble
The States Parties to this Convention,

Concerned about the seriousness of problems and
threats posed by corruption to the stability and
security of societies, undermining the institutions
and values of democracy, ethical values and justice
and jeopardizing sustainable development and the
rule of law,

Concerned also about the links between corruption
and other forms of crime, in particular organized
crime and economic crime, including money-
laundering,

Concerned further about cases of corruption that
involve vast quantities of assets, which may
constitute a substantial proportion of the resources
of States, and that threaten the political stability
and sustainable development of those States,

Convinced that corruption is no longer a local
matter but a transnational phenomenon that affects
all societies and economies, making international
cooperation to prevent and control it essential,

Convinced also that a comprehensive and
multidisciplinary approach is required to prevent
and combat corruption effectively,

Convinced further that the availability of technical
assistance can play an important role in enhancing
the ability of States, including by strengthening
capacity and by institution-building, to prevent and
combat corruption effectively,

Convinced that the illicit acquisition of personal wealth can be particularly damaging to democratic institutions, national economies and the rule of law,

Determined to prevent, detect and deter in a more effective manner international transfers of illicitly acquired assets and to strengthen international cooperation in asset recovery,

Acknowledging the fundamental principles of due process of law in criminal proceedings and in civil or administrative proceedings to adjudicate property rights,

Bearing in mind that the prevention and eradication of corruption is a responsibility of all States and that they must cooperate with one another, with the support and involvement of individuals and groups outside the public sector, such as civil society, non-governmental organizations and community-based organizations, if their efforts in this area are to be effective,

Bearing also in mind the principles of proper management of public affairs and public property, fairness, responsibility and equality before the law and the need to safeguard integrity and to foster a culture of rejection of corruption,

Commending the work of the Commission on Crime Prevention and Criminal Justice and the United Nations Office on Drugs and Crime in preventing and combating corruption,

Recalling the work carried out by other international and regional organizations in this field, including the activities of the African Union, the Council of Europe, the Customs Cooperation Council (also known as the World Customs Organization), the European Union, the League of Arab States, the Organisation for Economic Cooperation and Development and the Organization of American States,

Taking note with appreciation of multilateral instruments to prevent and combat corruption, including, inter alia, the Inter-American Convention against Corruption, adopted by the Organization of American States on 29 March 1996,

1. the Convention on the Fight against Corruption involving Officials of the European Communities or Officials of Member States of the European Union, adopted by the Council of the European Union on 26 May 1997,
2. the Convention on Combating Bribery of Foreign Public Officials in International Business Transactions, adopted by the Organisation for Economic Cooperation and Development on 21 November 1997,
3. the Criminal Law Convention on Corruption, adopted by the Committee of Ministers of the Council of Europe on 27 January 1999,
4. the Civil Law Convention on Corruption, adopted by the Committee of Ministers of the Council of Europe on 4 November 1999,
5. and the African Union Convention on Preventing and Combating Corruption, adopted by the Heads of State and Government of the African Union on 12 July 2003,

Welcoming the entry into force on 29 September 2003 of the United Nations Convention against Transnational Organized Crime

Have agreed as follows:

Chapter I

General Provisions

Article 1

Statement of Purpose
The purposes of this Convention are:

(a) To promote and strengthen measures to prevent and combat corruption more efficiently and effectively;

(b) To promote, facilitate and support international cooperation and technical assistance in the prevention of and fight against corruption, including in asset recovery;

(c) To promote integrity, accountability and proper management of public affairs and public property.

Article 2

Use of Terms

For the purposes of this Convention:

(a) "Public official" shall mean: (i) any person holding a legislative, executive, administrative or judicial office of a State Party, whether appointed or elected, whether permanent or temporary, whether paid or unpaid, irrespective of that person's seniority; (ii) any other person who performs a public function, including for a public agency or public enterprise, or provides a public service, as defined in the domestic law of the State Party and as applied in the pertinent area of law of that State Party; (iii) any other person defined as a "public official" in the domestic law of a State Party. However, for the purpose of some specific measures contained in chapter II of this Convention, "public official" may mean any person who performs a public function or provides a public service as defined in the domestic law of the State Party and as applied in the pertinent area of law of that State Party;

(b) "Foreign public official" shall mean any person holding a legislative, executive, administrative or judicial office of a foreign country, whether appointed or elected; and any person exercising a public function for a foreign country, including for a public agency or public enterprise;

(c) "Official of a public international organization" shall mean an international civil servant or any person who is authorized by such an organization to act on behalf of that organization;

(d) "Property" shall mean assets of every kind, whether corporeal or incorporeal, movable or immovable, tangible or intangible, and legal doc-

uments or instruments evidencing title to or interest in such assets;

(e) "Proceeds of crime" shall mean any property derived from or obtained, directly or indirectly, through the commission of an offence;

(f) "Freezing" or "seizure" shall mean temporarily prohibiting the transfer, conversion, disposition or movement of property or temporarily assuming custody or control of property on the basis of an order issued by a court or other competent authority;

(g) "Confiscation", which includes forfeiture where applicable, shall mean the permanent deprivation of property by order of a court or other competent authority;

(h) "Predicate offence" shall mean any offence as a result of which proceeds have been generated that may become the subject of an offence as defined in article 23 of this Convention;

(i) "Controlled delivery" shall mean the technique of allowing illicit or suspect consignments to pass out of, through or into the territory of one or more States, with the knowledge and under the supervision of their competent authorities, with a view to the investigation of an offence and the identification of persons involved in the commission of the offence.

Article 3

Scope of Application

1. This Convention shall apply, in accordance with its terms, to the prevention, investigation and prosecution of corruption and to the freezing, seizure, confiscation and return of the proceeds of offences established in accordance with this Convention.

2. For the purposes of implementing this Convention, it shall not be necessary, except as otherwise stated herein, for the offences set forth in it to result in damage or harm to state property.

Article 4

Protection of Sovereignty
1. States Parties shall carry out their obligations under this Convention in a manner consistent with the principles of sovereign equality and territorial integrity of States and that of non-intervention in the domestic affairs of other States.

2. Nothing in this Convention shall entitle a State Party to undertake in the territory of another State the exercise of jurisdiction and performance of functions that are reserved exclusively for the authorities of that other State by its domestic law.

Chapter II

Preventive Measures

Article 5

Preventive Anti-Corruption Policies and Practices
1. Each State Party shall, in accordance with the fundamental principles of its legal system, develop and implement or maintain effective, coordinated anticorruption policies that promote the participation of society and reflect the principles of the rule of law, proper management of public affairs and public property, integrity, transparency and accountability.

2. Each State Party shall endeavour to establish and promote effective practices aimed at the prevention of corruption.

3. Each State Party shall endeavour to periodically evaluate relevant legal instruments and administrative measures with a view to determining their adequacy to prevent and fight corruption.

4. States Parties shall, as appropriate and in accordance with the fundamental principles of their legal system, collaborate with each other and with relevant international and regional organizations in promoting and developing the

measures referred to in this article. That collaboration may include participation in international programmes and projects aimed at the prevention of corruption.

Article 6

Preventive Anti-Corruption Body or Bodies
1. Each State Party shall, in accordance with the fundamental principles of its legal system, ensure the existence of a body or bodies, as appropriate, that prevent corruption by such means as:

(a) Implementing the policies referred to in article 5 of this Convention and, where appropriate, overseeing and coordinating the implementation of those policies;

(b) Increasing and disseminating knowledge about the prevention of corruption.

2. Each State Party shall grant the body or bodies referred to in paragraph 1 of this article the necessary independence, in accordance with the fundamental principles of its legal system, to enable the body or bodies to carry out its or their functions effectively and free from any undue influence. The necessary material resources and specialized staff, as well as the training that such staff may require to carry out their functions, should be provided.

3. Each State Party shall inform the Secretary-General of the United Nations of the name and address of the authority or authorities that may assist other States Parties in developing and implementing specific measures for the prevention of corruption.

Article 7

Public Sector
1. Each State Party shall, where appropriate and in accordance with the fundamental principles of its legal system, endeavour to adopt, maintain and strengthen systems for the recruitment, hiring, retention, promotion and retirement of civil

servants and, where appropriate, other non-elected public officials:

    (a) That are based on principles of efficiency, transparency and objective criteria such as merit, equity and aptitude;

    (b) That include adequate procedures for the selection and training of individuals for public positions considered especially vulnerable to corruption and the rotation, where appropriate, of such individuals to other positions;

    (c) That promote adequate remuneration and equitable pay scales, taking into account the level of economic development of the State Party;

    (d) That promote education and training programmes to enable them to meet the requirements for the correct, honourable and proper performance of public functions and that provide them with specialized and appropriate training to enhance their awareness of the risks of corruption inherent in the performance of their functions. Such programmes may make reference to codes or standards of conduct in applicable areas.

2. Each State Party shall also consider adopting appropriate legislative and administrative measures, consistent with the objectives of this Convention and in accordance with the fundamental principles of its domestic law, to prescribe criteria concerning candidature for and election to public office.

3. Each State Party shall also consider taking appropriate legislative and administrative measures, consistent with the objectives of this Convention and in accordance with the fundamental principles of its domestic law, to enhance transparency in the funding of candidatures for elected public office and, where applicable, the funding of political parties.

4. Each State Party shall, in accordance with the fundamental principles of its domestic law, endeavour to adopt, maintain and strengthen systems that promote transparency and prevent conflicts of interest.

Article 8

Codes of Conduct for Public Officials
1. In order to fight corruption, each State Party shall promote, inter alia, integrity, honesty and responsibility among its public officials, in accordance with the fundamental principles of its legal system.

2. In particular, each State Party shall endeavour to apply, within its own institutional and legal systems, codes or standards of conduct for the correct, honourable and proper performance of public functions.

3. For the purposes of implementing the provisions of this article, each State Party shall, where appropriate and in accordance with the fundamental principles of its legal system, take note of the relevant initiatives of regional, interregional and multilateral organizations, such as the International Code of Conduct for Public Officials contained in the annex to General Assembly resolution 51/59 of 12 December 1996.

4. Each State Party shall also consider, in accordance with the fundamental principles of its domestic law, establishing measures and systems to facilitate the reporting by public officials of acts of corruption to appropriate authorities, when such acts come to their notice in the performance of their functions.

5. Each State Party shall endeavour, where appropriate and in accordance with the fundamental principles of its domestic law, to establish measures and systems requiring public officials to make declarations to appropriate authorities regarding, inter alia, their outside activities, employment, investments, assets and substantial gifts or benefits from which a conflict of interest may result with respect to their functions as public officials.

6. Each State Party shall consider taking, in accordance with the fundamental principles of its domestic law, disciplinary or other measures against public officials who violate the codes or standards established in accordance with this article.

Article 9

Public Procurement and Management of Public Finances
1. Each State Party shall, in accordance with the fundamental principles of its legal system, take the necessary steps to establish appropriate systems of procurement, based on transparency, competition and objective criteria in decision-making, that are effective, inter alia, in preventing corruption. Such systems, which may take into account appropriate threshold values in their application, shall address, inter alia:

(a) The public distribution of information relating to procurement procedures and contracts, including information on invitations to tender and relevant or pertinent information on the award of contracts, allowing potential tenderers sufficient time to prepare and submit their tenders;

(b) The establishment, in advance, of conditions for participation, including selection and award criteria and tendering rules, and their publication;

(c) The use of objective and predetermined criteria for public procurement decisions, in order to facilitate the subsequent verification of the correct application of the rules or procedures;

(d) An effective system of domestic review, including an effective system of appeal, to ensure legal recourse and remedies in the event that the rules or procedures established pursuant to this paragraph are not followed;

(e) Where appropriate, measures to regulate matters regarding personnel responsible for procurement, such as declaration of interest in particular public procurements, screening procedures and training requirements.

2. Each State Party shall, in accordance with the fundamental principles of its legal system, take appropriate measures to promote transparency and accountability in the management of public finances. Such measures shall encompass, inter alia:

(a) Procedures for the adoption of the national budget;
(b) Timely reporting on revenue and expenditure;
(c) A system of accounting and auditing standards and related oversight;
(d) Effective and efficient systems of risk management and internal control; and
(e) Where appropriate, corrective action in the case of failure to comply with the requirements established in this paragraph.

3. Each State Party shall take such civil and administrative measures as may be necessary, in accordance with the fundamental principles of its domestic law, to preserve the integrity of accounting books, records, financial statements or other documents related to public expenditure and revenue and to prevent the falsification of such documents.

Article 10

Public Reporting
Taking into account the need to combat corruption, each State Party shall, in accordance with the fundamental principles of its domestic law, take such measures as may be necessary to enhance transparency in its public administration, including with regard to its organization, functioning and decision-making processes, where appropriate. Such measures may include, inter alia:

(a) Adopting procedures or regulations allowing members of the general public to obtain, where appropriate, information on the organization, functioning and decision-making processes of its public administration and, with due regard for the protection of privacy and personal data, on decisions and legal acts that concern members of the public;

(b) Simplifying administrative procedures, where appropriate, in order to facilitate public access to the competent decision-making authorities; and

(c) Publishing information, which may include periodic reports on the risks of corruption in its public administration.

Article 11

Measures Relating to the Judiciary and Prosecution Services

1. Bearing in mind the independence of the judiciary and its crucial role in combating corruption, each State Party shall, in accordance with the fundamental principles of its legal system and without prejudice to judicial independence, take measures to strengthen integrity and to prevent opportunities for corruption among members of the judiciary. Such measures may include rules with respect to the conduct of members of the judiciary.

2. Measures to the same effect as those taken pursuant to paragraph 1 of this article may be introduced and applied within the prosecution service in those States Parties where it does not form part of the judiciary but enjoys independence similar to that of the judicial service.

Article 12

Private Sector

1. Each State Party shall take measures, in accordance with the fundamental principles of its domestic law, to prevent corruption involving the private sector, enhance accounting and auditing standards in the private sector and, where appropriate, provide effective, proportionate and dissuasive civil, administrative or criminal penalties for failure to comply with such measures.

2. Measures to achieve these ends may include, inter alia:

(a) Promoting cooperation between law enforcement agencies and relevant private entities;

(b) Promoting the development of standards and procedures designed to safeguard the integrity of relevant private entities, including codes of conduct for the correct, honourable and proper performance of the activities of business and all relevant professions and the prevention of conflicts of interest, and for the promotion of the use of good commercial practices among businesses and in the contractual relations of businesses with the State;

(c) Promoting transparency among private entities, including, where appropriate, measures regarding the identity of legal and natural persons involved in the establishment and management of corporate entities;

(d) Preventing the misuse of procedures regulating private entities, including procedures regarding subsidies and licences granted by public authorities for commercial activities;

(e) Preventing conflicts of interest by imposing restrictions, as appropriate and for a reasonable period of time, on the professional activities of former public officials or on the employment of public officials by the private sector after their resignation or retirement, where such activities or employment relate directly to the functions held or supervised by those public officials during their tenure;

(f) Ensuring that private enterprises, taking into account their structure and size, have sufficient internal auditing controls to assist in preventing and detecting acts of corruption and that the accounts and required financial statements of such private enterprises are subject to appropriate auditing and certification procedures.

3. In order to prevent corruption, each State Party shall take such measures as may be necessary, in accordance with its domestic laws and regulations regarding the maintenance of books and records, financial statement disclosures and accounting and auditing standards, to prohibit the following acts carried out for the purpose of committing any of

the offences established in accordance with this Convention:

(a) The establishment of off-the-books accounts;

(b) The making of off-the-books or inadequately identified transactions;

(c) The recording of non-existent expenditure;

(d) The entry of liabilities with incorrect identification of their objects;

(e) The use of false documents; and

(f) The intentional destruction of bookkeeping documents earlier than foreseen by the law.

4. Each State Party shall disallow the tax deductibility of expenses that constitute bribes, the latter being one of the constituent elements of the offences established in accordance with articles 15 and 16 of this Convention and, where appropriate, other expenses incurred in furtherance of corrupt conduct.

Article 13

Participation of Society

1. Each State Party shall take appropriate measures, within its means and in accordance with fundamental principles of its domestic law, to promote the active participation of individuals and groups outside the public sector, such as civil society, non-governmental organizations and community-based organizations, in the prevention of and the fight against corruption and to raise public awareness regarding the existence, causes and gravity of and the threat posed by corruption. This participation should be strengthened by such measures as:

(a) Enhancing the transparency of and promoting the contribution of the public to decision-making processes;

(b) Ensuring that the public has effective access to information;

(c) Undertaking public information activities that contribute to non-tolerance of corruption, as well as public education programmes, including school and university curricula;

(d) Respecting, promoting and protecting the freedom to seek, receive, publish and disseminate information concerning corruption. That freedom may be subject to certain restrictions, but these shall only be such as are provided for by law and are necessary:

(i) For respect of the rights or reputations of others;

(ii) For the protection of national security or *ordre public* or of public health or morals.

2. Each State Party shall take appropriate measures to ensure that the relevant anti-corruption bodies referred to in this Convention are known to the public and shall provide access to such bodies, where appropriate, for the reporting, including anonymously, of any incidents that may be considered to constitute an offence established in accordance with this Convention.

Article 14

Measures to Prevent Money-Laundering

1. Each State Party shall:

(a) Institute a comprehensive domestic regulatory and supervisory regime for banks and non-bank financial institutions, including natural or legal persons that provide formal or informal services for the transmission of money or value and, where appropriate, other bodies particularly susceptible to money-laundering, within its competence, in order to deter and detect all forms of money-laundering, which regime shall emphasize requirements for customer and, where appropriate, beneficial owner identification, record-keeping and the reporting of suspicious transactions;

(b) Without prejudice to article 46 of this Convention, ensure that administrative, regulatory, law enforcement and other authorities dedicated to combating money-laundering (including, where appropriate under domestic law, judicial authorities) have the ability to cooperate and exchange information at the national and international levels within the conditions prescribed by its domestic law and, to that end, shall consider the establishment of a financial intelligence unit to serve as a national centre for the collection, analysis and dissemination of information regarding potential money-laundering.

2. States Parties shall consider implementing feasible measures to detect and monitor the movement of cash and appropriate negotiable instruments across their borders, subject to safeguards to ensure proper use of information and without impeding in any way the movement of legitimate capital. Such measures may include a requirement that individuals and businesses report the cross-border transfer of substantial quantities of cash and appropriate negotiable instruments.

3. States Parties shall consider implementing appropriate and feasible measures to require financial institutions, including money remitters:

(a) To include on forms for the electronic transfer of funds and related messages accurate and meaningful information on the originator;

(b) To maintain such information throughout the payment chain; and

(c) To apply enhanced scrutiny to transfers of funds that do not contain complete information on the originator.

4. In establishing a domestic regulatory and supervisory regime under the terms of this article, and without prejudice to any other article of this Convention, States Parties are called upon to use as a guideline the relevant initiatives of regional, interregional and multilateral organizations against money-laundering.

5. States Parties shall endeavour to develop and promote global, regional, subregional and bilateral cooperation among judicial, law enforcement and financial regulatory authorities in order to combat money-laundering.

Chapter III

Criminalization and Law Enforcement

Article 15

Bribery of National Public Officials
Each State Party shall adopt such legislative and other measures as may be necessary to establish as criminal offences, when committed intentionally:

(a) The promise, offering or giving, to a public official, directly or indirectly, of an undue advantage, for the official himself or herself or another person or entity, in order that the official act or refrain from acting in the exercise of his or her official duties;

(b) The solicitation or acceptance by a public official, directly or indirectly, of an undue advantage, for the official himself or herself or another person or entity, in order that the official act or refrain from acting in the exercise of his or her official duties.

Article 16

Bribery of Foreign Public Officials and Officials of Public International Organizations
1. Each State Party shall adopt such legislative and other measures as may be necessary to establish as a criminal offence, when committed intentionally, the promise, offering or giving to a foreign public official or an official of a public international organization, directly or indirectly, of an undue advantage, for the official himself or herself or another person or entity, in order that the official act or refrain from acting in the exercise of his or her official duties, in order to obtain or retain business or other undue advantage in relation to the conduct of international business.

2. Each State Party shall consider adopting such legislative and other measures as may be necessary to establish as a criminal offence, when committed intentionally, the solicitation or acceptance by a

foreign public official or an official of a public international organization, directly or indirectly, of an undue advantage, for the official himself or herself or another person or entity, in order that the official act or refrain from acting in the exercise of his or her official duties.

Article 17

Embezzlement, Misappropriation or Other Diversion of Property by a Public Official
Each State Party shall adopt such legislative and other measures as may be necessary to establish as criminal offences, when committed intentionally, the embezzlement, misappropriation or other diversion by a public official for his or her benefit or for the benefit of another person or entity, of any property, public or private funds or securities or any other thing of value entrusted to the public official by virtue of his or her position.

Article 18

Trading in Influence
Each State Party shall consider adopting such legislative and other measures as may be necessary to establish as criminal offences, when committed intentionally:

(a) The promise, offering or giving to a public official or any other person, directly or indirectly, of an undue advantage in order that the public official or the person abuse his or her real or supposed influence with a view to obtaining from an administration or public authority of the State Party an undue advantage for the original instigator of the act or for any other person;

(b) The solicitation or acceptance by a public official or any other person, directly or indirectly, of an undue advantage for himself or herself or for another person in order that the public official or the person abuse his or her real or supposed influence with a view to obtaining from an administration or public authority of the State Party an undue advantage.

Article 19

Abuse of Functions
Each State Party shall consider adopting such legislative and other measures as may be necessary to establish as a criminal offence, when committed intentionally, the abuse of functions or position, that is, the performance of or failure to perform an act, in violation of laws, by a public official in the discharge of his or her functions, for the purpose of obtaining an undue advantage for himself or herself or for another person or entity.

Article 20

Illicit Enrichment
Subject to its constitution and the fundamental principles of its legal system, each State Party shall consider adopting such legislative and other measures as may be necessary to establish as a criminal offence, when committed intentionally, illicit enrichment, that is, a significant increase in the assets of a public official that he or she cannot reasonably explain in relation to his or her lawful income.

Article 21

Bribery in the Private Sector
Each State Party shall consider adopting such legislative and other measures as may be necessary to establish as criminal offences, when committed intentionally in the course of economic, financial or commercial activities:

(a) The promise, offering or giving, directly or indirectly, of an undue advantage to any person who directs or works, in any capacity, for a private sector entity, for the person himself or herself or for another person, in order that he or she, in breach of his or her duties, act or refrain from acting;

(b) The solicitation or acceptance, directly or indirectly, of an undue advantage by any person who directs or works, in any capacity, for a private sector entity, for the person himself or herself or for another person, in order that he or she, in breach of his or her duties, act or refrain from acting.

Article 22

Embezzlement of Property in the Private Sector
Each State Party shall consider adopting such legislative and other measures as may be necessary to establish as a criminal offence, when committed intentionally in the course of economic, financial or commercial activities, embezzlement by a person who directs or works, in any capacity, in a private sector entity of any property, private funds or securities or any other thing of value entrusted to him or her by virtue of his or her position.

Article 23

Laundering of Proceeds of Crime
1. Each State Party shall adopt, in accordance with fundamental principles of its domestic law, such legislative and other measures as may be necessary to establish as criminal offences, when committed intentionally:

(a) (i) The conversion or transfer of property, knowing that such property is the proceeds of crime, for the purpose of concealing or disguising the illicit origin of the property or of helping any person who is involved in the commission of the predicate offence to evade the legal consequences of his or her action;

(ii) The concealment or disguise of the true nature, source, location, disposition, movement or ownership of or rights with respect to property, knowing that such property is the proceeds of crime;

(b) Subject to the basic concepts of its legal system:

(i) The acquisition, possession or use of property, knowing, at the time of receipt, that such property is the proceeds of crime;

(ii) Participation in, association with or conspiracy to commit, attempts to commit and aiding, abetting, facilitating and counselling the com-

mission of any of the offences established in accordance with this article.

2. For purposes of implementing or applying paragraph 1 of this article:

(a) Each State Party shall seek to apply paragraph 1 of this article to the widest range of predicate offences;

(b) Each State Party shall include as predicate offences at a minimum a comprehensive range of criminal offences established in accordance with this Convention;

(c) For the purposes of subparagraph (b) above, predicate offences shall include offences committed both within and outside the jurisdiction of the State Party in question. However, offences committed outside the jurisdiction of a State Party shall constitute predicate offences only when the relevant conduct is a criminal offence under the domestic law of the State where it is committed and would be a criminal offence under the domestic law of the State Party implementing or applying this article had it been committed there;

(d) Each State Party shall furnish copies of its laws that give effect to this article and of any subsequent changes to such laws or a description thereof to the Secretary-General of the United Nations;

(e) If required by fundamental principles of the domestic law of a State Party, it may be provided that the offences set forth in paragraph 1 of this article do not apply to the persons who committed the predicate offence.

Article 24

Concealment
Without prejudice to the provisions of article 23 of this Convention, each State Party shall consider adopting such legislative and other measures as may be necessary to establish as a criminal offence, when committed intentionally after the commission of any of the offences established in accordance with this Convention without having participated in such offences, the concealment or

continued retention of property when the person involved knows that such property is the result of any of the offences established in accordance with this Convention.

Article 25

Obstruction of Justice
Each State Party shall adopt such legislative and other measures as may be necessary to establish as criminal offences, when committed intentionally:

(a) The use of physical force, threats or intimidation or the promise, offering or giving of an undue advantage to induce false testimony or to interfere in the giving of testimony or the production of evidence in a proceeding in relation to the commission of offences established in accordance with this Convention;

(b) The use of physical force, threats or intimidation to interfere with the exercise of official duties by a justice or law enforcement official in relation to the commission of offences established in accordance with this Convention. Nothing in this sub-paragraph shall prejudice the right of States Parties to have legislation that protects other categories of public official.

Article 26

Liability of Legal Persons
1. Each State Party shall adopt such measures as may be necessary, consistent with its legal principles, to establish the liability of legal persons for participation in the offences established in accordance with this Convention.

2. Subject to the legal principles of the State Party, the liability of legal persons may be criminal, civil or administrative.

3. Such liability shall be without prejudice to the criminal liability of the natural persons who have committed the offences.

4. Each State Party shall, in particular, ensure that legal persons held liable in accordance with this article are subject to effective, proportionate and dissuasive criminal or non-criminal sanctions, including monetary sanctions.

Article 27

Participation and Attempt
1. Each State Party shall adopt such legislative and other measures as may be necessary to establish as a criminal offence, in accordance with its domestic law, participation in any capacity such as an accomplice, assistant or instigator in an offence established in accordance with this Convention.

2. Each State Party may adopt such legislative and other measures as may be necessary to establish as a criminal offence, in accordance with its domestic law, any attempt to commit an offence established in accordance with this Convention.

3. Each State Party may adopt such legislative and other measures as may be necessary to establish as a criminal offence, in accordance with its domestic law, the preparation for an offence established in accordance with this Convention.

Article 28

Knowledge, Intent and Purpose As Elements of an Offence
Knowledge, intent or purpose required as an element of an offence established in accordance with this Convention may be inferred from objective factual circumstances.

Article 29

Statute of Limitations
Each State Party shall, where appropriate, establish under its domestic law a long statute of limitations period in which to commence proceedings for any offence established in accordance with this Convention and establish a longer statute of

limitations period or provide for the suspension of the statute of limitations where the alleged offender has evaded the administration of justice.

Article 30

Prosecution, Adjudication and Sanctions
1. Each State Party shall make the commission of an offence established in accordance with this Convention liable to sanctions that take into account the gravity of that offence.

2. Each State Party shall take such measures as may be necessary to establish or maintain, in accordance with its legal system and constitutional principles, an appropriate balance between any immunities or jurisdictional privileges accorded to its public officials for the performance of their functions and the possibility, when necessary, of effectively investigating, prosecuting and adjudicating offences established in accordance with this Convention.

3. Each State Party shall endeavour to ensure that any discretionary legal powers under its domestic law relating to the prosecution of persons for offences established in accordance with this Convention are exercised to maximize the effectiveness of law enforcement measures in respect of those offences and with due regard to the need to deter the commission of such offences.

4. In the case of offences established in accordance with this Convention, each State Party shall take appropriate measures, in accordance with its domestic law and with due regard to the rights of the defence, to seek to ensure that conditions imposed in connection with decisions on release pending trial or appeal take into consideration the need to ensure the presence of the defendant at subsequent criminal proceedings.

5. Each State Party shall take into account the gravity of the offences concerned when considering the eventuality of early release or parole of persons convicted of such offences.

6. Each State Party, to the extent consistent with the fundamental principles of its legal system, shall consider establishing procedures through which a public official accused of an offence established in accordance with this Convention may, where appropriate, be removed, suspended or reassigned by the appropriate authority, bearing in mind respect for the principle of the presumption of innocence.

7. Where warranted by the gravity of the offence, each State Party, to the extent consistent with the fundamental principles of its legal system, shall consider establishing procedures for the disqualification, by court order or any other appropriate means, for a period of time determined by its domestic law, of persons convicted of offences established in accordance with this Convention from:

   (a) Holding public office; and
   (b) Holding office in an enterprise owned in whole or in part by the State.

8. Paragraph 1 of this article shall be without prejudice to the exercise of disciplinary powers by the competent authorities against civil servants.

9. Nothing contained in this Convention shall affect the principle that the description of the offences established in accordance with this Convention and of the applicable legal defences or other legal principles controlling the lawfulness of conduct is reserved to the domestic law of a State Party and that such offences shall be prosecuted and punished in accordance with that law.

10. States Parties shall endeavour to promote the reintegration into society of persons convicted of offences established in accordance with this Convention.

Article 31

Freezing, Seizure and Confiscation
1. Each State Party shall take, to the greatest extent possible within its domestic legal system, such measures as may be necessary to enable confiscation of:

(a) Proceeds of crime derived from offences established in accordance with this Convention or property the value of which corresponds to that of such proceeds;

(b) Property, equipment or other instrumentalities used in or destined for use in offences established in accordance with this Convention.

2. Each State Party shall take such measures as may be necessary to enable the identification, tracing, freezing or seizure of any item referred to in paragraph 1 of this article for the purpose of eventual confiscation.

3. Each State Party shall adopt, in accordance with its domestic law, such legislative and other measures as may be necessary to regulate the administration by the competent authorities of frozen, seized or confiscated property covered in paragraphs 1 and 2 of this article.

4. If such proceeds of crime have been transformed or converted, in part or in full, into other property, such property shall be liable to the measures referred to in this article instead of the proceeds.

5. If such proceeds of crime have been intermingled with property acquired from legitimate sources, such property shall, without prejudice to any powers relating to freezing or seizure, be liable to confiscation up to the assessed value of the intermingled proceeds.

6. Income or other benefits derived from such proceeds of crime, from property into which such proceeds of crime have been transformed or converted or from property with which such proceeds of crime have been intermingled shall also be liable to the measures referred to in this article, in the same manner and to the same extent as proceeds of crime.

7. For the purpose of this article and article 55 of this Convention, each State Party shall empower its courts or other competent authorities to order that bank, financial or commercial records be made available or seized. A State Party shall not decline to act under the provisions of this paragraph on the ground of bank secrecy.

8. States Parties may consider the possibility of requiring that an offender demonstrate the lawful origin of such alleged proceeds of crime or other property liable to confiscation, to the extent that such a requirement is consistent with the fundamental principles of their domestic law and with the nature of judicial and other proceedings.

9. The provisions of this article shall not be so construed as to prejudice the rights of bona fide third parties.

10. Nothing contained in this article shall affect the principle that the measures to which it refers shall be defined and implemented in accordance with and subject to the provisions of the domestic law of a State Party.

Article 32

Protection of Witnesses, Experts and Victims
1. Each State Party shall take appropriate measures in accordance with its domestic legal system and within its means to provide effective protection from potential retaliation or intimidation for witnesses and experts who give testimony concerning offences established in accordance with this Convention and, as appropriate, for their relatives and other persons close to them.

2. The measures envisaged in paragraph 1 of this article may include, inter alia, without prejudice to

the rights of the defendant, including the right to due process:

(a) Establishing procedures for the physical protection of such persons, such as, to the extent necessary and feasible, relocating them and permitting, where appropriate, non-disclosure or limitations on the disclosure of information concerning the identity and whereabouts of such persons;

(b) Providing evidentiary rules to permit witnesses and experts to give testimony in a manner that ensures the safety of such persons, such as permitting testimony to be given through the use of communications technology such as video or other adequate means.

3. States Parties shall consider entering into agreements or arrangements with other States for the relocation of persons referred to in paragraph 1 of this article.

4. The provisions of this article shall also apply to victims insofar as they are witnesses.

5. Each State Party shall, subject to its domestic law, enable the views and concerns of victims to be presented and considered at appropriate stages of criminal proceedings against offenders in a manner not prejudicial to the rights of the defence.

Article 33

Protection of Reporting Persons
Each State Party shall consider incorporating into its domestic legal system appropriate measures to provide protection against any unjustified treatment for any person who reports in good faith and on reasonable grounds to the competent authorities any facts concerning offences established in accordance with this Convention.

Article 34

Consequences of Acts of Corruption
With due regard to the rights of third parties acquired in good faith, each State Party shall take measures, in accordance with the fundamental principles of its domestic law, to address consequences of corruption. In this context, States Parties may consider corruption a relevant factor in legal proceedings to annul or rescind a contract, withdraw a concession or other similar instrument or take any other remedial action.

Article 35

Compensation for Damage
Each State Party shall take such measures as may be necessary, in accordance with principles of its domestic law, to ensure that entities or persons who have suffered damage as a result of an act of corruption have the right to initiate legal proceedings against those responsible for that damage in order to obtain compensation.

Article 36

Specialized Authorities
Each State Party shall, in accordance with the fundamental principles of its legal system, ensure the existence of a body or bodies or persons specialized in combating corruption through law enforcement. Such body or bodies or persons shall be granted the necessary independence, in accordance with the fundamental principles of the legal system of the State Party, to be able to carry out their functions effectively and without any undue influence. Such persons or staff of such body or bodies should have the appropriate training and resources to carry out their tasks.

Article 37

Cooperation with Law Enforcement Authorities
1. Each State Party shall take appropriate measures to encourage persons who participate or who have participated in the commission of an offence established in accordance with this Convention to supply information useful to competent authorities for investigative and evidentiary purposes and to provide factual, specific help to competent

authorities that may contribute to depriving offenders of the proceeds of crime and to recovering such proceeds.

2. Each State Party shall consider providing for the possibility, in appropriate cases, of mitigating punishment of an accused person who provides substantial cooperation in the investigation or prosecution of an offence established in accordance with this Convention.

3. Each State Party shall consider providing for the possibility, in accordance with fundamental principles of its domestic law, of granting immunity from prosecution to a person who provides substantial cooperation in the investigation or prosecution of an offence established in accordance with this Convention.

4. Protection of such persons shall be, mutatis mutandis, as provided for in article 32 of this Convention.

5. Where a person referred to in paragraph 1 of this article located in one State Party can provide substantial cooperation to the competent authorities of another State Party, the States Parties concerned may consider entering into agreements or arrangements, in accordance with their domestic law, concerning the potential provision by the other State Party of the treatment set forth in paragraphs 2 and 3 of this article.

Article 38

Cooperation between National Authorities
Each State Party shall take such measures as may be necessary to encourage, in accordance with its domestic law, cooperation between, on the one hand, its public authorities, as well as its public officials, and, on the other hand, its authorities responsible for investigating and prosecuting criminal offences. Such cooperation may include:

(a) Informing the latter authorities, on their own initiative, where there are reasonable grounds to believe that any of the offences established in accordance with articles 15, 21 and 23 of this Convention has been committed; or
(b) Providing, upon request, to the latter authorities all necessary information.

Article 39

Cooperation between National Authorities and the Private Sector
1. Each State Party shall take such measures as may be necessary to encourage, in accordance with its domestic law, cooperation between national investigating and prosecuting authorities and entities of the private sector, in particular financial institutions, relating to matters involving the commission of offences established in accordance with this Convention.

2. Each State Party shall consider encouraging its nationals and other persons with a habitual residence in its territory to report to the national investigating and prosecuting authorities the commission of an offence established in accordance with this Convention.

Article 40

Bank Secrecy
Each State Party shall ensure that, in the case of domestic criminal investigations of offences established in accordance with this Convention, there are appropriate mechanisms available within its domestic legal system to overcome obstacles that may arise out of the application of bank secrecy laws.

Article 41

Criminal Record
Each State Party may adopt such legislative or other measures as may be necessary to take into consideration, under such terms as and for the

purpose that it deems appropriate, any previous conviction in another State of an alleged offender for the purpose of using such information in criminal proceedings relating to an offence established in accordance with this Convention.

Article 42

Jurisdiction
1. Each State Party shall adopt such measures as may be necessary to establish its jurisdiction over the offences established in accordance with this Convention when:

(a) The offence is committed in the territory of that State Party; or

(b) The offence is committed on board a vessel that is flying the flag of that State Party or an aircraft that is registered under the laws of that State Party at the time that the offence is committed.

2. Subject to article 4 of this Convention, a State Party may also establish its jurisdiction over any such offence when:

(a) The offence is committed against a national of that State Party; or

(b) The offence is committed by a national of that State Party or a stateless person who has his or her habitual residence in its territory; or

(c) The offence is one of those established in accordance with article 23, paragraph 1 (b) (ii), of this Convention and is committed outside its territory with a view to the commission of an offence established in accordance with article 23, paragraph 1 (a) (i) or (ii) or (b) (i), of this Convention within its territory; or

(d) The offence is committed against the State Party.

3. For the purposes of article 44 of this Convention, each State Party shall take such measures as may be necessary to establish its jurisdiction over the offences established in accordance with this Convention when the alleged offender is present in its territory and it does not extradite such person solely on the ground that he or she is one of its nationals.

4. Each State Party may also take such measures as may be necessary to establish its jurisdiction over the offences established in accordance with this Convention when the alleged offender is present in its territory and it does not extradite him or her.

5. If a State Party exercising its jurisdiction under paragraph 1 or 2 of this article has been notified, or has otherwise learned, that any other States Parties are conducting an investigation, prosecution or judicial proceeding in respect of the same conduct, the competent authorities of those States Parties shall, as appropriate, consult one another with a view to coordinating their actions.

6. Without prejudice to norms of general international law, this Convention shall not exclude the exercise of any criminal jurisdiction established by a State Party in accordance with its domestic law.

Chapter IV

International Cooperation

Article 43

International Cooperation
1. States Parties shall cooperate in criminal matters in accordance with articles 44 to 50 of this Convention. Where appropriate and consistent with their domestic legal system, States Parties shall consider assisting each other in investigations of and proceedings in civil and administrative matters relating to corruption.

Article 48

Law Enforcement Cooperation
1. States Parties shall cooperate closely with one another, consistent with their respective domestic legal and administrative systems, to enhance the effectiveness of law enforcement action to combat the offences covered by this Convention. States Parties shall, in particular, take effective measures:

(a) To enhance and, where necessary, to establish channels of communication between their competent authorities, agencies and services in order to facilitate the secure and rapid exchange of information concerning all aspects of the offences covered by this Convention, including, if the States Parties concerned deem it appropriate, links with other criminal activities;

(b) To cooperate with other States Parties in conducting inquiries with respect to offences covered by this Convention concerning:

(i) The identity, whereabouts and activities of persons suspected of involvement in such offences or the location of other persons concerned;

(ii) The movement of proceeds of crime or property derived from the commission of such offences;

(iii) The movement of property, equipment or other instrumentalities used or intended for use in the commission of such offences;

(c) To provide, where appropriate, necessary items or quantities of substances for analytical or investigative purposes;

(d) To exchange, where appropriate, information with other States Parties concerning specific means and methods used to commit offences covered by this Convention, including the use of false identities, forged, altered or false documents and other means of concealing activities;

(e) To facilitate effective coordination between their competent authorities, agencies and services and to promote the exchange of personnel and other experts, including, subject to bilateral agreements or arrangements between the States Parties concerned, the posting of liaison officers;

(f) To exchange information and coordinate administrative and other measures taken as appropriate for the purpose of early identification of the offences covered by this Convention.

2. With a view to giving effect to this Convention, States Parties shall consider entering into bilateral or multilateral agreements or arrangements on direct cooperation between their law enforcement agencies and, where such agreements or arrangements already exist, amending them. In the absence of such agreements or arrangements between the States Parties concerned, the States Parties may consider this Convention to be the basis for mutual law enforcement cooperation in respect of the offences covered by this Convention. Whenever appropriate, States Parties shall make full use of agreements or arrangements, including international or regional organizations, to enhance the cooperation between their law enforcement agencies.

3. States Parties shall endeavour to cooperate within their means to respond to offences covered by this Convention committed through the use of modern technology.

7.
Council of Europe Convention on Cybercrime

The information revolution of the twenty-first century has dramatically altered the means by which governments, businesses, and private-sector organizations and individuals conduct business and engage in day-to-day activities. Electronic mailing via the Internet is but one example of how advances in communication technology have altered and enhanced our capability to send and receive vital information. Unfortunately, these capabilities that enhance our lives have also enabled criminal entrepreneurs to span national and international borders, thereby increasing their ability to engage in traditional as well as nontraditional criminal activity. At present, national laws and the agencies assigned to enforce them are not equipped to deal with this phenomenon. Hence, to enhance global security and protect ordinary citizens, regional and international cooperation among governments and private-sector institutions is needed. The Convention on Cybercrime is a step in that direction.

Source
Council of Europe, http://conventions.coe.int/Treaty/en/Treaties/Word/185.doc.

Preamble

The member States of the Council of Europe and the other States signatory hereto,

Considering that the aim of the Council of Europe is to achieve a greater unity between its members;

Recognising the value of fostering co-operation with the other States parties to this Convention;

Convinced of the need to pursue, as a matter of priority, a common criminal policy aimed at the protection of society against cybercrime, *inter alia*, by adopting appropriate legislation and fostering international co-operation;

Conscious of the profound changes brought about by the digitalisation, convergence and continuing globalisation of computer networks;

Concerned by the risk that computer networks and electronic information may also be used for committing criminal offences and that evidence relating to such offences may be stored and transferred by these networks;

Recognising the need for co-operation between States and private industry in combating cybercrime and the need to protect legitimate interests in the use and development of information technologies;

Believing that an effective fight against cybercrime requires increased, rapid and well-functioning international co-operation in criminal matters;

Convinced that the present Convention is necessary to deter action directed against the confidentiality, integrity and availability of computer systems, networks and computer data as well as the misuse of such systems, networks and data by providing for the criminalisation of such conduct, as described in this Convention, and the adoption of powers sufficient for effectively combating such criminal offences, by facilitating their detection, investigation and prosecution at both the domestic and international levels and by providing arrangements for fast and reliable international co-operation;

Mindful of the need to ensure a proper balance between the interests of law enforcement and respect for fundamental human rights as enshrined in the 1950 Council of Europe Convention for the Protection of Human Rights and Fundamental Freedoms, the 1966 United Nations International Covenant on Civil and Political Rights and other applicable international human rights treaties, which reaffirm the right of everyone to hold opinions without interference, as well as the right to freedom of expression, including the freedom to seek, receive, and impart information and ideas of all kinds, regardless of frontiers, and the rights concerning the respect for privacy;

Mindful also of the right to the protection of personal data, as conferred, for example, by the 1981 Council of Europe Convention for the Protection of Individuals with regard to Automatic Processing of Personal Data. Considering the 1989 United Nations Convention on the Rights of the Child and the 1999 International Labour Organization Worst Forms of Child Labour Convention;

Taking into account the existing Council of Europe conventions on co-operation in the penal field, as well as similar treaties which exist between Council of Europe member States and other States, and stressing that the present Convention is intended to supplement those conventions in order to make criminal investigations and proceedings concerning criminal offences related to computer systems and data more effective and to enable the collection of evidence in electronic form of a criminal offence;

Welcoming recent developments which further advance international understanding and co-operation in combating cybercrime, including action taken by the United Nations, the OECD, the European Union and the G8;

Recalling Committee of Ministers Recommendations No. R (85) 10 concerning the practical application of the European Convention on Mutual Assistance in Criminal Matters in respect of letters rogatory for the interception of telecommunications, No. R (88) 2 on piracy in the field of copyright and neighbouring rights, No. R (87) 15 regulating the use of personal data in the police sector, No. R (95) 4 on the protection of personal data in the area of telecommunication services, with particular reference to telephone services, as well as No. R (89) 9 on computer-related crime providing guidelines for national legislatures concerning the definition of certain computer crimes and No. R (95) 13 concerning problems of criminal procedural law connected with information technology;

Having regard to Resolution No. 1 adopted by the European Ministers of Justice at their 21st Conference (Prague, 10 and 11 June 1997), which recommended that the Committee of Ministers support the work on cybercrime carried out by the European Committee on Crime Problems (CDPC) in order to bring domestic criminal law provisions closer to each other and enable the use of effective means of investigation into such offences, as well as to Resolution No. 3 adopted at the 23rd Conference of the European Ministers of Justice (London, 8 and 9 June 2000), which encouraged the negotiating parties to pursue their efforts with a view to finding appropriate solutions to enable the largest possible number of States to become parties to the Convention and acknowledged the need for a swift and efficient system of international co-operation, which duly takes into account the specific requirements of the fight against cybercrime;

Having also regard to the Action Plan adopted by the Heads of State and Government of the Council of Europe on the occasion of their Second Summit (Strasbourg, 10 and 11 October 1997), to seek common responses to the development of the new information technologies based on the standards and values of the Council of Europe;

Have agreed as follows:

Chapter I—Use of Terms

Article 1—Definitions
For the purposes of this Convention:

a. "computer system" means any device or a group of interconnected or related devices, one or more of which, pursuant to a program, performs automatic processing of data;
b. "computer data" means any representation of facts, information or concepts in a form suitable for processing in a computer system, including a program suitable to cause a computer system to perform a function;
c. "service provider" means:
    i. any public or private entity that provides to users of its service the ability to communicate by means of a computer system, and
    ii. any other entity that processes or stores computer data on behalf of such communication service or users of such service;
d. "traffic data" means any computer data relating to a communication by means of a computer system, generated by a computer system that formed a part in the chain of communication, indicating the communication's origin, destination, route, time, date, size, duration, or type of underlying service.

Chapter II—Measures to Be Taken at the National Level

Section 1—Substantive Criminal Law

Title 1—Offences against the Confidentiality, Integrity and Availability of Computer Data and Systems

Article 2—Illegal Access

Each Party shall adopt such legislative and other measures as may be necessary to establish as criminal offences under its domestic law, when committed intentionally, the access to the whole or any part of a computer system without right. A Party may require that the offence be committed by infringing security measures, with the intent of obtaining computer data or other dishonest intent, or in relation to a computer system that is connected to another computer system.

Article 3—Illegal Interception

Each Party shall adopt such legislative and other measures as may be necessary to establish as criminal offences under its domestic law, when committed intentionally, the interception without right, made by technical means, of non-public transmissions of computer data to, from or within a computer system, including electromagnetic emissions from a computer system carrying such computer data. A Party may require that the offence be committed with dishonest intent, or in relation to a computer system that is connected to another computer system.

Article 4—Data Interference

1. Each Party shall adopt such legislative and other measures as may be necessary to establish as criminal offences under its domestic law, when committed intentionally, the damaging, deletion, deterioration, alteration or suppression of computer data without right.

2. A Party may reserve the right to require that the conduct described in paragraph 1 result in serious harm.

Article 5—System Interference

Each Party shall adopt such legislative and other measures as may be necessary to establish as criminal offences under its domestic law, when committed intentionally, the serious hindering without right of the functioning of a computer system by inputting, transmitting, damaging, deleting, deteriorating, altering or suppressing computer data.

Article 6—Misuse of Devices

1. Each Party shall adopt such legislative and other measures as may be necessary to establish as criminal offences under its domestic law, when committed intentionally and without right:

    a. the production, sale, procurement for use, import, distribution or otherwise making available of:

        i. a device, including a computer program, designed or adapted primarily for the purpose of committing any of the offences established in accordance with the above Articles 2 through 5;

        ii. a computer password, access code, or similar data by which the whole or any part of a computer system is capable of being accessed, with intent that it be used for the purpose of committing any of the offences established in Articles 2 through 5; and

    b. the possession of an item referred to in paragraphs a.i or ii above, with intent that it be used for the purpose of committing any of the offences established in Articles 2 through 5. A Party may require by law that a number of such items be possessed before criminal liability attaches.

2. This article shall not be interpreted as imposing criminal liability where the production, sale, procurement for use, import, distribution or otherwise making available or possession referred to in paragraph 1 of this article is not for the purpose of committing an offence established in accordance with Articles 2 through 5 of this Convention, such as for the authorised testing or protection of a computer system.

3. Each Party may reserve the right not to apply paragraph 1 of this article, provided that the reservation does not concern the sale, distribution or otherwise making available of the items referred to in paragraph 1 a.ii of this article.

Title 2—Computer-Related Offences

Article 7—Computer-Related Forgery
Each Party shall adopt such legislative and other measures as may be necessary to establish as criminal offences under its domestic law, when committed intentionally and without right, the input, alteration, deletion, or suppression of computer data, resulting in inauthentic data with the intent that it be considered or acted upon for legal purposes as if it were authentic, regardless whether or not the data is directly readable and intelligible. A Party may require an intent to defraud, or similar dishonest intent, before criminal liability attaches.

Article 8—Computer-Related Fraud
Each Party shall adopt such legislative and other measures as may be necessary to establish as criminal offences under its domestic law, when committed intentionally and without right, the causing of a loss of property to another person by:

a. any input, alteration, deletion or suppression of computer data;
b. any interference with the functioning of a computer system, with fraudulent or dishonest intent of procuring, without right, an economic benefit for oneself or for another person.

Title 3—Content-Related Offences

Article 9—Offences Related to Child Pornography
1. Each Party shall adopt such legislative and other measures as may be necessary to establish as criminal offences under its domestic law, when committed intentionally and without right, the following conduct:

a. producing child pornography for the purpose of its distribution through a computer system;
b. offering or making available child pornography through a computer system;
c. distributing or transmitting child pornography through a computer system;
d. procuring child pornography through a computer system for oneself or for another person;
e. possessing child pornography in a computer system or on a computer-data storage medium.

2. For the purpose of paragraph 1 above, the term "child pornography" shall include pornographic material that visually depicts:

a. a minor engaged in sexually explicit conduct;
b. a person appearing to be a minor engaged in sexually explicit conduct;
c. realistic images representing a minor engaged in sexually explicit conduct.

3. For the purpose of paragraph 2 above, the term "minor" shall include all persons under 18 years of age. A Party may, however, require a lower age-limit, which shall be not less than 16 years.

4. Each Party may reserve the right not to apply, in whole or in part, paragraphs 1, sub-paragraphs d. and e, and 2, sub-paragraphs b. and c.

Title 4—Offences Related to Infringements of Copyright and Related Rights

Article 10—Offences Related to Infringements of Copyright and Related Rights
1. Each Party shall adopt such legislative and other measures as may be necessary to establish as criminal offences under its domestic law the infringement of copyright, as defined under the law of that Party, pursuant to the obligations it has undertaken under the Paris Act of 24 July 1971 revising the Bern Convention for the Protection of Literary and Artistic Works, the Agreement on Trade-Related Aspects of Intellectual Property Rights and the WIPO Copyright Treaty, with the exception of any moral rights conferred by such conventions, where such acts are committed wilfully, on a commercial scale and by means of a computer system.

2. Each Party shall adopt such legislative and other measures as may be necessary to establish as

criminal offences under its domestic law the infringement of related rights, as defined under the law of that Party, pursuant to the obligations it has undertaken under the International Convention for the Protection of Performers, Producers of Phonograms and Broadcasting Organisations (Rome Convention), the Agreement on Trade-Related Aspects of Intellectual Property Rights and the WIPO Performances and Phonograms Treaty, with the exception of any moral rights conferred by such conventions, where such acts are committed wilfully, on a commercial scale and by means of a computer system.

3. A Party may reserve the right not to impose criminal liability under paragraphs 1 and 2 of this article in limited circumstances, provided that other effective remedies are available and that such reservation does not derogate from the Party's international obligations set forth in the international instruments referred to in paragraphs 1 and 2 of this article.

Title 5—Ancillary Liability and Sanctions

Article 11—Attempt and Aiding or Abetting
1. Each Party shall adopt such legislative and other measures as may be necessary to establish as criminal offences under its domestic law, when committed intentionally, aiding or abetting the commission of any of the offences established in accordance with Articles 2 through 10 of the present Convention with intent that such offence be committed.

2. Each Party shall adopt such legislative and other measures as may be necessary to establish as criminal offences under its domestic law, when committed intentionally, an attempt to commit any of the offences established in accordance with Articles 3 through 5, 7, 8, and 9.1.a and c. of this Convention.

3. Each Party may reserve the right not to apply, in whole or in part, paragraph 2 of this article.

Article 12—Corporate Liability
1. Each Party shall adopt such legislative and other measures as may be necessary to ensure that legal persons can be held liable for a criminal offence established in accordance with this Convention, committed for their benefit by any natural person, acting either individually or as part of an organ of the legal person, who has a leading position within it, based on:

    a. a power of representation of the legal person;
    b. an authority to take decisions on behalf of the legal person;
    c. an authority to exercise control within the legal person.

2. In addition to the cases already provided for in paragraph 1 of this article, each Party shall take the measures necessary to ensure that a legal person can be held liable where the lack of supervision or control by a natural person referred to in paragraph 1 has made possible the commission of a criminal offence established in accordance with this Convention for the benefit of that legal person by a natural person acting under its authority.

3. Subject to the legal principles of the Party, the liability of a legal person may be criminal, civil or administrative.

4. Such liability shall be without prejudice to the criminal liability of the natural persons who have committed the offence.

Article 13—Sanctions and Measures
1. Each Party shall adopt such legislative and other measures as may be necessary to ensure that the criminal offences established in accordance with Articles 2 through 11 are punishable by effective, proportionate and dissuasive sanctions, which include deprivation of liberty.

2. Each Party shall ensure that legal persons held liable in accordance with Article 12 shall be subject to effective, proportionate and dissuasive criminal

or non-criminal sanctions or measures, including monetary sanctions.

Section 2—Procedural Law

Title 1—Common Provisions

Article 14—Scope of Procedural Provisions
1. Each Party shall adopt such legislative and other measures as may be necessary to establish the powers and procedures provided for in this section for the purpose of specific criminal investigations or proceedings.

2. Except as specifically provided otherwise in Article 21, each Party shall apply the powers and procedures referred to in paragraph 1 of this article to:

    a. the criminal offences established in accordance with Articles 2 through 11 of this Convention;
    b. other criminal offences committed by means of a computer system; and
    c. the collection of evidence in electronic form of a criminal offence.

3. a. Each Party may reserve the right to apply the measures referred to in Article 20 only to offences or categories of offences specified in the reservation, provided that the range of such offences or categories of offences is not more restricted than the range of offences to which it applies the measures referred to in Article 21. Each Party shall consider restricting such a reservation to enable the broadest application of the measure referred to in Article 20.
    b. Where a Party, due to limitations in its legislation in force at the time of the adoption of the present Convention, is not able to apply the measures referred to in Articles 20 and 21 to communications being transmitted within a computer system of a service provider, which system:
      i. is being operated for the benefit of a closed group of users, and

      ii. does not employ public communications networks and is not connected with another computer system, whether public or private,

that Party may reserve the right not to apply these measures to such communications. Each Party shall consider restricting such a reservation to enable the broadest application of the measures referred to in Articles 20 and 21.

[. . .]

Chapter III—International Co-operation

Section 1—General Principles

Title 1—General Principles Relating to International Co-operation

Article 23—General Principles Relating to International Co-operation
The Parties shall co-operate with each other, in accordance with the provisions of this chapter, and through the application of relevant international instruments on international co-operation in criminal matters, arrangements agreed on the basis of uniform or reciprocal legislation, and domestic laws, to the widest extent possible for the purposes of investigations or proceedings concerning criminal offences related to computer systems and data, or for the collection of evidence in electronic form of a criminal offence.

Title 2—Principles Relating to Extradition

Article 24—Extradition
1. a. This article applies to extradition between Parties for the criminal offences established in accordance with Articles 2 through 11 of this Convention, provided that they are punishable under the laws of both Parties concerned by deprivation of liberty for a maximum period of at least one year, or by a more severe penalty.
b. Where a different minimum penalty is to be applied under an arrangement agreed on the basis of uniform or reciprocal legislation or an extradition treaty, including the European

Convention on Extradition (ETS No. 24), applicable between two or more parties, the minimum penalty provided for under such arrangement or treaty shall apply.

2. The criminal offences described in paragraph 1 of this article shall be deemed to be included as extraditable offences in any extradition treaty existing between or among the Parties. The Parties undertake to include such offences as extraditable offences in any extradition treaty to be concluded between or among them.

3. If a Party that makes extradition conditional on the existence of a treaty receives a request for extradition from another Party with which it does not have an extradition treaty, it may consider this Convention as the legal basis for extradition with respect to any criminal offence referred to in paragraph 1 of this article.

4. Parties that do not make extradition conditional on the existence of a treaty shall recognise the criminal offences referred to in paragraph 1 of this article as extraditable offences between themselves.

5. Extradition shall be subject to the conditions provided for by the law of the requested Party or by applicable extradition treaties, including the grounds on which the requested Party may refuse extradition.

6. If extradition for a criminal offence referred to in paragraph 1 of this article is refused solely on the basis of the nationality of the person sought, or because the requested Party deems that it has jurisdiction over the offence, the requested Party shall submit the case at the request of the requesting Party to its competent authorities for the purpose of prosecution and shall report the final outcome to the requesting Party in due course. Those authorities shall take their decision and conduct their investigations and proceedings in the same manner as for any other offence of a comparable nature under the law of that Party.

7. a. Each Party shall, at the time of signature or when depositing its instrument of ratification, acceptance, approval or accession, communicate to the Secretary General of the Council of Europe the name and address of each authority responsible for making or receiving requests for extradition or provisional arrest in the absence of a treaty.
b. The Secretary General of the Council of Europe shall set up and keep updated a register of authorities so designated by the Parties. Each Party shall ensure that the details held on the register are correct at all times.

Title 3—General Principles Relating to Mutual Assistance
[. . .]

Article 32—Trans-Border Access to Stored Computer Data with Consent or Where Publicly Available
A Party may, without the authorisation of another Party:

a. access publicly available (open source) stored computer data, regardless of where the data is located geographically; or
b. access or receive, through a computer system in its territory, stored computer data located in another Party, if the Party obtains the lawful and voluntary consent of the person who has the lawful authority to disclose the data to the Party through that computer system.

Article 33—Mutual Assistance in the Real-Time Collection of Traffic Data
1. The Parties shall provide mutual assistance to each other in the real-time collection of traffic data associated with specified communications in their territory transmitted by means of a computer system. Subject to the provisions of paragraph 2, this assistance shall be governed by the conditions and procedures provided for under domestic law.

2. Each Party shall provide such assistance at least with respect to criminal offences for which real-

time collection of traffic data would be available in a similar domestic case.

Article 34—Mutual Assistance Regarding the Interception of Content Data
The Parties shall provide mutual assistance to each other in the real-time collection or recording of content data of specified communications transmitted by means of a computer system to the extent permitted under their applicable treaties and domestic laws.

8.
Additional Protocol to the Convention on Cybercrime, concerning the Criminalisation of Acts of a Racist and Xenophobic Nature Committed through Computer Systems

On 7 November 2002, the Council of Europe adopted an additional protocol to the Convention on Cybercrime. This protocol addresses ethnic and racial discrimination and Internet dissemination of racist and xenophobic material. The protocol also calls for international cooperation and appeals to all parties to "adopt such legislative and other measures as may be necessary" to criminalize the distribution of this material.

Source
Council of Europe, http://conventions.coe.int/Treaty/en/Treaties/Html/189.htm.

The member States of the Council of Europe and the other States Parties to the Convention on Cybercrime, opened for signature in Budapest on 23 November 2001, signatory hereto;

Considering that the aim of the Council of Europe is to achieve a greater unity between its members;

Recalling that all human beings are born free and equal in dignity and rights;

Stressing the need to secure a full and effective implementation of all human rights without any discrimination or distinction, as enshrined in European and other international instruments;

Convinced that acts of a racist and xenophobic nature constitute a violation of human rights and a threat to the rule of law and democratic stability;

Considering that national and international law need to provide adequate legal responses to propaganda of a racist and xenophobic nature committed through computer systems;

Aware of the fact that propaganda to such acts is often subject to criminalisation in national legislation;

Having regard to the Convention on Cybercrime, which provides for modern and flexible means of international co-operation and convinced of the need to harmonise substantive law provisions concerning the fight against racist and xenophobic propaganda;

Aware that computer systems offer an unprecedented means of facilitating freedom of expression and communication around the globe;

Recognising that freedom of expression constitutes one of the essential foundations of a democratic society, and is one of the basic conditions for its progress and for the development of every human being;

Concerned, however, by the risk of misuse or abuse of such computer systems to disseminate racist and xenophobic propaganda;

Mindful of the need to ensure a proper balance between freedom of expression and an effective fight against acts of a racist and xenophobic nature;

Recognising that this Protocol is not intended to affect established principles relating to freedom of expression in national legal systems;

Taking into account the relevant international legal instruments in this field, and in particular the Convention for the Protection of Human Rights and Fundamental Freedoms and its Protocol No. 12 concerning the general prohibition of discrimination, the existing Council of Europe conventions on co-operation in the penal field, in particular the Convention on Cybercrime, the United Nations International Convention on the Elimination of All Forms of Racial Discrimination of 21 December 1965, the European Union Joint Action of 15 July 1996 adopted by the Council on the basis of Article K.3 of the Treaty on European Union, concerning action to combat racism and xenophobia;

Welcoming the recent developments which further advance international understanding and co-operation in combating cybercrime and racism and xenophobia;

Having regard to the Action Plan adopted by the Heads of State and Government of the Council of Europe on the occasion of their Second Summit (Strasbourg, 10–11 October 1997) to seek common responses to the developments of the new technologies based on the standards and values of the Council of Europe;

Have agreed as follows:

Chapter I—Common Provisions

Article 1—Purpose
The purpose of this Protocol is to supplement, as between the Parties to the Protocol, the provisions of the Convention on Cybercrime, opened for signature in Budapest on 23 November 2001 (hereinafter referred to as "the Convention"), as regards the criminalisation of acts of a racist and

xenophobic nature committed through computer systems.

Article 2—Definition
1. For the purposes of this Protocol:

"*racist and xenophobic material*" means any written material, any image or any other representation of ideas or theories, which advocates, promotes or incites hatred, discrimination or violence, against any individual or group of individuals, based on race, colour, descent or national or ethnic origin, as well as religion if used as a pretext for any of these factors.

2. The terms and expressions used in this Protocol shall be interpreted in the same manner as they are interpreted under the Convention.

Chapter II—Measures to Be Taken at National Level

Article 3—Dissemination of Racist and Xenophobic Material through Computer Systems
1. Each Party shall adopt such legislative and other measures as may be necessary to establish as criminal offences under its domestic law, when committed intentionally and without right, the following conduct:

distributing, or otherwise making available, racist and xenophobic material to the public through a computer system.

2. A Party may reserve the right not to attach criminal liability to conduct as defined by paragraph 1 of this article, where the material, as defined in Article 2, paragraph 1, advocates, promotes or incites discrimination that is not associated with hatred or violence, provided that other effective remedies are available.

3. Notwithstanding paragraph 2 of this article, a Party may reserve the right not to apply paragraph 1 to those cases of discrimination for which, due to

established principles in its national legal system concerning freedom of expression, it cannot provide for effective remedies as referred to in the said paragraph 2.

Article 4—Racist and Xenophobic Motivated Threat

1. Each Party shall adopt such legislative and other measures as may be necessary to establish as criminal offences under its domestic law, when committed intentionally and without right, the following conduct:

threatening, through a computer system, with the commission of a serious criminal offence as defined under its domestic law, (i) persons for the reason that they belong to a group, distinguished by race, colour, descent or national or ethnic origin, as well as religion, if used as a pretext for any of these factors, or (ii) a group of persons which is distinguished by any of these characteristics.

Article 5—Racist and Xenophobic Motivated Insult

1. Each Party shall adopt such legislative and other measures as may be necessary to establish as criminal offences under its domestic law, when committed intentionally and without right, the following conduct:

insulting publicly, through a computer system, (i) persons for the reason that they belong to a group distinguished by race, colour, descent or national or ethnic origin, as well as religion, if used as a pretext for any of these factors; or (ii) a group of persons which is distinguished by any of these characteristics.

2. A Party may either:

   a. require that the offence referred to in paragraph 1 of this article has the effect that the person or group of persons referred to in paragraph 1 is exposed to hatred, contempt or ridicule; or

   b. reserve the right not to apply, in whole or in part, paragraph 1 of this article.

Article 6—Denial, Gross Minimisation, Approval or Justification of Genocide or Crimes against Humanity

1. Each Party shall adopt such legislative measures as may be necessary to establish the following conduct as criminal offences under its domestic law, when committed intentionally and without right:

distributing or otherwise making available, through a computer system to the public, material which denies, grossly minimises, approves or justifies acts constituting genocide or crimes against humanity, as defined by international law and recognised as such by final and binding decisions of the International Military Tribunal, established by the London Agreement of 8 August 1945, or of any other international court established by relevant international instruments and whose jurisdiction is recognised by that Party.

2. A Party may either

   a. require that the denial or the gross minimisation referred to in paragraph 1 of this article is committed with the intent to incite hatred, discrimination or violence against any individual or group of individuals, based on race, colour, descent or national or ethnic origin, as well as religion if used as a pretext for any of these factors, or otherwise

   b. reserve the right not to apply, in whole or in part, paragraph 1 of this article.

Article 7—Aiding and Abetting

Each Party shall adopt such legislative and other measures as may be necessary to establish as criminal offences under its domestic law, when committed intentionally and without right, aiding or abetting the commission of any of the offences established in accordance with this Protocol, with intent that such offence be committed.

Chapter III—Relations between the Convention and This Protocol

Article 8—Relations between the Convention and This Protocol
1. Articles 1, 12, 13, 22, 41, 44, 45 and 46 of the Convention shall apply, *mutatis mutandis,* to this Protocol.

2. The Parties shall extend the scope of application of the measures defined in Articles 14 to 21 and Articles 23 to 35 of the Convention, to Articles 2 to 7 of this Protocol.

Chapter IV—Final Provisions

Article 9—Expression of Consent to Be Bound
1. This Protocol shall be open for signature by the States which have signed the Convention, which may express their consent to be bound by either:

   a. signature without reservation as to ratification, acceptance or approval; or
   b. subject to ratification, acceptance or approval, followed by ratification, acceptance or approval.

2. A State may not sign this Protocol without reservation as to ratification, acceptance or approval, or deposit an instrument of ratification, acceptance or approval, unless it has already deposited or simultaneously deposits an instrument of ratification, acceptance or approval of the Convention.

3. The instruments of ratification, acceptance or approval shall be deposited with the Secretary General of the Council of Europe.

9.
Convention on International Trade in Endangered Species of Wild Fauna and Flora

The Convention on International Trade in Endangered Species of Wild Fauna and Flora is an international agreement that was adopted in an effort to regulate the trade in all species of wild fauna and flora that are presently facing extinction or may face that inevitability in the future without legislation to protect and regulate their trade. Enforcement measures are addressed in Article VIII. Article XII provides for the appointment of a secretariat. This individual, appointed by the United Nations Environment Program, will oversee the provisions of this convention and, "where appropriate, make recommendations for improving the effectiveness of the present Convention."

Source
Convention on International Trade in Endangered Species of Wild Fauna and Flora, http://www.cites.org/eng/disc/text.shtml.

Signed at Washington, D.C., on 3 March 1973

Amended at Bonn, on 22 June 1979

The Contracting States,

Recognizing that wild fauna and flora in their many beautiful and varied forms are an irreplaceable part of the natural systems of the earth which must be protected for this and the generations to come;

Conscious of the ever-growing value of wild fauna and flora from aesthetic, scientific, cultural, recreational and economic points of view;

Recognizing that peoples and States are and should be the best protectors of their own wild fauna and flora;

Recognizing, in addition, that international co-operation is essential for the protection of certain species of wild fauna and flora against over-exploitation through international trade;

Convinced of the urgency of taking appropriate measures to this end; *Have agreed* as follows:

Article I

Definitions

For the purpose of the present Convention, unless the context otherwise requires:

 (a) "Species" means any species, subspecies, or geographically separate population thereof;

 (b) "Specimen" means:

  (i) any animal or plant, whether alive or dead;

  (ii) in the case of an animal: for species included in Appendices I and II, any readily recognizable part or derivative thereof; and for species included in Appendix III, any readily recognizable part or derivative thereof specified in Appendix III in relation to the species; and

  (iii) in the case of a plant: for species included in Appendix I, any readily recognizable part or derivative thereof; and for species included in Appendices II and III, any readily recognizable part or derivative thereof specified in Appendices II and III in relation to the species;

 (c) "Trade" means export, re-export, import and introduction from the sea;

 (d) "Re-export" means export of any specimen that has previously been imported;

 (e) "Introduction from the sea" means transportation into a State of specimens of any species which were taken in the marine environment not under the jurisdiction of any State;

 (f) "Scientific Authority" means a national scientific authority designated in accordance with Article IX;

 (g) "Management Authority" means a national management authority designated in accordance with Article IX;

 (h) "Party" means a State for which the present Convention has entered into force.

Article II

Fundamental Principles

1. Appendix I shall include all species threatened with extinction which are or may be affected by trade. Trade in specimens of these species must be subject to particularly strict regulation in order not to endanger further their survival and must only be authorized in exceptional circumstances.

2. Appendix II shall include:

 (a) all species which although not necessarily now threatened with extinction may become so unless trade in specimens of such species is subject to strict regulation in order to avoid utilization incompatible with their survival; and

 (b) other species which must be subject to regulation in order that trade in specimens of certain species referred to in sub-paragraph (a) of this paragraph may be brought under effective control.

3. Appendix III shall include all species which any Party identifies as being subject to regulation within its jurisdiction for the purpose of preventing or restricting exploitation, and as needing the co-operation of other Parties in the control of trade.

4. The Parties shall not allow trade in specimens of species included in Appendices I, II and III except in accordance with the provisions of the present Convention.

Article III

Regulation of Trade in Specimens of Species Included in Appendix I

1. All trade in specimens of species included in Appendix I shall be in accordance with the provisions of this Article.

2. The export of any specimen of a species included in Appendix I shall require the prior grant and presentation of an export permit. An export permit shall only be granted when the following conditions have been met:

 (a) a Scientific Authority of the State of export has advised that such export will not be detrimental to the survival of that species;

(b) a Management Authority of the State of export is satisfied that the specimen was not obtained in contravention of the laws of that State for the protection of fauna and flora;

(c) a Management Authority of the State of export is satisfied that any living specimen will be so prepared and shipped as to minimize the risk of injury, damage to health or cruel treatment; and

(d) a Management Authority of the State of export is satisfied that an import permit has been granted for the specimen.

3. The import of any specimen of a species included in Appendix I shall require the prior grant and presentation of an import permit and either an export permit or a re-export certificate. An import permit shall only be granted when the following conditions have been met:

(a) a Scientific Authority of the State of import has advised that the import will be for purposes which are not detrimental to the survival of the species involved;

(b) a Scientific Authority of the State of import is satisfied that the proposed recipient of a living specimen is suitably equipped to house and care for it; and

(c) a Management Authority of the State of import is satisfied that the specimen is not to be used for primarily commercial purposes.

4. The re-export of any specimen of a species included in Appendix I shall require the prior grant and presentation of a re-export certificate. A re-export certificate shall only be granted when the following conditions have been met:

(a) a Management Authority of the State of re-export is satisfied that the specimen was imported into that State in accordance with the provisions of the present Convention;

(b) a Management Authority of the State of re-export is satisfied that any living specimen will be so prepared and shipped as to minimize the risk of injury, damage to health or cruel treatment; and

(c) a Management Authority of the State of re-export is satisfied that an import permit has been granted for any living specimen.

5. The introduction from the sea of any specimen of a species included in Appendix I shall require the prior grant of a certificate from a Management Authority of the State of introduction. A certificate shall only be granted when the following conditions have been met:

(a) a Scientific Authority of the State of introduction advises that the introduction will not be detrimental to the survival of the species involved;

(b) a Management Authority of the State of introduction is satisfied that the proposed recipient of a living specimen is suitably equipped to house and care for it; and

(c) a Management Authority of the State of introduction is satisfied that the specimen is not to be used for primarily commercial purposes.

Article IV

Regulation of Trade in Specimens of Species Included in Appendix II

1. All trade in specimens of species included in Appendix II shall be in accordance with the provisions of this Article.

2. The export of any specimen of a species included in Appendix II shall require the prior grant and presentation of an export permit. An export permit shall only be granted when the following conditions have been met:

(a) a Scientific Authority of the State of export has advised that such export will not be detrimental to the survival of that species;

(b) a Management Authority of the State of export is satisfied that the specimen was not obtained in contravention of the laws of that State for the protection of fauna and flora; and

(c) a Management Authority of the State of export is satisfied that any living specimen will be so prepared and shipped as to minimize the risk of injury, damage to health or cruel treatment.

3. A Scientific Authority in each Party shall monitor both the export permits granted by that State for specimens of species included in Appendix II and the actual exports of such specimens. Whenever a Scientific Authority determines that the export of specimens of any such species should be limited in order to maintain that species throughout its range at a level consistent with its role in the ecosystems in which it occurs and well above the level at which that species might become eligible for inclusion in Appendix I, the Scientific Authority shall advise the appropriate Management Authority of suitable measures to be taken to limit the grant of export permits for specimens of that species.

4. The import of any specimen of a species included in Appendix II shall require the prior presentation of either an export permit or a re-export certificate.

5. The re-export of any specimen of a species included in Appendix II shall require the prior grant and presentation of a re-export certificate. A re-export certificate shall only be granted when the following conditions have been met:

    (a) a Management Authority of the State of re-export is satisfied that the specimen was imported into that State in accordance with the provisions of the present Convention; and

    (b) a Management Authority of the State of re-export is satisfied that any living specimen will be so prepared and shipped as to minimize the risk of injury, damage to health or cruel treatment.

6. The introduction from the sea of any specimen of a species included in Appendix II shall require the prior grant of a certificate from a Management Authority of the State of introduction. A certificate shall only be granted when the following conditions have been met:

    (a) a Scientific Authority of the State of introduction advises that the introduction will not be detrimental to the survival of the species involved; and

    (b) a Management Authority of the State of introduction is satisfied that any living specimen will be so handled as to minimize the risk of injury, damage to health or cruel treatment.

7. Certificates referred to in paragraph 6 of this Article may be granted on the advice of a Scientific Authority, in consultation with other national scientific authorities or, when appropriate, international scientific authorities, in respect of periods not exceeding one year for total numbers of specimens to be introduced in such periods.

Article V

Regulation of Trade in Specimens of Species Included in Appendix III

1. All trade in specimens of species included in Appendix III shall be in accordance with the provisions of this Article.

2. The export of any specimen of a species included in Appendix III from any State which has included that species in Appendix III shall require the prior grant and presentation of an export permit. An export permit shall only be granted when the following conditions have been met:

    (a) a Management Authority of the State of export is satisfied that the specimen was not obtained in contravention of the laws of that State for the protection of fauna and flora; and

    (b) a Management Authority of the State of export is satisfied that any living specimen will be so prepared and shipped as to minimize the risk of injury, damage to health or cruel treatment.

3. The import of any specimen of a species included in Appendix III shall require, except in circumstances to which paragraph 4 of this Article applies, the prior presentation of a certificate of origin and, where the import is from a State which

has included that species in Appendix III, an export permit.

4. In the case of re-export, a certificate granted by the Management Authority of the State of re-export that the specimen was processed in that State or is being re-exported shall be accepted by the State of import as evidence that the provisions of the present Convention have been complied with in respect of the specimen concerned.

Article VI

Permits and Certificates
1. Permits and certificates granted under the provisions of Articles III, IV, and V shall be in accordance with the provisions of this Article.

2. An export permit shall contain the information specified in the model set forth in Appendix IV, and may only be used for export within a period of six months from the date on which it was granted.

3. Each permit or certificate shall contain the title of the present Convention, the name and any identifying stamp of the Management Authority granting it and a control number assigned by the Management Authority.

4. Any copies of a permit or certificate issued by a Management Authority shall be clearly marked as copies only and no such copy may be used in place of the original, except to the extent endorsed thereon.

5. A separate permit or certificate shall be required for each consignment of specimens.

6. A Management Authority of the State of import of any specimen shall cancel and retain the export permit or re-export certificate and any corresponding import permit presented in respect of the import of that specimen.

7. Where appropriate and feasible a Management Authority may affix a mark upon any specimen to assist in identifying the specimen. For these purposes "mark" means any indelible imprint, lead seal or other suitable means of identifying a specimen, designed in such a way as to render its imitation by unauthorized persons as difficult as possible.

Article VII

Exemptions and Other Special Provisions Relating to Trade
1. The provisions of Articles III, IV and V shall not apply to the transit or transhipment of specimens through or in the territory of a Party while the specimens remain in Customs control.

2. Where a Management Authority of the State of export or re-export is satisfied that a specimen was acquired before the provisions of the present Convention applied to that specimen, the provisions of Articles III, IV and V shall not apply to that specimen where the Management Authority issues a certificate to that effect.

3. The provisions of Articles III, IV and V shall not apply to specimens that are personal or household effects. This exemption shall not apply where:

(a) in the case of specimens of a species included in Appendix I, they were acquired by the owner outside his State of usual residence, and are being imported into that State; or
(b) in the case of specimens of species included in Appendix II:
  (i) they were acquired by the owner outside his State of usual residence and in a State where removal from the wild occurred;
  (ii) they are being imported into the owner's State of usual residence; and
  (iii) the State where removal from the wild occurred requires the prior grant of export permits before any export of such specimens; unless a Management Authority is satisfied

that the specimens were acquired before the provisions of the present Convention applied to such specimens.

4. Specimens of an animal species included in Appendix I bred in captivity for commercial purposes, or of a plant species included in Appendix I artificially propagated for commercial purposes, shall be deemed to be specimens of species included in Appendix II.

5. Where a Management Authority of the State of export is satisfied that any specimen of an animal species was bred in captivity or any specimen of a plant species was artificially propagated, or is a part of such an animal or plant or was derived there from, a certificate by that Management Authority to that effect shall be accepted in lieu of any of the permits or certificates required under the provisions of Article III, IV or V.

6. The provisions of Articles III, IV and V shall not apply to the non-commercial loan, donation or exchange between scientists or scientific institutions registered by a Management Authority of their State, of herbarium specimens, other preserved, dried or embedded museum specimens, and live plant material, which carry a label issued or approved by a Management Authority.

7. A Management Authority of any State may waive the requirements of Articles III, IV and V and allow the movement without permits or certificates of specimens which form part of a travelling zoo, circus, menagerie, plant exhibition or other travelling exhibition provided that:

(a) the exporter or importer registers full details of such specimens with that Management Authority;
(b) the specimens are in either of the categories specified in paragraph 2 or 5 of this Article; and
(c) the Management Authority is satisfied that any living specimen will be so transported and cared for as to minimize the risk of injury, damage to health or cruel treatment.

Article VIII

Measures to Be Taken by the Parties
1. The Parties shall take appropriate measures to enforce the provisions of the present Convention and to prohibit trade in specimens in violation thereof. These shall include measures:

(a) to penalize trade in, or possession of, such specimens, or both; and
(b) to provide for the confiscation or return to the State of export of such specimens.

2. In addition to the measures taken under paragraph 1 of this Article, a Party may, when it deems it necessary, provide for any method of internal reimbursement for expenses incurred as a result of the confiscation of a specimen traded in violation of the measures taken in the application of the provisions of the present Convention.

3. As far as possible, the Parties shall ensure that specimens shall pass through any formalities required for trade with a minimum of delay. To facilitate such passage, a Party may designate ports of exit and ports of entry at which specimens must be presented for clearance. The Parties shall ensure further that all living specimens, during any period of transit, holding or shipment, are properly cared for so as to minimize the risk of injury, damage to health or cruel treatment.

4. Where a living specimen is confiscated as a result of measures referred to in paragraph 1 of this Article:

(a) the specimen shall be entrusted to a Management Authority of the State of confiscation;
(b) the Management Authority shall, after consultation with the State of export, return the specimen to that State at the expense of that State, or to a rescue centre or such other place as the Management Authority deems appropriate and consistent with the purposes of the present Convention; and

(c) the Management Authority may obtain the advice of a Scientific Authority, or may, whenever it considers it desirable, consult the Secretariat in order to facilitate the decision under sub-paragraph (b) of this paragraph, including the choice of a rescue centre or other place.

5. A rescue centre as referred to in paragraph 4 of this Article means an institution designated by a Management Authority to look after the welfare of living specimens, particularly those that have been confiscated.

6. Each Party shall maintain records of trade in specimens of species included in Appendices I, II and III which shall cover:

(a) the names and addresses of exporters and importers; and

(b) the number and type of permits and certificates granted; the States with which such trade occurred; the numbers or quantities and types of specimens, names of species as included in Appendices I, II and III and, where applicable, the size and sex of the specimens in question.

7. Each Party shall prepare periodic reports on its implementation of the present Convention and shall transmit to the Secretariat:

(a) an annual report containing a summary of the information specified in sub-paragraph (b) of paragraph 6 of this Article; and

(b) a biennial report on legislative, regulatory and administrative measures taken to enforce the provisions of the present Convention.

8. The information referred to in paragraph 7 of this Article shall be available to the public where this is not inconsistent with the law of the Party concerned.

Article IX

Management and Scientific Authorities
1. Each Party shall designate for the purposes of the present Convention:

(a) one or more Management Authorities competent to grant permits or certificates on behalf of that Party; and

(b) one or more Scientific Authorities.

2. A State depositing an instrument of ratification, acceptance, approval or accession shall at that time inform the Depositary Government of the name and address of the Management Authority authorized to communicate with other Parties and with the Secretariat.

3. Any changes in the designations or authorizations under the provisions of this Article shall be communicated by the Party concerned to the Secretariat for transmission to all other Parties.

4. Any Management Authority referred to in paragraph 2 of this Article shall, if so requested by the Secretariat or the Management Authority of another Party, communicate to it impression of stamps, seals or other devices used to authenticate permits or certificates.

Article X

Trade with States Not Party to the Convention
Where export or re-export is to, or import is from, a State not a Party to the present Convention, comparable documentation issued by the competent authorities in that State which substantially conforms with the requirements of the present Convention for permits and certificates may be accepted in lieu thereof by any Party.

Article XI

Conference of the Parties
1. The Secretariat shall call a meeting of the Conference of the Parties not later than two years after the entry into force of the present Convention.

2. Thereafter the Secretariat shall convene regular meetings at least once every two years, unless the

Conference decides otherwise, and extraordinary meetings at any time on the written request of at least one-third of the Parties.

3. At meetings, whether regular or extraordinary, the Parties shall review the implementation of the present Convention and may:

(a) make such provision as may be necessary to enable the Secretariat to carry out its duties, and adopt financial provisions;

(b) consider and adopt amendments to Appendices I and II in accordance with Article XV;

(c) review the progress made towards the restoration and conservation of the species included in Appendices I, II and III;

(d) receive and consider any reports presented by the Secretariat or by any Party; and

(e) where appropriate, make recommendations for improving the effectiveness of the present Convention.

4. At each regular meeting, the Parties may determine the time and venue of the next regular meeting to be held in accordance with the provisions of paragraph 2 of this Article.

5. At any meeting, the Parties may determine and adopt rules of procedure for the meeting.

6. The United Nations, its Specialized Agencies and the International Atomic Energy Agency, as well as any State not a Party to the present Convention, may be represented at meetings of the Conference by observers, who shall have the right to participate but not to vote.

7. Any body or agency technically qualified in protection, conservation or management of wild fauna and flora, in the following categories, which has informed the Secretariat of its desire to be represented at meetings of the Conference by observers, shall be admitted unless at least one-third of the Parties present object:

(a) international agencies or bodies, either governmental or non-governmental, and national governmental agencies and bodies; and

(b) national non-governmental agencies or bodies which have been approved for this purpose by the State in which they are located. Once admitted, these observers shall have the right to participate but not to vote.

Article XII

The Secretariat
1. Upon entry into force of the present Convention, a Secretariat shall be provided by the Executive Director of the United Nations Environment Programme. To the extent and in the manner he considers appropriate, he may be assisted by suitable inter-governmental or non-governmental international or national agencies and bodies technically qualified in protection, conservation and management of wild fauna and flora.

2. The functions of the Secretariat shall be:

(a) to arrange for and service meetings of the Parties;

(b) to perform the functions entrusted to it under the provisions of Articles XV and XVI of the present Convention;

(c) to undertake scientific and technical studies in accordance with programmes authorized by the Conference of the Parties as will contribute to the implementation of the present Convention, including studies concerning standards for appropriate preparation and shipment of living specimens and the means of identifying specimens;

(d) to study the reports of Parties and to request from Parties such further information with respect thereto as it deems necessary to ensure implementation of the present Convention;

(e) to invite the attention of the Parties to any matter pertaining to the aims of the present Convention;

(f) to publish periodically and distribute to the Parties current editions of Appendices I, II and III together with any information which will facilitate identification of specimens of species included in those Appendices;

(g) to prepare annual reports to the Parties on its work and on the implementation of the present Convention and such other reports as meetings of the Parties may request;

(h) to make recommendations for the implementation of the aims and provisions of the present Convention, including the exchange of information of a scientific or technical nature;

(i) to perform any other function as may be entrusted to it by the Parties.

Article XIII

International Measures

1. When the Secretariat in the light of information received is satisfied that any species included in Appendix I or II is being affected adversely by trade in specimens of that species or that the provisions of the present Convention are not being effectively implemented, it shall communicate such information to the authorized Management Authority of the Party or Parties concerned.

2. When any Party receives a communication as indicated in paragraph 1 of this Article, it shall, as soon as possible, inform the Secretariat of any relevant facts insofar as its laws permit and, where appropriate, propose remedial action. Where the Party considers that an inquiry is desirable, such inquiry may be carried out by one or more persons expressly authorized by the Party.

3. The information provided by the Party or resulting from any inquiry as specified in paragraph 2 of this Article shall be reviewed by the next Conference of the Parties which may make whatever recommendations it deems appropriate.

Article XIV

Effect on Domestic Legislation and International Conventions

1. The provisions of the present Convention shall in no way affect the right of Parties to adopt:

(a) stricter domestic measures regarding the conditions for trade, taking, possession or transport of specimens of species included in Appendices I, II and III, or the complete prohibition thereof; or

(b) domestic measures restricting or prohibiting trade, taking, possession or transport of species not included in Appendix I, II or III.

2. The provisions of the present Convention shall in no way affect the provisions of any domestic measures or the obligations of Parties deriving from any treaty, convention, or international agreement relating to other aspects of trade, taking, possession or transport of specimens which is in force or subsequently may enter into force for any Party including any measure pertaining to the Customs, public health, veterinary or plant quarantine fields.

3. The provisions of the present Convention shall in no way affect the provisions of, or the obligations deriving from, any treaty, convention or international agreement concluded or which may be concluded between States creating a union or regional trade agreement establishing or maintaining a common external Customs control and removing Customs control between the parties thereto insofar as they relate to trade among the States members of that union or agreement.

4. A State party to the present Convention, which is also a party to any other treaty, convention or international agreement which is in force at the time of the coming into force of the present Convention and under the provisions of which protection is afforded to marine species included in Appendix II, shall be relieved of the obligations imposed on it under the provisions of the present Convention with respect to trade in specimens of

species included in Appendix II that are taken by ships registered in that State and in accordance with the provisions of such other treaty, convention or international agreement.

5. Notwithstanding the provisions of Articles III, IV and V, any export of a specimen taken in accordance with paragraph 4 of this Article shall only require a certificate from a Management Authority of the State of introduction to the effect that the specimen was taken in accordance with the provisions of the other treaty, convention or international agreement in question.

6. Nothing in the present Convention shall prejudice the codification and development of the law of the sea by the United Nations Conference on the Law of the Sea convened pursuant to Resolution 2750 C (XXV) of the General Assembly of the United Nations nor the present or future claims and legal views of any State concerning the law of the sea and the nature and extent of coastal and flag State jurisdiction.

Article XV

Amendments to Appendices I and II
1. The following provisions shall apply in relation to amendments to Appendices I and II at meetings of the Conference of the Parties:

(a) Any Party may propose an amendment to Appendix I or II for consideration at the next meeting. The text of the proposed amendment shall be communicated to the Secretariat at least 150 days before the meeting. The Secretariat shall consult the other Parties and interested bodies on the amendment in accordance with the provisions of sub-paragraphs (b) and (c) of paragraph 2 of this Article and shall communicate the response to all Parties not later than 30 days before the meeting.

(b) Amendments shall be adopted by a two-thirds majority of Parties present and voting. For these purposes "Parties present and voting" means Parties present and casting an affirmative or negative vote. Parties abstaining from voting shall not be counted among the two-thirds required for adopting an amendment.

(c) Amendments adopted at a meeting shall enter into force 90 days after that meeting for all Parties except those which make a reservation in accordance with paragraph 3 of this Article.

2. The following provisions shall apply in relation to amendments to Appendices I and II between meetings of the Conference of the Parties:

(a) Any Party may propose an amendment to Appendix I or II for consideration between meetings by the postal procedures set forth in this paragraph.

(b) For marine species, the Secretariat shall, upon receiving the text of the proposed amendment, immediately communicate it to the Parties. It shall also consult inter-governmental bodies having a function in relation to those species especially with a view to obtaining scientific data these bodies may be able to provide and to ensuring co-ordination with any conservation measures enforced by such bodies. The Secretariat shall communicate the views expressed and data provided by these bodies and its own findings and recommendations to the Parties as soon as possible.

(c) For species other than marine species, the Secretariat shall, upon receiving the text of the proposed amendment, immediately communicate it to the Parties, and, as soon as possible thereafter, its own recommendations.

(d) Any Party may, within 60 days of the date on which the Secretariat communicated its recommendations to the Parties under sub-paragraph (b) or (c) of this paragraph, transmit to the Secretariat any comments on the proposed amendment together with any relevant scientific data and information.

(e) The Secretariat shall communicate the replies received together with its own recommendations to the Parties as soon as possible.

(f) If no objection to the proposed amendment is received by the Secretariat within 30 days of the date the replies and recommendations were communicated under the provisions of sub-paragraph (e) of this paragraph, the amendment shall enter into force 90 days later for all Parties except those which make a reservation in accordance with paragraph 3 of this Article.

(g) If an objection by any Party is received by the Secretariat, the proposed amendment shall be submitted to a postal vote in accordance with the provisions of sub-paragraphs (h), (i) and (j) of this paragraph.

(h) The Secretariat shall notify the Parties that notification of objection has been received.

(i) Unless the Secretariat receives the votes for, against or in abstention from at least one-half of the Parties within 60 days of the date of notification under sub-paragraph (h) of this paragraph, the proposed amendment shall be referred to the next meeting of the Conference for further consideration.

(j) Provided that votes are received from one-half of the Parties, the amendment shall be adopted by a two-thirds majority of Parties casting an affirmative or negative vote.

(k) The Secretariat shall notify all Parties of the result of the vote.

(l) If the proposed amendment is adopted it shall enter into force 90 days after the date of the notification by the Secretariat of its acceptance for all Parties except those which make a reservation in accordance with paragraph 3 of this Article.

3. During the period of 90 days provided for by sub-paragraph (c) of paragraph 1 or sub-paragraph (l) of paragraph 2 of this Article any Party may by notification in writing to the Depositary Government make a reservation with respect to the amendment. Until such reservation is withdrawn the Party shall be treated as a State not a Party to the present Convention with respect to trade in the species concerned.

Article XVI

Appendix III and Amendments Thereto

1. Any Party may at any time submit to the Secretariat a list of species which it identifies as being subject to regulation within its jurisdiction for the purpose mentioned in paragraph 3 of Article II. Appendix III shall include the names of the Parties submitting the species for inclusion therein, the scientific names of the species so submitted, and any parts or derivatives of the animals or plants concerned that are specified in relation to the species for the purposes of sub-paragraph (b) of Article I.

2. Each list submitted under the provisions of paragraph 1 of this Article shall be communicated to the Parties by the Secretariat as soon as possible after receiving it. The list shall take effect as part of Appendix III 90 days after the date of such communication. At any time after the communication of such list, any Party may by notification in writing to the Depositary Government enter a reservation with respect to any species or any parts or derivatives, and until such reservation is withdrawn, the State shall be treated as a State not a Party to the present Convention with respect to trade in the species or part or derivative concerned.

3. A Party which has submitted a species for inclusion in Appendix III may withdraw it at any time by notification to the Secretariat which shall communicate the withdrawal to all Parties. The withdrawal shall take effect 30 days after the date of such communication.

4. Any Party submitting a list under the provisions of paragraph 1 of this Article shall submit to the Secretariat a copy of all domestic laws and regulations applicable to the protection of such species, together with any interpretations which the Party may deem appropriate or the Secretariat may request. The Party shall, for as long as the species in question is included in Appendix III,

submit any amendments of such laws and regulations or any interpretations as they are adopted.

Article XVII

Amendment of the Convention
1. An extraordinary meeting of the Conference of the Parties shall be convened by the Secretariat on the written request of at least one-third of the Parties to consider and adopt amendments to the present Convention. Such amendments shall be adopted by a two-thirds majority of Parties present and voting. For these purposes "Parties present and voting" means Parties present and casting an affirmative or negative vote. Parties abstaining from voting shall not be counted among the two-thirds required for adopting an amendment.

2. The text of any proposed amendment shall be communicated by the Secretariat to all Parties at least 90 days before the meeting.

3. An amendment shall enter into force for the Parties which have accepted it 60 days after two-thirds of the Parties have deposited an instrument of acceptance of the amendment with the Depositary Government. Thereafter, the amendment shall enter into force for any other Party 60 days after that Party deposits its instrument of acceptance of the amendment.

Article XVIII

Resolution of Disputes
1. Any dispute which may arise between two or more Parties with respect to the interpretation or application of the provisions of the present Convention shall be subject to negotiation between the Parties involved in the dispute.

2. If the dispute can not be resolved in accordance with paragraph 1 of this Article, the Parties may, by mutual consent, submit the dispute to arbitration, in particular that of the Permanent Court of

Arbitration at The Hague, and the Parties submitting the dispute shall be bound by the arbitral decision.

10.

International Convention for the Suppression of Acts of Nuclear Terrorism, United Nations, 2005

Since the events of 11 September 2001, there has been a growing concern in the international community that criminals or terrorists could acquire nuclear and radioactive munitions and material. The signatories to the International Convention for the Suppression of Acts of Nuclear Terrorism were deeply concerned about the increasing acts of terrorism globally in different forms. They were aware of the fact that nuclear terrorism would pose the greatest danger and that present legal provisions were not sufficient to deal with this potential threat. Article 2 criminalized the possession of radioactive material with the motive of causing death and injury or damaging property or the environment. Each country would take appropriate measures to punish the offender and cooperate with other countries by exchanging information.

Source
United Nations Office on Drugs and Crime, http://untreaty.un.org/English/Terrorism/English_18_15.pdf.

The States Parties to this Convention,

Having in mind the purposes and principles of the Charter of the United Nations concerning the maintenance of international peace and security and the promotion of good-neighbourliness and friendly relations and cooperation among States,

Recalling the Declaration on the Occasion of the Fiftieth Anniversary of the United Nations of 24 October 1995,

Recognizing the right of all States to develop and apply nuclear energy for peaceful purposes and their legitimate interests in the potential benefits to be derived from the peaceful application of nuclear energy,

Bearing in mind the Convention on the Physical Protection of Nuclear Material of 1980,

Deeply concerned about the worldwide escalation of acts of terrorism in all its forms and manifestations,

Recalling the Declaration on Measures to Eliminate International Terrorism annexed to General Assembly resolution 49/60 of 9 December 1994, in which, inter alia, the States Members of the United Nations solemnly reaffirm their unequivocal condemnation of all acts, methods and practices of terrorism as criminal and unjustifiable, wherever and by whomever committed, including those which jeopardize the friendly relations among States and peoples and threaten the territorial integrity and security of States,

Noting that the Declaration also encouraged States to review urgently the scope of the existing international legal provisions on the prevention, repression and elimination of terrorism in all its forms and manifestations, with the aim of ensuring that there is a comprehensive legal framework covering all aspects of the matter,

Recalling General Assembly resolution 51/210 of 17 December 1996 and the Declaration to Supplement the 1994 Declaration on Measures to Eliminate International Terrorism annexed thereto,

Recalling also that, pursuant to General Assembly resolution 51/210, an ad hoc committee was established to elaborate, inter alia, an international convention for the suppression of acts of nuclear terrorism to supplement related existing international instruments,

Noting that acts of nuclear terrorism may result in the gravest consequences and may pose a threat to international peace and security,

Noting also that existing multilateral legal provisions do not adequately address those attacks,

Being convinced of the urgent need to enhance international cooperation between States in devising and adopting effective and practical measures for the prevention of such acts of terrorism and for the prosecution and punishment of their perpetrators,

Noting that the activities of military forces of States are governed by rules of international law outside of the framework of this Convention and that the exclusion of certain actions from the coverage of this Convention does not condone or make lawful otherwise unlawful acts, or preclude prosecution under other laws,

Have agreed as follows:

Article 1
For the purposes of this Convention:

1. "Radioactive material" means nuclear material and other radioactive substances which contain nuclides which undergo spontaneous disintegration (a process accompanied by emission of one or more types of ionizing radiation, such as alpha-, beta-, neutron particles and gamma rays) and which may, owing to their radiological or fissile properties, cause death, serious bodily injury or substantial damage to property or to the environment.

2. "Nuclear material" means plutonium, except that with isotopic concentration exceeding 80 per cent in plutonium-238; uranium-233; uranium enriched in the isotope 235 or 233; uranium containing the mixture of isotopes as occurring in nature other than in the form of ore or ore residue; or any material containing one or more of the foregoing;

Whereby "uranium enriched in the isotope 235 or 233" means uranium containing the isotope 235 or 233 or both in an amount such that the abundance ratio of the sum of these isotopes to the isotope 238 is greater than the ratio of the isotope 235 to the isotope 238 occurring in nature.

3. "Nuclear facility" means:

(a) Any nuclear reactor, including reactors installed on vessels, vehicles, aircraft or space objects for use as an energy source in order to propel such vessels, vehicles, aircraft or space objects or for any other purpose;

(b) Any plant or conveyance being used for the production, storage, processing or transport of radioactive material.

4. "Device" means:

(a) Any nuclear explosive device; or

(b) Any radioactive material dispersal or radiation-emitting device which may, owing to its radiological properties, cause death, serious bodily injury or substantial damage to property or to the environment.

5. "State or government facility" includes any permanent or temporary facility or conveyance that is used or occupied by representatives of a State, members of a Government, the legislature or the judiciary or by officials or employees of a State or any other public authority or entity or by employees or officials of an intergovernmental organization in connection with their official duties.

6. "Military forces of a State" means the armed forces of a State which are organized, trained and equipped under its internal law for the primary purpose of national defence or security and persons acting in support of those armed forces who are under their formal command, control and responsibility.

Article 2

1. Any person commits an offence within the meaning of this Convention if that person unlawfully and intentionally:

(a) Possesses radioactive material or makes or possesses a device:

(i) With the intent to cause death or serious bodily injury; or

(ii) With the intent to cause substantial damage to property or to the environment;

(b) Uses in any way radioactive material or a device, or uses or damages a nuclear facility in a manner which releases or risks the release of radioactive material:

(i) With the intent to cause death or serious bodily injury; or

(ii) With the intent to cause substantial damage to property or to the environment; or

(iii) With the intent to compel a natural or legal person, an international organization or a State to do or refrain from doing an act.

2. Any person also commits an offence if that person:

(a) Threatens, under circumstances which indicate the credibility of the threat, to commit an offence as set forth in paragraph 1 (b) of the present article; or

(b) Demands unlawfully and intentionally radioactive material, a device or a nuclear facility by threat, under circumstances which indicate the credibility of the threat, or by use of force.

3. Any person also commits an offence if that person attempts to commit an offence as set forth in paragraph 1 of the present article.

4. Any person also commits an offence if that person:

(a) Participates as an accomplice in an offence as set forth in paragraph 1, 2 or 3 of the present article; or

(b) Organizes or directs others to commit an offence as set forth in paragraph 1, 2 or 3 of the present article; or

(c) In any other way contributes to the commission of one or more offences as set forth in paragraph 1, 2 or 3 of the present article by a group of persons acting with a common purpose; such contribution shall be intentional and either be made with the aim of furthering the general criminal activity or purpose of the group or be made in the knowledge of the intention of the group to commit the offence or offences concerned.

Article 3

This Convention shall not apply where the offence is committed within a single State, the alleged offender and the victims are nationals of that State, the alleged offender is found in the territory of that State and no other State has a basis under article 9, paragraph 1 or 2, to exercise jurisdiction, except that the provisions of articles 7, 12, 14, 15, 16 and 17 shall, as appropriate, apply in those cases.

Article 4

1. Nothing in this Convention shall affect other rights, obligations and responsibilities of States and individuals under international law, in particular the purposes and principles of the Charter of the United Nations and international humanitarian law.

2. The activities of armed forces during an armed conflict, as those terms are understood under international humanitarian law, which are governed by that law are not governed by this Convention, and the activities undertaken by military forces of a State in the exercise of their official duties, inasmuch as they are governed by other rules of international law, are not governed by this Convention.

3. The provisions of paragraph 2 of the present article shall not be interpreted as condoning or making lawful otherwise unlawful acts, or precluding prosecution under other laws.

4. This Convention does not address, nor can it be interpreted as addressing, in any way, the issue of the legality of the use or threat of use of nuclear weapons by States.

Article 5

Each State Party shall adopt such measures as may be necessary:

(a) To establish as criminal offences under its national law the offences set forth in article 2;

(b) To make those offences punishable by appropriate penalties which take into account the grave nature of these offences.

Article 6

Each State Party shall adopt such measures as may be necessary, including, where appropriate, domestic legislation, to ensure that criminal acts within the scope of this Convention, in particular where they are intended or calculated to provoke a state of terror in the general public or in a group of persons or particular persons, are under no circumstances justifiable by considerations of a political, philosophical, ideological, racial, ethnic, religious or other similar nature and are punished by penalties consistent with their grave nature.

Article 7

1. States Parties shall cooperate by:

(a) Taking all practicable measures, including, if necessary, adapting their national law, to prevent and counter preparations in their respective territories for the commission within or outside their territories of the offences set forth in article 2, including measures to prohibit in their territories illegal activities of persons, groups and organizations that encourage, instigate, organize, knowingly finance or knowingly provide technical assistance or information or engage in the perpetration of those offences;

(b) Exchanging accurate and verified information in accordance with their national law and in the manner and subject to the conditions specified herein, and coordinating administrative and other measures taken as appropriate to detect, prevent, suppress and investigate the offences set forth in article 2 and also in order to institute criminal proceedings against persons alleged to have committed those crimes. In particular, a State Party shall take appropriate measures in order to inform without delay the other States referred to in article 9 in respect of the commission of the offences set forth in article 2 as well as preparations to commit such offences about which it has learned, and also to inform, where appropriate, international organizations.

2. States Parties shall take appropriate measures consistent with their national law to protect the confidentiality of any information which they receive in confidence by virtue of the provisions of this Convention from another State Party or through participation in an activity carried out for the implementation of this Convention. If States Parties provide information to international organizations in confidence, steps shall be taken to ensure that the confidentiality of such information is protected.

3. States Parties shall not be required by this Convention to provide any information which they are not permitted to communicate pursuant to national law or which would jeopardize the security of the State concerned or the physical protection of nuclear material.

4. States Parties shall inform the Secretary-General of the United Nations of their competent authorities and liaison points responsible for sending and receiving the information referred to in the present article. The Secretary-General of the United Nations shall communicate such information regarding competent authorities and liaison points to all States Parties and the International Atomic Energy Agency. Such authorities and liaison points must be accessible on a continuous basis.

Article 8

For purposes of preventing offences under this Convention, States Parties shall make every effort to adopt appropriate measures to ensure the protection of radioactive material, taking into account relevant recommendations and functions of the International Atomic Energy Agency.

Article 9

1. Each State Party shall take such measures as may be necessary to establish its jurisdiction over the offences set forth in article 2 when:

   (a) The offence is committed in the territory of that State; or
   (b) The offence is committed on board a vessel flying the flag of that State or an aircraft which is registered under the laws of that State at the time the offence is committed; or
   (c) The offence is committed by a national of that State.

2. A State Party may also establish its jurisdiction over any such offence when:

   (a) The offence is committed against a national of that State; or
   (b) The offence is committed against a State or government facility of that State abroad, including an embassy or other diplomatic or consular premises of that State; or
   (c) The offence is committed by a stateless person who has his or her habitual residence in the territory of that State; or
   (d) The offence is committed in an attempt to compel that State to do or abstain from doing any act; or
   (e) The offence is committed on board an aircraft which is operated by the Government of that State.

3. Upon ratifying, accepting, approving or acceding to this Convention, each State Party shall notify the Secretary-General of the United Nations of the jurisdiction it has established under its national law in accordance with paragraph 2 of the present article. Should any change take place, the State

Party concerned shall immediately notify the Secretary-General.

4. Each State Party shall likewise take such measures as may be necessary to establish its jurisdiction over the offences set forth in article 2 in cases where the alleged offender is present in its territory and it does not extradite that person to any of the States Parties which have established their jurisdiction in accordance with paragraph 1 or 2 of the present article.

5. This Convention does not exclude the exercise of any criminal jurisdiction established by a State Party in accordance with its national law.

Article 10
1. Upon receiving information that an offence set forth in article 2 has been committed or is being committed in the territory of a State Party or that a person who has committed or who is alleged to have committed such an offence may be present in its territory, the State Party concerned shall take such measures as may be necessary under its national law to investigate the facts contained in the information.

2. Upon being satisfied that the circumstances so warrant, the State Party in whose territory the offender or alleged offender is present shall take the appropriate measures under its national law so as to ensure that person's presence for the purpose of prosecution or extradition.

3. Any person regarding whom the measures referred to in paragraph 2 of the present article are being taken shall be entitled:

(a) To communicate without delay with the nearest appropriate representative of the State of which that person is a national or which is otherwise entitled to protect that person's rights or, if that person is a stateless person, the State in the territory of which that person habitually resides;
(b) To be visited by a representative of that State;

(c) To be informed of that person's rights under sub-paragraphs (a) and (b).

4. The rights referred to in paragraph 3 of the present article shall be exercised in conformity with the laws and regulations of the State in the territory of which the offender or alleged offender is present, subject to the provision that the said laws and regulations must enable full effect to be given to the purposes for which the rights accorded under paragraph 3 are intended.

5. The provisions of paragraphs 3 and 4 of the present article shall be without prejudice to the right of any State Party having a claim to jurisdiction in accordance with article 9, paragraph 1 (c) or 2 (c), to invite the International Committee of the Red Cross to communicate with and visit the alleged offender.

6. When a State Party, pursuant to the present article, has taken a person into custody, it shall immediately notify, directly or through the Secretary-General of the United Nations, the States Parties which have established jurisdiction in accordance with article 9, paragraphs 1 and 2, and, if it considers it advisable, any other interested States Parties, of the fact that that person is in custody and of the circumstances which warrant that person's detention. The State which makes the investigation contemplated in paragraph 1 of the present article shall promptly inform the said States Parties of its findings and shall indicate whether it intends to exercise jurisdiction.

Article 11
1. The State Party in the territory of which the alleged offender is present shall, in cases to which article 9 applies, if it does not extradite that person, be obliged, without exception whatsoever and whether or not the offence was committed in its territory, to submit the case without undue delay to its competent authorities for the purpose of prosecution, through proceedings in accordance with the laws of that State. Those authorities shall

take their decision in the same manner as in the case of any other offence of a grave nature under the law of that State.

2. Whenever a State Party is permitted under its national law to extradite or otherwise surrender one of its nationals only upon the condition that the person will be returned to that State to serve the sentence imposed as a result of the trial or proceeding for which the extradition or surrender of the person was sought, and this State and the State seeking the extradition of the person agree with this option and other terms they may deem appropriate, such a conditional extradition or surrender shall be sufficient to discharge the obligation set forth in paragraph 1 of the present article.

Article 12

Any person who is taken into custody or regarding whom any other measures are taken or proceedings are carried out pursuant to this Convention shall be guaranteed fair treatment, including enjoyment of all rights and guarantees in conformity with the law of the State in the territory of which that person is present and applicable provisions of international law, including international law of human rights.

Article 13

1. The offences set forth in article 2 shall be deemed to be included as extraditable offences in any extradition treaty existing between any of the States Parties before the entry into force of this Convention. States Parties undertake to include such offences as extraditable offences in every extradition treaty to be subsequently concluded between them.

2. When a State Party which makes extradition conditional on the existence of a treaty receives a request for extradition from another State Party with which it has no extradition treaty, the requested State Party may, at its option, consider this Convention as a legal basis for extradition in respect of the offences set forth in article 2.

Extradition shall be subject to the other conditions provided by the law of the requested State.

3. States Parties which do not make extradition conditional on the existence of a treaty shall recognize the offences set forth in article 2 as extraditable offences between themselves, subject to the conditions provided by the law of the requested State.

4. If necessary, the offences set forth in article 2 shall be treated, for the purposes of extradition between States Parties, as if they had been committed not only in the place in which they occurred but also in the territory of the States that have established jurisdiction in accordance with article 9, paragraphs 1 and 2.

5. The provisions of all extradition treaties and arrangements between States Parties with regard to offences set forth in article 2 shall be deemed to be modified as between States Parties to the extent that they are incompatible with this Convention.

Article 14

1. States Parties shall afford one another the greatest measure of assistance in connection with investigations or criminal or extradition proceedings brought in respect of the offences set forth in article 2, including assistance in obtaining evidence at their disposal necessary for the proceedings.

2. States Parties shall carry out their obligations under paragraph 1 of the present article in conformity with any treaties or other arrangements on mutual legal assistance that may exist between them. In the absence of such treaties or arrangements, States Parties shall afford one another assistance in accordance with their national law.

Article 15

None of the offences set forth in article 2 shall be regarded, for the purposes of extradition or mutual legal assistance, as a political offence or as an offence connected with a political offence or as an offence inspired by political motives. Accordingly, a request for extradition or for mutual legal assistance based on such an offence may not be refused on the sole ground that it concerns a political offence or an offence connected with a political offence or an offence inspired by political motives.

Article 16

Nothing in this Convention shall be interpreted as imposing an obligation to extradite or to afford mutual legal assistance if the requested State Party has substantial grounds for believing that the request for extradition for offences set forth in article 2 or for mutual legal assistance with respect to such offences has been made for the purpose of prosecuting or punishing a person on account of that person's race, religion, nationality, ethnic origin or political opinion or that compliance with the request would cause prejudice to that person's position for any of these reasons.

Article 17

1. A person who is being detained or is serving a sentence in the territory of one State Party whose presence in another State Party is requested for purposes of testimony, identification or otherwise providing assistance in obtaining evidence for the investigation or prosecution of offences under this Convention may be transferred if the following conditions are met:

(a) The person freely gives his or her informed consent; and

(b) The competent authorities of both States agree, subject to such conditions as those States may deem appropriate.

2. For the purposes of the present article:

(a) The State to which the person is transferred shall have the authority and obligation to keep the person transferred in custody, unless otherwise requested or authorized by the State from which the person was transferred;

(b) The State to which the person is transferred shall without delay implement its obligation to return the person to the custody of the State from which the person was transferred as agreed beforehand, or as otherwise agreed, by the competent authorities of both States;

(c) The State to which the person is transferred shall not require the State from which the person was transferred to initiate extradition proceedings for the return of the person;

(d) The person transferred shall receive credit for service of the sentence being served in the State from which he or she was transferred for time spent in the custody of the State to which he or she was transferred.

3. Unless the State Party from which a person is to be transferred in accordance with the present article so agrees, that person, whatever his or her nationality, shall not be prosecuted or detained or subjected to any other restriction of his or her personal liberty in the territory of the State to which that person is transferred in respect of acts or convictions anterior to his or her departure from the territory of the State from which such person was transferred.

Article 18

1. Upon seizing or otherwise taking control of radioactive material, devices or nuclear facilities, following the commission of an offence set forth in article 2, the State Party in possession of such items shall:

(a) Take steps to render harmless the radioactive material, device or nuclear facility;

(b) Ensure that any nuclear material is held in accordance with applicable International Atomic Energy Agency safeguards; and

(c) Have regard to physical protection recommendations and health and safety standards published by the International Atomic Energy Agency.

2. Upon the completion of any proceedings connected with an offence set forth in article 2, or sooner if required by international law, any

radioactive material, device or nuclear facility shall be returned, after consultations (in particular, regarding modalities of return and storage) with the States Parties concerned to the State Party to which it belongs, to the State Party of which the natural or legal person owning such radioactive material, device or facility is a national or resident, or to the State Party from whose territory it was stolen or otherwise unlawfully obtained.

3. (*a*) Where a State Party is prohibited by national or international law from returning or accepting such radioactive material, device or nuclear facility or where the States Parties concerned so agree, subject to paragraph 3 (*b*) of the present article, the State Party in possession of the radioactive material, devices or nuclear facilities shall continue to take the steps described in paragraph 1 of the present article; such radioactive material, devices or nuclear facilities shall be used only for peaceful purposes;

3. (*b*) Where it is not lawful for the State Party in possession of the radioactive material, devices or nuclear facilities to possess them, that State shall ensure that they are placed as soon as possible in the possession of a State for which such possession is lawful and which, where appropriate, has provided assurances consistent with the requirements of paragraph 1 of the present article in consultation with that State, for the purpose of rendering it harmless; such radioactive material, devices or nuclear facilities shall be used only for peaceful purposes.

4. If the radioactive material, devices or nuclear facilities referred to in paragraphs 1 and 2 of the present article do not belong to any of the States Parties or to a national or resident of a State Party or was not stolen or otherwise unlawfully obtained from the territory of a State Party, or if no State is willing to receive such items pursuant to paragraph 3 of the present article, a separate decision concerning its disposition shall, subject to paragraph 3 (*b*) of the present article, be taken after consultations between the States concerned and any relevant international organizations.

5. For the purposes of paragraphs 1, 2, 3 and 4 of the present article, the State Party in possession of the radioactive material, device or nuclear facility may request the assistance and cooperation of other States Parties, in particular the States Parties concerned, and any relevant international organizations, in particular the International Atomic Energy Agency. States Parties and the relevant international organizations are encouraged to provide assistance pursuant to this paragraph to the maximum extent possible.

6. The States Parties involved in the disposition or retention of the radioactive material, device or nuclear facility pursuant to the present article shall inform the Director General of the International Atomic Energy Agency of the manner in which such an item was disposed of or retained. The Director General of the International Atomic Energy Agency shall transmit the information to the other States Parties.

7. In the event of any dissemination in connection with an offence set forth in article 2, nothing in the present article shall affect in any way the rules of international law governing liability for nuclear damage, or other rules of international law.

Article 19
The State Party where the alleged offender is prosecuted shall, in accordance with its national law or applicable procedures, communicate the final outcome of the proceedings to the Secretary-General of the United Nations, who shall transmit the information to the other States Parties.

Article 20
States Parties shall conduct consultations with one another directly or through the Secretary-General of the United Nations, with the assistance of international organizations as necessary, to ensure effective implementation of this Convention.

Article 21

The States Parties shall carry out their obligations under this Convention in a manner consistent with the principles of sovereign equality and territorial integrity of States and that of non-intervention in the domestic affairs of other States.

Article 22

Nothing in this Convention entitles a State Party to undertake in the territory of another State Party the exercise of jurisdiction and performance of functions which are exclusively reserved for the authorities of that other State Party by its national law.

Article 23

1. Any dispute between two or more States Parties concerning the interpretation or application of this Convention which cannot be settled through negotiation within a reasonable time shall, at the request of one of them, be submitted to arbitration. If, within six months of the date of the request for arbitration, the parties are unable to agree on the organization of the arbitration, any one of those parties may refer the dispute to the International Court of Justice, by application, in conformity with the Statute of the Court.

2. Each State may, at the time of signature, ratification, acceptance or approval of this Convention or accession thereto, declare that it does not consider itself bound by paragraph 1 of the present article. The other States Parties shall not be bound by paragraph 1 with respect to any State Party which has made such a reservation.

3. Any State which has made a reservation in accordance with paragraph 2 of the present article may at any time withdraw that reservation by notification to the Secretary-General of the United Nations.

11.
The Global Congress/World Customs Organization Regional Forum on Protection of Intellectual Property Rights

In the following regional forum, held in Shanghai, China, during 22–23 November 2004, the Global Congress/World Customs Organization made recommendations to strengthen law enforcement efforts to combat counterfeiting relative to intellectual property rights. The congress sought to improve cooperation between the public and private sectors in the fight against global counterfeiting. Countries were also encouraged to strengthen their borders and promote cooperation and information exchange between state custom authorities.

Source

Global Congress, http://www.ccapcongress.net/Files/Shanghai%20Initiative%20-%20Final.doc.

The Shanghai Initiative

(Final)

Preamble

The Global Congress/World Customs Organization (WCO) Regional Forum on Protection of Intellectual Property Rights (IPR) was held in Shanghai, China from the 22nd to 23rd of November 2004. The participating international representatives invited by the WCO and the General Administration of Customs of People's Republic of China carried out a thorough discussion on the impact of counterfeiting and piracy, countermeasures employed, the constraints and development of IPR protection, and enforcement cooperation between Customs, other agencies and the private sector.

WHEREAS

1. As noted in the Outcomes Statement from the First Global Congress on Combating Counterfeiting and the Rome Declaration from the

International Conference in Italy—the trade in counterfeits is a large and growing problem and requires governments at all levels to place a higher priority against it.

2. Widespread concern has been expressed regarding:

- The negative social and economic impacts of counterfeiting and the demonstrated linkages with international organized crime groups;
- The fact that many counterfeit products endanger the health, safety and security of consumers;
- The potential for corruption emanating from the trade in counterfeit products;

3. The governments of the Asia/Pacific region, their agencies and private sector partners have identified counterfeiting as a major problem causing significant harm to national and business interests through the loss of tax and company revenues, diversion of government resources, higher costs for law enforcement and negative impacts on economic development, employment and investment;

NOTING THE FOLLOWING FACTORS

1. The governments and customs administrations in the Asia-Pacific region have increased their attention on IPR protection and their cooperation with business resulting in improvements in combating the trade in counterfeit goods.

2. The economy in the Asia-Pacific region is growing rapidly and has become one of the most vigorous economies in the world. Maintaining this favourable environment is one of the most important responsibilities of governments, their agencies and departments.

3. With globalization, counterfeiting and piracy have become a major concern. The establishment and optimization of effective IPR legal protection and enforcement systems will play a significant and unique role in promoting social wealth and economic development.

4. IPR border protection is one of the most important Customs' responsibilities. In the framework of the *WTO Agreement on Trade-Related Aspects of Intellectual Property Rights* (TRIPs), customs in many countries are striving to establish and improve a more complete legal framework and enforcement system for IPR border protection. They are intensifying enforcement capabilities and improving the effectiveness of customs enforcement.

5. Customs and the private sector have the same goals and aspirations regarding IPR border protection. The effective customs-business cooperation in the areas of information exchange, training, and legal proceeding coordination plays an important role in facilitating IPR border protection.

6. The initiative of the World Customs Organization IPR Strategic Group in establishing an Asia Pacific Secretariat to co-ordinate efforts to assist Customs administrations improve their capacity to implement effective border measures against IPR crime; and to further enhance the partnership between rights holders, customs administrations and other competent national agencies throughout the Region.

7. A number of countries and regions have announced anti-counterfeit initiatives, the most recent being the European Commission which, in November 2004, adopted a strategy for the enforcement of intellectual property rights (IPR) in third countries. The EC action plan focuses on vigorous and effective implementation and enforcement of existing IPR laws and providing technical cooperation and assistance to help third countries fight counterfeiting. The Commission will foster awareness raising of consumers in third countries and support the creation of public-private partnerships for enforcement.

8. Encouraging progress has been made at the First Global Congress on Combating Counterfeiting in Brussels, the International Conference in Rome, Italy and the Regional Forum in Shanghai in raising awareness of the counterfeit issue but there remains a strong need to engage all governments at the political and policy-maker levels on the issue;

9. The Global Congress Steering Committee has been established to improve levels of cooperation among international authorities and the private sector, and now must urgently develop the recommendations from Brussels, Rome and Shanghai into priorities and concrete action plans;

10. The World Customs Organization is planning to enhance its anti-counterfeit capabilities by broadening its capacity building programs and targeting counterfeit products under its security and facilitation initiative to secure the international supply chain;

11. Interpol has formally established an Intellectual Property Crimes Unit and is about to launch its pilot project in South America;

12. The World Intellectual Property Organization is enhancing its efforts to convince governments of the need for effective enforcement systems and the benefits of entrusting judges with special experience in dealing with intellectual property cases;

13. The private sector has made progress in identifying mechanisms to quantify the size and extent of the global counterfeit problem and its impacts on consumer health and safety and the growth of organized crime networks.

CONCLUDES

That the Global Congress/WCO Asia Pacific Regional Forum on the Protection of Intellectual Property Rights provided an important venue for customs administrations from the Asia/Pacific region and global representatives from the public and private sectors to enhance cooperation and identify areas for improving synergy and action. In doing so, they built upon the recommendations arising from the First Global Congress on Combating Counterfeiting and the subsequent International Conference in Rome. All participating Asia Pacific countries considered the protection of IP rights as key to economic development and agreed to continue to enhance their efforts to make IP enforcement more effective.

AND RECOMMENDS[†]

Asia-Pacific Countries

Legislation and Procedures

1. Improving understanding at the political and policy-making level of the serious consequences of the counterfeiting trade and the vital role that enforcement authorities in the region can play in fighting IP crime.

2. Encouraging countries to modernize their Customs legislation on border measures for IP protection, taking into account the WCO Model Law (published on the website www.wcoipr.org) to further enhance anti-counterfeit capabilities, specifically by:

—Reducing or eliminating the requirement for IP owners to pay bonds for counterfeiting cases;
—Facilitating further simplification of procedures for obtaining court orders;
—Empowering customs officials to conduct in-depth investigations into counterfeiting and piracy cases;

3. Encouraging Customs—with the assistance of right owners where appropriate—to transfer more

---

[†] The recommendations contained in the Shanghai Initiative are in addition to, or enhancements of, the recommendations in the Brussels Global Congress Outcomes Statement and the Rome Declaration.

cases to the police and other competent authorities for investigation and criminal prosecutions.

4. Implementing protection for industrial products design and patents for inventions similar to the protection currently offered for trademarks.

Risk Analysis, Information Sharing and Communication

5. Establishing channels for strengthening exchange of information between the customs administrations of the Asia-Pacific region and other foreign customs administrations to effectively share information concerning the infringing trade in counterfeit goods.

6. Expanding and promoting understanding, information-sharing and cooperation between customs, other enforcement agencies and the private sector to effectively facilitate combating IPR abuses;

7. Establishing a regular regional IPR forum to ensure that the relationship between business, customs and other enforcement authorities continues to develop;

8. Enhancing the role of the WCO Regional Intelligence Liaison Office (RILO) in the Asia/Pacific region to include coordinating customs information and intelligence gathering on counterfeiting and piracy and providing regular analyses and reports;

9. Designing protocols on the exchange of IPR information between customs authorities and rights holders and vice versa;

Capacity Building

10. Providing advanced communication tools to customs to facilitate investigations;

11. Intensifying enforcement capabilities and sanctions particularly with respect to the enormous illegal profits and relatively low risk costs associated with the counterfeiting and piracy trade;

12. Developing a comprehensive programme of IPR technical assistance and capacity building for enforcement authorities including the exploration of funding sources;

13. Conducting a WCO exercise in the Asia-Pacific region to identify and intercept counterfeit and pirate products in containers. The WCO will manage the arrangements for sharing information via the Customs Enforcement Network;

Internationally

14. Conducting a meeting of embassy attachés in Brussels as a means of exploring opportunities to increase political and policy-maker awareness of the serious consequences of the trade in counterfeit products;

15. Developing the WCO's e-learning program on counterfeiting to provide national customs administrations with the latest strategies and knowledge on combating the illegal trade;

16. Sharing the results, as appropriate, of Interpol's intellectual property crimes exercise, Operation Jupiter, in South America and identifying other potential countries where Operation Jupiter could be run;

17. Increasing the number of activities of the World Intellectual Property Organization to facilitate the exchange of information between law enforcement agencies and to render advice and assistance to Governments on the protection and enforcement of intellectual property rights including by developing and making use of practical training scenarios;

18. Securing private and public sector financial support for the OECD to finalize its plans to conduct an extensive research project on the global counterfeit trade;

19. Establishing a study group to investigate and recommend how enforcement authorities and business can best harness the new inspection and security technologies to improve IPR border control capabilities.

12.
Establishing Provisions Aimed at Combating Organized Crime and Enacting Other Provisions

Among the Latin American nations, Colombia had taken the most important steps against money laundering. The profit-making cocaine and heroin trade had made severe inroads into the economy of Colombia. Dollars accrued from drug smuggling were exchanged for pesos in Colombia. Narcotics-related foreign currency was also smuggled out of the country and deposited in other Latin American countries. The Criminal Code of 21 February 1997 criminalized money laundering proceeds connected with crimes such as drug trafficking, extortion, and kidnapping. Article 2 stipulated the closure of organizations that were engaged in criminal activities. Penalties for violation of these drug laws may also include imprisonment, fine, house arrest, disqualification from public office, or rights forfeiture.

Source
United Nations Office on Drugs and Crime, http://www.unodc.org/unodc/en/legal_library/co/legal_library_2001-06-01_2001-41.html.

E/NL.2001/41 LAW No. 365 of 1997

THE CONGRESS OF THE REPUBLIC

DECREES

Article 1
Article 42, paragraph 4, of the Criminal Code shall read as follows:

"4. Prohibition of the pursuit of an occupation, trade, craft, business or enterprise."

Article 2
The Code of Criminal Procedure shall have an article 61A, reading as follows:

"ARTICLE 61A: Revocation of the legal personality of companies and organizations devoted to the pursuit of criminal activities or closure of their premises or establishments open to the public.

At any stage in the course of proceedings, if the judicial officer deems it a proven fact that juridical persons, companies or organizations have been devoted entirely or partly to the pursuit of criminal activities, that officer shall order the competent authority, subject to the fulfilment of the relevant established legal requirements, to revoke the legal personality thereof or to close premises or establishments thereof that are open to the public."

Article 3
Article 44 of the Criminal Code shall read as follows:

"ARTICLE 44: Length of sentence

The maximum length of the sentence shall be as follows:

—Long-term imprisonment, up to sixty (60) years;
—Short-term imprisonment, up to eight (8) years;
—House arrest, up to five (5) years;
—Forfeiture of rights and disqualification from public office, up to ten (10) years;
—Prohibition of the pursuit of an occupation, trade, craft, business or enterprise, up to five (5) years;
—Loss of parental rights, up to fifteen (15) years."

Article 4
Article 58 of the Criminal Code shall read as follows:

"ARTICLE 58: Prohibition of the pursuit of a business, enterprise, occupation, trade or craft

In the case of an offence involving abuse of a function relating to pursuits of a business, enterprise, occupation, trade or craft, or violation of the obligations deriving from such pursuit, the judge, in awarding sentence, may disqualify the offender from continued pursuit of the business, enterprise, occupation, trade or craft in question for a period of up to five (5) years."

Article 5
The Criminal Code shall have an article 63A, reading as follows:

"ARTICLE 63A: Aggravation of the offence through place of commission

If the punishable act was directed or committed, entirely or in part, from within a place of imprisonment by an inmate, or entirely or in part outside the national territory, the sentence shall be increased by up to one half, provided that such circumstance does not constitute a separate punishable act or ingredient thereof."

Article 6
Article 176 of the Criminal Code shall have an additional clause, reading as follows:

"ADDITIONAL CLAUSE: If assistance is provided for the purpose of evading prosecution or interfering in the investigation of the punishable acts of extortion, illicit enrichment, kidnapping with extortion, or trafficking in narcotic drugs or toxic or psychotropic substances, the penalty imposed shall be a term of imprisonment of four (4) to twelve (12) years."

Article 7
Article 177 of the Criminal Code shall read as follows:

"ARTICLE 177: Receiving stolen goods

Any person who, without having taken part in the commission of an offence, acquires, possesses, converts or transfers movable or removable property derived directly or indirectly from an offence, or who performs some other act to disguise or conceal the illicit origin of such property, shall be liable to a term of imprisonment of one (1) to five (5) years and a fine of five (5) to five hundred (500) times the statutory minimum monthly wage, provided that the act does not constitute a separate, more serious, offence.

If the act in question relates to property with a value greater than one thousand (1,000) times the statutory minimum monthly wage, the custodial sentence shall be increased by a proportion of from one third to one half."

Article 8
Article 186 of the Criminal Code shall read as follows:

"ARTICLE 186: Conspiracy to commit a crime

When several persons conspire to commit a crime, each such person shall be liable, for this fact alone, to a term of imprisonment of three (3) to six (6) years.

Such an offence committed in an uninhabited area or with the use of weapons shall be punishable by a term of imprisonment of three (3) to nine (9) years.

When the conspiracy is aimed at the commission of offences of terrorism, drug trafficking, kidnapping with extortion, extortion or the formation of death squads, vigilante squads or bands of hired assassins, it shall be punishable by a term of imprisonment of ten (10) to fifteen (15) years and a fine of two thousand (2,000) to fifty thousand (50,000) times the statutory minimum monthly wage.

The aforementioned penalty shall be doubled to tripled for any person who organizes, encourages, promotes, directs, leads, forms or funds a conspiracy or association to commit a crime."

Article 9
Book II, Title VII, of the Criminal Code shall have a Chapter Three entitled "Money-laundering", containing the following articles:

"ARTICLE 247 A: Money-laundering

Any person who acquires, guards, invests, transports, processes, has in safe keeping or administers property deriving directly or indirectly from activities involving extortion, illicit enrichment, kidnapping with extortion or revolt, or related to trafficking in narcotic drugs or toxic or psychotropic substances and who gives to property deriving from such activities the appearance of legality or legalizes it or conceals or disguises the true nature, origin, location, purpose or movement of such property or of title thereto, or performs any other act to conceal or disguise its illicit origin shall be liable, for such act alone, to a term of imprisonment of six (6) to fifteen (15) years and a fine of five hundred (500) to fifty thousand (50,000) times the statutory minimum monthly wage.

The same penalty shall apply if the acts described in the preceding paragraph were performed in respect of property which, pursuant to the additional clause of article 340 of the Code of Criminal Procedure, has been declared to be of illicit origin.

ADDITIONAL CLAUSE 1: Money-laundering shall be a punishable offence even if the offence from which the property is derived or the acts punishable under the above-mentioned provisions were entirely or partly committed abroad.

ADDITIONAL CLAUSE 2: The penalties established in this article shall be increased by a proportion of from one third (1/3) to one half (1/2)

if the performance of the acts concerned involved exchange or foreign trade transactions or the importation of goods into national territory.

ADDITIONAL CLAUSE 3: The increase in penalty established in the preceding additional clause shall also apply in the case of the importation of smuggled goods into the national territory.

ARTICLE 247 B: Failure to apply measures of control

Any employee or executive manager of a financial institution or savings and loans cooperative who, with the aim of concealing or disguising the illicit origin of the money concerned, fails to apply any or all of the control mechanisms established by articles 103 and 104 of Decree No. 663 of 1993 for cash transactions shall be liable, for this act alone, to a term of imprisonment of two (2) to six (6) years and a fine of one hundred (100) to ten thousand (10,000) times the statutory minimum monthly wage.

ARTICLE 247 C: Specific aggravating circumstances

The custodial sentences specified in article 247 A shall be increased by a proportion of from one third to one half if the conduct in question is performed by a person belonging to an entity which is a juridical person, company or organization devoted to money-laundering and by a proportion of from one half to three quarters if it is performed by the chiefs, administrators or executives of such an entity.

ARTICLE 247 D: Imposition of accessory penalties

If the acts envisaged in article 247 A and 247 B were performed by an employer in any line of business, an administrator, employee, executive manager or intermediary in the financial, stock exchange or insurance sector, as the case may be, or a public servant in the discharge of his or her duties, in addition to the corresponding penalty there shall also be imposed the penalty of disqualification from public office or official duties, or prohibition of the pursuit of that person's occupation, trade, craft, business or enterprise for a period of not less than three (3) and not more than five (5) years."

Article 10
Article 369 A, paragraph (d), of the Code of Criminal Procedure shall read as follows:

"(d) Bringing of charges against the leaders of criminal organizations, accompanied by effective proofs of guilt."

Article 11
Article 37 of the Code of Criminal Procedure shall read as follows:

"ARTICLE 37: Early sentence

After a decision defining the legal situation has been made enforceable and pending termination of the investigation, the defendant may request pronouncement of an early sentence.

In response to such request, the prosecutor may, if he or she deems it necessary, extend the preliminary investigation and examine evidence during a maximum period of eight (8) days. The counts of the indictment formulated by the prosecutor and their admission by the defendant shall be recorded in a record signed by all parties to such proceedings.

The judicial proceedings shall be transmitted to the competent judge who, within a period of ten (10) working days, shall pronounce a sentence on the basis of the accepted facts and circumstances, provided that no violation of fundamental guarantees has taken place.

The judge shall determine the appropriate penalty, reducing the amount of the penalty by a proportion of one third (1/3) if the defendant enters a guilty plea.

An early sentence may also be pronounced if, once the indictment order has been issued and before the date for a public hearing has been set, the defendant pleads guilty to all the charges listed therein. The penalty may then be reduced by one eighth (1/8)."

Article 12
Article 37 B of the Code of Criminal Procedure shall read as follows:

"ARTICLE 37 B: Common provisions

In the cases of articles 37 and 37 A of this Code the following provisions shall apply:

1. Concurrent reductions of penalty

The reduction of penalty established in article 299 of this Code may be accumulated with a reduction envisaged in article 37 or with the reduction indicated in article 37 A, but in no circumstances may the latter reductions be accumulated with each other.

2. Equivalence to the indictment order

The document containing the charges accepted by the defendant in the case of article 37 and the document containing the agreement referred to by article 37 A are equivalent to the indictment order.

3. Rupture of the unity of proceedings

Where the proceedings involve several defendants or offences, partial agreements of pleas of guilt may be filed, in which case the unity of proceedings shall be deemed broken.

4. Interest in recourse

A sentence is appealable by the prosecutor, the Department of Public Prosecutions, the defendant and the defendant's counsel, but by the latter two parties only in respect of the gravity of the sentence, the imposition of a conditional sentence or the extinction of ownership rights to property.

5. Exclusion of a third party with civil liability and of the party to civil proceedings

If an early sentence is awarded in the circumstances envisaged in articles 37 or 37 A of this Code, the court order in question shall not determine matters of civil liability."

Article 13
Article 71 of the Code of Criminal Procedure shall contain a new paragraph as follows:

"6. Proceedings in respect of offences of conspiracy to commit a crime in the cases envisaged in article 186, paragraph 3, of the Criminal Code, as well as proceedings in respect of offences covered by articles 247 A and 247 B of the Criminal Code."

Article 14
Article 340 of the Code of Criminal Procedure shall read as follows:

"ARTICLE 340: Extinction of ownership rights

Ownership of property acquired by means of illicit enrichment or causing financial loss to the Treasury or serious damage to social moral standards shall be declared to be extinguished by judicial sentence. For such purposes, the offences established in the National Narcotics Statute and its amending and supplementing provisions, as well as the offences of kidnapping, kidnapping with extortion, extortion, money-laundering and engaging in dummy operations, crimes against the social economic order, crimes against natural resources, the manufacture of and trafficking in weapons and ammunition for the exclusive use of the military forces, misappropriation of public funds, bribery, influence peddling, rebellion, sedition and unlawful assembly are considered offences that cause serious damage to social moral standards. In all cases, the rights of third parties of good faith shall be safeguarded. Property and assets to which ownership rights have been extinguished shall, without exception, revert to the Fund for Rehabilitation, Social Investment and Organized Crime Control for allocation by the National Narcotics Board.

ADDITIONAL CLAUSE: In criminal investigations and proceedings in respect of offences of extortion, kidnapping with extortion, engaging in dummy operations, money-laundering, offences covered by the National Narcotics Statute and its amending or supplementing provisions, the illicit enrichment of public servants or private persons, embezzlement of public funds, illicit interest in the conclusion of contracts, the conclusion of contracts in breach of legal requirements, the illegal issuing of currency or of assets or securities with equivalent value to currency, illicit engaging in monopolistic activities or activities relating to revenue taxation, theft of assets or equipment intended for national security and defence, crimes against property affecting State assets, improper use of privileged information or use of confidential or classified information, the declaration that movable or immovable property is of illicit origin is independent from the criminal responsibility of the accused and the abatement of the action or extinction of the penalty. In such cases extinction of ownership shall proceed in conformity with the provisions of the law governing such action *in rem.*

Unless the proceedings conclude by demonstrating non-existence of the offence, the declaration that movable or immovable property is of illicit origin shall be made in the restraining order, in the order of proscription of the investigation, in the writ of termination of proceedings or in the sentence. In the same order, and with a view to furthering the process of extinction of ownership, there shall be issued an order for the attachment and seizure of property declared to be of illicit origin."

Article 15
Article 369 H of the Code of Criminal Procedure shall contain a paragraph as follows:

"ADDITIONAL CLAUSE: Any person convicted on charges of conspiracy to commit a crime aggravated by the circumstance of organizing, encouraging, promoting, directing, leading, forming or funding a conspiracy or association, in combination with a different offence, may have recourse to an early sentence or to a special hearing and may be eligible for a reduced sentence in return for entering a guilty plea or for effectively assisting the course of justice, but in no case may the penalty imposed be lower than that imposable without any reductions for the more serious offence."

Article 16
Article 508, paragraph 4, of the Code of Criminal Procedure shall read as follows:

"4. In the case of a prohibition on the pursuit of an occupation, trade, craft, business or enterprise, an issue shall be ordered to annul the document permitting such pursuit and the issuing authority shall be duly notified."

Article 17
Article 33 of Law No. 30 of 1986 shall read as follows:

"ARTICLE 33: Any person not in possession of a licence issued by a competent authority who, except as provided by law governing the permitted dosage for personal consumption, introduces into the country, in transit or otherwise, or exports from it, transports, carries, stores, conserves, manufactures, sells, offers, acquires, finances or supplies in any capacity addictive drugs shall be liable to a term of imprisonment of six (6) to twenty (20) years and a fine of one hundred (100) to fifty thousand (50,000) times the statutory minimum monthly wage.

If the quantity of drugs in question is not greater than one thousand (1,000) grams of marijuana, two hundred (200) grams of hashish, one hundred (100) grams of cocaine or narcotic substance based on cocaine or twenty (20) grams of opium derivative, or two hundred (200) grams of methaqualone or synthetic drug, the penalty shall be a term of imprisonment of one (1) to three (3) years and a fine of two (2) to one hundred (100) times the statutory minimum monthly wage.

If the quantity of drugs in question is greater than the maximum limits established in the preceding paragraph but not greater than ten thousand (10,000) grams of marijuana, three thousand (3,000) grams of hashish, two thousand (2,000) grams of cocaine or narcotic substance based on cocaine, or sixty (60) grams of opium derivative, or four thousand (4,000) grams of methaqualone or synthetic drug, the penalty shall be a term of imprisonment of four (4) to twelve (12) years and a fine of ten (10) to one hundred (100) times the statutory minimum monthly wage."

Article 18
Article 34 of Law No. 30 of 1986 shall read as follows:

"ARTICLE 34: Any person who illicitly uses movable or immovable property for the purpose of manufacturing, storing or transporting, selling or utilizing any of the drugs referred to in article 32 above or who authorizes or tolerates such use by others shall be liable to term of imprisonment of four (4) to twelve (12) years and a fine of one thousand (1,000) to fifty thousand (50,000) times the statutory minimum monthly wage, without prejudice to the provisions of articles 124 and 125 of Decree-Law No. 522 of 1971 (article 208, paragraph 5, and 214, paragraph 3, of the National Police Code).

If the quantity of drugs in question is not greater than one thousand (1,000) grams of marijuana, three hundred (300) grams of hashish, one hundred (100) grams of cocaine or narcotic substance based on cocaine, twenty (20) grams of opium derivative or two hundred (200) grams of methaqualone or synthetic drug, the penalty shall be a term of imprisonment of one (1) to three (3) years and a fine of two (2) to one hundred (100) times the statutory minimum monthly wage.

If the quantity of drug in question is greater than the maximum limits established in the preceding paragraph but not greater than ten thousand (10,000) grams of marijuana, three thousand (3,000) grams of hashish, two thousand (2,000) grams of cocaine or narcotic substance based on cocaine, sixty (60) grams of opium derivative or four thousand (4,000) grams of methaqualone or synthetic drug, the penalty shall be a term of imprisonment of three (3) to eight (8) years and a fine of ten (10) to eight hundred (800) times the statutory minimum monthly wage."

Article 19
Article 40 of Law No. 30 of 1986 shall read as follows:

"ARTICLE 40: In the order imposing a protective measure of custody in respect of any of the offences established in articles 33, 34 or 43 of this Law, the judicial officer shall decree the seizure and attachment of property belonging to the accused which has not already been confiscated in connection with the punishable act in an amount deemed sufficient to guarantee payment of the fine stipulated in those articles and shall appoint a depositary. Once seizure and attachment have been decreed, both their execution and the procedures for contesting such action and decision-taking on such recourse shall proceed in conformity with the relevant provisions of the Code of Civil Procedure.

The sentence delivered shall order the sale of any property seized and attached as part of proceedings, for which purpose regard shall be had to the procedures laid down in the Code of Civil Procedure."

Article 20
Article 43 of Law No. 30 of 1986 shall read as follows:

"ARTICLE 43: Any person who illegally introduces into the country, or exports from it, transports or has in his possession elements which may be used for processing cocaine or any other addictive drug such as the following: ethyl ether, acetone, ammonium, potassium permanganate, carbonate light, hydrochloric acid, sulphuric acid, thinners, solvents and other substances which, according to pre-established criteria of the National Narcotics Board, are used for such purpose, shall be liable to a term of imprisonment of three (3) to ten (10) years and a fine of two thousand (2,000) to fifty thousand (50,000) times the statutory minimum monthly wage.

Except as provided by article 54 of Decree-Law No. 099 of 1991, adopted as permanent legislation under article 1 of Decree-Law No. 2271 of 1991, once such elements have been established by expert opinion as belonging to the aforementioned category, they shall be placed by a judicial officer at the disposal of the National Narcotics Office, which may order their immediate utilization by an official entity, their sale for duly verified licit purposes, or their destruction in cases where they present a serious risk to public health or safety.

In cases where the quantity of the substances concerned is not greater than triple those quantities indicated in the resolutions issued by the National Narcotics Office, the penalty shall be a term of imprisonment of two (2) to five (5) years and a fine of ten (10) to one hundred (100) times the statutory minimum monthly wage."

Article 21
The following additional clause is hereby added to article 209 of the Organizational Statute of the Financial System:

"ADDITIONAL CLAUSE: In cases where the offending acts referred to in this article relate to provisions contained in Chapter XVI of the Third Part of the Organizational Statute of the Financial System, the fine imposable shall be up to fifty million pesos ($50,000,000) payable to the National Treasury. This amount shall be readjustable in the manner indicated in the first paragraph of this article.

This fine may be renewable until such time as the requirement is met and shall be applied without prejudice to any penal sanctions imposed in respect of each offence committed.

In addition, the head of the Bank Supervisory Authority may demand immediate dismissal of the offender and transmit such decision to all entities under the supervision of that Authority."

Article 22
The following paragraph is hereby added to article 211 of the Organizational Statute of the Financial System:

"3. Provisions on the prevention of criminal conduct

In cases where the offence referred to in the first paragraph of this article relates to the provisions contained in Chapter XVI of the Third Part of the Organizational Statute of the Financial System, the fine imposable shall be up to one thousand million pesos ($1,000,000,000).

In addition, the head of the Bank Supervisory Authority may order the establishment awarded such fine to allocate an amount of up to one thousand million pesos ($1,000,000,000) for the implementation of internal reforms to be agreed with that supervisory body.

The aforementioned amounts shall be readjustable in the manner indicated in the first paragraph of this article."

Article 23

Cooperatives Which Engage in Savings and Credit Activities
In addition to high-level cooperatives [*entidades Cooperativas de Grado Superior*] which fall within the responsibility of the Bank Supervisory Authority, all cooperatives which engage in savings and credit activities shall also be governed by the provisions of articles 102 to 107 of the Organizational Statute of the Financial System.

In the case of entities not supervised by the Bank Supervisory Authority, the National Administrative Department for Cooperatives (Dancoop) shall determine the lower threshold amounts for the reporting requirement for cash transactions.

Furthermore, Dancoop shall prescribe rules governing, and shall collect, periodical reports on the number of cash transactions referred to in article 104 of the Organizational Statute of the Financial System, as well as monthly reports on the registration of multiple cash transactions referred to in article 103, paragraph 2, of that Statute undertaken by cooperative entities not supervised by the Bank Supervisory Authority.

The obligations set out in this article shall enter into effect on the date specified by the National Government.

13.
Council of Europe Convention on Laundering, Search, Seizure, and Confiscation of the Proceeds from Crime and on the Financing of Terrorism

The Council of Europe Convention on Laundering, Search, Seizure, and Confiscation of the Proceeds of Crime and on the Financing of Terrorism updates the 1990 Strasbourg Convention. This updated instrument incorporates provisions to prevent the financing of terrorist organizations and seeks to ensure "that logistical cells cannot find financial safe havens anywhere in Europe." This convention calls for international cooperation by all parties.

Source
Council of Europe, http://conventions.coe.int/Treaty/EN/Treaties/Html/198.htm.

Preamble
The member States of the Council of Europe and the other Signatories hereto,

Considering that the aim of the Council of Europe is to achieve a greater unity between its members;

Convinced of the need to pursue a common criminal policy aimed at the protection of society;

Considering that the fight against serious crime, which has become an increasingly international problem, calls for the use of modern and effective methods on an international scale;

Believing that one of these methods consists in depriving criminals of the proceeds from crime and instrumentalities;

Considering that for the attainment of this aim a well-functioning system of international co-operation also must be established;

Bearing in mind the Council of Europe Convention on Laundering, Search, Seizure and Confiscation of the Proceeds from Crime (ETS No. 141—hereinafter referred to as "the 1990 Convention");

Recalling also Resolution 1373(2001) on threats to international peace and security caused by terrorist acts adopted by the Security Council of the United Nations on 28 September 2001, and particularly its paragraph 3.d;

Recalling the International Convention for the Suppression of the Financing of Terrorism, adopted by the General Assembly of the United Nations on 9 December 1999 and particularly its Articles 2 and 4, which oblige States Parties to establish the financing of terrorism as a criminal offence;

Convinced of the necessity to take immediate steps to ratify and to implement fully the International Convention for the Suppression of the Financing of Terrorism, cited above,

Have agreed as follows:

Chapter I—Use of Terms

Article 1—Use of Terms
For the purposes of this Convention:

a. "proceeds" means any economic advantage, derived from or obtained, directly or indirectly, from criminal offences. It may consist of any property as defined in sub-paragraph b of this article;

b. "property" includes property of any description, whether corporeal or incorporeal, movable or immovable, and legal documents or instruments evidencing title to or interest in such property;

c. "instrumentalities" means any property used or intended to be used, in any manner, wholly or in part, to commit a criminal offence or criminal offences;

d. "confiscation" means a penalty or a measure, ordered by a court following proceedings in relation to a criminal offence or criminal offences resulting in the final deprivation of property;

e. "predicate offence" means any criminal offence as a result of which proceeds were generated that may become the subject of an offence as defined in Article 9 of this Convention.

f. "financial intelligence unit" (hereinafter referred to as "FIU") means a central, national agency responsible for receiving (and, as permitted, requesting), analysing and disseminating to the competent authorities, disclosures of financial information

  i. concerning suspected proceeds and potential financing of terrorism, or

  ii. required by national legislation or regulation,in order to combat money laundering and financing of terrorism;

g. "freezing" or "seizure" means temporarily prohibiting the transfer, destruction, conversion, disposition or movement of property or temporarily assuming custody or control of property on the basis of an order issued by a court or other competent authority;

h. "financing of terrorism" means the acts set out in Article 2 of the International Convention for the Suppression of the Financing of Terrorism, cited above.

Chapter II—Financing of Terrorism

Article 2—Application of the Convention to the Financing of Terrorism
1. Each Party shall adopt such legislative and other measures as may be necessary to enable it to apply the provisions contained in Chapters III, IV and V of this Convention to the financing of terrorism.

2. In particular, each Party shall ensure that it is able to search, trace, identify, freeze, seize and confiscate property, of a licit or illicit origin, used or allocated to be used by any means, in whole or in part, for the financing of terrorism, or the proceeds of this offence, and to provide co-operation to this end to the widest possible extent.

Chapter III—Measures to Be Taken at National Level

Section 1—General Provisions

Article 3—Confiscation Measures
1. Each Party shall adopt such legislative and other measures as may be necessary to enable it to confiscate instrumentalities and proceeds or property the value of which corresponds to such proceeds and laundered property.

2. Provided that paragraph 1 of this article applies to money laundering and to the categories of offences in the appendix to the Convention, each Party may, at the time of signature or when depositing its instrument of ratification, acceptance, approval or accession, by a declaration addressed to the Secretary General of the Council of Europe, declare that paragraph 1 of this article applies

a. only in so far as the offence is punishable by deprivation of liberty or a detention order for a maximum of more than one year. However, each Party may make a declaration on this provision in respect of the confiscation of the proceeds from tax offences for the sole purpose of being able to confiscate such proceeds, both nationally and through international cooperation, under national and international tax-debt recovery legislation; and/or

b. only to a list of specified offences.

3. Parties may provide for mandatory confiscation in respect of offences which are subject to the confiscation regime. Parties may in particular include in this provision the offences of money laundering, drug trafficking, trafficking in human beings and any other serious offence.

4. Each Party shall adopt such legislative or other measures as may be necessary to require that, in respect of a serious offence or offences as defined by national law, an offender demonstrates the origin of alleged proceeds or other property liable

to confiscation to the extent that such a requirement is consistent with the principles of its domestic law.

Article 4—Investigative and Provisional Measures
Each Party shall adopt such legislative and other measures as may be necessary to enable it to identify, trace, freeze or seize rapidly property which is liable to confiscation pursuant to Article 3, in order in particular to facilitate the enforcement of a later confiscation.

Article 5—Freezing, Seizure and Confiscation
Each Party shall adopt such legislative and other measures as may be necessary to ensure that the measures to freeze, seize and confiscate also encompass:

    a. the property into which the proceeds have been transformed or converted;

    b. property acquired from legitimate sources, if proceeds have been intermingled, in whole or in part, with such property, up to the assessed value of the intermingled proceeds;

    c. income or other benefits derived from proceeds, from property into which proceeds of crime have been transformed or converted or from property with which proceeds of crime have been intermingled, up to the assessed value of the intermingled proceeds, in the same manner and to the same extent as proceeds.

Article 6—Management of Frozen or Seized Property
Each Party shall adopt such legislative or other measures as may be necessary to ensure proper management of frozen or seized property in accordance with Articles 4 and 5 of this Convention.

Article 7—Investigative Powers and Techniques
1. Each Party shall adopt such legislative and other measures as may be necessary to empower its courts or other competent authorities to order that bank, financial or commercial records be made available or be seized in order to carry out the actions referred to in Articles 3, 4 and 5. A Party shall not decline to act under the provisions of this article on grounds of bank secrecy.

2. Without prejudice to paragraph 1, each Party shall adopt such legislative and other measures as may be necessary to enable it to:

    a. determine whether a natural or legal person is a holder or beneficial owner of one or more accounts, of whatever nature, in any bank located in its territory and, if so obtain all of the details of the identified accounts;

    b. obtain the particulars of specified bank accounts and of banking operations which have been carried out during a specified period through one or more specified accounts, including the particulars of any sending or recipient account;

    c. monitor, during a specified period, the banking operations that are being carried out through one or more identified accounts; and,

    d. ensure that banks do not disclose to the bank customer concerned or to other third persons that information has been sought or obtained in accordance with sub-paragraphs a, b, or c, or that an investigation is being carried out.

Parties shall consider extending this provision to accounts held in non-bank financial institutions.

3. Each Party shall consider adopting such legislative and other measures as may be necessary to enable it to use special investigative techniques facilitating the identification and tracing of proceeds and the gathering of evidence related thereto, such as observation, interception of telecommunications, access to computer systems and order to produce specific documents.

Article 8—Legal Remedies
Each Party shall adopt such legislative and other measures as may be necessary to ensure that interested parties affected by measures under Articles 3, 4 and 5 and such other provisions in this

Section as are relevant, shall have effective legal remedies in order to preserve their rights.

Article 9—Laundering Offences
1. Each Party shall adopt such legislative and other measures as may be necessary to establish as offences under its domestic law, when committed intentionally:

a. the conversion or transfer of property, knowing that such property is proceeds, for the purpose of concealing or disguising the illicit origin of the property or of assisting any person who is involved in the commission of the predicate offence to evade the legal consequences of his actions;

b. the concealment or disguise of the true nature, source, location, disposition, movement, rights with respect to, or ownership of, property, knowing that such property is proceeds; and, subject to its constitutional principles and the basic concepts of its legal system;

c. the acquisition, possession or use of property, knowing, at the time of receipt, that such property was proceeds;

d. participation in, association or conspiracy to commit, attempts to commit and aiding, abetting, facilitating and counselling the commission of any of the offences established in accordance with this article.

2. For the purposes of implementing or applying paragraph 1 of this article:

a. it shall not matter whether the predicate offence was subject to the criminal jurisdiction of the Party;

b. it may be provided that the offences set forth in that paragraph do not apply to the persons who committed the predicate offence;

c. knowledge, intent or purpose required as an element of an offence set forth in that paragraph may be inferred from objective, factual circumstances.

3. Each Party may adopt such legislative and other measures as may be necessary to establish as an offence under its domestic law all or some of the acts referred to in paragraph 1 of this article, in

either or both of the following cases where the offender

a. suspected that the property was proceeds,

b. ought to have assumed that the property was proceeds.

4. Provided that paragraph 1 of this article applies to the categories of predicate offences in the appendix to the Convention, each State or the European Community may, at the time of signature or when depositing its instrument of ratification, acceptance, approval or accession, by a declaration addressed to the Secretary General of the Council of Europe, declare that paragraph 1 of this article applies:

a. only in so far as the predicate offence is punishable by deprivation of liberty or a detention order for a maximum of more than one year, or for those Parties that have a minimum threshold for offences in their legal system, in so far as the offence is punishable by deprivation of liberty or a detention order for a minimum of more than six months; and/or

b. only to a list of specified predicate offences; and/or

c. to a category of serious offences in the national law of the Party.

5. Each Party shall ensure that a prior or simultaneous conviction for the predicate offence is not a prerequisite for a conviction for money laundering.

6. Each Party shall ensure that a conviction for money laundering under this Article is possible where it is proved that the property, the object of paragraph 1.a or b of this article, originated from a predicate offence, without it being necessary to establish precisely which offence.

7. Each Party shall ensure that predicate offences for money laundering extend to conduct that occurred in another State, which constitutes an offence in that State, and which would have constituted a predicate offence had it occurred domestically. Each Party may provide that the only

prerequisite is that the conduct would have constituted a predicate offence had it occurred domestically.

Article 10—Corporate Liability
1. Each Party shall adopt such legislative and other measures as may be necessary to ensure that legal persons can be held liable for the criminal offences of money laundering established in accordance with this Convention, committed for their benefit by any natural person, acting either individually or as part of an organ of the legal person, who has a leading position within the legal person, based on:

   a. a power of representation of the legal person; or
   b. an authority to take decisions on behalf of the legal person; or
   c. an authority to exercise control within the legal person,

as well as for involvement of such a natural person as accessory or instigator in the above-mentioned offences.

2. Apart from the cases already provided for in paragraph 1, each Party shall take the necessary measures to ensure that a legal person can be held liable where the lack of supervision or control by a natural person referred to in paragraph 1 has made possible the commission of the criminal offences mentioned in paragraph 1 for the benefit of that legal person by a natural person under its authority.

3. Liability of a legal person under this Article shall not exclude criminal proceedings against natural persons who are perpetrators, instigators of, or accessories to, the criminal offences mentioned in paragraph 1.

4. Each Party shall ensure that legal persons held liable in accordance with this Article, shall be subject to effective, proportionate and dissuasive criminal or non-criminal sanctions, including monetary sanctions.

Article 11—Previous Decisions
Each Party shall adopt such legislative and other measures as may be necessary to provide for the possibility of taking into account, when determining the penalty, final decisions against a natural or legal person taken in another Party in relation to offences established in accordance with this Convention.

Section 2—Financial Intelligence Unit (FIU) and Prevention

Article 12—Financial Intelligence Unit (FIU)
1. Each Party shall adopt such legislative and other measures as may be necessary to establish an FIU as defined in this Convention.

2. Each Party shall adopt such legislative and other measures as may be necessary to ensure that its FIU has access, directly or indirectly, on a timely basis to the financial, administrative and law enforcement information that it requires to properly undertake its functions, including the analysis of suspicious transaction reports.

Article 13—Measures to Prevent Money Laundering
1. Each Party shall adopt such legislative and other measures as may be necessary to institute a comprehensive domestic regulatory and supervisory or monitoring regime to prevent money laundering and shall take due account of applicable international standards, including in particular the recommendations adopted by the Financial Action Task Force on Money Laundering (FATF).

2. In that respect, each Party shall adopt, in particular, such legislative and other measures as may be necessary to:

   a. require legal and natural persons which engage in activities which are particularly likely to be used for money laundering purposes, and as far as these activities are concerned, to:

i. identify and verify the identity of their customers and, where applicable, their ultimate beneficial owners, and to conduct ongoing due diligence on the business relationship, while taking into account a risk based approach;

ii. report suspicions on money laundering subject to safeguard;

iii. take supporting measures, such as record keeping on customer identification and transactions, training of personnel and the establishment of internal policies and procedures, and if appropriate, adapted to their size and nature of business;

b. prohibit, as appropriate, the persons referred to in sub-paragraph a from disclosing the fact that a suspicious transaction report or related information has been transmitted or that a money laundering investigation is being or may be carried out;

c. ensure that the persons referred to in sub-paragraph a are subject to effective systems for monitoring, and where applicable supervision, with a view to ensure their compliance with the requirements to combat money laundering, where appropriate on a risk sensitive basis.

3. In that respect, each Party shall adopt such legislative or other measures as may be necessary to detect the significant physical cross border transportation of cash and appropriate bearer negotiable instruments.

Article 14—Postponement of Domestic Suspicious Transactions

Each Party shall adopt such legislative and other measures as may be necessary to permit urgent action to be taken by the FIU or, as appropriate, by any other competent authorities or body, when there is a suspicion that a transaction is related to money laundering, to suspend or withhold consent to a transaction going ahead in order to analyse the transaction and confirm the suspicion. Each party may restrict such a measure to cases where a suspicious transaction report has been submitted. The maximum duration of any suspension or withholding of consent to a transaction shall be subject to any relevant provisions in national law.

Chapter IV—International Co-operation

Section 1—Principles of International Co-operation

Article 15—General Principles and Measures for International Co-operation

1. The Parties shall mutually co-operate with each other to the widest extent possible for the purposes of investigations and proceedings aiming at the confiscation of instrumentalities and proceeds.

2. Each Party shall adopt such legislative or other measures as may be necessary to enable it to comply, under the conditions provided for in this chapter, with requests:

a. for confiscation of specific items of property representing proceeds or instrumentalities, as well as for confiscation of proceeds consisting in a requirement to pay a sum of money corresponding to the value of proceeds;

b. for investigative assistance and provisional measures with a view to either form of confiscation referred to under a above.

3. Investigative assistance and provisional measures sought in paragraph 2.b shall be carried out as permitted by and in accordance with the internal law of the requested Party. Where the request concerning one of these measures specifies formalities or procedures which are necessary under the law of the requesting Party, even if unfamiliar to the requested Party, the latter shall comply with such requests to the extent that the action sought is not contrary to the fundamental principles of its law.

4. Each Party shall adopt such legislative or other measures as may be necessary to ensure that the requests coming from other Parties in order to identify, trace, freeze or seize the proceeds and

instrumentalities, receive the same priority as those made in the framework of internal procedures.

Section 2—Investigative Assistance

Article 16—Obligation to Assist
The Parties shall afford each other, upon request, the widest possible measure of assistance in the identification and tracing of instrumentalities, proceeds and other property liable to confiscation. Such assistance shall include any measure providing and securing evidence as to the existence, location or movement, nature, legal status or value of the aforementioned property.

Article 17—Requests for Information on Bank Accounts
1. Each Party shall, under the conditions set out in this article, take the measures necessary to determine, in answer to a request sent by another Party, whether a natural or legal person that is the subject of a criminal investigation holds or controls one or more accounts, of whatever nature, in any bank located in its territory and, if so, provide the particulars of the identified accounts.

2. The obligation set out in this article shall apply only to the extent that the information is in the possession of the bank keeping the account.

3. In addition to the requirements of Article 37, the requesting party shall, in the request:

   a. state why it considers that the requested information is likely to be of substantial value for the purpose of the criminal investigation into the offence;
   b. state on what grounds it presumes that banks in the requested Party hold the account and specify, to the widest extent possible, which banks and/or accounts may be involved; and
   c. include any additional information available which may facilitate the execution of the request.

4. The requested Party may make the execution of such a request dependant on the same conditions as it applies in respect of requests for search and seizure.

5. Each State or the European Community may, at the time of signature or when depositing its instrument of ratification, acceptance, approval or accession, by a declaration addressed to the Secretary General of the Council of Europe, declare that this article applies only to the categories of offences specified in the list contained in the appendix to this Convention.

6. Parties may extend this provision to accounts held in non-bank financial institutions. Such extension may be made subject to the principle of reciprocity.

Article 18—Requests for Information on Banking Transactions
1. On request by another Party, the requested Party shall provide the particulars of specified bank accounts and of banking operations which have been carried out during a specified period through one or more accounts specified in the request, including the particulars of any sending or recipient account.

2. The obligation set out in this article shall apply only to the extent that the information is in the possession of the bank holding the account.

3. In addition to the requirements of Article 37, the requesting Party shall in its request indicate why it considers the requested information relevant for the purpose of the criminal investigation into the offence.

4. The requested Party may make the execution of such a request dependant on the same conditions as it applies in respect of requests for search and seizure.

5. Parties may extend this provision to accounts held in non-bank financial institutions. Such

extension may be made subject to the principle of reciprocity.

Article 19—Requests for the Monitoring of Banking Transactions
1. Each Party shall ensure that, at the request of another Party, it is able to monitor, during a specified period, the banking operations that are being carried out through one or more accounts specified in the request and communicate the results thereof to the requesting Party.

2. In addition to the requirements of Article 37, the requesting Party shall in its request indicate why it considers the requested information relevant for the purpose of the criminal investigation into the offence.

3. The decision to monitor shall be taken in each individual case by the competent authorities of the requested Party, with due regard for the national law of that Party.

4. The practical details regarding the monitoring shall be agreed between the competent authorities of the requesting and requested Parties.

5. Parties may extend this provision to accounts held in non-bank financial institutions.

Article 20—Spontaneous Information
Without prejudice to its own investigations or proceedings, a Party may without prior request forward to another Party information on instrumentalities and proceeds, when it considers that the disclosure of such information might assist the receiving Party in initiating or carrying out investigations or proceedings or might lead to a request by that Party under this chapter.

Section 3—Provisional Measures

Article 21—Obligation to Take Provisional Measures
1. At the request of another Party which has instituted criminal proceedings or proceedings for the purpose of confiscation, a Party shall take the necessary provisional measures, such as freezing or seizing, to prevent any dealing in, transfer or disposal of property which, at a later stage, may be the subject of a request for confiscation or which might be such as to satisfy the request.

2. A Party which has received a request for confiscation pursuant to Article 23 shall, if so requested, take the measures mentioned in paragraph 1 of this article in respect of any property which is the subject of the request or which might be such as to satisfy the request.

Article 22—Execution of Provisional Measures
1. After the execution of the provisional measures requested in conformity with paragraph 1 of Article 21, the requesting Party shall provide spontaneously and as soon as possible to the requested Party all information which may question or modify the extent of these measures. The requesting Party shall also provide without delays all complementary information requested by the requested Party and which is necessary for the implementation of and the follow up to the provisional measures.

2. Before lifting any provisional measure taken pursuant to this article, the requested Party shall, wherever possible, give the requesting Party an opportunity to present its reasons in favour of continuing the measure.

Section 4—Confiscation

Article 23—Obligation to Confiscate
1. A Party, which has received a request made by another Party for confiscation concerning

instrumentalities or proceeds, situated in its territory, shall:

   a. enforce a confiscation order made by a court of a requesting Party in relation to such instrumentalities or proceeds; or

   b. submit the request to its competent authorities for the purpose of obtaining an order of confiscation and, if such order is granted, enforce it.

2. For the purposes of applying paragraph 1.b of this article, any Party shall whenever necessary have competence to institute confiscation proceedings under its own law.

3. The provisions of paragraph 1 of this article shall also apply to confiscation consisting in a requirement to pay a sum of money corresponding to the value of proceeds, if property on which the confiscation can be enforced is located in the requested Party. In such cases, when enforcing confiscation pursuant to paragraph 1, the requested Party shall, if payment is not obtained, realise the claim on any property available for that purpose.

4. If a request for confiscation concerns a specific item of property, the Parties may agree that the requested Party may enforce the confiscation in the form of a requirement to pay a sum of money corresponding to the value of the property.

5. The Parties shall co-operate to the widest extent possible under their domestic law with those Parties which request the execution of measures equivalent to confiscation leading to the deprivation of property, which are not criminal sanctions, in so far as such measures are ordered by a judicial authority of the requesting Party in relation to a criminal offence, provided that it has been established that the property constitutes proceeds or other property in the meaning of Article 5 of this Convention.

Article 24—Execution of Confiscation
1. The procedures for obtaining and enforcing the confiscation under Article 23 shall be governed by the law of the requested Party.

2. The requested Party shall be bound by the findings as to the facts in so far as they are stated in a conviction or judicial decision of the requesting Party or in so far as such conviction or judicial decision is implicitly based on them.

3. Each State or the European Community may, at the time of signature or when depositing its instrument of ratification, acceptance, approval or accession, by a declaration addressed to the Secretary General of the Council of Europe, declare that paragraph 2 of this article applies only subject to its constitutional principles and the basic concepts of its legal system.

4. If the confiscation consists in the requirement to pay a sum of money, the competent authority of the requested Party shall convert the amount thereof into the currency of that Party at the rate of exchange ruling at the time when the decision to enforce the confiscation is taken.

5. In the case of Article 23, paragraph 1.a, the requesting Party alone shall have the right to decide on any application for review of the confiscation order.

Article 25—Confiscated Property
1. Property confiscated by a Party pursuant to Articles 23 and 24 of this Convention, shall be disposed of by that Party in accordance with its domestic law and administrative procedures.

2. When acting on the request made by another Party in accordance with Articles 23 and 24 of this Convention, Parties shall, to the extent permitted by domestic law and if so requested, give priority consideration to returning the confiscated property to the requesting Party so that it can give

compensation to the victims of the crime or return such property to their legitimate owners.

3. When acting on the request made by another Party in accordance with Articles 23 and 24 of this Convention, a Party may give special consideration to concluding agreements or arrangements on sharing with other Parties, on a regular or case-by-case basis, such property, in accordance with its domestic law or administrative procedures.

Article 26—Right of Enforcement and Maximum Amount of Confiscation
1. A request for confiscation made under Articles 23 and 24 does not affect the right of the requesting Party to enforce itself the confiscation order.

2. Nothing in this Convention shall be so interpreted as to permit the total value of the confiscation to exceed the amount of the sum of money specified in the confiscation order. If a Party finds that this might occur, the Parties concerned shall enter into consultations to avoid such an effect.

Article 27—Imprisonment in Default
The requested Party shall not impose imprisonment in default or any other measure restricting the liberty of a person as a result of a request under Article 23, if the requesting Party has so specified in the request.

Section 5—Refusal and Postponement of Co-operation

Article 28—Grounds for Refusal
1. Co-operation under this chapter may be refused if:

   a. the action sought would be contrary to the fundamental principles of the legal system of the requested Party; or

   b. the execution of the request is likely to prejudice the sovereignty, security, ordre public or other essential interests of the requested Party; or

   c. in the opinion of the requested Party, the importance of the case to which the request relates does not justify the taking of the action sought; or

   d. the offence to which the request relates is a fiscal offence, with the exception of the financing of terrorism;

   e. the offence to which the request relates is a political offence, with the exception of the financing of terrorism; or

   f. the requested Party considers that compliance with the action sought would be contrary to the principle of "*ne bis in idem*"; or

   g. the offence to which the request relates would not be an offence under the law of the requested Party if committed within its jurisdiction. However, this ground for refusal applies to co-operation under Section 2 only in so far as the assistance sought involves coercive action. Where dual criminality is required for co-operation under this chapter, that requirement shall be deemed to be satisfied regardless of whether both Parties place the offence within the same category of offences or denominate the offence by the same terminology, provided that both Parties criminalise the conduct underlying the offence.

2. Co-operation under Section 2, in so far as the assistance sought involves coercive action, and under Section 3 of this chapter, may also be refused if the measures sought could not be taken under the domestic law of the requested Party for the purposes of investigations or proceedings, had it been a similar domestic case.

3. Where the law of the requested Party so requires, co-operation under Section 2, in so far as the assistance sought involves coercive action, and under Section 3 of this chapter may also be refused if the measures sought or any other measures having similar effects would not be permitted under the law of the requesting Party, or, as regards the competent authorities of the requesting Party,

if the request is not authorised by either a judge or another judicial authority, including public prosecutors, any of these authorities acting in relation to criminal offences.

4. Co-operation under Section 4 of this chapter may also be refused if:

    a. under the law of the requested Party confiscation is not provided for in respect of the type of offence to which the request relates; or

    b. without prejudice to the obligation pursuant to Article 23, paragraph 3, it would be contrary to the principles of the domestic law of the requested Party concerning the limits of confiscation in respect of the relationship between an offence and:

        i. an economic advantage that might be qualified as its proceeds; or

        ii. property that might be qualified as its instrumentalities; or

    c. under the law of the requested Party confiscation may no longer be imposed or enforced because of the lapse of time; or

    d. without prejudice to Article 23, paragraph 5, the request does not relate to a previous conviction, or a decision of a judicial nature or a statement in such a decision that an offence or several offences have been committed, on the basis of which the confiscation has been ordered or is sought; or

    e. confiscation is either not enforceable in the requesting Party, or it is still subject to ordinary means of appeal; or

    f. the request relates to a confiscation order resulting from a decision rendered in absentia of the person against whom the order was issued and, in the opinion of the requested Party, the proceedings conducted by the requesting Party leading to such decision did not satisfy the minimum rights of defence recognised as due to everyone against whom a criminal charge is made.

5. For the purpose of paragraph 4.f of this article a decision is not considered to have been rendered *in absentia* if:

    a. it has been confirmed or pronounced after opposition by the person concerned; or

    b. it has been rendered on appeal, provided that the appeal was lodged by the person concerned.

6. When considering, for the purposes of paragraph 4.f of this article if the minimum rights of defence have been satisfied, the requested Party shall take into account the fact that the person concerned has deliberately sought to evade justice or the fact that that person, having had the possibility of lodging a legal remedy against the decision made *in absentia,* elected not to do so. The same will apply when the person concerned, having been duly served with the summons to appear, elected not to do so nor to ask for adjournment.

7. A Party shall not invoke bank secrecy as a ground to refuse any co-operation under this chapter. Where its domestic law so requires, a Party may require that a request for co-operation which would involve the lifting of bank secrecy be authorised by either a judge or another judicial authority, including public prosecutors, any of these authorities acting in relation to criminal offences.

8. Without prejudice to the ground for refusal provided for in paragraph 1.a of this article:

    a. the fact that the person under investigation or subjected to a confiscation order by the authorities of the requesting Party is a legal person shall not be invoked by the requested Party as an obstacle to affording any co-operation under this chapter;

    b. the fact that the natural person against whom an order of confiscation of proceeds has been issued has died or the fact that a legal person against whom an order of confiscation of proceeds has been issued has subsequently been dissolved shall not be invoked as an obstacle to render assistance in accordance with Article 23, paragraph 1.a;

    c. the fact that the person under investigation or subjected to a confiscation order by the authorities of the requesting Party is mentioned in the request both as the author of the underlying criminal offence and of the offence of money laundering, in accordance with Article 9.2.b of this Convention, shall not be invoked by the requested Party as an obstacle to affording any co-operation under this chapter.

Article 29—Postponement
The requested Party may postpone action on a request if such action would prejudice investigations or proceedings by its authorities.

Article 30—Partial or Conditional Granting of a Request
Before refusing or postponing co-operation under this chapter, the requested Party shall, where appropriate after having consulted the requesting Party, consider whether the request may be granted partially or subject to such conditions as it deems necessary.

Section 6—Notification and Protection of Third Parties' Rights

Article 31—Notification of Documents
1. The Parties shall afford each other the widest measure of mutual assistance in the serving of judicial documents to persons affected by provisional measures and confiscation.

2. Nothing in this article is intended to interfere with:

a. the possibility of sending judicial documents, by postal channels, directly to persons abroad;
b. the possibility for judicial officers, officials or other competent authorities of the Party of origin to effect service of judicial documents directly through the consular authorities of that Party or through judicial officers, officials or other competent authorities of the Party of destination, unless the Party of destination makes a declaration to the contrary to the Secretary General of the Council of Europe at the time of signature or when

depositing its instrument of ratification, acceptance, approval or accession.

3. When serving judicial documents to persons abroad affected by provisional measures or confiscation orders issued in the sending Party, this Party shall indicate what legal remedies are available under its law to such persons.

Article 32—Recognition of Foreign Decisions
1. When dealing with a request for co-operation under Sections 3 and 4, the requested Party shall recognise any judicial decision taken in the requesting Party regarding rights claimed by third parties.

2. Recognition may be refused if:

a. third parties did not have adequate opportunity to assert their rights; or
b. the decision is incompatible with a decision already taken in the requested Party on the same matter; or
c. it is incompatible with the ordre public of the requested Party; or
d. the decision was taken contrary to provisions on exclusive jurisdiction provided for by the law of the requested Party.

Section 7—Procedural and Other General Rules

Article 33—Central Authority
1. The Parties shall designate a central authority or, if necessary, authorities, which shall be responsible for sending and answering requests made under this chapter, the execution of such requests or the transmission of them to the authorities competent for their execution.

2. Each Party shall, at the time of signature or when depositing its instrument of ratification, acceptance, approval or accession, communicate to the Secretary General of the Council of Europe the names and addresses of the authorities

designated in pursuance of paragraph 1 of this article.

Article 34—Direct Communication
1. The central authorities shall communicate directly with one another.

2. In the event of urgency, requests or communications under this chapter may be sent directly by the judicial authorities, including public prosecutors, of the requesting Party to such authorities of the requested Party. In such cases a copy shall be sent at the same time to the central authority of the requested Party through the central authority of the requesting Party.

3. Any request or communication under paragraphs 1 and 2 of this article may be made through the International Criminal Police Organisation (Interpol).

4. Where a request is made pursuant to paragraph 2 of this article and the authority is not competent to deal with the request, it shall refer the request to the competent national authority and inform directly the requesting Party that it has done so.

5. Requests or communications under Section 2 of this chapter, which do not involve coercive action, may be directly transmitted by the competent authorities of the requesting Party to the competent authorities of the requested Party.

6. Draft requests or communications under this chapter may be sent directly by the judicial authorities of the requesting Party to such authorities of the requested Party prior to a formal request to ensure that it can be dealt with efficiently upon receipt and contains sufficient information and supporting documentation for it to meet the requirements of the legislation of the requested Party.

Article 35—Form of Request and Languages
1. All requests under this chapter shall be made in writing. They may be transmitted electronically, or by any other means of telecommunication, provided that the requesting Party is prepared, upon request, to produce at any time a written record of such communication and the original. However each Party may, at any time, by a declaration addressed to the Secretary General of the Council of Europe, indicate the conditions in which it is ready to accept and execute requests received electronically or by any other means of communication.

2. Subject to the provisions of paragraph 3 of this article, translations of the requests or supporting documents shall not be required.

3. At the time of signature or when depositing its instrument of ratification, acceptance, approval or accession, any State or the European Community may communicate to the Secretary General of the Council of Europe a declaration that it reserves the right to require that requests made to it and documents supporting such requests be accompanied by a translation into its own language or into one of the official languages of the Council of Europe or into such one of these languages as it shall indicate. It may on that occasion declare its readiness to accept translations in any other language as it may specify. The other Parties may apply the reciprocity rule.

Article 36—Legalisation
Documents transmitted in application of this chapter shall be exempt from all legalisation formalities.

Article 37—Content of Request
1. Any request for co-operation under this chapter shall specify:

  a. the authority making the request and the authority carrying out the investigations or proceedings;
  b. the object of and the reason for the request;

c. the matters, including the relevant facts (such as date, place and circumstances of the offence) to which the investigations or proceedings relate, except in the case of a request for notification;

d. insofar as the co-operation involves coercive action:

    i. the text of the statutory provisions or, where this is not possible, a statement of the relevant law applicable; and

    ii. an indication that the measure sought or any other measures having similar effects could be taken in the territory of the requesting Party under its own law;

e. where necessary and in so far as possible:

    i. details of the person or persons concerned, including name, date and place of birth, nationality and location, and, in the case of a legal person, its seat; and

    ii. the property in relation to which co-operation is sought, its location, its connection with the person or persons concerned, any connection with the offence, as well as any available information about other persons, interests in the property; and

f. any particular procedure the requesting Party wishes to be followed.

2. A request for provisional measures under Section 3 in relation to seizure of property on which a confiscation order consisting in the requirement to pay a sum of money may be realised shall also indicate a maximum amount for which recovery is sought in that property.

3. In addition to the indications mentioned in paragraph 1, any request under Section 4 shall contain:

a. in the case of Article 23, paragraph 1.a:

    i. a certified true copy of the confiscation order made by the court in the requesting Party and a statement of the grounds on the basis of which the order was made, if they are not indicated in the order itself;

    ii. an attestation by the competent authority of the requesting Party that the confiscation order is enforceable and not subject to ordinary means of appeal;

    iii. information as to the extent to which the enforcement of the order is requested; and

    iv. information as to the necessity of taking any provisional measures;

b. in the case of Article 23, paragraph 1.b, a statement of the facts relied upon by the requesting Party sufficient to enable the requested Party to seek the order under its domestic law;

c. when third parties have had the opportunity to claim rights, documents demonstrating that this has been the case.

Article 38—Defective Requests

1. If a request does not comply with the provisions of this chapter or the information supplied is not sufficient to enable the requested Party to deal with the request, that Party may ask the requesting Party to amend the request or to complete it with additional information.

2. The requested Party may set a time-limit for the receipt of such amendments or information.

3. Pending receipt of the requested amendments or information in relation to a request under Section 4 of this chapter, the requested Party may take any of the measures referred to in Sections 2 or 3 of this chapter.

Article 39—Plurality of Requests

1. Where the requested Party receives more than one request under Sections 3 or 4 of this chapter in respect of the same person or property, the plurality of requests shall not prevent that Party from dealing with the requests involving the taking of provisional measures.

2. In the case of plurality of requests under Section 4 of this chapter, the requested Party shall consider consulting the requesting Parties.

Article 40—Obligation to Give Reasons
The requested Party shall give reasons for any decision to refuse, postpone or make conditional any co-operation under this chapter.

Article 41—Information
1. The requested Party shall promptly inform the requesting Party of:

    a. the action initiated on a request under this chapter;

    b. the final result of the action carried out on the basis of the request;

    c. a decision to refuse, postpone or make conditional, in whole or in part, any co-operation under this chapter;

    d. any circumstances which render impossible the carrying out of the action sought or are likely to delay it significantly; and

    e. in the event of provisional measures taken pursuant to a request under Sections 2 or 3 of this chapter, such provisions of its domestic law as would automatically lead to the lifting of the provisional measure.

2. The requesting Party shall promptly inform the requested Party of:

    a. any review, decision or any other fact by reason of which the confiscation order ceases to be wholly or partially enforceable; and

    b. any development, factual or legal, by reason of which any action under this chapter is no longer justified.

3. Where a Party, on the basis of the same confiscation order, requests confiscation in more than one Party, it shall inform all Parties which are affected by an enforcement of the order about the request.

Article 42—Restriction of Use
1. The requested Party may make the execution of a request dependent on the condition that the information or evidence obtained will not, without its prior consent, be used or transmitted by the authorities of the requesting Party for investigations or proceedings other than those specified in the request.

2. Each State or the European Community may, at the time of signature or when depositing its instrument of ratification, acceptance, approval or accession, by declaration addressed to the Secretary General of the Council of Europe, declare that, without its prior consent, information or evidence provided by it under this chapter may not be used or transmitted by the authorities of the requesting Party in investigations or proceedings other than those specified in the request.

Article 43—Confidentiality
1. The requesting Party may require that the requested Party keep confidential the facts and substance of the request, except to the extent necessary to execute the request. If the requested Party cannot comply with the requirement of confidentiality, it shall promptly inform the requesting Party.

2. The requesting Party shall, if not contrary to basic principles of its national law and if so requested, keep confidential any evidence and information provided by the requested Party, except to the extent that its disclosure is necessary for the investigations or proceedings described in the request.

3. Subject to the provisions of its domestic law, a Party which has received spontaneous information under Article 20 shall comply with any requirement of confidentiality as required by the Party which supplies the information. If the other Party cannot comply with such requirement, it shall promptly inform the transmitting Party.

Article 44—Costs
The ordinary costs of complying with a request shall be borne by the requested Party. Where costs of a substantial or extraordinary nature are necessary to comply with a request, the Parties shall consult in order to agree to the conditions on

which the request is to be executed and how the costs shall be borne.

Article 45—Damages
1. When legal action on liability for damages resulting from an act or omission in relation to co-operation under this chapter has been initiated by a person, the Parties concerned shall consider consulting each other, where appropriate, to determine how to apportion any sum of damages due.

2. A Party which has become subject of a litigation for damages shall endeavour to inform the other Party of such litigation if that Party might have an interest in the case.

Chapter V—Co-operation between FIUs

Article 46—Co-operation between FIUs
1. Parties shall ensure that FIUs, as defined in this Convention, shall cooperate for the purpose of combating money laundering, to assemble and analyse, or, if appropriate, investigate within the FIU relevant information on any fact which might be an indication of money laundering in accordance with their national powers.

2. For the purposes of paragraph 1, each Party shall ensure that FIUs exchange, spontaneously or on request and either in accordance with this Convention or in accordance with existing or future memoranda of understanding compatible with this Convention, any accessible information that may be relevant to the processing or analysis of information or, if appropriate, to investigation by the FIU regarding financial transactions related to money laundering and the natural or legal persons involved.

3. Each Party shall ensure that the performance of the functions of the FIUs under this article shall not be affected by their internal status, regardless of whether they are administrative, law enforcement or judicial authorities.

4. Each request made under this article shall be accompanied by a brief statement of the relevant facts known to the requesting FIU. The FIU shall specify in the request how the information sought will be used.

5. When a request is made in accordance with this article, the requested FIU shall provide all relevant information, including accessible financial information and requested law enforcement data, sought in the request, without the need for a formal letter of request under applicable conventions or agreements between the Parties.

6. An FIU may refuse to divulge information which could lead to impairment of a criminal investigation being conducted in the requested Party or, in exceptional circumstances, where divulging the information would be clearly disproportionate to the legitimate interests of a natural or legal person or the Party concerned or would otherwise not be in accordance with fundamental principles of national law of the requested Party. Any such refusal shall be appropriately explained to the FIU requesting the information.

7. Information or documents obtained under this article shall only be used for the purposes laid down in paragraph 1. Information supplied by a counterpart FIU shall not be disseminated to a third party, nor be used by the receiving FIU for purposes other than analysis, without prior consent of the supplying FIU.

8. When transmitting information or documents pursuant to this article, the transmitting FIU may impose restrictions and conditions on the use of information for purposes other than those stipulated in paragraph 7. The receiving FIU shall comply with any such restrictions and conditions.

9. Where a Party wishes to use transmitted information or documents for criminal investigations or prosecutions for the purposes laid

down in paragraph 7, the transmitting FIU may not refuse its consent to such use unless it does so on the basis of restrictions under its national law or conditions referred to in paragraph 6. Any refusal to grant consent shall be appropriately explained.

10. FIUs shall undertake all necessary measures, including security measures, to ensure that information submitted under this article is not accessible by any other authorities, agencies or departments.

11. The information submitted shall be protected, in conformity with the Council of Europe Convention of 28 January 1981 for the Protection of Individuals with regard to Automatic Processing of Personal Data (ETS No. 108) and taking account of Recommendation No R(87)15 of 15 September 1987 of the Committee of Ministers of the Council of Europe Regulating the Use of Personal Data in the Police Sector, by at least the same rules of confidentiality and protection of personal data as those that apply under the national legislation applicable to the requesting FIU.

12. The transmitting FIU may make reasonable enquiries as to the use made of information provided and the receiving FIU shall, whenever practicable, provide such feedback.

13. Parties shall indicate the unit which is an FIU within the meaning of this article.

Article 47—International Co-operation for Postponement of Suspicious Transactions
1. Each Party shall adopt such legislative or other measures as may be necessary to permit urgent action to be initiated by a FIU, at the request of a foreign FIU, to suspend or withhold consent to a transaction going ahead for such periods and depending on the same conditions as apply in its domestic law in respect of the postponement of transactions.

2. The action referred to in paragraph 1 shall be taken where the requested FIU is satisfied, upon justification by the requesting FIU, that:

a. the transaction is related to money laundering; and
b. the transaction would have been suspended, or consent to the transaction going ahead would have been withheld, if the transaction had been the subject of a domestic suspicious transaction report.

Chapter VI—Monitoring Mechanism and Settlement of Disputes

Article 48—Monitoring Mechanism and Settlement of Disputes
1. The Conference of the Parties (COP) shall be responsible for following the implementation of the Convention. The COP:

a. shall monitor the proper implementation of the Convention by the Parties;
b. shall, at the request of a Party, express an opinion on any question concerning the interpretation and application of the Convention.

2. The COP shall carry out the functions under paragraph 1.a above by using any available Select Committee of Experts on the Evaluation of Anti-Money Laundering Measures (Moneyval) public summaries (for Moneyval countries) and any available FATF public summaries (for FATF countries), supplemented by periodic self assessment questionnaires, as appropriate. The monitoring procedure will deal with areas covered by this Convention only in respect of those areas which are not covered by other relevant international standards on which mutual evaluations are carried out by the FATF and Moneyval.

3. If the COP concludes that it requires further information in the discharge of its functions, it shall liaise with the Party concerned, taking advantage, if so required by the COP, of the procedure and mechanism of Moneyval. The Party concerned

shall then report back to the COP. The COP shall on this basis decide whether or not to carry out a more in-depth assessment of the position of the Party concerned. This may, but need not necessarily, involve, a country visit by an evaluation team.

4. In case of a dispute between Parties as to the interpretation or application of the Convention, they shall seek a settlement of the dispute through negotiation or any other peaceful means of their choice, including submission of the dispute to the COP, to an arbitral tribunal whose decisions shall be binding upon the Parties, or to the International Court of Justice, as agreed upon by the Parties concerned.

5. The COP shall adopt its own rules of procedure.

6. The Secretary General of the Council of Europe shall convene the COP not later than one year following the entry into force of this Convention. Thereafter, regular meetings of the COP shall be held in accordance with the rules of procedure adopted by the COP.

Note by the Secretariat: See the Declaration formulated by the European Community and the Member States of the European Union upon the adoption of the Convention by the Committee of Ministers of the Council of Europe, on 3 May 2005:

"The European Community/European Union and its Member States reaffirm that their objective in requesting the inclusion of a 'disconnection clause' is to take account of the institutional structure of the Union when acceding to international conventions, in particular in case of transfer of sovereign powers from the Member States to the Community.

This clause is not aimed at reducing the rights or increasing the obligations of a non-European Union Party vis-à-vis the European Community/European Union and its Member States, inasmuch as the latter are also parties to this Convention.

The disconnection clause is necessary for those parts of the Convention which fall within the competence of the Community/Union, in order to indicate that European Union Member States cannot invoke and apply the rights and obligations deriving from the Convention directly among themselves (or between themselves and the European Community/Union). This does not detract from the fact that the Convention applies fully between the European Community/European Union and its Member States on the one hand, and the other Parties to the Convention, on the other; the Community and the European Union Members States will be bound by the Convention and will apply it like any Party to the Convention, if necessary, through Community/Union legislation. They will thus guarantee the full respect of the Convention's provisions vis-à-vis non-European Union Parties."

Appendix

   a. participation in an organised criminal group and racketeering;

   b. terrorism, including financing of terrorism;

   c. trafficking in human beings and migrant smuggling;

   d. sexual exploitation, including sexual exploitation of children;

   e. illicit trafficking in narcotic drugs and psychotropic substances;

   f. illicit arms trafficking;

   g. illicit trafficking in stolen and other goods;

   h. corruption and bribery;

   i. fraud;

   j. counterfeiting currency;

   k. counterfeiting and piracy of products;

   l. environmental crime;

   m. murder, grievous bodily injury;

   n. kidnapping, illegal restraint and hostage-taking;

   o. robbery or theft;

p. smuggling;

q. extortion;

r. forgery;

s. piracy; and

t. insider trading and market manipulation.

14.
Combating Money Laundering

The Organization of American States at its eighth plenary session on 7 June 1996 signed a resolution to check money laundering. The meeting at Buenos Aires one year earlier had called for the establishment of an inter-American convention for combating money laundering. The resolution appealed to the member states to strengthen their domestic system and establish close international efforts to stop the practice of money laundering.

Source
Organization of American States, Department of International Legal Affairs, Office of Legal Cooperation, http://www.oas.org/juridico/english/ga-res96/res-1396.htm.

AG/RES. 1396 (XXVI-O/96)

(Resolution adopted at the eighth plenary session, held on June 7, 1996)

THE GENERAL ASSEMBLY,

HAVING SEEN the Report of the Permanent Council on Money Laundering (AG/doc.3334/96 rev. 1);

CONSIDERING:

The decision reached by the heads of state and government at the Summit of the Americas, held in Miami in December 1994, on the need to "hold a working-level conference, to be followed by a ministerial conference, to study and agree on a coordinated hemispheric response, including

consideration of an inter-American convention, to combat money laundering"; and

The recommendation made by participants at the "Ministerial Conference concerning the Laundering of Proceeds and Instrumentalities of Crime," held in Buenos Aires on December 2, 1995, who, in order to carry out fully the mandate from the heads of state and government, called for establishment of a working group within the Organization of American States to consider the suggestion of an inter-American convention to combat money laundering and identify priorities for basic harmonization of national laws;

REAFFIRMING that the transfer, exchange, and investment of illicit proceeds from drug trafficking and other illegal activities are serious crimes and a challenge to law enforcement and can jeopardize financial systems and trade; and

BEARING IN MIND the work of CICAD, especially its decision at its nineteenth regular session, to convene for June 1996 the Group of Experts that developed the "Model Regulations concerning Laundering Offenses Connected to Illicit Drug Trafficking and Related Offenses," so that it might propose a plan of action defining the role of CICAD in relation to the recommendations of the ministerial conference held in Buenos Aires in December 1995,

RESOLVES:

1. To receive with satisfaction the report of the Permanent Council on the activities of the Working Group on Money Laundering, which has been instructed to "study and agree on a coordinated hemispheric response, including consideration of an inter-American convention, to combat money laundering," and to "identify priorities for basic harmonization of national laws" for that purpose.

2. To urge all governments to adopt as soon as possible, in accordance with their domestic laws,

such measures as may be necessary to strengthen their legal, judicial, and administrative systems and to develop such mechanisms as may be required to establish close international cooperation, including the exchange of information and evidence, to put a stop to the money laundering and the proceeds and instrumentalities of this criminal activity.

3. To take note of the interest expressed by the Inter-American Drug Abuse Control Commission (CICAD) in supporting the countries in the evaluation they are conducting to implement the Buenos Aires Plan of Action, as well as its interest in cooperating, in areas within its competence, with the working group set up by the Permanent Council to consider the proposal for an inter-American convention to combat money laundering and to identify priorities for basic harmonization of national laws for that purpose.

4. To instruct the Group of Experts convened by CICAD at its nineteenth regular session to pay special attention to identifying priorities for basic harmonization of laws on this subject and submit a working procedure and other suggestions for appropriate action.

5. To instruct the Permanent Council's Working Group on Money Laundering to continue consideration of an inter-American convention to combat money laundering.

6. To request the Permanent Council to submit a report on the implementation of this resolution to the General Assembly at its twenty-seventh regular session.

15.
The Law of Combating Money Laundering

The Kingdom of Saudi Arabia, one of the key allies of the United States and the world's largest oil exporter, faced criticism following the events of 11 September 2001. Fifteen of the nineteen hijackers who participated in the events of that day were from Saudi Arabia. Abdullah ibn Abdulaziz as-Saud (1924–), the crown prince (1982–2005) and king of Saudi Arabia (2005–), was determined to stamp out terrorist activities from his country. Money laundering has been the lifeblood for terrorists for financing their activities. Saudi Arabia, a victim of terrorist attacks, passed a law to check the illegal financing of terrorist organizations. Abdullah and his advisors were determined to stop the funding sources of terrorists. A Royal Decree, No. M/39, the Law of Combating Money Laundering, was passed on 23 August 2003. The financing of terrorism and terrorist acts were to be treated as criminal offenses. Harsh penalties, such as jail sentences of fifteen years and fines up to $1.8 million, were to be meted out to the offender.

Source
Royal Embassy of Saudi Arabia, http://www.saudiembassy.net/Country/Laws/MoneyLaundering2003.asp.

Article One
The following terms and phrases, wherever mentioned in this Law, shall have the meanings following them, unless the context requires otherwise.

Money laundering: Committing or attempting to commit any act for the purpose of concealing or falsifying the true origin of funds acquired by means contrary to Shari'ah or law, thus making them appear as if they came from a legitimate source.

Funds: Assets or properties of whatever type, material or intangible, movable or immovable, along with the legal documents and deeds proving the ownership of the assets or any right pertaining thereto.

Proceeds: Any funds obtained or acquired, through direct or indirect means, by committing a crime punishable pursuant to the provisions of this Law.

Means: Anything used or prepared for use in any form for committing a crime punishable pursuant to the provisions of this Law.

Financial and non-financial institutions: Any institution in the Kingdom undertaking one or more of the financial, commercial or economic activities such as banks, exchange bureaus, investment or insurance companies, commercial companies, sole proprietorships, vocational activities or any other similar activity specified by the implementing regulations of this Law.

Transaction: Any disposal of funds, properties or proceeds in cash or in kind including, for example: deposit, withdrawal, transfer, sale, purchase, lending, exchange or use of safe deposit boxes and the like as specified by the implementing regulations of this Law.

Criminal activity: Any activity constituting a crime punishable by Shari'ah or law including the financing of terrorism, terrorist acts and terrorist organizations.

Preventive Seizure: Temporary ban on transport, transfer, exchange, disposal, movement, possession, or seizure of funds and proceeds, pursuant to an order issued by a court or a competent authority.

Confiscation: Permanent dispossession and deprivation of funds, proceeds or means used in a crime, pursuant to a judiciary judgment issued by a competent court.

Monitoring body: The governmental authority empowered to grant licenses to financial and non-financial institutions and to monitor and supervise these institutions.

Competent authority: Any governmental agency entrusted, according to its jurisdiction, with combating money laundering transactions.

Article Two
Anyone who carries out any of the following acts shall be committing the crime of money laundering:

(a) Conducting any transaction involving funds or proceeds, with the knowledge that they are the result of a criminal activity or have an illegitimate or illegal source.

(b) Transporting, acquiring, using, keeping, receiving, or transferring funds or proceeds, with the knowledge that they are the result of a criminal activity or have an illegitimate or illegal source.

(c) Concealing or falsifying the nature of funds or proceeds or their source, movement or ownership, place or means of disposal, with the knowledge that they are the result of a criminal activity or have an illegitimate or illegal source.

(d) Financing of terrorism, terrorist acts and terrorist organizations.

(e) Participating through agreement, assistance, incitement, providing of consultation and advice, facilitating, colluding, covering up or attempting to commit any of the acts specified in this article.

Article Three
Anyone who carries out or participates in any of the acts specified in Article Two of this Law shall be committing a money laundering crime, including chairmen of the boards of directors of financial and non-financial institutions, board members, owners, employees, authorized representatives, auditors or their hired hands who act under these capacities, without prejudice to the criminal liability of the financial and non-financial institutions if that crime has been committed in their names or for their account.

Article Four
Financial and non-financial institutions shall not carry out any financial or commercial transaction or otherwise under a fake or unknown name. The identity of the clients shall be verified according to official documents, at the initiation of dealing with the clients or when concluding commercial deals

whether directly or on the clients' behalf. These institutions shall verify the official documents of the entities of corporate capacity that show the name of the institution, its address, names of proprietors and managers authorized to sign on its behalf and so forth, as provided for by the implementing regulations of this Law.

Article Five
Financial and non-financial institutions shall keep—for a period of not less than ten years from the date of expiry of the transaction or of closing the account—all records and documents, for the purpose of clarifying financial, commercial and cash transactions, whether domestic or foreign as well as preserving the account files, commercial correspondence and photocopies of documents of personal identities.

Article Six
Financial and non-financial institutions shall establish precautionary measures and internal monitoring to discover and suppress any of the crimes specified in this Law and comply with the instructions issued by the competent monitoring bodies in this regard.

Article Seven
Upon availability of sufficient indications and evidence indicating that a complex, huge or unusual deal and transaction have been performed or that a transaction raises doubt and suspicion concerning its nature and purpose, or is related to money laundering, financing of terrorism, terrorist acts, or terrorist organizations, financial and non-financial institutions shall promptly take the following measures:

(a) Immediately reporting said transaction to the Financial Investigation Unit, provided for in Article Eleven of this Law.
(b) Filing a report including all available data and information about the transactions and the parties involved, and providing the Investigation Unit with said report.

Article Eight
As an exception to the provisions concerning banking confidentiality, financial and non-financial institutions shall submit documents, records and information to judicial or competent authorities upon request.

Article Nine
Financial and non-financial institutions as well as their staff and others who are bound by the provisions of this Law shall not alert the clients or allow for their alert or alert other related parties of suspicion regarding their activities.

Article Ten
Financial and non-financial institutions shall introduce programs for combating money laundering transactions, provided that said programs include the following as a minimum:

(a) Developing and implementing policies, plans, procedures and internal guidelines, including the appointment of competent officers at the higher administrative level for their implementation.
(b) Introducing internal audit and control systems for monitoring the availability of basic requirements in the field of combating money laundering.
(c) Preparing continuous training programs for the employees concerned, to acquaint them with the latest developments in the field of money laundering transactions and improve their abilities to recognize those transactions, their forms and ways of combating them.

Article Eleven
A unit for combating money laundering shall be established under the name of "Financial Investigation Unit". Part of its responsibility shall be receiving notifications, analyzing them and preparing reports regarding suspicious transactions in all financial and non-financial institutions. The implementing regulations of this Law shall specify the seat of this unit, its formation, powers, method of discharging its duties as well as its affiliation.

Article Twelve

The Financial Investigation Unit, upon establishment of suspicion, shall request the authority with jurisdiction as regard the investigation to apply preventive seizure to the funds, properties and means associated with the crime of money laundering, for a period not exceeding twenty days. Should there be a need for the preventive seizure to continue for a longer period, it shall be pursuant to a judicial order from the competent court.

Article Thirteen

Information disclosed by financial and non-financial institutions may be exchanged—according to the provisions of article (Eight) of this Law—between these institutions and the competent authorities, should this information be related to the violation of the provisions of this Law. The competent authorities shall abide by the confidentiality of this information and not disclose it, except as necessary for use in investigations or lawsuits pertinent to the violation of the provisions of this Law.

Article Fourteen

The implementing regulations of this Law shall specify the rules and procedures of the disclosure of cash and precious metals permitted to enter or leave the Kingdom and shall determine the amounts of money and weights required to be disclosed.

Article Fifteen

If a judgment confiscating funds, proceeds or means is rendered pursuant to the provisions of this Law, and they are not required to be destroyed, the competent authority shall dispose of them according to the law or share them with the countries that are signatories to agreements and treaties in force with the Kingdom.

Article Sixteen

Anyone who commits a crime of money laundering, as provided for in article (Two) of this Law, shall be punished by imprisonment for a period not exceeding ten years and a fine not exceeding five million riyals or by either punishment, along with the confiscation of funds, proceeds and means associated with the crime. Should the funds and proceeds be mixed with funds acquired from legitimate sources, said funds shall be subject to confiscation within the limits equivalent to the estimated value of the illegitimate proceeds.

The competent court may exempt from these punishments the owner of the funds or proceeds subject of the criminal violation, the possessor or user if he notifies the authorities—prior to their knowledge—of the sources of the funds or proceeds and the identity of accomplices, without himself benefiting from their revenue.

Article Seventeen

The punishment of imprisonment shall be for a period not exceeding fifteen years and a fine not exceeding seven million riyals, if the crime of money laundering is coupled with one of the following cases:

(a) The perpetrator commits the crime through an organized crime syndicate.
(b) The perpetrator uses violence or weapons.
(c) The perpetrator occupies a public post to which the crime is connected or exploits his authorities or powers in the commission of the crime.
(d) Deceiving and exploiting women or minors.
(e) Committing the crime through a correctional, charitable, or educational institution or in a social service facility.
(f) Issuance of previous local or foreign judgments convicting the perpetrator, especially in similar crimes.

Article Eighteen

Without prejudice to other laws, any of the chairmen of the boards of directors of financial and non-financial institutions, or board members, owners, managers, employees, authorized representatives, hired hands who act under these capacities, shall be punished by imprisonment for a period not exceeding two years and a fine not exceeding five hundred thousand riyals or by either punishment, if they violate any of the obligations specified in articles Four, Five, Six, Seven, Eight, Nine and Ten of this Law. The punishment shall be applied to those performing the activity without obtaining the required licenses.

Article Nineteen

Upon referral by the competent authority and based on a judgment, a fine of not less than one hundred thousand riyals and not exceeding the value of funds subject of the crime may be imposed on financial and non-financial institutions whose responsibility is proven pursuant to the provisions of articles Two and Three of this Law.

Article Twenty

With exception to the punishments specified in this Law, anyone violating its provisions shall be punished by imprisonment for a period not exceeding six months and a fine not exceeding one hundred thousand riyals, or by either punishment.

Article Twenty-One

The punishments specified in this Law shall not apply to those who violate its provisions in good faith.

Article Twenty-Two

Information disclosed by financial and non-financial institutions may be exchanged between these institutions and the competent authorities in other countries which are signatories with the Kingdom to agreements and treaties in force or on the basis of reciprocity, pursuant to established legal procedures without violation of the provisions and customs related to business confidentiality of financial and non-financial institutions.

Article Twenty-Three

Upon request from a competent court or authority in another country which is a signatory with the Kingdom to an agreement or a treaty in force or on the basis of reciprocity, the judicial authority may order seizure of funds, proceeds or means associated with a money laundering crime, according to the laws in force in the Kingdom.

Upon request from a competent authority in another country which is a signatory with the Kingdom to an agreement or treaty in force or on the basis of reciprocity, the competent authority may order tracking of funds, proceeds or means associated with a money laundering crime, according to the laws in force in the Kingdom.

Article Twenty-Four

Any conclusive judicial judgment providing for the confiscation of funds, revenues or means related to money laundering crimes, issued by a competent court in another country which is a signatory to an agreement or treaty in force with the Kingdom or on the basis of reciprocity, may be recognized and enforced if the funds, proceeds or means provided for in this judgment may be subject to confiscation, according to the law in force in the Kingdom.

Article Twenty-Five

Chairmen of the boards of directors of financial and non-financial institutions, board members, owners, employees, hired hands, or their authorized representatives shall be exempted from criminal, civil or administrative liability which may result from the implementation of the duties provided for in this Law or upon infringement of any restriction imposed to ensure information confidentiality, unless their actions are proven to be in bad faith, with the intent to harm the transaction holder.

Article Twenty-Six

General courts shall have jurisdiction to decide on all crimes provided for in this Law.

Article Twenty-Seven
The Bureau of Investigation and Prosecution shall investigate and prosecute before general courts as to crimes provided for in this Law.

16.

Financial Action Task Force on Money Laundering, Forty Recommendations and Nine Special Recommendations on Terrorist Financing

The Financial Action Task Force's (FATF) "Forty Recommendations" were adopted in April 1990 in an effort to provide comprehensive regulation and oversight to the international financial system. The recommendations were implemented to address the growing problem of money laundering. They were revised in 1996 and again in 2003. The "Nine Special Recommendations" on terrorist financing were adopted in October 2001 following the attacks of 11 September 2001. The "Forty Recommendations" are considered the international standard to assist countries in combating the crime of money laundering. Although these recommendations are not mandatory, countries are encouraged to institute legislative measures and enforcement protocols in order to comply with these recommendations, which serve as an international blueprint for the global community in the fight against money laundering and terrorist financing.

Sources

Financial Action Task Force on Money Laundering, "The Forty Recommendations," http://www.fatf-gafi.org/dataoecd/7/40/34849567.PDF, and "Special Recommendations on Terrorist Financing," http://www.fatf-gafi.org/dataoecd/8/17/34849466.pdf.

The Forty Recommendations

Introduction
Money laundering methods and techniques change in response to developing counter-measures. In recent years, the Financial Action Task Force (FATF)[1] has noted increasingly sophisticated combinations of techniques, such as the increased use of *legal persons* to disguise the true ownership and control of illegal proceeds, and an increased use of professionals to provide advice and assistance in laundering criminal funds. These factors, combined with the experience gained through the FATF's *Non-Cooperative Countries and Territories* process, and a number of national and international initiatives, led the FATF to review and revise the Forty Recommendations into a new comprehensive framework for combating money laundering and *terrorist financing*. The FATF now calls upon all countries to take the necessary steps to bring their national systems for combating money laundering and terrorist financing into compliance with the new FATF Recommendations, and to effectively implement these measures.

The review process for revising the Forty Recommendations was an extensive one, open to FATF *members, non-members, observers,* financial and other affected sectors and interested parties. This consultation process provided a wide range of input, all of which was considered in the review process.

The revised Forty Recommendations now apply not only to money laundering but also to terrorist financing, and when combined with the *Nine Special Recommendations on Terrorist Financing* provide an enhanced, comprehensive and consistent framework of measures for combating money laundering and terrorist financing. The FATF recognises that countries have diverse legal

---

[1] The FATF is an inter-governmental body which sets standards, and develops and promotes policies to combat money laundering and terrorist financing. It currently has 33 members: 31 countries and governments and two international organisations; and more than 20 observers: five FATF-style regional bodies and more than 15 other international organisations or bodies. A list of all members and observers can be found on the FATF website.

and financial systems and so all cannot take identical measures to achieve the common objective, especially over matters of detail. The Recommendations therefore set minimum standards for action for countries to implement the detail according to their particular circumstances and constitutional frameworks. The Recommendations cover all the measures that national systems should have in place within their criminal justice and regulatory systems; the preventive measures to be taken by *financial institutions* and certain other businesses and professions; and international co-operation.

The original FATF Forty Recommendations were drawn up in 1990 as an initiative to combat the misuse of financial systems by persons laundering drug money. In 1996 the Recommendations were revised for the first time to reflect evolving money laundering typologies. The 1996 Forty Recommendations have been endorsed by more than 130 countries and are the international anti-money laundering standard.

In October 2001 the FATF expanded its mandate to deal with the issue of the financing of terrorism, and took the important step of creating the Nine Special Recommendations on Terrorist Financing. These Recommendations contain a set of measures aimed at combating the funding of terrorist acts and terrorist organisations, and are complementary to the Forty Recommendations.[2]

A key element in the fight against money laundering and the financing of terrorism is the need for countries systems to be monitored and evaluated, with respect to these international standards. The mutual evaluations conducted by the FATF and FATF-style regional bodies, as well as the assessments conducted by the IMF and World Bank, are a vital mechanism for ensuring

[2] The FATF Forty and Nine Special Recommendations have been recognised by the International Monetary Fund and the World Bank as the international standards for combating money laundering and the financing of terrorism.

that the FATF Recommendations are effectively implemented by all countries.

Legal Systems

Scope of the Criminal Offence of Money Laundering

Recommendation 1

Countries should criminalise money laundering on the basis of United Nations Convention against Illicit Traffic in Narcotic Drugs and Psychotropic Substances, 1988 (the Vienna Convention) and United Nations Convention against Transnational Organized Crime, 2000 (the Palermo Convention).

Countries should apply the crime of money laundering to all serious offences, with a view to including the widest range of predicate offences. Predicate offences may be described by reference to all offences, or to a threshold linked either to a category of serious offences or to the penalty of imprisonment applicable to the predicate offence (threshold approach), or to a list of predicate offences, or a combination of these approaches.

Where countries apply a threshold approach, predicate offences should at a minimum comprise all offences that fall within the category of serious offences under their national law or should include offences which are punishable by a maximum penalty of more than one year's imprisonment or for those countries that have a minimum threshold for offences in their legal system, predicate offences should comprise all offences, which are punished by a minimum penalty of more than six months imprisonment.

Whichever approach is adopted, each country should at a minimum include a range of offences within each of the designated categories of offences.[3]

[3] See the definition of "designated categories of offences" in the Glossary (p. 597).

Predicate offences for money laundering should extend to conduct that occurred in another country, which constitutes an offence in that country, and which would have constituted a predicate offence had it occurred domestically. Countries may provide that the only prerequisite is that the conduct would have constituted a predicate offence had it occurred domestically.

Countries may provide that the offence of money laundering does not apply to persons who committed the predicate offence, where this is required by fundamental principles of their domestic law.

Recommendation 2

Countries should ensure that:

a) The intent and knowledge required to prove the offence of money laundering is consistent with the standards set forth in the Vienna and Palermo Conventions, including the concept that such mental state may be inferred from objective factual circumstances.

b) Criminal liability, and, where that is not possible, civil or administrative liability, should apply to legal persons. This should not preclude parallel criminal, civil or administrative proceedings with respect to legal persons in countries in which such forms of liability are available. Legal persons should be subject to effective, proportionate and dissuasive sanctions. Such measures should be without prejudice to the criminal liability of individuals.

Provisional Measures and Confiscation

Recommendation 3

Countries should adopt measures similar to those set forth in the Vienna and Palermo Conventions, including legislative measures, to enable their competent authorities to confiscate property laundered, proceeds from money laundering or predicate offences, instrumentalities used in or intended for use in the commission of these offences, or property of corresponding value, without prejudicing the rights of bona fide third parties.

Such measures should include the authority to: (a) identify, trace and evaluate property which is subject to confiscation; (b) carry out provisional measures, such as freezing and seizing, to prevent any dealing, transfer or disposal of such property; (c) take steps that will prevent or void actions that prejudice the State's ability to recover property that is subject to confiscation; and (d) take any appropriate investigative measures.

Countries may consider adopting measures that allow such proceeds or instrumentalities to be confiscated without requiring a criminal conviction, or which require an offender to demonstrate the lawful origin of the property alleged to be liable to confiscation, to the extent that such a requirement is consistent with the principles of their domestic law.

Measures to Be Taken by Financial Institutions and Non-financial Businesses and Professions to Prevent Money Laundering and Terrorist Financing

Recommendation 4

Countries should ensure that financial institution secrecy laws do not inhibit implementation of the FATF Recommendations.

Customer Due Diligence and Record-keeping

Recommendation 5

Financial institutions should not keep anonymous accounts or accounts in obviously fictitious names.

Financial institutions should undertake customer due diligence measures, including identifying and verifying the identity of their customers, when:

- establishing business relations;
- carrying out occasional transactions: (i) above the applicable designated threshold; or (ii) that are

wire transfers in the circumstances covered by the Interpretative Note to Special Recommendation VII;

- there is a suspicion of money laundering or terrorist financing; or
- the financial institution has doubts about the veracity or adequacy of previously obtained customer identification data.

The customer due diligence (CDD) measures to be taken are as follows:

a) Identifying the customer and verifying that customer's identity using reliable, independent source documents, data or information.[4]

b) Identifying the beneficial owner, and taking reasonable measures to verify the identity of the beneficial owner such that the financial institution is satisfied that it knows who the beneficial owner is. For legal persons and arrangements this should include financial institutions taking reasonable measures to understand the ownership and control structure of the customer.

c) Obtaining information on the purpose and intended nature of the business relationship.

d) Conducting ongoing due diligence on the business relationship and scrutiny of transactions undertaken throughout the course of that relationship to ensure that the transactions being conducted are consistent with the institution's knowledge of the customer, their business and risk profile, including, where necessary, the source of funds.

Financial institutions should apply each of the CDD measures under (a) to (d) above, but may determine the extent of such measures on a risk sensitive basis depending on the type of customer, business relationship or transaction. The measures that are taken should be consistent with any guidelines issued by competent authorities. For higher risk categories, financial institutions should perform enhanced due diligence. In certain circumstances, where there are low risks, countries

may decide that financial institutions can apply reduced or simplified measures.

Financial institutions should verify the identity of the customer and beneficial owner before or during the course of establishing a business relationship or conducting transactions for occasional customers. Countries may permit financial institutions to complete the verification as soon as reasonably practicable following the establishment of the relationship, where the money laundering risks are effectively managed and where this is essential not to interrupt the normal conduct of business.

Where the financial institution is unable to comply with paragraphs (a) to (c) above, it should not open the account, commence business relations or perform the transaction; or should terminate the business relationship; and should consider making a suspicious transactions report in relation to the customer.

These requirements should apply to all new customers, though financial institutions should also apply this Recommendation to existing customers on the basis of materiality and risk, and should conduct due diligence on such existing relationships at appropriate times.

(See Interpretative Notes: Recommendation 5 and Recommendations 5, 12 and 16)

Recommendation 6

Financial institutions should, in relation to politically exposed persons, in addition to performing normal due diligence measures:

a) Have appropriate risk management systems to determine whether the customer is a politically exposed person.

b) Obtain senior management approval for establishing business relationships with such customers.

c) Take reasonable measures to establish the source of wealth and source of funds.

---

[4] Reliable, independent source documents, data or information will hereafter be referred to as "identification data".

d) Conduct enhanced ongoing monitoring of the business relationship.

Recommendation 7

Financial institutions should, in relation to cross-border correspondent banking and other similar relationships, in addition to performing normal due diligence measures:

a) Gather sufficient information about a respondent institution to understand fully the nature of the respondent's business and to determine from publicly available information the reputation of the institution and the quality of supervision, including whether it has been subject to a money laundering or terrorist financing investigation or regulatory action.

b) Assess the respondent institution's anti-money laundering and terrorist financing controls.

c) Obtain approval from senior management before establishing new correspondent relationships.

d) Document the respective responsibilities of each institution.

e) With respect to "payable-through accounts", be satisfied that the respondent bank has verified the identity of and performed on-going due diligence on the customers having direct access to accounts of the correspondent and that it is able to provide relevant customer identification data upon request to the correspondent bank.

Recommendation 8

Financial institutions should pay special attention to any money laundering threats that may arise from new or developing technologies that might favour anonymity, and take measures, if needed, to prevent their use in money laundering schemes. In particular, financial institutions should have policies and procedures in place to address any specific risks associated with non-face to face business relationships or transactions.

Recommendation 9

Countries may permit financial institutions to rely on intermediaries or other third parties to perform elements (a)–(c) of the CDD process or to introduce business, provided that the criteria set out below are met. Where such reliance is permitted, the ultimate responsibility for customer identification and verification remains with the financial institution relying on the third party.

The criteria that should be met are as follows:

a) A financial institution relying upon a third party should immediately obtain the necessary information concerning elements (a)–(c) of the CDD process. Financial institutions should take adequate steps to satisfy themselves that copies of identification data and other relevant documentation relating to the CDD requirements will be made available from the third party upon request without delay.

b) The financial institution should satisfy itself that the third party is regulated and supervised for, and has measures in place to comply with CDD requirements in line with Recommendations 5 and 10.

It is left to each country to determine in which countries the third party that meets the conditions can be based, having regard to information available on countries that do not or do not adequately apply the FATF Recommendations.

Recommendation 10

Financial institutions should maintain, for at least five years, all necessary records on transactions, both domestic or international, to enable them to comply swiftly with information requests from the competent authorities. Such records must be sufficient to permit reconstruction of individual transactions (including the amounts and types of currency involved if any) so as to provide, if necessary, evidence for prosecution of criminal activity.

Financial institutions should keep records on the identification data obtained through the customer due diligence process (e.g. copies or records of official identification documents like passports, identity cards, driving licenses or similar documents), account files and business correspondence for at least five years after the business relationship is ended.

The identification data and transaction records should be available to domestic competent authorities upon appropriate authority.

Recommendation 11

Financial institutions should pay special attention to all complex, unusual large transactions, and all unusual patterns of transactions, which have no apparent economic or visible lawful purpose. The background and purpose of such transactions should, as far as possible, be examined, the findings established in writing, and be available to help competent authorities and auditors.

(See Interpretative Note on p. 597)

Recommendation 12

The customer due diligence and record-keeping requirements set out in Recommendations 5, 6, and 8 to 11 apply to designated non-financial businesses and professions in the following situations:

a) Casinos—when customers engage in financial transactions equal to or above the applicable designated threshold.

b) Real estate agents—when they are involved in transactions for their client concerning the buying and selling of real estate.

c) Dealers in precious metals and dealers in precious stones—when they engage in any cash transaction with a customer equal to or above the applicable designated threshold.

d) Lawyers, notaries, other independent legal professionals and accountants when they prepare for or carry out transactions for their client concerning the following activities:

- buying and selling of real estate;
- managing of client money, securities or other assets;

- management of bank, savings or securities accounts;
- organisation of contributions for the creation, operation or management of companies;
- creation, operation or management of legal persons or arrangements, and buying and selling of business entities.

e) Trust and company service providers when they prepare for or carry out transactions for a client concerning the activities listed in the definition in the Glossary.

Reporting of Suspicious Transactions and Compliance

Recommendation 13

If a financial institution suspects or has reasonable grounds to suspect that funds are the proceeds of a criminal activity, or are related to terrorist financing, it should be required, directly by law or regulation, to report promptly its suspicions to the financial intelligence unit (FIU).

Recommendation 14

Financial institutions, their directors, officers and employees should be:

a) Protected by legal provisions from criminal and civil liability for breach of any restriction on disclosure of information imposed by contract or by any legislative, regulatory or administrative provision, if they report their suspicions in good faith to the FIU, even if they did not know precisely what the underlying criminal activity was, and regardless of whether illegal activity actually occurred.

b) Prohibited by law from disclosing the fact that a suspicious transaction report (STR) or related information is being reported to the FIU.

Recommendation 15

Financial institutions should develop programmes against money laundering and terrorist financing. These programmes should include:

a) The development of internal policies, procedures and controls, including appropriate compliance management arrangements, and adequate screening procedures to ensure high standards when hiring employees.

b) An ongoing employee training programme.

c) An audit function to test the system.

Recommendation 16

The requirements set out in Recommendations 13 to 15, and 21 apply to all designated non-financial businesses and professions, subject to the following qualifications:

a) Lawyers, notaries, other independent legal professionals and accountants should be required to report suspicious transactions when, on behalf of or for a client, they engage in a financial transaction in relation to the activities described in Recommendation 12(d). Countries are strongly encouraged to extend the reporting requirement to the rest of the professional activities of accountants, including auditing.

b) Dealers in precious metals and dealers in precious stones should be required to report suspicious transactions when they engage in any cash transaction with a customer equal to or above the applicable designated threshold.

c) Trust and company service providers should be required to report suspicious transactions for a client when, on behalf of or for a client, they engage in a transaction in relation to the activities referred to Recommendation 12(e).

Lawyers, notaries, other independent legal professionals, and accountants acting as independent legal professionals, are not required to report their suspicions if the relevant information was obtained in circumstances where they are subject to professional secrecy or legal professional privilege. (See Interpretative Notes: Recommendation 16 and Recommendations 5, 12, and 16).

Other Measures to Deter Money Laundering and Terrorist Financing

Recommendation 17

Countries should ensure that effective, proportionate and dissuasive sanctions, whether criminal, civil or administrative, are available to deal with natural or legal persons covered by these Recommendations that fail to comply with anti-money laundering or terrorist financing requirements.

Recommendation 18

Countries should not approve the establishment or accept the continued operation of shell banks. Financial institutions should refuse to enter into, or continue, a correspondent banking relationship with shell banks. Financial institutions should also guard against establishing relations with respondent foreign financial institutions that permit their accounts to be used by shell banks.

Recommendation 19

Countries should consider the feasibility and utility of a system where banks and other financial institutions and intermediaries would report all domestic and international currency transactions above a fixed amount, to a national central agency with a computerised data base, available to competent authorities for use in money laundering or terrorist financing cases, subject to strict safeguards to ensure proper use of the information. (Modified 22 October 2004)

Recommendation 20

Countries should consider applying the FATF Recommendations to businesses and professions, other than designated non-financial businesses and professions, that pose a money laundering or terrorist financing risk.

Countries should further encourage the development of modern and secure techniques of money management that are less vulnerable to money laundering.

Measures to Be Taken with Respect to Countries That Do Not or Insufficiently Comply with the FATF Recommendations

Recommendation 21

Financial institutions should give special attention to business relationships and transactions with persons, including companies and financial institutions, from countries which do not or insufficiently apply the FATF Recommendations. Whenever these transactions have no apparent economic or visible lawful purpose, their background and purpose should, as far as possible, be examined, the findings established in writing, and be available to help competent authorities. Where such a country continues not to apply or insufficiently applies the FATF Recommendations, countries should be able to apply appropriate countermeasures.

Recommendation 22

Financial institutions should ensure that the principles applicable to financial institutions, which are mentioned above are also applied to branches and majority owned subsidiaries located abroad, especially in countries which do not or insufficiently apply the FATF Recommendations, to the extent that local applicable laws and regulations permit. When local applicable laws and regulations prohibit this implementation, competent authorities in the country of the parent institution should be informed by the financial institutions that they cannot apply the FATF Recommendations.

Regulation and Supervision

Recommendation 23

Countries should ensure that financial institutions are subject to adequate regulation and supervision and are effectively implementing the FATF Recommendations. Competent authorities should take the necessary legal or regulatory measures to prevent criminals or their associates from holding or being the beneficial owner of a significant or controlling interest or holding a management function in a financial institution.

For financial institutions subject to the Core Principles, the regulatory and supervisory measures that apply for prudential purposes and which are also relevant to money laundering, should apply in a similar manner for anti-money laundering and terrorist financing purposes.

Other financial institutions should be licensed or registered and appropriately regulated, and subject to supervision or oversight for anti-money laundering purposes, having regard to the risk of money laundering or terrorist financing in that sector. At a minimum, businesses providing a service of money or value transfer, or of money or currency changing should be licensed or registered, and subject to effective systems for monitoring and ensuring compliance with national requirements to combat money laundering and terrorist financing.

Recommendation 24

Designated non-financial businesses and professions should be subject to regulatory and supervisory measures as set out below.

a) Casinos should be subject to a comprehensive regulatory and supervisory regime that ensures that they have effectively implemented the necessary anti-money laundering and terrorist-financing measures. At a minimum:

- casinos should be licensed;
- competent authorities should take the necessary legal or regulatory measures to prevent criminals or their associates from holding or being the beneficial owner of a significant or controlling interest, holding a management function in, or being an operator of a casino;
- competent authorities should ensure that casinos are effectively supervised for compliance with requirements to combat money laundering and terrorist financing.

b) Countries should ensure that the other categories of designated non-financial businesses and professions are subject to effective systems for monitoring and ensuring their compliance with requirements to combat money laundering and terrorist financing. This should be performed on a risk-sensitive basis. This may be performed by a government authority or by an appropriate self-regulatory organisation, provided that such an organisation can ensure that its members comply with their obligations to combat money laundering and terrorist financing.

Recommendation 25

The competent authorities should establish guidelines, and provide feedback which will assist financial institutions and designated non-financial businesses and professions in applying national measures to combat money laundering and terrorist financing, and in particular, in detecting and reporting suspicious transactions.

Institutional and Other Measures Necessary in Systems for Combating Money Laundering and Terrorist Financing

Competent Authorities, Their Powers and Resources

Recommendation 26

Countries should establish a FIU that serves as a national centre for the receiving (and, as permitted, requesting), analysis and dissemination of STR and other information regarding potential money laundering or terrorist financing. The FIU should have access, directly or indirectly, on a timely basis to the financial, administrative and law enforcement information that it requires to properly undertake its functions, including the analysis of STR.

(See Interpretative Note on p. 597)

Recommendation 27

Countries should ensure that designated law enforcement authorities have responsibility for money laundering and terrorist financing investigations. Countries are encouraged to support and develop, as far as possible, special investigative techniques suitable for the investigation of money laundering, such as controlled delivery, undercover operations and other relevant techniques. Countries are also encouraged to use other effective mechanisms such as the use of permanent or temporary groups specialised in asset investigation, and co-operative investigations with appropriate competent authorities in other countries.

Recommendation 28

When conducting investigations of money laundering and underlying predicate offences, competent authorities should be able to obtain documents and information for use in those investigations, and in prosecutions and related actions. This should include powers to use compulsory measures for the production of records held by financial institutions and other persons, for the search of persons and premises, and for the seizure and obtaining of evidence.

Recommendation 29

Supervisors should have adequate powers to monitor and ensure compliance by financial institutions with requirements to combat money laundering and terrorist financing, including the authority to conduct inspections. They should be authorised to compel production of any information from financial institutions that is relevant to monitoring such compliance, and to impose adequate administrative sanctions for failure to comply with such requirements.

Recommendation 30

Countries should provide their competent authorities involved in combating money laundering and terrorist financing with adequate financial, human and technical resources. Countries should have in place processes to ensure that the staff of those authorities are of high integrity.

Recommendation 31

Countries should ensure that policy makers, the FIU, law enforcement and supervisors have effective mechanisms in place which enable them to co-operate, and where appropriate co-ordinate domestically with each other concerning the development and implementation of policies and activities to combat money laundering and terrorist financing.

Recommendation 32

Countries should ensure that their competent authorities can review the effectiveness of their systems to combat money laundering and terrorist financing systems by maintaining comprehensive statistics on matters relevant to the effectiveness and efficiency of such systems. This should include statistics on the STR received and disseminated; on money laundering and terrorist financing investigations, prosecutions and convictions; on property frozen, seized and confiscated; and on mutual legal assistance or other international requests for co-operation.

Transparency of Legal Persons and Arrangements

Recommendation 33

Countries should take measures to prevent the unlawful use of legal persons by money launderers. Countries should ensure that there is adequate, accurate and timely information on the beneficial ownership and control of legal persons that can be obtained or accessed in a timely fashion by competent authorities. In particular, countries that have legal persons that are able to issue bearer shares should take appropriate measures to ensure that they are not misused for money laundering and be able to demonstrate the adequacy of those measures. Countries could consider measures to facilitate access to beneficial ownership and control information to financial institutions undertaking the requirements set out in Recommendation 5.

Recommendation 34

Countries should take measures to prevent the unlawful use of legal arrangements by money launderers. In particular, countries should ensure that there is adequate, accurate and timely information on express trusts, including information on the settlor, trustee and beneficiaries, that can be obtained or accessed in a timely fashion by competent authorities. Countries could consider measures to facilitate access to beneficial ownership and control information to financial institutions undertaking the requirements set out in Recommendation 5.

International Co-operation

Recommendation 35

Countries should take immediate steps to become party to and implement fully the Vienna Convention, the Palermo Convention, and the 1999 United Nations International Convention for the Suppression of the Financing of Terrorism. Countries are also encouraged to ratify and implement other relevant international conventions, such as the 1990 Council of Europe Convention on Laundering, Search, Seizure and Confiscation of the Proceeds from Crime and the 2002 Inter-American Convention against Terrorism.

Mutual Legal Assistance and Extradition

Recommendation 36

Countries should rapidly, constructively and effectively provide the widest possible range of mutual legal assistance in relation to money laundering and terrorist financing investigations, prosecutions, and related proceedings. In particular, countries should:

a) Not prohibit or place unreasonable or unduly restrictive conditions on the provision of mutual legal assistance.

b) Ensure that they have clear and efficient processes for the execution of mutual legal assistance requests.

c) Not refuse to execute a request for mutual legal assistance on the sole ground that the offence is also considered to involve fiscal matters.

d) Not refuse to execute a request for mutual legal assistance on the grounds that laws require financial institutions to maintain secrecy or confidentiality.

Countries should ensure that the powers of their competent authorities required under Recommendation 28 are also available for use in response to requests for mutual legal assistance, and if consistent with their domestic framework, in response to direct requests from foreign judicial or law enforcement authorities to domestic counterparts.

To avoid conflicts of jurisdiction, consideration should be given to devising and applying mechanisms for determining the best venue for prosecution of defendants in the interests of justice in cases that are subject to prosecution in more than one country.

Recommendation 37

Countries should, to the greatest extent possible, render mutual legal assistance notwithstanding the absence of dual criminality.

Where dual criminality is required for mutual legal assistance or extradition, that requirement should be deemed to be satisfied regardless of whether both countries place the offence within the same category of offence or denominate the offence by the same terminology, provided that both countries criminalise the conduct underlying the offence.

Recommendation 38

There should be authority to take expeditious action in response to requests by foreign countries to identify, freeze, seize and confiscate property laundered, proceeds from money laundering or predicate offences, instrumentalities used in or intended for use in the commission of these offences, or property of corresponding value. There should also be arrangements for co-ordinating seizure and confiscation proceedings, which may include the sharing of confiscated assets.

Recommendation 39

Countries should recognise money laundering as an extraditable offence. Each country should either extradite its own nationals, or where a country does not do so solely on the grounds of nationality, that country should, at the request of the country seeking extradition, submit the case without undue delay to its competent authorities for the purpose of prosecution of the offences set forth in the request. Those authorities should take their decision and conduct their proceedings in the same manner as in the case of any other offence of a serious nature under the domestic law of that country. The countries concerned should cooperate with each other, in particular on procedural and evidentiary aspects, to ensure the efficiency of such prosecutions.

Subject to their legal frameworks, countries may consider simplifying extradition by allowing direct transmission of extradition requests between appropriate ministries, extraditing persons based only on warrants of arrests or judgements, and/or introducing a simplified extradition of consenting persons who waive formal extradition proceedings.

Other Forms of Co-operation

Recommendation 40

Countries should ensure that their competent authorities provide the widest possible range of international co-operation to their foreign counterparts. There should be clear and effective gateways to facilitate the prompt and constructive exchange directly between counterparts, either spontaneously or upon request, of information relating to both money laundering and the underlying predicate offences. Exchanges should be permitted without unduly restrictive conditions. In particular:

a) Competent authorities should not refuse a request for assistance on the sole ground that the request is also considered to involve fiscal matters.

b) Countries should not invoke laws that require financial institutions to maintain secrecy or confidentiality as a ground for refusing to provide co-operation.

c) Competent authorities should be able to conduct inquiries; and where possible, investigations; on behalf of foreign counterparts.

Where the ability to obtain information sought by a foreign competent authority is not within the mandate of its counterpart, countries are also encouraged to permit a prompt and constructive exchange of information with non-counterparts. Co-operation with foreign authorities other than counterparts could occur directly or indirectly. When uncertain about the appropriate avenue to follow, competent authorities should first contact their foreign counterparts for assistance.

Countries should establish controls and safeguards to ensure that information exchanged by competent authorities is used only in an authorised manner, consistent with their obligations concerning privacy and data protection.

Special Recommendations on Terrorist Financing

Recognising the vital importance of taking action to combat the financing of terrorism, the FATF has agreed these Recommendations, which, when combined with the FATF Forty Recommendations on money laundering, set out the basic framework to detect, prevent and suppress the financing of terrorism and terrorist acts.

I. Ratification and Implementation of UN Instruments

Each country should take immediate steps to ratify and to implement fully the 1999 United Nations International Convention for the Suppression of the Financing of Terrorism.

Countries should also immediately implement the United Nations resolutions relating to the prevention and suppression of the financing of terrorist acts, particularly United Nations Security Council Resolution 1373.

II. Criminalising the Financing of Terrorism and Associated Money Laundering

Each country should criminalise the financing of terrorism, terrorist acts and terrorist organisations. Countries should ensure that such offences are designated as money laundering predicate offences.

III. Freezing and Confiscating Terrorist Assets

Each country should implement measures to freeze without delay funds or other assets of terrorists, those who finance terrorism and terrorist organisations in accordance with the United Nations resolutions relating to the prevention and suppression of the financing of terrorist acts.

Each country should also adopt and implement measures, including legislative ones, which would enable the competent authorities to seize and confiscate property that is the proceeds of, or used in, or intended or allocated for use in, the financing of terrorism, terrorist acts or terrorist organisations.

IV. Reporting Suspicious Transactions Related to Terrorism

If financial institutions, or other businesses or entities subject to anti-money laundering obligations, suspect or have reasonable grounds to suspect that funds are linked or related to, or are to be used for terrorism, terrorist acts or by terrorist organisations, they should be required to report promptly their suspicions to the competent authorities.

V. International Co-operation

Each country should afford another country, on the basis of a treaty, arrangement or other mechanism for mutual legal assistance or information exchange, the greatest possible measure of assistance in connection with criminal, civil enforcement, and administrative investigations, inquiries and proceedings relating to the financing of terrorism, terrorist acts and terrorist organisations.

Countries should also take all possible measures to ensure that they do not provide safe havens for individuals charged with the financing of terrorism, terrorist acts or terrorist organisations, and should have procedures in place to extradite, where possible, such individuals.

VI. Alternative Remittance

Each country should take measures to ensure that persons or legal entities, including agents, that provide a service for the transmission of money or value, including transmission through an informal money or value transfer system or network, should be licensed or registered and subject to all the FATF Recommendations that apply to banks and non-bank financial institutions. Each country should ensure that persons or legal entities that carry out this service illegally are subject to administrative, civil or criminal sanctions.

VII. Wire Transfers

Countries should take measures to require financial institutions, including money remitters, to include accurate and meaningful originator information (name, address and account number) on funds transfers and related messages that are sent, and the information should remain with the transfer or related message through the payment chain.

Countries should take measures to ensure that financial institutions, including money remitters, conduct enhanced scrutiny of and monitor for suspicious activity funds transfers which do not contain complete originator information (name, address and account number).

VIII. Non-profit Organisations

Countries should review the adequacy of laws and regulations that relate to entities that can be abused for the financing of terrorism. Non-profit organisations are particularly vulnerable, and countries should ensure that they cannot be misused:

- by terrorist organisations posing as legitimate entities;
- to exploit legitimate entities as conduits for terrorist financing, including for the purpose of escaping asset freezing measures; and
- to conceal or obscure the clandestine diversion of funds intended for legitimate purposes to terrorist organisations.

IX. Cash Couriers

Countries should have measures in place to detect the physical cross-border transportation of currency and bearer negotiable instruments, including a declaration system or other disclosure obligation.

Countries should ensure that their competent authorities have the legal authority to stop or restrain currency or bearer negotiable instruments that are suspected to be related to terrorist financing or money laundering, or that are falsely declared or disclosed.

Countries should ensure that effective, proportionate and dissuasive sanctions are available to deal with persons who make false declaration(s) or disclosure(s). In cases where the currency or bearer negotiable instruments are related to terrorist financing or money laundering, countries should also adopt measures, including legislative ones consistent with Recommendation 3 and Special Recommendation III, which would enable the confiscation of such currency or instruments.

Note:

With the adoption of Special Recommendation IX, the FATF now deletes paragraph 19(a) of Recommendation 19 and the Interpretative Note to Recommendation 19 in order to ensure internal consistency amongst the FATF Recommendations. The modified text of recommendation 19 reads as follows:

Recommendation 19

Countries should consider the feasibility and utility of a system where banks and other financial institutions and intermediaries would report all domestic and international currency transactions above a fixed amount, to a national central agency with a computerised data base, available to competent authorities for use in money laundering or terrorist financing cases, subject to strict safeguards to ensure proper use of the information.

Glossary

In these Recommendations the following abbreviations and references are used:

"Beneficial owner" refers to the natural person(s) who ultimately owns or controls a customer and/or the person on whose behalf a transaction is being conducted. It also incorporates those persons who exercise ultimate effective control over a legal person or arrangement.

"Core Principles" refers to the Core Principles for Effective Banking Supervision issued by the Basel Committee on Banking Supervision, the Objectives and Principles for Securities Regulation issued by the International Organization of Securities Commissions, and the Insurance Supervisory Principles issued by the International Association of Insurance Supervisors.

"Designated categories of offences" means:

- participation in an organised criminal group and racketeering;
- terrorism, including terrorist financing;
- trafficking in human beings and migrant smuggling;
- sexual exploitation, including sexual exploitation of children;
- illicit trafficking in narcotic drugs and psychotropic substances;
- illicit arms trafficking;
- illicit trafficking in stolen and other goods;
- corruption and bribery;
- fraud;
- counterfeiting currency;
- counterfeiting and piracy of products;
- environmental crime;
- murder, grievous bodily injury;
- kidnapping, illegal restraint and hostage-taking;
- robbery or theft;
- smuggling;
- extortion;
- forgery;
- piracy; and
- insider trading and market manipulation.

When deciding on the range of offences to be covered as predicate offences under each of the categories listed above, each country may decide, in accordance with its domestic law, how it will define those offences and the nature of any particular elements of those offences that make them serious offences.

"Designated non-financial businesses and professions" means:

a) Casinos (which also includes internet casinos).
b) Real estate agents.
c) Dealers in precious metals.
d) Dealers in precious stones.
e) Lawyers, notaries, other independent legal professionals and accountants—this refers to sole practitioners, partners or employed professionals within professional firms. It is not meant to refer to 'internal' professionals that are employees of other types of businesses, nor to professionals working for government agencies, who may already be subject to measures that would combat money laundering.

f) Trust and Company Service Providers refers to all persons or businesses that are not covered elsewhere under these Recommendations, and which as a business, provide any of the following services to third parties:

- acting as a formation agent of legal persons;
- acting as (or arranging for another person to act as) a director or secretary of a company, a partner of a partnership, or a similar position in relation to other legal persons;
- providing a registered office; business address or accommodation, correspondence or administrative address for a company, a partnership or any other legal person or arrangement;
- acting as (or arranging for another person to act as) a trustee of an express trust;
- acting as (or arranging for another person to act as) a nominee shareholder for another person.

"*Designated threshold*" refers to the amount set out in the Interpretative Notes.

"*Financial institutions*" means any person or entity who conducts as a business one or more of the following activities or operations for or on behalf of a customer:

1. Acceptance of deposits and other repayable funds from the public.[5]
2. Lending.[6]
3. Financial leasing.[7]
4. The transfer of money or value.[8]
5. Issuing and managing means of payment (e.g. credit and debit cards, cheques, traveller's cheques, money orders and bankers' drafts, electronic money).
6. Financial guarantees and commitments.
7. Trading in:
   (a) money market instruments (cheques, bills, CDs, derivatives etc.);
   (b) foreign exchange;
   (c) exchange, interest rate and index instruments;
   (d) transferable securities;
   (e) commodity futures trading.
8. Participation in securities issues and the provision of financial services related to such issues.
9. Individual and collective portfolio management.
10. Safekeeping and administration of cash or liquid securities on behalf of other persons.
11. Otherwise investing, administering or managing funds or money on behalf of other persons.
12. Underwriting and placement of life insurance and other investment related insurance.[9]
13. Money and currency changing.

When a financial activity is carried out by a person or entity on an occasional or very limited basis (having regard to quantitative and absolute criteria) such that there is little risk of money laundering activity occurring, a country may decide that the application of anti-money laundering measures is not necessary, either fully or partially.

In strictly limited and justified circumstances, and based on a proven low risk of money laundering, a country may decide not to apply some or all of the Forty Recommendations to some of the financial activities stated above.

"*FIU*" means financial intelligence unit.

"*Legal arrangements*" refers to express trusts or other similar legal arrangements.

"*Legal persons*" refers to bodies corporate, foundations, anstalt, partnerships, or associations, or any similar bodies that can establish a

---

[5] This also captures private banking.

[6] This includes inter alia: consumer credit; mortgage credit; factoring, with or without recourse; and finance of commercial transactions (including forfeiting).

[7] This does not extend to financial leasing arrangements in relation to consumer products.

[8] This applies to financial activity in both the formal or informal sector e.g. alternative remittance activity. See the Interpretative Note to Special Recommendation VI. It does not apply to any natural or legal person that provides financial institutions solely with message or other support systems for transmitting funds. See the Interpretative Note to Special Recommendation VII.

[9] This applies both to insurance undertakings and to insurance intermediaries (agents and brokers).

permanent customer relationship with a financial institution or otherwise own property.

"*Payable-through accounts*" refers to correspondent accounts that are used directly by third parties to transact business on their own behalf.

"*Politically Exposed Persons*" (PEPs) are individuals who are or have been entrusted with prominent public functions in a foreign country, for example Heads of State or of government, senior politicians, senior government, judicial or military officials, senior executives of state owned corporations, important political party officials. Business relationships with family members or close associates of PEPs involve reputational risks similar to those with PEPs themselves. The definition is not intended to cover middle ranking or more junior individuals in the foregoing categories.

"*Shell bank*" means a bank incorporated in a jurisdiction in which it has no physical presence and which is unaffiliated with a regulated financial group.

"*STR*" refers to suspicious transaction reports.

"*Supervisors*" refers to the designated competent authorities responsible for ensuring compliance by financial institutions with requirements to combat money laundering and terrorist financing.

"*the FATF Recommendations*" refers to these Recommendations and to the FATF Special Recommendations on Terrorist Financing.

17.
Council Decision of 22 December 2004 on Tackling Vehicle Crime with Cross-Border Implications

Organized crime is responsible for a large percentage of stolen motor vehicles in the European Union (EU). The Council Decision of 22 December 2004 provides measures to deal with the cross-border implications of motor vehicle theft. This decision calls for mutual cooperation between all EU members in order to further the objectives as laid down by this decision. Specifically, it calls for mutual cooperation between the "national competent authorities" of each member state and the private sector. The term "national competent authorities" refers to "any national authorities designated by the Member States for the purposes of this Decision, and may include, as appropriate, police, customs, border guards and judicial authorities." Article 8 addresses vehicle registration certificates recovery.

Source
EUR-Lex, Official Journal of the European Union, http://eur-lex.europa.eu/LexUriServ/site/en/oj/2004/l_389/l_38920041230en00280030.pdf.

THE COUNCIL OF THE EUROPEAN UNION,

Having regard to the Treaty on European Union, and in particular Article 30(1)(a) and Article 34(2)(c) thereof,

Having regard to the initiative of the Kingdom of the Netherlands,

Having regard to the Opinion of the European Parliament,

Whereas:

(1) An estimated 1.2 million motor vehicles are stolen each year in the Member States of the European Union.

(2) These thefts involve considerable damage amounting to at least EUR 15 billion per year.

(3) A large proportion of these vehicles, estimated at 30 to 40%, are stolen by organised crime and then converted and exported to other States within and outside the European Union.

(4) Besides causing material damage, this is also seriously damaging to citizens' sense of justice and feeling of security. Vehicle crime may be accompanied by serious forms of violence.

(5) Consequently, attainment of the objective in Article 29 of the Treaty, to provide citizens with a high level of safety within an area of freedom, security and justice, is hampered.

(6) The Council has adopted a Resolution of 27 May 1999 on combating international crime with fuller cover of the routes used (1).

(7) Vehicle crime may also be linked internationally to other forms of crime, such as trafficking in drugs, firearms and human beings.

(8) Tackling vehicle crime is a matter for the law enforcement agencies of the Member States. However, a common approach involving—wherever practicable and necessary—cooperation between the Member States and law enforcement authorities of the Member States is necessary and proportional in order to address the cross-border aspects of this form of crime.

(9) Cooperation between law enforcement authorities and vehicle registration authorities is of particular importance, as is the provision of information to the relevant parties.

(10) Cooperation with Europol is equally important as Europol can provide analyses and reports on the matter.

(11) The European Police College offers police forces in the Member States, via the European Police Learning Net (EPLN), a library function in the field of vehicle crime for consulting information and expertise. Via its discussion function, EPLN also provides the possibility of exchanging knowledge and experience.

(12) The fight against vehicle crime will be intensified by an increase in the number of Member States acceding to the Treaty concerning a European Vehicle and Driving Licence Information System (EUCARIS) of 29 June 2000.

(13) A number of specific measures will need to be taken if vehicle crime with an international dimension is to be combated effectively,

HAS DECIDED AS FOLLOWS:

Article 1

Definitions
For the purposes of this Decision, the following definitions apply:

1. 'Vehicle' shall mean any motor vehicle, trailer or caravan as defined in the provisions relating to the Schengen Information System (SIS).
2. 'National competent authorities' shall mean any national authorities designated by the Member States for the purposes of this Decision, and may include, as appropriate, police, customs, border guards and judicial authorities.

L 389/28 EN Official Journal of the European Union 30.12.2004

(1) OJ C 162, 9.6.1999, p. 1.

Article 2

Objective
1. The objective of this Decision is to achieve improved cooperation within the European Union with the aim of preventing and combating cross-border vehicle crime.

2. Particular attention shall be given to the relationship between vehicle theft and the illegal car trade and forms of organised crime, such as trafficking in drugs, firearms and human beings.

Article 3

Cooperation between National Competent Authorities
1. Member States shall take the necessary steps, in accordance with national law, to enhance mutual cooperation between national competent authorities

in order to combat cross-border vehicle crime, such as by means of cooperation agreements.

2. Specific attention shall be given to cooperation with respect to export control, taking into account respective competences in the Member States.

Article 4

Cooperation between Competent Authorities and the Private Sector
1. Member States shall take the necessary steps to organise periodic consultations, as appropriate, among national competent authorities, in accordance with national law, and may involve representatives of the private sector (such as holders of private registers of missing vehicles, insurers and the car trade) in such consultations with a view to coordination of information and mutual alignment of activities in this area.

2. Member States shall facilitate procedures, in accordance with national law, for a quick repatriation of vehicles released by national competent authorities following their seizure.

Article 5

Vehicle Crime Contact Points
1. By 30 March 2005, Member States shall designate, within their law enforcement authorities, a contact point for tackling cross-border vehicle crime.

2. Member States shall authorise the contact points to exchange experience, expertise as well as general and technical information concerning vehicle crime on the basis of existing applicable legislation. Information exchange shall extend to methods and best practices of prevention of vehicle crime. Such exchanges shall not include exchanges of personal data.

3. Information concerning the designated national contact points, including subsequent changes, shall

be notified to the General Secretariat of the Council for publication in the *Official Journal of the European Union.*

Article 6

Issuing Alerts for Stolen Vehicles and Registration Certificates
1. Whenever a vehicle is reported stolen, Member States' competent authorities shall immediately enter a stolen vehicle alert in the SIS, in accordance with national law, and, where possible, in Interpol's Stolen Motor Vehicle database.

2. An alert in the search register shall, in accordance with national law, be immediately withdrawn by the Member State which issued it as soon as the reason for issuing an alert on the vehicle ceases to exist.

3. Whenever registration certificates are reported stolen, Member States' competent authorities shall immediately enter an alert thereon in the SIS, in accordance with national law.

Article 7

Registration
1. Each Member State shall ensure that its competent authorities shall take the necessary steps to prevent abuse and theft of vehicle registration documents.

2. The national vehicle registration authorities shall be informed by law enforcement authorities whether a vehicle, that is in the process of being registered, is known as having been stolen. Access to databases to that end shall take place with due respect to provisions of Community law.

30.12.2004 EN Official Journal of the European Union L 389/29

Article 8

Preventing Abuse of Vehicle Registration Certificates
1. In order to prevent abuse of vehicle registration certificates, each Member State shall, in accordance with national law, ensure that its competent authorities take the necessary steps to recover a vehicle owner's or vehicle holder's registration certificate if the vehicle has been seriously damaged in an accident (total loss).

2. A registration certificate shall also be recovered, in accordance with national law, where, during a check by the law enforcement agency, it is suspected that there has been an infringement concerning the vehicle's identity markings, such as the vehicle identification number.

3. Registration certificates shall be returned only following examination and positive verification of the vehicle's identity, and in accordance with national law.

Article 9

Europol
Each Member State shall ensure that its law enforcement authorities keep Europol informed on vehicle crime perpetrators as necessary, within the scope of that mandate and tasks.

Article 10

Promotion of Expertise and Training
Member States shall take the necessary steps to ensure that national institutes responsible for the training of relevant law enforcement authorities promote in their curricula, where appropriate in cooperation with the European Police College, specialist training in the field of vehicle crime prevention and detection. Such training may include input from Europol, in accordance with its sphere of competence.

Article 11

Meeting of Contact Points and Annual Report to the Council
Vehicle crime contact points shall hold a meeting at least once a year under the auspices of the Member State holding the Presidency of the Council. Europol shall be invited to participate in that meeting. The Presidency shall report to the Council on the progress of relevant practical cooperation among law enforcement authorities.

Article 12

Evaluation
The Council shall evaluate the implementation of this Decision by 30 December 2007.

Article 13

Entry into Effect

This Decision shall take effect on the day of its publication in the *Official Journal of the European Union.*

For those Member States in which the provisions of the Schengen acquis relating to the SIS have not yet been put into effect, the obligations of this Decision relating to the SIS shall take effect on the date on which those provisions start applying, as specified in a Council Decision adopted to that effect in accordance with the applicable procedures.

Done at Brussels, 22 December 2004

For the Council
The President
C. VEERMAN
L 389/30 EN Official Journal of the European Union 30.12.2004

18.
Government of Afghanistan Counter-Narcotics Law

Afghanistan is a part of the Golden Crescent, which includes Iran and Pakistan. After the fall of the Taliban regime, the new government of Afghanistan took steps to curb poppy cultivation and the illicit opium market, which has been a major corrupting force in the country since the Soviet invasion of 1979. The antinarcotics law passed by the government became a milestone in checking drug trafficking and production. However, since the U.S.-led Coalition invasion of that country in 2001, poppy cultivation has steadily increased. Although the cultivation and trafficking of opium are now illegal in Afghanistan, the country remains the world's largest producer of that crop.

Source
Islamic Republic of Afghanistan, Ministry of Counter Narcotics, http://www.mcn.gov.af/eng/downloads/documents/drug_law.pdf.

Chapter I

General Provisions

Article 1

Basis
This Law is enacted pursuant to Article 7 of the Constitution of Afghanistan in order to prevent the cultivation of opium poppy, cannabis plants, and coca bush, and the trafficking of narcotic drugs, and to control psychotropic substances, chemical precursors, and equipment used in manufacturing, producing, or processing of narcotic drugs and psychotropic substances.

Article 2

Objectives
The objectives of this Law are:

1. To prevent the cultivation of opium poppy, cannabis plants, and coca bush, and prescribe penalties for persons engaging in these activities.
2. To regulate and control narcotic drugs, psychotropic substances, chemical precursors, and substances and equipment used in the manufacture, production, or processing of narcotic drugs and psychotropic substances in order to prevent their use for illicit purposes and to ensure their use for medical, scientific, research and industrial purposes in accordance with the provisions of the law.
3. To prescribe penalties for persons engaging in and to prevent the cultivation, production, processing, acquisition, possession, distribution, manufacture, trade, brokering, importation, exportation, transportation, offering, use, storage, and concealment of narcotic drugs and psychotropic substances, and of the chemical precursors, other illicit substances, and equipment used for these illicit activities.
4. To coordinate, monitor, and evaluate the counter narcotics activities, policies, and programs of the Government of the Islamic Republic of Afghanistan.
5. To encourage farmers to cultivate licit crops instead of opium poppy, coca bush, and cannabis plants.
6. To establish health centers for detoxification, treatment, rehabilitation, and harm reduction services for drug-addicted and drug dependent persons in order to reintegrate them into society.
7. To attract the cooperation and assistance of national and international organizations in the task of combating cultivation, trafficking and use of narcotic drugs, psychotropic substances, and the chemical precursors used in their production, manufacturing, and processing.

Article 3

Definitions
Terms: The following terms have the following meanings in this law:

1) "Narcotic Drug" means a plant, substance or preparation classified as such in the Tables annexed to this law.

2) "Analogue" means any substance which is not included in any of the Tables annexed to this law but whose chemical structure combination and whose psychotropic effects are similar to those of a substance included in the Tables annexed to this law.

3) "Controlled delivery" means allowing the transportation and passage of illicit or suspected consignments of prohibited articles, including drugs, precursors, analogues or substances substituted for them, equipment of clandestine laboratories, or laundered money into or through Afghanistan or one or more countries, with the knowledge and under the supervision of the competent law enforcement authorities, in efforts to identify persons and investigate and establish proof of criminal offenses.

4) "Dependence" is a condition in which the use of drugs is compulsive, and stopping gives rise to psychological and even physical disorders, which leads the person to continue using the drug.

5) "Detoxification treatment" means treatment intended to eliminate physical dependence on a drug.

6) "Drug abuse" and "illicit drug use" mean the use of any regulated drug without a medical prescription and medical instructions for non-scientific and non-medical purposes.

7) "Drug addict" means a person in a state of physical and/or psychic dependence on a drug.

8) "Industrial use" of a drug means its exclusive use in a manufacturing process.

9) "Medical prescription" means a written document signed by a physician or a person holding a medical license, issued for the medical treatment of a patient and authorizing the dispensing by a pharmacist to that person of a specific quantity of controlled drugs.

10) "Medical use" means the consumption or use of drugs controlled by this law under a medical prescription and in accordance with international conventions.

11) "Money-laundering" means the same concepts as defined under article 3 of the Law against Money-Laundering and Criminal Proceeds published in the Official Gazette No. 840 on 10.08.1383.

12) "Precursor" means a substance used in drug manufacture or processing and classified as such under Table IV of this law.

13) "Psychotropic substance" means a drug in one of the Tables annexed to the 1971 Convention on Psychotropic Substances.

14) "Regulated drugs" are defined as all plants and substances, including their chemical preparations and their derivatives, and chemical precursors that are listed in Tables 1–4, derived from the United Nations International Conventions on Drugs, attached to this law.

15) "Mixture" or "Compound" means any preparation that contains any detectable amount of a controlled or regulated drug substance under this law.

16) "Covert Operations" means the investigation of criminal offences by law enforcement agencies' use of methods that include surveillance, the use of informants, undercover operations and the exchange of intelligence with appropriate law enforcement agencies or other organisations.

17) "Vehicle" means any mode of transportation used in drug-trafficking.

18) "Undercover Operations" means operations carried out in secret by the police in which the officers' identities are concealed from third parties by the use of an alias and false identity so as to enable the infiltration of existing criminal groups in order to arrest suspected criminals.

19) "Surveillance" means the covert watching of a person or group of persons or the covert listening to their conversations over a period of time by a human being or through the use of technical devices.

20) "Secret or Electronic Surveillance" means surveillance authorized by a competent court in accordance with the provisions of law. This surveillance includes the following activities:

- watching in private places using human or technical means;
- interception of communications;
- opening of mail; and,
- inspection of bank accounts and records of other financial activity.

21) "Conspiracy" or "Complicity" means the same as defined under article 49 of the 1355 Penal Code published in the Official Gazette No. 347.

22) "Possession" means the ability to exert control over an object, including cases where a person is not in physical contact with the object, but has the power to exercise control over it, either directly or through others.

23) "Distribution" is the transfer or attempted transfer of possession from one person to another.

24) "Aid" or "abet" means the same as defined under article 39 of the 1355 Penal Code published in the Official Gazette No. 347.

25) "Attempt" means the same as defined under article 29 of the 1355 Penal Code published in the Official Gazette No. 347.

26) "Public official" shall mean any officer, employee, or person acting for, on behalf, or under the authority of a government agency.

27) "Official act" shall mean any decision or action on any matter, controversy, or legal proceeding by a public official.

28) "Bribe" shall mean corruptly giving, offering, or promising anything of value to any person or entity, directly or indirectly, with the purpose of:
   (1) influencing an official act;
   (2) influencing a public official to commit or omit any act in violation of his lawful duty; or
   (3) influencing witnesses, detection, investigation, or trial proceedings;
   (4) compelling any witness to be absent from any legal or court proceedings;
   (5) influencing any agency, commission, or officer authorized by the law to hear and record the testimony of witnesses.

29) "Weapon" means any beating or injuring tools and devices, firearms, and explosives capable of inflicting injury or destruction, or that can cause death.

Chapter II

Classification and Regulation of Narcotic Drugs, Psychotropic Substances, and Chemicals Used in the Manufacture, Production, or Processing of Narcotic Drugs and Psychotropic Substances

Article 4

Classification and Regulation of Narcotic Drugs
1. For purposes of this law, regulated drugs are defined as all plants and substances that are listed in Tables 1–3, including their chemical derivatives, and all chemical precursors that are listed in Table 4 of the Tables attached hereto. The regulated drugs covered by this law shall be classified in four tables:
   - Table 1: Prohibited plants and substances with no medical use;
   - Table 2: Strictly controlled plants and substances with a medical use;
   - Table 3: Controlled plants and substances with a medical use;
   - Table 4: Chemical precursors and other substances used in the illicit manufacture or processing of narcotic drugs and psychotropic substances.

Article 5

Drug Regulation Committee
1) A Drug Regulation Committee is hereby established which shall be composed of five members with the following composition:

   a) One medical and one pharmaceutical expert from the Ministry of Public Health;
   b) Two experts from the Ministry of Counter-Narcotics;
   c) One customs expert from the Ministry of Finance.

2) Members of the Drug Regulation Committee mentioned in paragraph 1 of this Article shall be appointed by their respective ministries for a period of four years. The Chairperson of the Drug Regulation Committee shall be appointed by the

Minister of Counter-Narcotics from among its members.

3) Decisions and regulations of the Drug Regulation Committee shall be made by a majority of its members and shall be recorded in a special book.

4) In case any member of the Drug Regulation Committee fails to carry out his/her duties in a satisfactory fashion, he/she can be removed from his membership in the Committee by the Minister of Counter Narcotics.

5) The administrative costs of the Drug Regulation Committee and those of its secretariat shall be paid directly from the budget of the Ministry of Counter Narcotics. Members of the Drug Regulation Committee shall be paid appropriate attendance fees by the Ministry of Counter-Narcotics.

6) The Drug Regulation Committee shall prepare one quarterly and one annual report to the Minister of Counter Narcotics on its activities. The Minister may direct the Drug Regulation Committee to provide the necessary information in accordance with this Law and relevant regulations.

7) The Drug Regulation Committee will hereinafter be called the Committee.

Article 6

Duties of the Committee
1. The classifications of the regulated drugs in Tables 1 through 4 shall be established and amended, in particular by new inclusions, deletions, or transfers from one Table to another, by the Committee, taking into account any amendments or additions ordered by the United Nations Commission on Narcotic Drugs. Plants and substances shall be included under their international nonproprietary name or, failing this, under their commercial, scientific, or common name.

2. The Committee may not include an internationally controlled substance in a Table subject to a regime less strict than that required under the United Nations Conventions for the substance in question.

3. The Committee shall not transfer any substance from Table 1 to Table 2 or 3, except as provided in paragraph 1 of this Article.

4. Inclusions, deletions or transfers from one Table to another in accordance with paragraphs 1, 2, and 3 above shall be valid when they are published in the official gazette.

5. Except as otherwise provided by this law, a preparation, compound, or mixture of any regulated drug shall be subject to the same regulations, prohibitions, and penalties as the regulated drug which it contains, and if it contains two or more regulated drugs it shall be subject to the conditions governing the most strictly controlled regulated drug that it contains.

6. A preparation, compound, or mixture containing a substance listed in Tables 2, 3 or 4 that is compounded in such a way as to present no, or a negligible, risk of abuse or diversion and from which the substance cannot be recovered by readily applicable means in a quantity liable to illicit use, abuse, or diversion may be exempt from certain of the control measures set forth in this law by decision of the Committee.

7. If the substances listed in Tables 2 and 3 and their preparations can be used in medicine they shall be subject to the provisions applicable to all substances and preparations intended for use in human or veterinary medicine to the extent that such provisions are compatible with those established in this law.

Chapter III

Licensing, Cultivation, Production, Manufacture, Trade, Distribution, and Use of Plants, Substances and Preparations Listed in Tables 1, 2, 3, and 4

Article 7

Licenses

1. No person shall cultivate, produce, process, manufacture, trade, distribute, possess, supply, traffic, transport, transfer, acquire, purchase, sell, import, export, or transit, plants, substances and preparations listed in Tables 2 and 3 in the territory of Afghanistan, unless he has been licensed by the Committee.

2. No person may engage in any of the operations set forth in paragraph 1 of this article at any building or on any premises not expressly identified on a license issued under this Article, or separately licensed by the Committee for use by specially designated State enterprises, or exempt from licensing under this law.

3. The Committee may issue a license to cultivate, manufacture, distribute (including dispensing), import or export one or more of the plants, substances and preparations listed in Tables 1, 2 and 3 at the building or on the premises identified in the license. Such a license shall permit any of the operations set forth in the first paragraph of this article that are necessarily involved in the licensed activity.

4. A license to engage in the operations set forth in paragraph 1 of this article may be issued only if the use of the plants, substances and preparations in question is restricted to medical or scientific purposes. This license shall be valid for one year. Licensing shall be subject to verification of the character and professional qualifications of the applicant. A license may not be granted to any person convicted of a narcotics or money laundering offense.

5. The industrial production and use of a substance listed in Tables 1, 2 or 3 for other than medical or scientific purposes may be authorized by the Committee if the applicant satisfactorily shows that such production or use is necessary to a industrial process, he shall ensure that the products manufactured, other than another regulated drug subject to this Law, cannot be abused or produce harmful effects, and he shall ensure that any regulated drug included in this authorization and used in the composition of the products manufactured cannot be easily recovered. The person or entity so authorized shall destroy all quantities of the regulated drug included in this authorization that cannot be rendered harmless or sufficiently irretrievable and reports to the Committee the quantity of the regulated drug produced, used or destroyed.

6. A person can operate in places set forth in paragraphs 3 and 7 of this article which have been designated for the manufacture, distribution (including dispensing), importation or exportation of regulated drugs only when those places comply with the security standards established by the Committee.

7. State enterprises specially designated by the Committee to engage in the operations set forth in paragraph 1 of this article shall be required to apply for a license to use buildings and premises for such operations, and the Committee may issue such license in accordance with the requirements of paragraph 6 of this Article.

8. For the better implementation of this article, the Committee may establish regulations, in particular those governing applications for and the granting, content, scope, withdrawal and suspension of licenses.

Article 8

Possessing Needed Amounts of Narcotic Drugs
1. Authorized regulated drug manufacturers and distributors may hold the quantities of the various regulated drugs required for the smooth functioning of business. The distributors who only dispense regulated drugs are excepted from this provision.

2. The Committee shall establish for each year, taking into account the prevailing market conditions, the anticipated medical, scientific, research, and industrial needs for the regulated drugs in Tables 1, 2 and 3, and the anticipated lawful exports of such regulated drugs, the maximum quantities of these regulated drugs that shall be manufactured and the maximum quantities that each licensee and each specially designated State enterprise shall be entitled to manufacture. These limits may be changed during the year if necessary.

3. The Committee may establish and publish regulations and procedures for the implementation of this Article.

Article 9

Exports and Imports
1. The export and import of substances on Tables 1, 2 and 3 shall be subject to separate authorization issued by the Committee.

2. This authorization shall be subject to the completion of a form which includes the requirements established by the Committee and the United Nations Economic and Social Council.

3. The Committee may authorize an importation of a substance listed in Tables 1, 2, or 3 only to meet legitimate medical, scientific, and industrial needs. The import authorization shall not be necessary in the event of a catastrophe or an emergency as determined by the Committee, but the importer shall maintain a record of the importation as prescribed by the Committee.

4. The Committee may authorize an exportation of a substance listed on Tables 1, 2, or 3 only to a country that maintains effective controls over the use of the regulated drug and only if the regulated drug is to be used for medical, scientific, or other legitimate purposes.

5. An authorization for the importation or exportation of a substance listed on Tables 1, 2, or 3 is not transferable.

6. An application for import or export authorization of a substance listed on Tables 1, 2, or 3 shall indicate the following:

a) The name and address of the importer or exporter;
b) The names and addresses of any consignee, if known;
c) The international non-proprietary name of each substance or, failing this, the name of the substance in the tables of the international conventions;
d) The pharmaceutical form and characteristics of each substance and, in the case of a preparation, its trade name;
e) The quantity of each substance and preparation involved in the operation;
f) The period during which the operation is to take place;
g) The mode of transport or shipment; and
h) The border custom house of the importation and exportation.

7. An import certificate or other documentation issued by the Government of the importing country shall be attached to the export application.

8. An import or export authorization shall contain, in addition to the expiration date and the name of the issuing authority, the same types of details as the application.

9. The import authorization shall specify whether the import is to be effected in a single consignment or may be effected in more than one consignment, and shall establish the time in which the import of all consignments must be effected.

10. The export authorization shall also indicate the number and date of the import certificate issued by the Government of the importing country.

11. A copy of the export authorization shall accompany each consignment and the Committee shall send a copy to the Government of the importing country.

12. If the quantity of plants, substances or preparations actually exported is smaller than that specified in the export authorization, and is certified by the customs office, the Committee shall note that fact on the related document and on all official copies thereof.

13. Once the consignment has entered the national territory or when the period stipulated in the import authorization has expired, the Committee shall send the export authorization to the Government of the exporting country, with an endorsement specifying the quantity of each regulated drug actually imported.

14. Commercial documents such as invoices, cargo manifests, customs or transport documents and other shipping documents shall include the name of the plants and substances as set out in the tables of the international conventions and the trade name of the preparations, the quantities exported from the national territory or to be imported into it, and the names and addresses of the exporter, the importer and the consignee.

15. Exports from the national territory of consignments to the address or account of a person other than the person named in the import certificate issued by the Government of the importing country or in other documentation

demonstrating authorization for the import into that country shall be prohibited. This same provision shall apply to the importation of consignments into the national territory.

16. Exports from the national territory of consignments to a bonded warehouse shall be prohibited unless the Government of the importing country certifies on the import certificate or other authorization that it has approved such a consignment.

17. Imports to the national territory of consignments to a bonded warehouse shall be prohibited unless the Government certifies on the import certificate that it approves such a consignment. Withdrawal from the bonded warehouse shall require a permit from the authorities having jurisdiction over the warehouse. In the case of a consignment to a foreign destination, such withdrawal shall be treated as if it were a new export within the meaning of the present Article. The regulated drugs stored in the bonded warehouse may not be subjected to any process, which would modify their nature, nor may their packaging be altered without the permission of the authorities having jurisdiction over the warehouse.

18. A consignment entering or leaving the national territory which is not accompanied by a proper import or export authorization or does not comply with the authorization shall be detained by the competent authorities until the legitimacy of the consignment is established or until a court rules on its status.

19. The Committee shall specify those customs offices operating in the national territory that are to deal with the import or export of the regulated drugs listed in Tables 1, 2 and 3.

20. The transit of any consignment of plants, substances or preparations listed in Tables 1, 2 and 3 through the national territory shall be prohibited,

whether or not the consignment is removed from the conveyance in which it is carried, unless a copy of the export authorization issued by the Government of the exporting country for such consignment is produced to the department designated by the Committee.

21. The route specified by the export license for a consignment which is in transit in Afghanistan shall not be changed.

22. An application for authorization to change the itinerary or the consignee shall be treated as if the export in question were from the national territory to the new country or consignee concerned.

23. No consignment of plants, substances and preparations in transit through the national territory may be subjected to any process that might change their nature, nor may its packaging be altered without the permission of the Committee.

24. If there is a conflict between the provisions of this article and those of an international agreement that Afghanistan has signed, the provisions of the international agreement prevail.

25. The provisions of this article shall not apply where the consignment in question is transported by air to another country. If the aircraft stops over or makes an emergency landing in the national territory, the consignment shall be treated as an export from the national territory to the country of destination only if it is removed from the aircraft.

26. Free ports and free trade zones shall be subject to the same controls and supervision as other parts of the national territory regarding the importation of plants, substances, or preparations listed in Tables 1, 2 and 3.

27. Transport companies and enterprises shall abide by the regulations of the Committee with regard to taking reasonable measures to prevent the use of their means of transport for illicit trafficking in the regulated drugs covered by the present law, and shall also be required:

- To submit cargo manifests in advance, whenever possible;
- To keep the products in sealed containers having tamper-resistant, individually verifiable seals, and in which every kind of alteration should be easily discernable;
- To report to the appropriate authorities, at the earliest opportunity, any suspicious consignments.

Article 10

Retail Trade and Distribution
1. Purchases of regulated drugs listed in Tables 2 and 3 for the purpose of professional supply may be made only from a private individual or state enterprise holding a license issued under this law.

2. Only the following persons and state entities may, without having to apply for a license, purchase and hold plants and regulated drugs listed in Tables 2 and 3 for their professional needs:

- Pharmacists holding a license to practice when acting in the usual course of business as an agent or employee of a person or entity holding a valid license to distribute regulated drugs;
- Pharmacists at a public or private hospital or health care institution that is licensed to distribute regulated drugs when acting in the usual course of business as an agent or employee of that hospital or health care institutions;
- Pharmacists holding a license to practice in charge of public or private warehouses;
- Hospitals or health care institutions without a pharmacist in charge, in emergency cases and unanticipated events provided that a qualified physician attached to the establishment who holds a license to practice and to dispense regulated drugs has agreed to take responsibility for the stocks in question;
- Physicians, dental surgeons, and veterinary surgeons holding a license to practice and authorized

to dispense regulated drugs, including the preparations included in a list drawn up by the Committee;

3. Physicians, dental surgeons, and veterinary surgeons holding a license to practice may, without having to apply for a drug distribution license, purchase and hold the needed quantities of preparations included in a list drawn up by the Committee.

4. Dental surgeons, midwives, and nurses holding a license to practice may, without having to apply for a license, purchase and hold for their professional activities quantities of preparations included in a list drawn up by the Committee.

5. The regulated drugs listed in Tables 2 and 3 may be prescribed to individuals and animals only in the form of pharmaceutical preparations and only on a medical prescription issued by one of the following professionals:

- A physician holding a license to practice and to dispense regulated drugs;
- A dental surgeon holding a license to practice and to dispense regulated drugs, for treatment of a dental nature;
- A veterinary surgeon holding a license to practice and to dispense regulated drugs, for treatment of animals;
- A nurse or midwife holding a license to practice for treatment connected with their professional duties and within the limits set by the competent authority.

6. Pharmaceutical preparations listed in Tables 2 and 3 may be dispensed only by:

- Dispensing pharmacists holding a license;
- Pharmacists at public or private hospitals or health care institutions when such hospitals or institutions hold a license to dispense regulated drugs;
- Physicians and veterinary surgeons holding a license to practice and authorized to dispense regulated drugs;
- Nurses and midwives in the conduct of their professional duties.

7. The Committee, if the situation so requires and under such conditions as it may determine, may authorize, in all or part of the national territory, licensed pharmacists or any other licensed retail distributors to supply, without prescription, small quantities of therapeutic doses of pharmaceutical preparations containing one or more of the regulated drugs listed in Table 3.

8. The Committee shall establish regulations for the implementation of this Article, in particular the rules concerning the writing and filling of prescriptions for pharmaceutical preparations listed in Tables 2 and 3.

Article 11

Private Institutions and State Enterprises
1. Private institutions and State enterprises holding licenses to engage in operations involving regulated drugs shall furnish to the Committee in respect of their activities:

- Not later than 15 days after the end of each quarter, a quarterly report on the quantities of each substance and each preparation imported or exported, indicating the country of origin and the country of destination;
- Not later than 5 May of each year, a report for the previous calendar year indicating:
  - The quantities of each substance and each preparation produced or manufactured;
  - The quantities of each substance used for producing preparations and other:
    - Other substances covered by the present legislation; and
    - Substances not covered by the present legislation;
  - The quantities of each substance and each preparation supplied for retail distribution, medical or scientific research or teaching;
  - The quantities of each substance and each preparation in stock as of 29 March of the year to which the information refers;
  - The quantities of each substance necessary for the new calendar year.

2. The Committee shall establish procedures for the purchase of and placing orders for plants,

substances and preparations listed in Tables 2, 3, and 4 required for the conduct of professional activities.

3. The Committee shall establish procedures for any purchase, transfer, export, import or dispensing of plants, substances and preparations listed in Table 2, and all related transactions shall be recorded in accordance with regulations established by the Committee.

4. Any person, private enterprise, or state enterprise holding, for professional purposes, any plants, substances and preparations listed in Tables 2, 3, and 4 shall be required to keep them under regulations established by the Committee so as to prevent theft or any other form of diversion.

5. Any person, private enterprise, State enterprise, medical or scientific institution engaged in any activity or operation involving plants, substances or preparations covered by the present law shall be controlled and monitored by regulations established by the Committee. Such control and monitoring shall extend to the compartments containing first-aid kits of public transport conveyances engaged in international travel. The Committee shall, in particular, arrange for inspectors or any other body legally empowered to conduct inspections to make ordinary inspections of the establishments, premises, stocks and records at least once every two years. Extraordinary inspections can be done at any time.

Article 12

Monitoring and Control
1. State enterprises, private enterprises, medical and scientific institutions and other persons referred to in Article 11 shall be required, at the beginning of each year, to make an inventory of the plants, substances and preparations listed in Tables 1, 2 and 3 held by them and to compare the total quantities in stock at the time of the previous inventory, calculated together with those entered

over the previous year and the total quantities withdrawn during the year, with those held at the time of the latest inventory.

2. Licensees, pharmacists and persons authorized to dispense drugs through wholesale pharmacies or drugstores shall be required to make an inventory and calculate the balance as stipulated in paragraph 1 of this article.

3. Any discrepancies noted in a balance or between the results of the balance and those of the inventory shall be immediately reported by the licensee, pharmacist or person authorized to dispense drugs to the Committee, which shall acknowledge receipt of the notification.

4. It shall be forbidden to distribute substances and preparations listed in Tables 2 and 3 unless they are enclosed in wrappers or containers bearing their name and, in the case of consignments of substances and preparations listed in Table 2, a double red band.

5. The outer wrappings of parcels described in paragraph 4 shall bear no information other than the names and addresses of the sender and the consignee. They shall be sealed with the sender's mark.

6. The label under which a preparation is offered for sale shall indicate the names of the substances listed in Tables 1, 2 and 3 that it contains, together with their weight and percentage.

7. Labels accompanying packages for retail sale or distribution as described in paragraph 4 shall indicate the directions for use as well as the cautions and warnings necessary for the safety of the user.

8. If necessary, additional requirements in respect of packaging and labeling shall be stipulated by regulations established by the Committee.

Article 13

Regulation of Substances (Precursors) in Table 4
1. The manufacture, distribution or trading of the substances listed in Table 4 shall be subject to the provisions of this article.

2. Import or export authorizations shall be refused if a consignment is possibly [?!!!] intended for the illicit manufacture of narcotic drugs or psychotropic substances.

3. Export or import consignments of substances listed in Table 4 annexed to this law shall be clearly labeled to show their contents.

4. Any person who, because of his job requirements, becomes aware of the economic, industrial, trade or professional secrets or trade processes of the substances listed on Table 4 annexed to this law shall be required to avoid disclosing the same to other people.

5. Manufacturers, importers, exporters, wholesalers and retailers shall be required to enter in a register established by the Committee any purchase or transfer of substances listed in Table 4. The entry shall be made with no blank spaces, erasures or overwriting. It shall indicate the date of the transaction, the name and the quantity of the product purchased or transferred and the name, address and occupation of the purchaser and seller. However, retailers shall not be required to enter the name of the purchaser. The registers shall be kept for ten years pursuant to regulations established by the Committee.

6. Manufacturers, importers, exporters, wholesalers and retailers of the substances listed in Table 4 shall be required to inform the appropriate police authority of any orders or transactions that appear suspicious, in particular by reason of the quantity of the substances being purchased or ordered, the repetition of such orders or purchases or the means of payment or transport used.

7. If there is strong evidence to warrant the suspicion that a substance listed in Table 4 is for use in the illicit manufacture of a narcotic drug, such substance shall be immediately seized pending the outcome of a judicial investigation.

8. The Committee shall submit to the Minister of Counter-Narcotics information on the import and export of precursor substances listed in Table 4.

Article 14

Medical and Scientific Research and Teaching
1. For purposes of medical or scientific research, teaching or forensic work, the Committee may authorize, in accordance with a separate procedure and without requiring the licenses referred to in this Chapter, the cultivation, manufacturing, acquiring, importation, use, or possession of plants, substances and preparations in Tables 1, 2 and 3 in quantities not exceeding those strictly necessary for the purpose in question.

2. The applicant of the authorization referred to in paragraph 1 of this article shall enter in a register, which he shall keep for 5 years, the quantities of plants, substances and preparations that he imports, acquires, manufactures, uses, and destroys. He shall also record the dates of the operations and the names of his suppliers. He shall furnish the Committee with an annual report on the quantities used or destroyed and those held in stock. The Committee shall be entitled to inspect registers maintained in accordance with this provision.

Chapter IV

Offenses and Penalties

Article 15

Drug Trafficking Offenses and Penalties
1. Any person who engages in the following acts without a license or authorization issued according

to the provisions of this law has committed a drug trafficking offense and shall be punished in accordance with the provisions of this law:

(a) The production, manufacture, distribution, possession, extraction, preparation, processing, offering for sale, purchasing, selling, delivery, brokerage, dispatch, transportation, importation, exportation, purchase, concealment, or storage of any substance or mixture containing a substance listed in Tables 1 through 3 annexed to this law;

(b) Any of the operations referred to in paragraph 1 of this article in relation to any chemicals or precursors listed in Table 4 for the illicit cultivation, production or manufacture of narcotic drugs or psychotropic substances.

Article 16

Drug Trafficking Penalties
1. Whoever commits a drug trafficking offense involving the following quantities of heroin, morphine, or cocaine, or any mixture containing those substances, shall be sentenced as follows:

(i) Less than 10 grams, imprisonment for between 6 months and one year, and a fine of between 30,000 Afs and 50,000 Afs.

(ii) Between 10 grams and 100 grams, imprisonment for between one and three years, and a fine of between 50,000 and 100,000 Afs.

(iii) Between 100 grams and 500 grams, imprisonment for between three and five years, and a fine of between 100,000 Afs and 250,000 Afs.

(iv) Between 500g and 1kg, imprisonment for between seven and ten years, and a fine of between 300,000 Afs and 500,000 Afs.

(v) Between 1kg and 5kg, imprisonment for between ten and fifteen years, and a fine of between 500,000 Afs and 1,000,000 Afs.

(vi) Over 5kg, life imprisonment, and a fine of between 1,000,000 Afs and 10,000,000 Afs.

2. Whoever commits a drug trafficking offense involving the following quantities of opium or any mixture containing that substance shall be sentenced as follows:

(i) Less than 10 grams, imprisonment for up to three months, and a fine of between 5000 Afs and 10,000 Afs.

(ii) Between 10 grams and 100g, imprisonment between six months and one year, and a fine of between 10,000 Afs and 50,000 Afs.

(iii) Between 100g and 500g, imprisonment for between one and three years, and a fine of between 50,000 and 100,000 Afs.

(iv) Between 500g and 1kg, imprisonment for between three and five years, and a fine of between 100,000 Afs and 500,000 Afs.

(v) Between 1kg and 5kg, imprisonment for between five and ten years, and a fine of between 500,000 Afs and 1,000,000 Afs.

(vi) Between 5kg and 50kg, imprisonment for between ten and fifteen years, and a fine of between 700,000 Afs and 1,500,000 Afs.

(vii) Over 50kg, life imprisonment and a fine of between 1,500,000 Afs and 5,000,000 Afs.

3. Whoever commits a drug trafficking offense involving the following quantities of the substances or any mixture containing substances listed in Tables 1 through 4, with the exception of heroin, morphine, cocaine, and opium, shall be sentenced as follows:

(i) Less than 250 grams, imprisonment for up to three months, and a fine of between 5000 Afs and 10,000 Afs.

(ii) Between 250 grams and 500g, imprisonment for between three months and six months and a fine of between 10,000 Afs and 50,000 Afs.

(iii) Between 500g and 1 kg, imprisonment for between six months and 1 year, and a fine of between 50,000 Afs and 100,000 Afs.

(iv) Between 1kg and 5kg, imprisonment for between one and three years, and a fine of between 100,000 Afs and 500,000 Afs.

(v) Between 5kg and 10kg, imprisonment for between five and ten years and a fine of between 500,000 Afs and up to 1,000,000 Afs.

(vi) Over 10kg, imprisonment for between ten and fifteen years, and a fine of between 1,000,000 Afs and 1,500,000 Afs.

4. Any person who, during the course of any of the offenses set forth in paragraphs 1, 2, and 3 of this article, directs, controls, organizes, finances, or guides three or more persons, shall be sentenced to penalties thrice as severe as the maximum penalties prescribed for that crime under the sub-paragraphs of paragraphs 1, 2, and 3 of this article, provided that the term of imprisonment does not exceed 20 years.

Article 17

Aggregation of Amounts
1. If several persons are responsible for the commission of a drug trafficking offense, and the amounts of drugs trafficked by each of them is known, each of the offenders shall be punished under the provisions of this law pursuant to his share in the overall amount trafficked.

2. If several persons are responsible for the commission of a drug trafficking offense, but the share of each in the amount of drug trafficked is not known, each of them shall be sentenced to a penalty prescribed for the total amount trafficked.

Article 18

Conspiracy, Aiding, Abetting, Facilitation, Incitement
Any person who attempts, conspires, or engages in preparatory acts to commit any offense under this law shall be subject to the same penalties as the principal offender.

Article 19

Drug Laboratories, Manufacturing, and Storage
Whoever without authorization under this law opens, maintains, manages, or controls any property, building, room, or facility, as an owner, lessee, manager, agent, employee, or mortgagee, and intentionally rents, leases, or makes available for use, with or without compensation, such a place for the purpose of cultivating, manufacturing, processing, storing, concealing, or distributing any substance or mixture listed in Tables 1 through 4, or participates in or obtains an income from such activity, shall be sentenced to a term of imprisonment between 10 and 20 years and a fine of between 500,000 Afs. and 1,000,000 Afs.

Article 20

Importation or Use of Equipment for Drug Trafficking
1. Whoever imports equipment or materials used in or for the production and processing of regulated drugs without having a license, shall be sentenced to imprisonment for 5 to 10 years and a fine of between 100,000 and 500,000 Afs, and shall have the equipment or materials confiscated.

2. Whoever lawfully imports equipment or materials used in or for the production and processing of drugs but uses them in the illicit production or processing of the regulated drugs, shall be sentenced to imprisonment for 10 to 15 years and a fine of between 500,000 and 1,000,000 Afs, and shall have the equipment or materials confiscated.

3. Whoever possesses or uses the equipment or materials referred to in paragraph 1 of this article for the illicit production or processing of regulated drugs, shall be sentenced to imprisonment for 15 to 20 years and a fine of between 1,000,000 and 2,000,000 Afs, and shall have the equipment and materials confiscated.

Article 21

Drug-Related Corruption and Intimidation
1. Any public official who intentionally commits one of the following acts shall be sentenced to

imprisonment for 5 to 10 years and shall be fined twice the amount of the bribe:

(a) facilitating or assisting any offense under this law;

(b) obstructing an official investigation of an offense under this law or obstructing a trial of any offense under this law, including by failing to carry out lawful obligations; or

(c) directly or indirectly demanding, seeking, receiving, accepting, or agreeing to accept or receive a bribe in relation to drug trafficking or any official duty connected directly or indirectly to drug law enforcement,

A bribe-giver and a bribe-agent shall be sentenced to the same penalties as the bribe-taker.

2. Any person who threatens or intimidates another for the purpose of committing the following acts shall be sentenced to imprisonment between 5 and 8 years and fined between 500,000 and 1,000,000 Afs.

(a) committing or facilitating an offense under this law; or

(b) impeding a drug trafficking investigation or prosecution,

3. Any person who receives or accepts any benefit for the purpose of impeding or interfering with an investigation or criminal trial of a drug trafficking offense shall be sentenced to imprisonment for between 5 and 10 years, and shall relinquish the benefit.

4. Any person who threatens or seeks to intimidate any public official in connection with the detection of any drug trafficking offense, or an investigation or criminal trial of any drug trafficking offense, shall be sentenced to imprisonment for between 5 and 10 years, and a fine of between 1,000,000 Afs and 2,000,000 Afs.

5. Any person who injures any public official in connection with the detection, investigation or criminal trial of any drug trafficking offense, shall

be sentenced to imprisonment between 10 to 15 years, and a fine of between 1,000,000 Afs and 3,000,000 Afs.

6. Subject to the provisions of Chapter Seven of the Penal Code, the penalties set forth in paragraphs 1, 2, 3, 4, and 5 of this article shall be in addition to other penalties that an offender may be sentenced to for committing other criminal offenses.

Article 22

Use of Weapons
1. Any person who uses, or causes the use of, any weapon during or in relation to any drug trafficking offense shall be punished by a term of five to ten years imprisonment, and a fine between 500,000 Afs and 1000,000 Afs.

2. Any person who carries or possesses any weapon, or causes another person to carry or possess any weapon, during or in relation to any drug trafficking offense shall be punished by a term of 3 to 5 years imprisonment, and a fine of between 500,000 Afs and 1,000,000 Afs.

Article 23

Intimidation Leading to Drug-Related Offenses
Any person who intentionally commits the following acts shall be sentenced to a term of imprisonment of between 5 and 8 years, and a fine of between 50,000 Afs and 200,000 Afs.

(a) Compelling another by force or intimidation to cultivate, manufacture, distribute, possess, sell, transport, store, or use substances or any mixture containing substances on Tables 1 through 4;

(b) Mixing substances on Tables 1 through 4 in food or drink intending that they be consumed by others;

(c) Distributing or sells any substance or mixture containing substances on Tables 1 through 4 to a child or to a person with mental health problems;

(d) Distributing any substance or mixture containing substances on Tables 1 through 4 in educational, military training, health or social service centers, or prisons;

(e) Employing or using a child to commit a drug trafficking offense; or

(f) Allowing the consumption of substances or any mixture containing substances on Tables 1 through 4 in restaurants, hotels, shops or any other premises.

Article 24

Illicit Prescription of Drugs
Any person who intentionally commits the following acts shall be sentenced to a term of imprisonment of between 3 and 5 years, and a fine of between 50,000 Afs and 100,000 Afs.

(a) Prescribing a regulated drug knowing it is to be used illegally; or

(b) Selling and buying regulated drugs using fraudulent prescriptions,

Article 25

Prohibition on Cultivation
1. Planting or cultivating opium poppy and seeds, coca bush, and cannabis plants within Afghanistan is a criminal offense and prohibited.

2. The owners, occupiers, or cultivators of lands are obligated to destroy opium poppy, coco bush, and cannabis plants growing on their lands. If they fail to do so shall be punished pursuant to the provisions of Article 26.

Article 26

Penalties for Cultivation
1. Whoever plants or cultivates less than 1 jerib of opium poppy or coca bush without having a license shall be sentenced to a term of imprisonment between 6 months and 1 year and a fine between 10,000 Afs and 50,000 Afs.

2. Whoever plants or cultivates 1 jerib or more of opium poppy or coca bush shall, for each "beswa" (100 square meters) in excess of 1 jerib, be sentenced to imprisonment for 1 month and fine of 5,000 Afs, which penalty shall be in addition to the penalty prescribed in paragraph 1 of this article.

3. Whoever plants or cultivates less than 1 jerib of cannabis plants shall be sentenced to imprisonment for 3 to 9 months and a fine between 5,000 and 20,000 Afs.

4. Whoever plants or cultivates more than 1 jerib of cannabis plants, shall, for each beswa in excess of 1 jerib, be sentenced to imprisonment for 15 days and a fine of 2,500 Afs, which penalty shall be in addition to the penalty prescribed in paragraph 3 of this article.

5. Whoever encourages, causes, incites, or finances any person to plant or cultivate opium poppy, coca bush, or cannabis plants shall be sentenced to twice the penalties of the farmer in accordance with the provisions of paragraphs 1, 2, 3, and 4 of this article.

6. Illicit opium poppy, coca bush, or cannabis plants shall be destroyed and any person associated with the cultivation or planting shall not be entitled to any compensation, in addition to the penalties set forth in this article.

Article 27

Consumption of Illegal Drugs, and Treatment of Dependant Persons or Addicts
1. Any person who uses or possesses for the purpose of personal consumption any substance or mixture containing a substance listed in Tables 1 through 4, other than as authorized for medical treatment or by this law, shall be punished as follows:

(a) Heroin, morphine, and cocaine, or any mixture containing those substances: 6 months to 1 year imprisonment and a fine between 20,000 to 50,000 Afs.

(b) Opium or any mixture containing that substance: 3 months to 6 months imprisonment and a fine of between 10,000 Afs to 25,000 Afs.

(c) Substances or any mixture containing substances listed in Tables 1 through 4, with the exception of those in paragraphs 1 and 2 of this article: 1 month to 3 months imprisonment and a fine of between 5,000 Afs to 10,000 Afs.

(d) Possession of more than 1 gram of heroin, morphine, or cocaine, or 10 grams of opium or hashish, shall be subject to the penalties set forth in Article 16.

2. If a medical doctor certifies that a person is addicted to an illegal drug substance listed in Tables 1 through 4, the court may exempt the person from imprisonment and fine. In this case, the court may require an addicted person to attend a detoxification or drug treatment center.

3. Detoxification or drug treatment centers shall report to the sentencing court through the office of the prosecutor every 15 days on the health condition of persons sentenced to detention and treatment. On the basis of the report received, the court can abrogate or extend the period of detention and treatment.

4. Any person sentenced to a period of detention in a detoxification or drug treatment center shall receive credit on any sentence of imprisonment for the time served in the treatment center.

5. Any person in control of a vehicle while under the influence of any narcotic or psychotropic substance listed in Tables 1 through 3 shall be sentenced to a term of imprisonment of between six months and one year and a fine of 10,000 to 20,000 Afs.

Article 28

Vehicles

1. Whoever without legal authorization intentionally carries, transports, or conceals more than 10 grams of heroin, morphine, or cocaine; or more than 20 grams of opium; or more than 100 grams of hashish or any other substance listed in Tables 1 through 4 in his vehicle shall have the vehicle confiscated, in addition to the punishment prescribed in this law.

2. Any vehicle owner who without legal authorization intentionally allows a vehicle to be used to carry, transport, or conceal more than 10 grams of heroin, morphine, or cocaine; or more than 20 grams of opium; or more than 100 grams of hashish or any other substance listed in Tables 1 through 4 shall be punished as an accomplice to the crime and shall have the vehicle confiscated.

3. Any vehicle seized in relation to a drug-trafficking offense shall be registered and officially handed over to the nearest customs office and following the completion of its confiscation in accordance with the provisions of the relevant law, it shall be placed on sale and the proceeds be deposited to the government treasury.

[. . .]

19.
The Narcotic Drug Control Act

Laundered money has remained a major problem for the People's Republic of China. These laundered funds emanate from corruption, smuggling, fraud, and drug trafficking. Regulatory measures were initiated by the People's Bank of China and the State Administration of Foreign Exchange. The Criminal Code of 1997 made money laundering an offense pertaining to organized crime, smuggling, and drug trafficking. A major effort was established to control narcotic drugs by enacting the Narcotic Drug Control Act. Article 3 of the act included under narcotic drugs: cannabis, opiates, cocaine, synthetic narcotic drugs, and medicinal plants with their preparations. Cultivation of narcotic plants along with distribution, import, and export of narcotic drugs were prohibited by Article 4. Punishment for the offender depended on the seriousness of the crime as per the provisions of Article 30.

Source

United Nations Office on Drugs and Crime, http://www.unodc.org/unodc/en/legal_library/cn/legal_library_1997-11-19_1997-66.html.

Chapter I—General Provisions

Article 1

This Act is enacted in accordance with the Drug Administration Law of the People's Republic of China to strengthen the control of narcotic drugs, assure the safety of narcotic drugs used in medical practice, education and scientific research.

Article 2

The term "Narcotic drug" refers to those addictive substances that, when used continuously, can give rise to physical dependence.

Article 3

The scope of narcotic drugs includes opiates, cocaine, cannabis, synthetic narcotic drugs and medicinal plants and their preparations assigned by the Ministry of Public Health that are liable to be abused.

Article 4

The cultivation of narcotic plants and the production, distribution, importation and exportation of narcotic drugs are strictly controlled by the State, narcotic drugs are not to be used except for medical, educational or scientific purposes.

Chapter II—The Cultivation of Narcotic Plants and the Production of Narcotic Drugs

Article 5

Narcotic plant growing units should be approved by the Ministry of Public Health in concurrence with the Ministry of Agriculture, Animal Husbandry and Fishery and the State Bureau of Pharmaceutical Industry. The Ministry of Public Security should be notified of the approval.

Narcotic drug producing units should be approved by the Ministry of Public Health in concurrence with the State Bureau of Pharmaceutical Industry. No unit or individual may be engaged in the production of narcotic drugs without authorization.

Article 6

The annual plan for the cultivation of narcotic plants should be approved by the Ministry of Public Health in concurrence with the Ministry of Agriculture, Animal Husbandry and Fishery. The annual plan for the production of narcotic drugs should be approved by the Ministry of Public Health in concurrence with the State Bureau of Pharmaceutical Industry and conveyed jointly to all institutions concerned, the cultivating or producing units are not allowed to alter the plans at liberty. In every cultivating or producing unit, a definite person should be nominated to assure the safekeeping of all finished products, intermediate products, opium poppy shells and seeds, they are not to be sold or used at liberty.

Article 7

Quality control should be strengthened in the production of narcotic drugs, the quality of each product must comply with its national standard.

Article 8

The plan for the development of a new narcotic drug must be submitted to the Ministry of Public Health for approval. When the research activities come to an end, the new product should be subjected to the procedures of New Drug

Approval, in the mean time, the new product should be stored and used properly, diversion should be avoided.

Chapter III—The Supply of Narcotic Drugs

Article 9
Narcotic drugs should be supplied in a planned way according to the need in medical practice, education and scientific research. The plan for supply should be elaborated by an institution designated by the State Bureau of Pharmaceutical Industry and submitted to the Ministry of Public Health and the State Bureau of Pharmaceutical Industry for approval.

Article 10
The setting of narcotic drug handling units should be submitted, by the health authorities of provinces, autonomous regions and municipalities in concurrence with the pharmaceutical managing institutions, to the Ministry of Public Health and the State Bureau of Pharmaceutical Industry for approval. Narcotic drugs can only be supplied, in the basis of the fixed limited amounts, to those units qualified by the health authorities. No narcotic drugs should be supplied to any other units or individuals.

Article 11
The supply of medicine opium poppy shells should be handled solely by those units authorized by the State Bureau of Pharmaceutical Industry and the pharmaceutical managing institutions of provinces, autonomous regions and municipalities. Opium poppy shells should be distributed according to the plan jointly approved by the Ministry of Public Health and the State Bureau of Pharmaceutical Industry. Opium poppy shells can be dispensed by medical units and handling units assigned by health authorities above county level, pursuant to a physician's prescription which bears the seal of a medical unit, but they are not to be sold at retail. The amount of opium poppy shells planned for the manufacture of formulated products should be balanced by the pharmaceutical managing institutions and approved by the health authorities of provinces, autonomous regions and municipalities.

Article 12
Narcotic drugs must be stored in special warehouses or cabinets, special individual should be assigned to take charge of the distribution and transportation of narcotic drugs.

Chapter IV—The Transportation of Narcotic Drugs

Article 13
The transportation of opium must go through formalities by the holder of a licence issued by the Ministry of Public Health. Opium dispatched from the cultivating unit to the warehouse should be escorted by the consigner; opium dispatched from the warehouse to drug manufacturing enterprises should be escorted by the consignee. The number of escort must comply with the provision of the transport agency. The transport licence is provided exclusively by the Ministry of Public Health.

Article 14
When the consignment is a narcotic drug other than opium, or is opium poppy shell, the words "Narcotic Drug" must be written clearly on the bill of transportation, and a seal used especially for narcotic drugs should be stamped on the bill of transportation.

Article 15
Transport agencies should pay all attention and give priority to a consignment of narcotic drug or opium poppy shell, shorten their standing time on railway stations, wharves or airports. Open carriage should not be used for the transportation of narcotic drugs by train, the consignment should not be loaded on the surface of a cabin when it is transported by ship, and if it is transported by truck, it should be tightly covered and securely bundled.

Article 16
Narcotic drugs lost on the way of transportation must be traced urgently, and the local Public Security and Public Health authorities should be informed immediately.

Chapter V—The Importation and Exportation of Narcotic Drugs

Article 17
The importation and exportation of narcotic drugs should be handled solely by foreign trade agencies assigned by the Ministry of Foreign Trade and Economic Relations. Annual plan for the importation and exportation of narcotic drugs should be submitted to the Ministry of Public Health for approval.

Article 18
The importation of narcotic drugs for the purpose of medical treatment, education or scientific research should be approved by the Ministry of Public Health, no importation is permitted without a "Narcotic Drug Import Certificate".

Article 19
An import certificate issued by the competent authority of the importing country should be produced when an application for the exportation of a narcotic drug is submitted to the Ministry of Public Health, no exportation is permitted without a "Narcotic Drug Export Certificate".

Article 20
Narcotic Drug Import (or Export) Certificate is provided exclusively by the Ministry of Public Health.

Chapter VI—The Use of Narcotic Drugs

Article 21
The use of narcotic drugs is restricted to medical treatment, education and scientific research. Medical units equipped with beds, capable of performing operations or those considered to be

qualified may apply for a "Narcotic Drug Purchasing Card", the application should be submitted to the local health authority and approved by the health authority at a higher level. The holder of a "Narcotic Drug Purchasing Card" may purchase narcotic drugs at a definite handling unit, provided that the amount of narcotic drug purchased does not exceed a specified limit.

Educational and scientific research units in need of narcotic drugs should submit their application to the health authority at a higher level for approval.

The criteria for the classification of narcotic drug purchasers and the corresponding limits are stipulated by the Ministry of Public Health.

Article 22
Narcotic drugs should be purchased by sending a "Narcotic Drug Order" to the handling unit. The handling unit should check the seals and quantity carefully. The quarterly purchasing limit for various narcotic drugs is specified by the Ministry of Public Health.

Article 23
Narcotic drugs can also be purchased by mail, but orders and bills should be mailed by registered post. The delivery note should be stamped with a seal used especially for narcotic drugs. An invoice stamped with such a seal can serve as a certificate for mailing narcotic drugs.

Article 24
Preparations falling into the scope of narcotic drugs under control must be purchased at handling units specialized in narcotic drugs. Preparations not included in the scope of control or not commercially available can only be prepared by medical units with the permission of health authorities above the county level.

Article 25
Medical personnel permitted to prescribe narcotic drugs must be of a vocational rank above

"physician" and proved to be able to use narcotic drugs properly.

Medical personnel specialized in planned birth surgery and proved to be able to use narcotic drugs properly are also entitled to prescribe narcotic drugs in the course of an operation.

Article 26

In each prescription of narcotic drugs, the quantity of injection prescribed should not exceed two usual daily doses; the quantity of tablets, tincture or syrup should not exceed three usual daily doses. Narcotic drugs should not be used continuously for a period longer than seven days. Prescriptions should be written neatly and distinctly and signed by the prescriber. The dispensing should be checked carefully, both the dispenser and the person who has checked the dispensing should put down their signature. All prescriptions should be registered. Medical personnel should not prescribe narcotic drugs for themselves.

Article 27

Health authorities above the county level may issue a "Narcotic Drug Demanding Card" to a very ill patient if, according to the diagnosis, the use of narcotic drug is justifiable, the patient may then be supplied with narcotic drugs by the designated medical unit. As a result of increased consumption of narcotic drugs by patients holding "Narcotic Drug Demanding Card", the quarterly supply of narcotic drugs may be increased if it is insufficient to meet the demand by the approval of health authority at a higher level.

Article 28

Medical units should strengthen the control of narcotic drugs. Illegal use, storage, transfer or lending of narcotic drug is prohibited. Special individual should be assigned to take care of narcotic drugs, cabinets used for the storage of narcotic drugs must be locked, special accounting book, prescription paper and register book should

be used for narcotic drugs. Prescriptions of narcotic drugs should be reserved for three years.

Medical units are authorized to refuse an abuser's illegal demand of narcotic drugs, any case of abuse should be reported to the local health authority timely.

Article 29

Narcotic drugs needed in case of emergency should be supplied immediately, but the quantity is limited to one single dose, formalities can be completed afterwards.

Chapter VII—Punishment

Article 30

In case of an offence against this Act, or if one of the following conducts has been committed, all of the narcotic drug and the illicit income should be confiscated by the local health authority, and depending on how serious the case is, a fine equivalent to 5–10 times of the illicit income may be imposed, or the activities of the enterprise may be suspended until it has been consolidated, or its "Drug Manufacturer Certificate", "Drug Handler Certificate" or "Drug Dispensing Certificate" shall be revoked:

(1) Carry out the production of narcotic drugs without authorization or alter the plan of production so as to increase the variety of narcotic products;
(2) Carry out the handling of narcotic drugs and opium poppy shells without authorization;
(3) Carry out the supply of narcotic drugs to an unqualified unit or individual, or the quantity supplied exceeds the normal limit;
(4) Carry out the dispensing and sale of narcotic preparations without authorization;
(5) Carry out the importation or exportation of narcotic drugs without authorization;
(6) Arrange the clinical trial of a new narcotic drug without authorization or carry out the production of a new narcotic drug without approval.

Article 31

An administrative penalty should be imposed on the person directly responsible for the issue of an illegal prescription for other person or for oneself to gain access of narcotic drugs for abusing.

Article 32

Illicit cultivation of opium poppy and dope taking should be punished pursuant to the relevant regulation stipulated by the public security institution.

Article 33

Penal liability should be sought in case a crime is committed due to the illicit manufacture, trafficking or vending of narcotic drugs or opium poppy shells.

Article 34

Any objection to the decision of an administrative penalty should be referred, within a period of 15 days counting from the date of notification of the penalty, to the institution at a higher level than the one who has made such a decision. The institution at a higher level should respond to the appeal within a period of 10 days counting from the date of receipt of the appeal. Any objection to the response should be referred to the People's Court within a period of 15 days counting from the date of receipt of the response. In case the decision has not been enforced and the time limit for an appeal has elapsed, the People's Court shall order its compulsory execution at the request of the institution that has made such a decision.

20.
The Anti-Narcotic Drugs Law of Iran

The Parliament of Iran enacted legislation on 1 July 1989 in an attempt to eliminate the narcotics trade. The cultivation of opium poppies and the selling, transport, import, and export of narcotics were prohibited by this antinarcotics drug law. Article 33 cre-

ated a body called Headquarters, with the president as chairperson with full executive and judicial powers. The punishment for the offender was very severe. Apart from the usual fine or imprisonment, the guilty person could get thirty to seventy lashes for a second offense. For a fourth offense, the death sentence would be carried out either in public or on the premises of the offender's house.

Source
United Nations Office of Drugs and Crime, http://www.unodc.org/unodc/en/legal_library/ir/legal_library_1991-02-28_1991-3.html.

Article 1

The following acts are considered as crimes and the perpetrator shall be sentenced to the punishments prescribed hereunder.

1. Cultivating poppies, absolutely, and cannabis for the purpose of production of narcotics.
2. Importing, exporting and producing any kind of narcotics.
3. Keeping, carrying, purchasing, distributing and selling narcotic drugs.
4. Setting up or running places for the use of drugs.
5. Using drugs in any form or manner except for cases provided for by law.
6. Causing to escape or giving protection to drug offenders and perpetrators who are under prosecution or have been arrested.
7. Destroying or concealing evidence of offenders' crimes.

Article 2

Anybody who cultivates poppies or cannabis for the purpose of producing narcotic drugs shall be sentenced, in addition to his crop being destroyed, to the following punishments for each time according to the amount of his cultivation:

1. The first time, a fine in an amount up to ten million rials in cash.
2. Second time, a fine in the amount of five to fifty million rials in cash, plus 30 to 70 lashes.

3. Third time, a fine in the amount of ten to one hundred million rials in cash, plus 1 to 70 lashes together with two to five years of imprisonment.
4. Fourth time, death penalty.

Note: In the event that it is proved that cultivation of poppy or cannabis has taken place under the instruction of the landlord(s) or the tenant or their legal Deputies, the instructor who was the cause (of the crime), if he is in a higher position than the agent, shall be sentenced to the punishments prescribed in this Article, and the agent who took the charge of cultivation shall be condemned to a fine in the amount of one to three million rials in cash and fifteen to forty lashes.

Article 3

Anybody who stores, conceals, carries the seeds or capsules of poppy or flowering or fruiting top of cannabis shall be sentenced to a fine in the amount of one hundred thousand to three million rials in cash as well as to one to seventy lashes.

In the case of flowering or fruiting top of cannabis the intention of producing narcotics from them must be established.

Article 4

Anybody who smuggles in or out, produces, distributes, deals in or puts on sale bhang, Indian hemp juice, opium and opium juice or opium residue (Shireh) shall be sentenced to the following punishments, taking into account the quantity of said materials:

1. Up to 50 grams, a fine in the amount of up to five hundred thousand rials in cash, plus up to fifty lashes.
2. More than fifty grams up to five hundred grams, a fine in the amount of four million to ten million rials in cash, plus twenty to seventy four lashes and one to five years of imprisonment.
3. More than five hundred grams to five kilograms, a fine in the amount of ten to forty million rials in cash, plus fifty to seventy four lashes and three to fifteen years of imprisonment.

4. More than five kilograms, death penalty and confiscation of property, excepting the provision of the normal living costs for the family of the convicted.

Note: If it is established that the perpetrator of the crime under paragraph 4 of this Article has committed the crime for the first time and has not succeeded in distributing or selling narcotic drugs he shall be sentenced to life imprisonment plus seventy four lashes and confiscation of property, excepting the provision of the normal living cost for his family.

Article 5

Anyone who keeps, conceals, carries opium and other drugs mentioned in Article 4 shall be sentenced to the following punishments, taking into consideration the quantity of the drugs.

1. Up to fifty grams, a fine in the amount of up to two hundred rials in cash, plus up to thirty lashes.
2. More than fifty grams up to five hundred grams, a fine in the amount of three to seven million rials in cash, plus up to sixty lashes and six months to three years of imprisonment.
3. More than five hundred grams up to five kilograms, a fine in the amount of seven million to thirty million rials in cash plus forty to seventy four lashes and two to ten years of imprisonment.
4. More than five kilograms, a fine in the amount of thirty to fifty million rials in cash, plus ten to twenty five years of imprisonment, and in the event of recidivism, death penalty and confiscation of property, excepting the provision of the normal living cost for his family.

Article 6

The punishment of the perpetrator of the crimes mentioned in paragraphs 1, 2 and 3 of the Articles 4 and 5 shall be increased for the second time to one and a half of the punishments set forth in each paragraph, and for the third time to twice as much as the punishments prescribed in each paragraph and in subsequent instances two and a half, three, three and a half . . . times as much as the punishments provided for in each paragraph.

The punishment of whipping for the second time onwards shall be seventy four lashes at the maximum.

In the instances mentioned above, if as a consequence of recidivism of the crime the total of the narcotic drugs amounts to more than five kilograms, the perpetrator of the crime being a corruptor on earth, shall be sentenced to death penalty. The execution, should it be deemed appropriate, shall be carried out in the place of residence of the convicted and in public.

Article 7

In case the perpetrator of the crimes mentioned in Articles 4 and 5 is an employee of the Government, Governmental companies, or Government affiliated agencies, organizations and companies, and he is not, according to employment laws, subject to dismissal from Government services, he shall be sentenced, for the first time to six months, for the second time to one year of dismissal from Government services, and for the third time to permanent expulsion.

Article 8

Anyone who imports, produces, distributes, exports, deals in, puts on sale, keeps or stores, conceals and carries (or transports) heroin, morphine, codeine, methadone and other chemical derivatives of morphine, cocaine and also chemical extract of hashish or hashish oil, shall be sentenced to the following punishments, taking into account the amount of said drugs:

1. Up to five centigrams, a fine in the amount of two hundred up to five hundred thousand rials in cash, plus twenty to fifty lashes.
2. More than five centigrams up to one gram, a fine in the amount of one million to three million rials cash, plus thirty to seventy lashes.
3. More than one gram to four grams, a fine in the amount of four million to ten million rials in cash, plus two to five years of imprisonment, and thirty to seventy lashes.
4. More than four grams up to fifteen grams, a fine in the amount of ten to twenty million rials in cash, plus three to eight years of imprisonment, and thirty to seventy four lashes.
5. More than fifteen up to thirty grams, a fine in the amount of twenty million to thirty million rials in cash, plus ten to fifteen years of imprisonment, and thirty to seventy four lashes.
6. More than thirty grams, death penalty and confiscation of property, excepting the provision of the normal living cost for the family of the convicted.

Note 1

If it is established that the perpetrator of the crime under paragraph 6 of this Article has committed it for the first time and has not succeeded in distributing or selling the drugs the court shall sentence him to life imprisonment with seventy four lashes, and confiscation of his property, excepting the provision of the normal cost of living for his family.

Note 2

In all the above cases, if the accused is an employee of the Government or Governmental companies or Government-affiliated companies and establishments, he shall be sentenced, in addition to the punishments mentioned in this Article, to permanent dismissal from government services.

Article 9

The punishment of the perpetrator of the crimes set forth at paragraphs 1 to 5 of the Article 8 shall be for the second time one and a half of and for the third time twice as much as the punishment mentioned in each paragraph. The punishment of whipping for the second time onwards shall be seventy four lashes at the maximum.

In the fourth time if the total of the narcotics as a result of repetition reaches thirty grams, the offender is considered as corruptor on earth and shall be sentenced to death penalty.

The death sentence, if deemed appropriate, shall be carried out on the premises of his residence and in public. In case the total of the narcotics in the fourth time as a result of repetition does not reach thirty grams, the offender shall be condemned to a fine in the amount of twenty to thirty million rials in cash, with ten to fifteen years of imprisonment, plus thirty to seventy four lashes.

Article 10
Drug addicts mentioned in Article 8 who carries or keep up to one gram of such drugs shall not be condemned to the punishments set forth in Articles 8 and 9.

Article 11
The punishment of armed smuggling of narcotic drugs, subject matter of this Act, shall be death penalty, and the death sentence, if deemed appropriate, shall be carried out on the premises of the offender and in public.

Article 12
Anyone who smuggles narcotic drugs into prisons, barracks, or rehabilitation centers for addicts, he shall be sentenced, as the case may be, to the maximum punishments mentioned in Articles 4 to 9, and in case the offender is a Government employee, he shall also be condemned to permanent expulsion from Government services.

In the event that as a consequence of negligence or omission of the persons in charge, narcotic drugs are smuggled into such centers, the failing officers shall be sentenced, as the case may be, to the punishment of:

   a) Demotion;
   b) Temporary dismissal;
   c) Permanent dismissal.

Article 13
Anybody who uses his industrial, commercial service and residential units for storing, producing and residential units for storing, producing and distributing narcotic drugs or make them available to others for such purposes, and also when the proprietor's representative commits such acts on his permission or knowledge, the respective permit for and approval in principle concerning the operation of industrial units or the business license of the service and commercial unit shall be cancelled, and the unit(s) mentioned in this Article shall be confiscated in favor of the Government.

Article 14
Anybody who establishes or runs a place for the use of narcotic drugs, he shall be sentenced to a fine in cash in an amount of five hundred thousand to one million rials, plus one to four years of imprisonment together with permanent removal from Government services. The punishment for recidivism of this offense shall be two to four times as much as the first one.

Note: If the place mentioned in this Article is producing commercial or service units, in addition to the punishment provided in this Article, the approval in principle concerning and the permit for operation of the producing unit and also the business license of the service and commercial unit shall be suspended for the period of one year, and in case of recidivism of the crime the unit shall be confiscated in favor of the Government.

Article 15
As of the date of the entry into force of this Act:

   a) All drug addicts mentioned in Article 8 are required to give up addiction within six months, and the (Anti-Drug Campaign) headquarters has the duty to take action, from the same date and in accordance to its plans and with due regard to priorities, with respect to introducing such drug addicts to rehabilitation centers.
   b) All the drug addicts referred to in Article 4 whose ages are under sixty are required to give up their addiction within six months. If after expiration of the prescribed deadline they have failed to do so, the public prosecutor shall send them to rehabili-

tation centers, and such addicts shall remain in said centers until they get rid of their addiction. The implementation of this project and the respective programming shall be the duty of the head-quarters.

Article 16

After the expiry of the time limit provided in the above Article, the drug addicts referred to in the Article 8 shall be sentenced to the following punishments:

1. The first time, a fine in cash in the amount of five hundred thousand up to one million rials with four to twelve months of imprisonment.
2. The second time, a cash fine in the amount of one million to four million rials and one to three years of imprisonment. And if the offender is a Government employee, in addition to the cash fine and the imprisonment, he shall be permanently dismissed from Government offices.
3. The third time onwards, the punishment prescribed in paragraph 2 shall be two to four-fold, plus fifty lashes.

Article 17

The punishment of the drug addicts referred to in Article 4, subject of paragraph (b), Article 15, who after their treatment in rehabilitation centers resume their addiction shall be as follows:

1. The first time, a cash fine in the amount of five hundred thousand to one million rials, plus four to twelve months of imprisonment.
2. The second time, a cash fine in the amount of one million to four million rials with one to three years of imprisonment plus permanent dismissal from Government services.
3. The third time, the punishment stipulated in paragraph 2 shall be two to four-fold, plus fifty lashes.

Article 18

If it is established that a person has intentionally caused another person to be addicted to the drugs mentioned in Article 8, he shall be sentenced for the first time to five to ten years, and for the

second time to ten to twenty years of imprisonment, and in case of repetition to death penalty.

Note 1

In the event that the offender is an employee of the Government, or Government affiliated companies and organizations, he shall be at the very first time also sentenced, in addition to the punishment of imprisonment, to permanent dismissal from Government services.

Note 2

In the event that the offender causes members of his family, school, university students or the personnel of the disciplinary or Armed Forces to get addicted, he shall be sentenced for the first time to ten to twenty years of imprisonment and permanent dismissal from government services and for the second time to death penalty.

Article 19

Non-addicts who use the narcotic drugs referred to in Article 4, shall be sentenced, proportionately, to ten to seventy four lashes or a fine of five thousand to thirty seven thousand rials, and the non-addicts who use the drugs mentioned in Article B, shall be condemned to twenty to seventy four lashes or a fine of ten thousand to thirty seven thousand rials.

Article 20

Anybody who produces equipment and instrument for the use or production of narcotic drugs shall be sentenced to pay a fine of five times as much as the value of the equipment and tools or to five to twenty lashes.

Article 21

Anybody, who gives protection to or causes to escape an offender subject of this Act, who is under prosecution or cooperates in securing protection for him or in causing him to escape, shall be sentenced to one-fifth to one half of the punishment of the crime, the perpetrator of which he has caused to escape or to whom he has given protection, unless he has had no ill intention in this connection. In the case of life imprisonment and death penalty, the offender shall be sentenced to four to ten years and ten to fifteen years of imprisonment, respectively.

Note: In case the offender is a member of the disciplinary personnel, a prison guards or a member of the judiciary, in addition to the afore-mentioned punishment, he shall be subjected to permanent dismissal from Government services.

Article 22

Anybody who extends protection or causes to escape an offender under this Act, in the process of arrest or after having been arrested, or gives protection to or causes to escape an offender subject of this Act or cooperates in this, shall be sentenced to one half of the punishment of the convicted or that of the principal offender. In the case of life imprisonment and death penalty, the accused shall be condemned to ten to twenty years of imprisonment respectively.

Note 1

If the perpetrator of the offence is a member of the disciplinary or security forces or a prison guards or a member of the judiciary, he shall be sentenced to the punishment of the convicted or that of the principal offender as well as to permanent dismissal from government functions; except for the death penalty, in case the punishment shall be consisted of twenty five years of prison and permanent dismissal from Government services.

Note 2

If the perpetrator of the crimes subject of this Act, who is not yet under prosecution, escapes or is given protection, the provider of protection or the person who has caused the offender to escape shall be condemned to one tenth to one fifth of the punishment of the principal offender.

In case of life imprisonment and death penalty, the offender shall be sentenced to two to four years and four to eight years of imprisonment respectively.

Article 23

Anybody who intentionally destroys or conceals evidence of narcotic crimes shall be sentenced to one fifth to one half of the punishment of the principal offender. In case of life imprisonment the perpetrator of the crime shall be condemned to four to ten years of imprisonment, and in case of death penalty, he shall have to face eight to twenty years of imprisonment.

Article 24

Any member of village Islamic Councils has as his duty, as soon as he learns of cultivation of poppies or cannabis in the rural area, to notify the matter in writing to the alderman and the closest Gendarmerie outpost or the Islamic Revolution Committee Corps.

The heads of the outpost or of the committee are required to report, immediately and simultaneously, to their higher authorities in the country, province and state, and to be present, together with the alderman, district officer or the representative of the village Islamic Council, at the premises of the cultivation and destroy it and to draw up a process-verbal to be forwarded, along with the accused, to competent judicial authorities.

Note: If the cultivation of poppies or cannabis is discovered in urban areas, the members of the municipality, the police, the committee or the Bassij members are required, as soon as they learn of the matter, to report it to the nearest Police station, the Committee or the Bassij outpost, and the concerned authorities shall take action together with the public Prosecutor's representative, in accordance with the provisions of this Article.

Article 25

If the persons referred to in Article 24 and the Note thereto refuse or fail, without any justifiable cause, to fulfill their duties, they shall be condemned for the first time to six months to one year of expulsion from Government functions, and for the second time, to permanent dismissal from Government services. Members of Islamic Councils also shall be, for the first time, for a period of six months up to one year, and for the second time, permanently divested of their membership of the Islamic Councils.

Article 26

Whoever places, in an attempt to accuse another person, narcotic drugs and the tools and equipments of their use in a locality, shall be sentenced to the maximum punishment attaching to the same offence.

Article 27

Anybody who, in an attempt to prosecute before judicial authorities intentionally, accuses another person, of any of the offences subject of this Act, shall be sentenced to twenty to seventy four lashes.

Article 28

Any property earned through smuggling shall be confiscated by the Government.

Article 29

The fines and other funds received through the enforcement of this Act shall be imbursed into a centralized account that will be opened with the Ministry of Economic Affairs and Finance. Such funds shall be expended by approval of the Headquarters mentioned in Article 33 and the endorsement of the president.

Article 30

Any vehicle transporting narcotic drugs shall be confiscated in favor of the Government, which shall be utilized by the approval of the Headquarters referred to in Article 33 and the endorsement of the president except for cases in which the transport of drugs has been affected without the knowledge or permission of the vehicle owner.

In the event that the driver allows, with or without the knowledge and permission of the owner, making false compartment for transportation of narcotic drugs, he shall be condemned, as the case may be, to one tenth to one half of the punishment of the principal offender, and in case of life imprisonment and death penalty, he shall be sentenced, respectively, to two to ten years, and four to twenty years of imprisonment; in addition, his driving license shall be withdrawn for a period of one to ten years; and in the event that during the transportation of the drugs the driver held no driving license, he shall also be sentenced, in addition to the above-mentioned punishment of driving without a license. In case of repetition of this offence drivers shall be deprived permanently of their licenses.

Article 31

The accused who are not in a position to pay the entire or part of the cash fine under a sentence, shall have to be detained, ten days in exchange of each thousand toman, in half-covered or uncovered prisons in occupational training centers. If during their stay in such centers, the behavior of the convicted is satisfactory, at the discretion of the center's authorities such stay shall be reduced to three days in exchange of each thousand toman.

Article 32

The death sentences issued by virtue of this Act shall be final and enforceable after the endorsement of the Chairman of the Supreme Court or the Prosecutor General.

In other cases, should the sentence be deemed probable, by the Chairman of the Supreme Court or the Prosecutor General, to contravene the law or the religious canon, or that the judge who pronounced the sentence is not competent, the Chairman of the Supreme Court or the Prosecutor General will be entitled to revise or quash the sentence; however, the existence of such entitlement shall not bar the sentence from being final and enforceable.

Article 32 bis[1]

Should the chairman of the Supreme Court confirm the competence of the judges, prosecutors and the heads of the public prosecutors' offices, they shall be entitled to pronounce sentences for the crimes referred to in Articles 16 and 17.

Article 33

In order to fight against smuggling narcotic drugs, of any kind, and their production, trafficking and use, as well as other instances mentioned in the present Act, a headquarters, presided over by the president,[2] shall be established, where all the related executive and juridical operations shall be centered. The members of this headquarters shall be consisted of the followings:

1. The president, who will act as the Chairman of the Headquarters.
2. The Prosecutor General
3. The Minister of Interior.
4. The Minister of Information.
5. The Minister of Health & Medical Education.
6. The Managing Director of the Islamic Republic of Iran Broadcasting (IPIB).
7. The Commander-In-Chief of the Islamic Revolution Committee Corps.
8. The Tehran Head of the Court and the Public Prosecutor's office for Anti-Drug Campaign.
9. The Head of the Organization of Prisons and Penitentiaries.
10. The Minister of Education.[3]

Note: During the membership period of the Head of the Court and the Public Prosecutor's office for Anti-Drug Campaign in the Headquarters, he will act independently.

---

[1] Amended the "anti-narcotic Drugs law" approved in the Meeting of 1 July 1989 of the High Council of Distinguish.
[2] Amended in the Meeting of 1 July 1989 of the High Council of Distinguish in conformity with the amendments of the constitutional law.
[3] Amended in the Meeting of 1 July 1989 of the High Council of Distinguish.

Article 34

The Headquarters has the duty to have, within two months as the date of their notification, approved by the Headquarters the executive, financial, employment and by-laws as well as the organization and the job description of the Headquarters and its respective units, and to commence the enforcement of this Act.

Article 35

Once this Act entered into force, the enforcement of all the laws inconsistent therewith shall be stopped, and the Headquarters shall exclusively carry out the Anti-Drug Campaign.

Note: The proposal for the elimination of the Article 35 has been presented by the Anti-Drug Campaign Headquarters to the High Council of Distinguish.

21.

United Nations Convention against Illicit Traffic in Narcotic Drugs and Psychotropic Substances

The increase in the production and demand for narcotics poses a serious danger to the welfare and health of humankind and has become an international security concern. Drug-related money laundering has also been one of the major organized criminal activities that helps finance terrorism. The United Nations Convention against Illicit Traffic in Narcotic Drugs and Psychotropic Substances was a major step toward combating the global abuse of drugs. The member countries signed the convention in Vienna on 20 December 1988. Article 2 stipulated that the members would cooperate with each other and take necessary steps to check drug trafficking. The cultivation, production, manufacture, transport, import, and export of narcotics and psychotropic substances was criminalized. The property of the offender would be confiscated as per Article 5. The crime committed was included as an extraditable offense.

Source
United Nations Office on Drugs and Crime,
http://www.unodc.org/pdf/convention_1988_en.pdf.

Final Act of the United Nations Conference for the Adoption of a Convention against Illicit Traffic in Narcotic Drugs and Psychotropic Substances

Article 1

Definitions

Except where otherwise expressly indicated or where the context otherwise requires, the following definitions shall apply throughout this Convention:

a) "Board" means the International Narcotics Control Board established by the Single Convention on Narcotic Drugs, 1961, and that Convention as amended by the 1972 Protocol Amending the Single Convention on Narcotic Drugs, 1961;

b) "Cannabis plant" means any plant of the genus Cannabis;

c) "Coca bush" means the plant of any species of the genus Erythroxylon;

d) "Commercial carrier" means any person or any public, private or other entity engaged in transporting persons, goods or mails for remuneration, hire or any other benefit;

e) "Commission" means the Commission on Narcotic Drugs of the Economic and Social Council of the United Nations;

f) "Confiscation", which includes forfeiture where applicable, means the permanent deprivation of property by order of a court or other competent authority;

g) "Controlled delivery" means the technique of allowing illicit or suspect consignments of narcotic drugs, psychotropic substances, substances in Table I and Table II annexed to this Convention, or substances substituted for them, to pass out of, through or into the territory of one or more countries, with the knowledge and under the supervision of their competent authorities, with a view to identifying persons involved in the commission of offences established in accordance with article 3, paragraph 1 of the Convention;

h) "1961 Convention" means the Single Convention on Narcotic Drugs, 1961;

i) "1961 Convention as amended" means the Single Convention on Narcotic Drugs, 1961, as amended by the 1972 Protocol Amending the Single Convention on Narcotic Drugs, 1961;

j) "1971 Convention" means the Convention on Psychotropic Substances, 1971;

k) "Council" means the Economic and Social Council of the United Nations;

l) "Freezing" or "seizure" means temporarily prohibiting the transfer, conversion, disposition or movement of property or temporarily assuming custody or control of property on the basis of an order issued by a court or a competent authority;

m) "Illicit traffic" means the offences set forth in article 3, paragraphs 1 and 2, of this Convention;

n) "Narcotic drug" means any of the substances, natural or synthetic, in Schedules I and II of the Single Convention on Narcotic Drugs, 1961, and that Convention as amended by the 1972 Protocol Amending the Single Convention on Narcotic Drugs, 1961;

o) "Opium poppy" means the plant of the species *Papaver somniferum L;*

p) "Proceeds" means any property derived from or obtained, directly or indirectly, through the commission of an offence established in accordance with article 3, paragraph 1;

q) "Property" means assets of every kind, whether corporeal or incorporeal, movable or immovable, tangible or intangible, and legal documents or instruments evidencing title to, or interest in, such assets;

r) "Psychotropic substance" means any substance, natural or synthetic, or any natural material in Schedules I, II, III and IV of the Convention on Psychotropic Substances, 1971;

s) "Secretary-General" means the Secretary-General of the United Nations;

t) "Table I" and "Table II" mean the correspondingly numbered lists of substances annexed to this

Convention, as amended from time to time in accordance with article 12,

u) "Transit State" means a State through the territory of which illicit narcotic drugs, psychotropic substances and substances in Table I and Table II are being moved, which is neither the place of origin nor the place of ultimate destination thereof.

Article 2

Scope of the Convention

1. The purpose of this Convention is to promote co-operation among the Parties so that they may address more effectively the various aspects of illicit traffic in narcotic drugs and psychotropic substances having an international dimension. In carrying out their obligations under the Convention, the Parties shall take necessary measures, including legislative and administrative measures, in conformity with the fundamental provisions of their respective domestic legislative systems.

2. The Parties shall carry out their obligations under this Convention in a manner consistent with the principles of sovereign equality and territorial integrity of States and that of non-intervention in the domestic affairs of other States.

3. A Party shall not undertake in the territory of another Party the exercise of jurisdiction and performance of functions which are exclusively reserved for the authorities of that other Party by its domestic law.

Article 3

Offences and Sanctions

1. Each Party shall adopt such measures as may be necessary to establish as criminal offences under its domestic law, when committed intentionally:

a) i) The production, manufacture, extraction; preparation, offering, offering for sale, distribution, sale, delivery on any terms whatsoever,

brokerage, dispatch, dispatch in transit, transport, importation or exportation of any narcotic drug or any psychotropic substance contrary to the provisions of the 1961 Convention, the 1961 Convention as amended or the 1971 Convention;

ii) The cultivation of opium poppy, coca bush or cannabis plant for the purpose of the production of narcotic drugs contrary to the provisions of the 1961 Convention and the 1961 Convention as amended;

iii) The possession or purchase of any narcotic drug or psychotropic substance for the purpose of any of the activities enumerated in i) above;

iv) The manufacture, transport or distribution of equipment, materials or of substances listed in Table I and Table II, knowing that they are to be used in or for the illicit cultivation, production or manufacture of narcotic drugs or psychotropic substances;

v) The organization, management or financing of any of the offences enumerated in i), ii), iii) or iv) above;

b) i) The conversion or transfer of property, knowing that such property is derived from any offence or offences established in accordance with subparagraph a) of this paragraph, or from an act of participation in such offence or offences, for the purpose of concealing or disguising the illicit origin of the property or of assisting any person who is involved in the commission of such an offence or offences to evade the legal consequences of his actions;

ii) The concealment or disguise of the true nature, source, location, disposition, movement, rights with respect to, or ownership of property, knowing that such property is derived from an offence or offences established in accordance with subparagraph a) of this paragraph or from an act of participation in such an offence or offences;

c) Subject to its constitutional principles and the basic concepts of its legal system:

i) The acquisition, possession or use of property, knowing, at the time of receipt, that such property was derived from an offence or offences established in accordance with subparagraph a) of this paragraph or from an act of participation in such offence or offences;

ii) The possession of equipment or materials or substances listed in Table I and Table II, knowing that they are being or are to be used in or for the illicit cultivation, production or

iii) Publicly inciting or inducing others, by any means, to commit any of the offences established in accordance with this article or to use narcotic drugs or psychotropic substances illicitly;

iv) Participation in, association or conspiracy to commit, attempts to commit and aiding, abetting, facilitating and counselling the commission of any of the offences established in accordance with this article.

2. Subject to its constitutional principles and the basic concepts of its legal system, each Party shall adopt such measures as may be necessary to establish as a criminal offence under its domestic law, when committed intentionally, the possession, purchase or cultivation of narcotic drugs or psychotropic substances for personal consumption contrary to the provisions of the 1961 Convention, the 1961 Convention as amended or the 1971 Convention.

3. Knowledge, intent or purpose required as an element of an offence set forth in paragraph 1 of this article may be inferred from objective factual circumstances.

4. a) Each Party shall make the commission of the offences established in accordance with paragraph 1 of this article liable to sanctions which take into account the grave nature of these offences, such as imprisonment or other forms of deprivation of liberty, pecuniary sanctions and confiscation.

b) The Parties may provide, in addition to conviction or punishment, for an offence established in accordance with paragraph 1 of this article, that the offender shall undergo measures such as treatment, education, aftercare, rehabilitation or social reintegration.

c) Notwithstanding the preceding subparagraphs, in appropriate cases of a minor nature, the Parties may provide, as alternatives to conviction or punishment, measures such as education, rehabilitation or social reintegration, as well as, when the offender is a drug abuser, treatment and aftercare.

d) The Parties may provide, either as an alternative to conviction or punishment, or in addition to conviction or punishment of an offence established in accordance with paragraph 2 of this article, measures for the treatment, education, aftercare, rehabilitation or social reintegration of the offender.

5. The Parties shall ensure that their courts and other competent authorities having jurisdiction can take into account factual circumstances which make the commission of the offences established in accordance with paragraph 1 of this article particularly serious, such as:

a) The involvement in the offence of an organized criminal group to which the offender belongs;

b) The involvement of the offender in other international organized criminal activities;

c) The involvement of the offender in other illegal activities facilitated by commission of the offence;

d) The use of violence or arms by the offender;

e) The fact that the offender holds a public office and that the offence is connected with the office in question;

f) The victimization or use of minors;

g) The fact that the offence is committed in a penal institution or in an educational institution or social service facility or in their immediate vicinity or in other places to which school children and students resort for educational, sports and social activities;

h) Prior conviction, particularly for similar offences, whether foreign or domestic, to the extent permitted under the domestic law of a Party.

6. The Parties shall endeavour to ensure that any discretionary legal powers under their domestic law relating to the prosecution of persons for

offences established in accordance with this article are exercised to maximize the effectiveness of law enforcement measures in respect of those offences, and with due regard to the need to deter the commission of such offences.

7. The Parties shall ensure that their courts or other competent authorities bear in mind the serious nature of the offences enumerated in paragraph 1 of this article and the circumstances enumerated in paragraph 5 of this article when considering the eventuality of early release or parole of persons convicted of such offences.

8. Each Party shall, where appropriate, establish under its domestic law a long statute of limitations period in which to commence proceedings for any offence established in accordance with paragraph 1 of this article, and a longer period where the alleged offender has evaded the administration of justice.

9. Each Party shall take appropriate measures, consistent with its legal system, to ensure that a person charged with or convicted of an offence established in accordance with paragraph 1 of this article, who is found within its territory, is present at the necessary criminal proceedings.

10. For the purpose of co-operation among the Parties under this Convention, including, in particular, co-operation under articles 5, 6, 7 and 9, offences established in accordance with this article shall not be considered as fiscal offences or as political offences or regarded as politically motivated, without prejudice to the constitutional limitations and the fundamental domestic law of the Parties.

11. Nothing contained in this article shall affect the principle that the description of the offences to which it refers and of legal defences thereto is reserved to the domestic law of a Party and that such offences shall be prosecuted and punished in conformity with that law.

Article 4

Jurisdiction

1. Each Party:

    a) Shall take such measures as may be necessary to establish its jurisdiction over the offences it has established in accordance with article 3, paragraph 1, when:

       i) The offence is committed in its territory;

      ii) The offence is committed on board a vessel flying its flag or an aircraft which is registered under its laws at the time the offence is committed;

    b) May take such measures as may be necessary to establish its jurisdiction over the offences it has established in accordance with article 3, paragraph 1, when:

       i) The offence is committed by one of its nationals or by a person who has his habitual residence in its territory;

      ii) The offence is committed on board a vessel concerning which that Party has been authorized to take appropriate action pursuant to article 17, provided that such jurisdiction shall be exercised only on the basis of agreements or arrangements referred to in paragraphs 4 and 9 of that article;

      iii) The offence is one of those established in accordance with article 3, paragraph 1, subparagraph c) iv), and is committed outside its territory with a view to the commission, within its territory, of an offence established in accordance with article 3, paragraph 1.

2. Each Party:

    a) Shall also take such measures as may be necessary to establish its jurisdiction over the offences it has established in accordance with article 3, paragraph 1, when the alleged offender is present in its territory and it does not extradite him to another Party on the ground:

       i) That the offence has been committed in its territory or on board a vessel flying its flag or an aircraft which was registered under its law at the time the offence was committed; or

ii) That the offence has been committed by one of its nationals;

b) May also take such measures as may be necessary to establish its jurisdiction over the offences it has established in accordance with article 3, paragraph 1, when the alleged offender is present in its territory and it does not extradite him to another Party.

3. This Convention does not exclude the exercise of any criminal jurisdiction established by a Party in accordance with its domestic law.

[. . .]

Article 12

Substances Frequently Used in the Illicit Manufacture of Narcotic Drugs or Psychotropic Substances
1. The Parties shall take the measures they deem appropriate to prevent diversion of substances in Table I and Table II used for the purpose of illicit manufacture of narcotic drugs or psychotropic substances, and shall co-operate with one another to this end.

2. If a Party or the Board has information which in its opinion may require the inclusion of a substance in Table I or Table II, it shall notify the Secretary-General and furnish him with the information in support of that notification. The procedure described in paragraphs 2 to 7 of this article shall also apply when a Party or the Board has information justifying the deletion of a substance from Table I or Table II, or the transfer of a substance from one Table to the other.

3. The Secretary-General shall transmit such notification, and any information which he considers relevant, to the Parties, to the Commission, and, where notification is made by a Party, to the Board. The Parties shall communicate their comments concerning the notification to the Secretary-General, together with all supplementary information which may assist the Board in establishing an assessment and the Commission in reaching a decision.

4. If the Board, taking into account the extent, importance and diversity of the licit use of the substance, and the possibility and ease of using alternate substances both for licit purposes and for the illicit manufacture of narcotic drugs or psychotropic substances, finds:

a) That the substance is frequently used in the illicit manufacture of a narcotic drug or psychotropic substance;

b) That the volume and extent of the illicit manufacture of a narcotic drug or psychotropic substance creates serious public health or social problems, so as to warrant international action, it shall communicate to the Commission an assessment of the substance, including the likely effect of adding the substance to either Table I or Table II on both licit use and illicit manufacture, together with recommendations of monitoring measures, if any, that would be appropriate in the light of its assessment.

5. The Commission, taking into account the comments submitted by the Parties and the comments and recommendations of the Board, whose assessment shall be determinative as to scientific matters, and also taking into due consideration any other relevant factors, may decide by a two-thirds majority of its members to place a substance in Table I or Table II.

6. Any decision of the Commission taken pursuant to this article shall be communicated by the Secretary-General to all States and other entities which are, or which are entitled to become, Parties to this Convention, and to the Board. Such decision shall become fully effective with respect to each Party one hundred and eighty days after the date of such communication.

7. a) The decisions of the Commission taken under this article shall be subject to review by the Council

upon the request of any Party filed within one hundred and eighty days after the date of notification of the decision. The request for review shall be sent to the Secretary-General, together with all relevant information upon which the request for review is based.

b) The Secretary-General shall transmit copies of the request for review and the relevant information to the Commission, to the Board and to all the Parties, inviting them to submit their comments within ninety days. All comments received shall be submitted to the Council for consideration.

c) The Council may confirm or reverse the decision of the Commission. Notification of the Council's decision shall be transmitted to all States and other entities which are, or which are entitled to become, Parties to this Convention, to the Commission and to the Board.

8. a) Without prejudice to the generality of the provisions contained in paragraph 1 of this article and the provisions of the 1961 Convention, the 1961 Convention as amended and the 1971 Convention, the Parties shall take the measures they deem appropriate to monitor the manufacture and distribution of substances in Table I and Table II which are carried out within their territory.

b) To this end, the Parties may:

i) Control all persons and enterprises engaged in the manufacture and distribution of such substances;

ii) Control under licence the establishment and premises in which such manufacture or distribution may take place;

ii) Require that licensees obtain a permit for conducting the aforesaid operations;

iv) Prevent the accumulation of such substances in the possession of manufacturers and distributors, in excess of the quantities required for the normal conduct of business and the prevailing market conditions.

9. Each Party shall, with respect to substances in Table I and Table II, take the following measures:

a) Establish and maintain a system to monitor international trade in substances in Table I and Table II in order to facilitate the identification of suspicious transactions. Such monitoring systems shall be applied in close co-operation with manufacturers, importers, exporters, wholesalers and retailers, who shall inform the competent authorities of suspicious orders and transactions.

b) Provide for the seizure of any substance in Table I or Table II if there is sufficient evidence that it is for use in the illicit manufacture of a narcotic drug or psychotropic substance.

c) Notify, as soon as possible, the competent authorities and services of the Parties concerned if there is reason to believe that the import, export or transit of a substance in Table I or Table II is destined for the illicit manufacture of narcotic drugs or psychotropic substances, including in particular information about the means of payment and any other essential elements which led to that belief.

d) Require that imports and exports be properly labelled and documented. Commercial documents such as invoices, cargo manifests, customs, transport and other shipping documents shall include the names, as stated in Table I or Table II, of the substances being imported or exported, the quantity being imported or exported, and the name and address of the exporter, the importer and, when available, the consignee.

e) Ensure that documents referred to in subparagraph d) of this paragraph are maintained for a period of not less than two years and may be made available for inspection by the competent authorities.

10. a) In addition to the provisions of paragraph 9, and upon request to the Secretary-General by the interested Party, each Party from whose territory a substance in Table I is to be exported shall ensure that, prior to such export, the following information is supplied by its competent authorities to the competent authorities of the importing country:

i) Name and address of the exporter and importer and, when available, the consignee;

ii) Name of the substance in Table I;

iii) Quantity of the substance to be exported;

iv) Expected point of entry and expected date of dispatch;

v) Any other information which is mutually agreed upon by the Parties.

b) A Party may adopt more strict or severe measures of control than those provided by this paragraph if, in its opinion, such measures are desirable or necessary.

11. Where a Party furnishes information to another Party in accordance with paragraphs 9 and 10 of this article, the Party furnishing such information may require that the Party receiving it keep confidential any trade, business, commercial or professional secret or trade process.

12. Each Party shall furnish annually to the Board, in the form and manner provided for by it and on forms made available by it, information on:

a) The amounts seized of substances in Table I and Table II and, when known, their origin;

b) Any substance not included in Table I or Table II which is identified as having been used in illicit manufacture of narcotic drugs or psychotropic substances, and which is deemed by the Party to be sufficiently significant to be brought to the attention of the Board;

c) Methods of diversion and illicit manufacture.

13. The Board shall report annually to the Commission on the implementation of this article and the Commission shall periodically review the adequacy and propriety of Table I and Table II.

14. The provisions of this article shall not apply to pharmaceutical preparations, nor to other preparations containing substances in Table I or Table II that are compounded in such a way that such substances cannot be easily used or recovered by readily applicable means.

Article 13

Materials and Equipment
The Parties shall take such measures as they deem appropriate to prevent trade in and the diversion of materials and equipment for illicit production or manufacture of narcotic drugs and psychotropic substances and shall co-operate to this end.

Article 14

Measures to Eradicate Illicit Cultivation of Narcotic Plants and to Eliminate Illicit Demand for Narcotic Drugs and Psychotropic Substances
1. Any measures taken pursuant to this Convention by Parties shall not be less stringent than the provisions applicable to the eradication of illicit cultivation of plants containing narcotic and psychotropic substances and to the elimination of illicit demand for narcotic drugs and psychotropic substances under the provisions of the 1961 Convention, the 1961 Convention as amended and the 1971 Convention.

2. Each Party shall take appropriate measures to prevent illicit cultivation of and to eradicate plants containing narcotic or psychotropic substances, such as opium poppy, coca bush and cannabis plants, cultivated illicitly in its territory. The measures adopted shall respect fundamental human rights and shall take due account of traditional licit uses, where there is historic evidence of such use, as well as the protection of the environment.

3. a) The Parties may co-operate to increase the effectiveness of eradication efforts. Such co-operation may, *inter alia,* include support, when appropriate, for integrated rural development leading to economically viable alternatives to illicit cultivation. Factors such as access to markets, the availability of resources and prevailing socio-economic conditions should be taken into account before such rural development programmes are

implemented. The Parties may agree on any other appropriate measures of co-operation.

b) The Parties shall also facilitate the exchange of scientific and technical information and the conduct of research concerning eradication.

c) Whenever they have common frontiers, the Parties shall seek to co-operate in eradication programmes in their respective areas along those frontiers.

4. The Parties shall adopt appropriate measures aimed at eliminating or reducing illicit demand for narcotic drugs and psychotropic substances, with a view to reducing human suffering and eliminating financial incentives for illicit traffic. These measures may be based, *inter alia*, on the recommendations of the United Nations, specialized agencies of the United Nations such as the World Health Organization, and other competent international organizations, and on the Comprehensive Multidisciplinary Outline adopted by the International Conference on Drug Abuse and Illicit Trafficking, held in 1987, as it pertains to governmental and non-governmental agencies and private efforts in the fields of prevention, treatment and rehabilitation. The Parties may enter into bilateral or multilateral agreements or arrangements aimed at eliminating or reducing illicit demand for narcotic drugs and psychotropic substances.

5. The Parties may also take necessary measures for early destruction or lawful disposal of the narcotic drugs, psychotropic substances and substances in Table I and Table II which have been seized or confiscated and for the admissibility as evidence of duly certified necessary quantities of such substances.

22.
ASEAN Plan of Action to Combat Transnational Crime

The ASEAN Plan of Action to Combat Transnational Crime calls for expanded efforts to fight many types of organized criminal activity, including "terrorism, drug trafficking, arms smuggling, money laundering, trafficking in persons and piracy." It calls for regional mutual cooperation in information exchange and in the area of law enforcement and training to enhance the capabilities of member states to more effectively combat criminal and terrorist activities.

Source
Association of Southeast Asian Nations,
http://www.aseansec.org/16134.htm.

A. Background

(a) The Mandate for ASEAN Cooperation in Combating Transnational Crime
One of the fundamental principles of the Association of Southeast Asian Nations (ASEAN) as enshrined in the Bangkok Declaration of 8 August 1967 was "strengthening the foundation for a prosperous and peaceful community of Southeast Asian Nations." ASEAN policies, plans, strategies and activities revolve around this principle. Transnational crime has the potential of eroding this central belief thereby affecting the political, economic and social well being of ASEAN. In recognizing the detrimental effects of transnational crime, ASEAN countries have taken concerted efforts to combat such crime since early 1970s.

ASEAN's initial efforts in combating transnational crime were focused on drug abuse and drug trafficking, the prevalent crime then, which affected the growth and vitality of ASEAN. With globalization, technological advancement and greater mobility of people and resources across national borders, transnational crime has become increasingly pervasive, diversified and organized. The region has to deal with many new forms of organized crimes that transcend national borders and political sovereignty such as terrorism, new types of drug abuse and trafficking, innovative forms of money laundering activities, arms smuggling, trafficking in women and children and piracy.

The resolve of ASEAN's Leaders in fighting illicit drugs, the prevalent transnational crime then, can be traced to the Declaration of ASEAN Concord of 24 February 1976. The ASEAN Leaders, in that landmark document, called for the "intensification of cooperation among member states as well as with the relevant international bodies in the prevention and eradication of the abuse of narcotics and the illegal trafficking of drugs."

Since then, all the ASEAN Summits have expressed concerns on narcotics abuse and illegal drug trafficking in the region. At the Fifth ASEAN Summit in December 1995 in Bangkok, the Leaders decided that "ASEAN shall further enhance cooperative efforts against drug abuse and illicit trafficking with special emphasis being given to demand reduction programs and information exchange and dissemination, with the aim of creating a drug-free ASEAN."

With transnational crime expanding in scope and becoming more organized, ASEAN's Leaders have called for a comprehensive and coordinated approach in combating crime at the regional level. At the First Informal Summit in November 1996, the ASEAN Leaders called upon the "relevant ASEAN bodies to study the possibility of regional cooperation on criminal matters, including extradition." At the Second Informal Summit in December 1997, they "resolved to take firm and stern measures to combat transnational crimes such as drug trafficking, trafficking in women and children as well as other transnational crime." The ASEAN Leaders also adopted the ASEAN Vision 2020 at the Second Informal Summit which, among others, envisioned the evolution of agreed rules of behavior and cooperative measures to deal with problems that can be met only on a regional scale, including drug trafficking, trafficking in women and children and other transnational crimes.

The ASEAN Foreign Ministers have also called for closer cooperation and coordinated actions on tackling transnational crime among ASEAN countries. At the 29th ASEAN Ministerial Meeting (AMM) in Jakarta in July 1996, the Foreign Ministers recognized the need to focus attention on such crimes as narcotics trafficking, economic crimes, including money laundering, environmental crimes and illegal migration. They "share(d) the view that the management of such transnational issues are urgently called for so that they would not affect the long-term viability of ASEAN and its individual member nations." At the 30th AMM in Subang Jaya in July 1997, the Foreign Ministers "stressed the need for sustained cooperation in addressing transnational concerns including the fight against terrorism, trafficking of people, illicit drugs and arms, piracy and communicable diseases." The Foreign Ministers, at the 31st AMM in Manila in July 1998 reiterated the need for enhancing regional efforts against transnational crimes, such as illicit drug trafficking, terrorism, money laundering, and trafficking in women and children. At the meeting, the Ministers also signed the Joint Declaration for a Drug-Free ASEAN to eradicate the production, processing, traffic and use of illicit drugs in Southeast Asia by the year 2020.

The ASEAN Finance Ministers echoed the sentiments of the ASEAN Leaders and the ASEAN Foreign Ministers on illicit drug trafficking when they signed the ASEAN Agreement on Customs at their inaugural meeting on 1 March 1997 in Phuket. The agreement, which apart from enhancing ASEAN cooperation in customs activities and expediting the early realization of AFTA, aims to strengthen cooperation in combating trafficking in narcotics and psychotropic substances, and will facilitate joint efforts in anti-smuggling and customs control.

(b) Other Significant Developments
Recognizing the urgency to tackle transnational crime from the regional dimension, the Philippines hosted the inaugural Meeting of the ASEAN Ministers of Interior/Home Affairs on Transnational Crime on 20 December 1997 in Manila. Apart from presenting an opportunity for the Interior and Home Ministers to exchange views on the transnational crime situation in ASEAN, the meeting also reflected on the detrimental impact of such on the Member Countries and the need for enhanced regional cooperation in fighting the crime. The highlight of the meeting was the signing of the ASEAN Declaration on Transnational Crime by the Ministers. The document reflected ASEAN's resolve in dealing with transnational crime and its intention to work together with the international community in combating transnational crime.

The Declaration also established the basic framework for regional cooperation on fighting transnational crime. Accordingly, the ASEAN Ministers Meeting on Transnational Crime was to convene once every two years to coordinate activities of relevant bodies such as the ASEAN Senior Officials on Drug Matters (ASOD) and the ASEAN Chiefs of National Police (ASEANAPOL). The Senior Officials Meeting Transnational Crime was to meet at least once in a year to assist the Ministers in accomplishing their task. The Declaration also outlined the following initiatives for regional cooperation on tackling transnational crime:

1. Hold discussions with a view to signing mutual legal assistance agreements, bilateral treaties, memorandum of understanding or other arrangements among Member Countries;
2. Consider the establishment of an ASEAN Centre on Combating Transnational Crime (ACTC), which will coordinate regional efforts against

transnational crime through intelligence sharing, harmonization of policies and coordination of operations;
3. Convene a high-level ad-hoc Experts Group within one year to accomplish the following with the assistance of the ASEAN Secretariat:
   a. ASEAN Plan of Action on Transnational Crime,
   b. Institutional Framework for ASEAN Cooperation on Transnational Crime; and,
   c. Feasibility study on the establishment of ACTC
4. Encourage Member Countries to consider assigning Police Attaches and/or Police Liaison Officers in each other's capital in order to facilitate cooperation for tackling transnational crime;
5. Encourage networking of the relevant national agencies or organizations in Member Countries dealing with transnational crime to further enhance information exchange and dissemination;
6. Expand the scope of Member Countries' efforts against transnational crime such as terrorism, illicit drug trafficking, arms smuggling, money laundering, traffic in person and piracy, and to request the ASEAN Secretary General to include these areas in the work programme of the ASEAN Secretariat.
7. Explore ways by which the Member Countries can work closer with relevant agencies and organizations in Dialogue Partner countries, other countries and international organizations, including the United Nations and its specialized agencies, Colombo Plan Bureau, INTERPOL and such other agencies, to combat transnational crime;
8. Cooperate and coordinate more closely with other ASEAN bodies such as the ASEAN Law Ministers and Attorneys-General, the ASEAN Chiefs of National Police, the ASEAN Finance Ministers, the Directors-General of Immigration and the Directors-General of Customs in the investigations, prosecution and rehabilitation of perpetrators of such crimes.

The ASEAN Member Countries also participated in the first Asian Regional Ministerial Meeting on Transnational Crime held on 23–25 March 1998 in Manila. The meeting was a follow-up to the Naples Political Declaration and Global Plan of Action

Against Transnational Crime adopted at the World Ministerial Conference on Organized Transnational Crime held in Italy in November 1994.

The meeting culminated with the adoption of a Manila Declaration on the Prevention and Control of Transnational Crime. The declaration reflects the concerns of the participating countries, including ASEAN, on the increase and expansion of transnational crimes and outlines the approaches to be undertaken, both at the national and regional levels, in fighting transnational crime.

B. Objectives

(a) General Objectives
The general objective of the Action Plan is to encourage ASEAN Member Countries to expand their efforts in combating transnational crime at the national and bilateral levels to the regional level. As espoused in the ASEAN Declaration on Transnational Crime, the overall focus of ASEAN collaboration will be to strengthen regional commitment and capacity to combat transnational crimes which include terrorism, drug trafficking, arms smuggling, money laundering, trafficking in persons and piracy. This is in recognition of the fact that tackling transnational crime requires a concerted regional effort in view of its global dimension and pervasive nature. Besides, such efforts will assist in complementing and contributing to the national and bilateral efforts undertaken by Member Countries in combating such crime.

(b) Specific Objectives
The specific objectives of the Plan of Action are to urge the ASEAN Member Countries to:

1. Develop a more cohesive, regional strategy aimed at preventing, controlling and neutralizing transnational crime;

2. Foster regional cooperation at the investigative, prosecutorial, and judicial level as well as the rehabilitation of perpetrators;
3. Enhance coordination among ASEAN bodies dealing with transnational crime;
4. Strengthen regional capacities and capabilities to deal with sophisticated nature of transnational crime; and
5. Develop sub-regional and regional treaties on cooperation in criminal justice, including mutual legal assistance and extradition.

C. Programme of Action/Priorities

In order to achieve the general and specific objectives, ASEAN Member Countries are encouraged to:

Information Exchange

1. Improve the ASEANAPOL regional database so as to further facilitate sharing and analysis of critical intelligence information, such as wanted and arrested persons, "modus operandi", syndicates, and maritime offences;

2. Establish a regional repository to compile summaries of national laws of ASEAN Member Countries pertaining to transnational crime;

3. Conduct typology studies to determine trends and "modus operandi" of transnational crime in the ASEAN region;

4. Maximize the use of modern telecommunications technology in facilitating the exchange of data on, among others, criminals, methodologies, arrests, legal documents, requests for assistance, and ensure its restricted transmission;

5. Identify relevant contact persons in the policy, legal, law enforcement, and academic institutions of ASEAN Member Countries, and facilitate networking and lateral coordination among persons and agencies with similar functions;

Legal Matters

6. Work for the criminalization in ASEAN Member Countries of specific transnational crimes, such as illicit drug trafficking, money laundering, terrorism, piracy, arms smuggling and trafficking in persons;

7. Ensure the harmonization of relevant national policies among ASEAN Member Countries;

8. Develop multilateral or bilateral legal arrangements to facilitate apprehension, investigation, prosecution, and extradition, exchange of witnesses, sharing of evidence, inquiry, seizure and forfeiture of the proceeds of the crime in order to enhance mutual legal and administrative assistance among ASEAN Member Countries;

9. Study the possibility of creating a regional programme on witness protection;

10. Coordinate with the ASEAN Senior Law Officials Meeting on the implementation of the ASEAN Legal Information Network System:

11. Strengthen the mechanisms for effective protection of the integrity of travel documents and government control of the ingress/egress of transnational criminal personalities;

12. Seek to ratify and support existing international treaties or agreements designed to combat transnational crime.

Law Enforcement Matters

13. Appoint Police Attaché or Police Liaison Officers, whenever feasible, in the capitals of ASEAN Member Countries;

14. Develop programmes for joint tactical exercises and simulations;

15. Develop an exchange programme among ASEAN officials in the policy, legal, law enforcement and academic fields;

16. Implement measures to ensure the protection of judges, prosecutors, witnesses, and law enforcement officials and personnel from retaliation by transnational criminal organizations;

17. Enhance cooperation and coordination in law enforcement, intelligence sharing, and in preventing the illegal trafficking and use of explosives, firearms, and other deadly weapons, as well as nuclear, chemical and biological materials.

Training

18. Develop regional training programmes, and conduct regular conferences to enhance existing capabilities in investigation, intelligence, surveillance, detection and monitoring, and reporting.

19. Exchange "best practices" of relevant institutions in ASEAN Member Countries involved in the combat against transnational crime, including transfer of technologies.

Institutional Capacity-Building

20. Establish the ASEAN Centre for Combating Transnational Crime (ACTC).

21. Rationalize the institutional framework on ASEAN cooperation in transnational crime by making the ASEAN Ministerial Meeting on Transnational Crime the highest policy-making body, with a supervisory role and consultative relations with relevant ASEAN institutions involved in the combat against transnational crime;

22. Promote the efficient networking of relevant national agencies/organizations in ASEAN Member Countries by creating inter-agency committees/task forces to enhance information exchange and dissemination;

23. Strengthen institutional linkages with the various ASEAN mechanisms involved in combating transnational crime particularly the ASEAN Finance Ministers Meeting, ASEAN Finance Officials Meeting, ASEAN Senior Officials on Drug Matters, ASEAN Directors General of Customs, ASEAN Directors General for Immigration and ASEAN Chiefs of National Police.

Extra-Regional Cooperation

24. Seek technical assistance from ASEAN Dialogue Partners and relevant specialized agencies of the United Nations and other international organizations, particularly with regard to training and acquisition of equipment.

25. Enhance information exchange with ASEAN Dialogue Partner, regional organizations, relevant specialized agencies of the United Nations and other international organizations, particularly towards the sharing of critical information on the identities, movements and activities of known transnational criminal organizations.

26. Urge ASEAN Dialogue Partners not yet party to existing international treaties against organized transnational crime, in its various forms, to accede to such agreements.

27. Promote interest and support in the international community for ASEAN initiatives against transnational crime through the participation of ASEAN Member Countries and the ASEAN Secretariat in relevant international conferences.

[. . .]

23.
Australia Criminal Code Act 1995

The Australia Criminal Code Act 1995 is a comprehensive 613-page legal instrument. Cited below are two divisions (73 and 360) that comprise a portion of this document. Division 73 addresses people smuggling when one victim is abducted and smuggled into a foreign country and when groups of five or more victims are involved. This division also addresses the falsification of travel or identity documents that helps facilitate the crime of people smuggling. The possession and/or destruction of a person's identification documents is also covered in this section. Division 360 deals with cross-border firearms trafficking and covers both the "disposal and acquisition of a firearm."

Source
Commonwealth of Australia Law, http://www.comlaw.gov.au/ComLaw/Legislation/ActCompilation1.nsf/0/D72BB78BACF1888DCA25719C0008E93A/$file/CriminalCode1995_WD02_Version4.doc.

Act No. 12 of 1995 as amended

This compilation was prepared on 27 June 2006

taking into account amendments up to Act No. 54 of 2006

Division 73—People Smuggling and Related Offences

Subdivision A—People Smuggling Offences

73.1—Offence of People Smuggling
(1) A person (the *first person*) is guilty of an offence if:

(a) the first person organises or facilitates the entry of another person (the *other person*) into a foreign country (whether or not via Australia); and
(b) the entry of the other person into the foreign country does not comply with the requirements under that country's law for entry into the country; and

(c) the other person is not a citizen or permanent resident of the foreign country; and

(d) the first person organises or facilitates the entry:
   (i) having obtained (whether directly or indirectly) a benefit to do so; or
   (ii) with the intention of obtaining (whether directly or indirectly) a benefit.
   Penalty: Imprisonment for 10 years or 1,000 penalty units, or both.

(2) Absolute liability applies to the paragraph (1)(c) element of the offence.

(3) For the purposes of this Code, an offence against subsection (1) is to be known as the offence of people smuggling.

73.2—Aggravated Offence of People Smuggling (Exploitation Etc.)

(1) A person (the *first person*) is guilty of an offence if the first person commits the offence of people smuggling in relation to another person (the *victim*) and any of the following applies:

(a) the first person commits the offence intending that the victim will be exploited after entry into the foreign country (whether by the first person or another);

(b) in committing the offence, the first person subjects the victim to cruel, inhuman or degrading treatment;

(c) in committing the offence, the first person's conduct:
   (i) gives rise to a danger of death or serious harm to the victim; and
   (ii) the first person is reckless as to the danger of death or serious harm to the victim that arises from the conduct.
   Penalty: Imprisonment for 20 years or 2,000 penalty units, or both.

(3) In this section:

forced labour means the condition of a person who provides labour or services (other than sexual services) and who, because of the use of force or threats:

(a) is not free to cease providing labour or services; or

(b) is not free to leave the place or area where the person provides labour or services.

sexual servitude has the same meaning as in Division 270.

slavery has the same meaning as in Division 270.

threat means:

(a) a threat of force; or

(b) a threat to cause a person's deportation; or

(c) a threat of any other detrimental action unless there are reasonable grounds for the threat of that action in connection with the provision of labour or services by a person.

73.3—Aggravated offence of people smuggling (at least 5 people)

(1) A person (the *first person*) is guilty of an offence if:

(a) the first person organises or facilitates the entry of a group of at least 5 persons (the *other persons*) into a foreign country (whether or not via Australia); and

(b) the entry of at least 5 of the other persons into the foreign country does not comply with the requirements under that country's law for entry into that country; and

(c) at least 5 of the other persons whose entry into the foreign country is covered by paragraph (b) are not citizens or permanent residents of the foreign country; and

(d) the first person organises or facilitates the entry:
   (i) having obtained (whether directly or indirectly) a benefit to do so; or
   (ii) with the intention of obtaining (whether directly or indirectly) a benefit.
   Penalty: Imprisonment for 20 years or 2,000 penalty units, or both.

(2) Absolute liability applies to the paragraph (1)(c) element of the offence.

(3) If, on a trial for an offence against subsection (1), the trier of fact is not satisfied that the defendant is guilty of that offence, but is satisfied beyond reasonable doubt that the defendant is guilty of an offence against subsection 73.1(1), the trier of fact may find the defendant not guilty of an offence against subsection (1) but guilty of an offence against subsection 73.1(1), so long as the defendant has been accorded procedural fairness in relation to that finding of guilt.

73.4—*Jurisdictional Requirement*
A person commits an offence against this Subdivision only if:

(a) both:
    (i) the person is an Australian citizen or a resident of Australia; and
    (ii) the conduct constituting the alleged offence occurs wholly outside Australia; or
(b) both:
    (i) the conduct constituting the alleged offence occurs wholly or partly in Australia; and
    (ii) a result of the conduct occurs, or is intended by the person to occur, outside Australia.

73.5—*Attorney-General's Consent Required*
(1) Proceedings for an offence against this Subdivision must not be commenced without the Attorney-General's written consent.

(2) However, a person may be arrested, charged, remanded in custody or released on bail in connection with an offence against this Subdivision before the necessary consent has been given.

Subdivision B—Document Offences Related to People Smuggling and Unlawful Entry into Foreign Countries

73.6—*Meaning of Travel or Identity Document*
(1) For the purposes of this Subdivision, a document is a *travel or identity document* if it is:
    (a) a travel document; or
    (b) an identity document.

73.7—*Meaning of False Travel or Identity Document*
(1) For the purposes of this Subdivision, a travel or identity document is a *false travel or identity document* if, and only if:

(a) the document, or any part of the document:
    (i) purports to have been made in the form in which it is made by a person who did not make it in that form; or
    (ii) purports to have been made in the form in which it is made on the authority of a person who did not authorise its making in that form; or
(b) the document, or any part of the document:
    (i) purports to have been made in the terms in which it is made by a person who did not make it in those terms; or
    (ii) purports to have been made in the terms in which it is made on the authority of a person who did not authorise its making in those terms; or
(c) the document, or any part of the document:
    (i) purports to have been altered in any respect by a person who did not alter it in that respect; or
    (ii) purports to have been altered in any respect on the authority of a person who did not authorise its alteration in that respect; or
(d) the document, or any part of the document:
    (i) purports to have been made or altered by a person who did not exist; or
    (ii) purports to have been made or altered on the authority of a person who did not exist; or
(e) the document, or any part of the document, purports to have been made or altered on a date on

which, at a time at which, at a place at which, or otherwise in circumstances in which, it was not made or altered.

(2) For the purposes of this Subdivision, a person is taken to *make* a false travel or identity document if the person alters a document so as to make it a false travel or identity document (whether or not it was already a false travel or identity document before the alteration).

(3) This section has effect as if a document that purports to be a true copy of another document were the original document.

73.8—*Making, Providing or Possessing a False Travel or Identity Document*

A person (the *first person*) is guilty of an offence if:

(a) the first person makes, provides or possesses a false travel or identity document; and

(b) the first person intends that the document will be used to facilitate the entry of another person (the *other person*) into a foreign country, where the entry of the other person into the foreign country would not comply with the requirements under that country's law for entry into the country; and

(c) the first person made, provided or possessed the document:

(i) having obtained (whether directly or indirectly) a benefit to do so; or

(ii) with the intention of obtaining (whether directly or indirectly) a benefit.

Penalty: Imprisonment for 10 years or 1,000 penalty units, or both.

73.9—*Providing or Possessing a Travel or Identity Document Issued or Altered Dishonestly or As a Result of Threats*

(1) A person (the *first person*) is guilty of an offence if:

(a) the first person provides or possesses a travel or identity document; and

(b) the first person knows that:

(i) the issue of the travel or identity document; or

(ii) an alteration of the travel or identity document; has been obtained dishonestly or by threats; and

(c) the first person intends that the document will be used to facilitate the entry of another person (the *other person*) into a foreign country, where the entry of the other person into the foreign country would not comply with the requirements under that country's law for entry into the country; and

(d) the first person provided or possessed the document:

(i) having obtained (whether directly or indirectly) a benefit to do so; or

(ii) with the intention of obtaining (whether directly or indirectly) a benefit.

Penalty: Imprisonment for 10 years or 1,000 penalty units, or both.

(2) For the purposes of subsection (1), a *threat* may be:

(a) express or implied; or

(b) conditional or unconditional.

(3) For the purposes of subsection (1), *dishonest* means:

(a) dishonest according to the standards of ordinary people; and

(b) known by the defendant to be dishonest according to the standards of ordinary people.

(4) In a prosecution for an offence against this section, the determination of dishonesty is a matter for the trier of fact.

73.10—*Providing or Possessing a Travel or Identity Document to Be Used by a Person Who Is Not the Rightful User*

A person (the *first person*) is guilty of an offence if:

(a) the first person provides or possesses a travel or identity document; and

(b) the first person intends that the document will be used to facilitate the entry of another person (the *other person*) into a foreign country, where the entry of the other person into the foreign country would not comply with the requirements under that country's law for entry into the country; and

(c) the first person knows that the other person is not the person to whom the document applies; and

(d) the first person provided or possessed the document:

    (i) having obtained (whether directly or indirectly) a benefit to do so; or

    (ii) with the intention of obtaining (whether directly or indirectly) a benefit.

Penalty: Imprisonment for 10 years or 1,000 penalty units, or both.

73.11—*Taking Possession of or Destroying Another Person's Travel or Identity Document*

A person (the *first person*) is guilty of an offence if:

(a) the first person takes possession of, or destroys, a travel or identity document that applies to another person (the *other person*); and

(b) the first person does so intending to conceal the other person's identity or nationality; and

(c) at the time of doing so, the first person intends to organise or facilitate the entry of the other person into a foreign country:

    (i) having obtained, or with the intention of obtaining, whether directly or indirectly, a benefit to organise or facilitate that entry; and

    (ii) where the entry of the other person into the foreign country would not comply with the requirements under that country's law for entry into the country.

Penalty: Imprisonment for 10 years or 1,000 penalty units, or both.

73.12—*Jurisdictional Requirement*

Section 15.2 (extended geographical jurisdiction—category B) applies to an offence against this Subdivision.

Part 9.4—Dangerous Weapons

Division 360—Cross-Border Firearms Trafficking

360.1—*Disposal and Acquisition of a Firearm*

(1) For the purposes of this Division, and without limitation, a person *disposes* of a firearm if any of the following applies:

(a) the person sells the firearm (whether or not the person to whom the firearm is sold also acquires physical control of the firearm);

(b) the person hires, leases or rents the firearm to another person;

(c) the person passes physical control of the firearm to another person (whether or not the person to whom physical control is passed also acquires ownership of the firearm).

(2) For the purposes of this Division, and without limitation, a person *acquires* a firearm if any of the following applies:

(a) the person purchases the firearm (whether or not the person also acquires physical control of the firearm);

(b) the person hires, leases or rents the firearm from another person;

(c) the person obtains physical control of the firearm (whether or not the person also acquires ownership of the firearm).

360.2—*Cross-Border Offence of Disposal or Acquisition of a Firearm*

(1) A person is guilty of an offence if:

(a) in the course of trade or commerce among the States, between Territories or between a Territory and a State, the person engages in conduct that constitutes an offence against a firearm law; and

(b) the primary element of the offence is:

    (i) the disposal of a firearm by the person; or

    (ii) the acquisition of a firearm by the person.

Penalty: Imprisonment for 10 years or a fine of 2,500 penalty units, or both.

(2) Absolute liability applies to the paragraph (1)(a) element of the offence.

(3) In this section:

firearm means a firearm within the meaning of the firearm law concerned.

firearm law means a law of a State or Territory which is prescribed by the regulations for the purposes of this Division.

360.3—Taking or Sending a Firearm across Borders

(1) A person is guilty of an offence if:

(a) in the course of trade or commerce among the States, between Territories or between a Territory and a State, the person takes or sends a firearm from one State or Territory to another State or Territory; and

(b) the person does so intending that the firearm will be disposed of in the other State or Territory (whether by the person or another); and

(c) the person knows that, or is reckless as to whether:
  (i) the disposal of the firearm; or
  (ii) any acquisition of the firearm that results from the disposal; would happen in circumstances that would constitute an offence against the firearm law of that other State or Territory.
  Penalty: Imprisonment for 10 years or a fine of 2,500 penalty units, or both.

(2) In this section:

firearm means a firearm within the meaning of the firearm law mentioned in paragraph (1)(c).

firearm law means a law of a State or Territory which is prescribed by the regulations for the purposes of this Division.

360.4—Concurrent Operation Intended
This Division is not intended to exclude or limit the concurrent operation of any law of a State or Territory.

24.
Communication from the Commission to the Council and the European Parliament: "Developing a Strategic Concept on Tackling Organised Crime"

The objective of this communication as set forth by the Commission of the European Communities is to outline a comprehensive strategy to deal with the growing problem of organized crime. At the outset, the commission addresses the inherent difficulty in developing such a comprehensive plan due to the definitional dilemma of what constitutes organized crime. This document addresses many initiatives such as "an enhanced ability to freeze and confiscate the proceeds of crime"; mutual cooperation, nationally as well as internationally; the exchange of information; an expansion of the scope and range of education and training programs; and the collection and dissemination of relevant data. This communication also stresses "social responsibility standards for the public and private sector to reduce crime opportunities."

Source
EUR-Lex, http://eur-lex.europa.eu/LexUriServ/LexUriServ.do?uri=CELEX:52005DC0232:EN:HTML.

Introduction
1. The European Council of 4/5 November 2004 asked the Council and the Commission, under The Hague Programme, to develop a strategic concept on tackling organised crime (OC) at EU-level with Union bodies such as Europol, Eurojust, CEPOL and the Police Chiefs. This Communication constitutes the Commission's contribution to the development of this strategy.

2. Since the Amsterdam Treaty's entry into force, several EU action plans on combating OC have been adopted, the latest being the Millennium Strategy on the prevention and control of OC of 2000. On the Dutch Council Presidency's initiative discussion began in 2004 leading to the adoption of Council conclusions on the development of a strategic concept on tackling OC on 2.12.2004.

3. Various legislative and non-legislative initiatives contributing to the prevention and fight against OC have been adopted at EU-level since the creation of an area of freedom, security and justice. Now time is needed to integrate the different tools and measures (preventive, criminal law and procedural law) taken at local, national or EU level and fill identified gaps. The Union should move to elaborate and implement a counter OC policy, with adequate financial support.

4. Since September 2001, the fight against terrorism became the focus of attention. Although links between OC and terrorism exist, OC continues to pose in itself a threat to society. OC undermines legitimate economies and is a destabilising factor for society's social and democratic fabric. It is therefore welcome that the European Council put combating OC high on the agenda. In fighting this scourge all actors must balance efficient law enforcement and prosecution of OC, and the protection of fundamental rights and freedoms.

5. To develop a strategic concept on tackling OC is a difficult task because the idea of OC remains complex despite several past initiatives defining "criminal organisation". Also, the priority topics identified by the Council on 2.12.2004 are cross-cutting, and include the knowledge base for reducing OC to prevention, law enforcement, judicial cooperation and external relations (cf. section 2). Measures proposed in the present context may therefore effect offences that are not, or not exclusively, OC-related. Conversely, initiatives which implement e.g. the principle of mutual recognition of judicial decisions in criminal matters, impact on many forms of serious cross-border crime. A strategic approach will ensure effective cooperation between all relevant actors.

6. Due to the strategic concept's broad scope priority-setting is inevitable within the Communication. Section 2 develops the objectives under the priority topics of the strategic concept on tackling OC. Some aspects are only covered summarily but set out in detail elsewhere. Section 3 summarises the follow-up to the mid-term evaluation of the Millennium Strategy, while section 4 points the way forward. Annex 1 lists the measures for implementing the strategic concept on tackling OC, and corresponding responsibilities with target dates and priority ratings. Annex 2 lists and summarises recently adopted Communications and Council conclusions which are relevant. Annex 3 details the follow-up to the mid-term evaluation of the Millennium Strategy.

Priority Topics and Objectives

Improve Knowledge of OC and Strengthen Information Gathering and Analysis
7. Technological evolution along with increasing globalisation provides new opportunities for OC groups. In order to prevent and counteract OC, knowledge about OC, OC groups and vulnerabilities of the licit sectors has to be gathered and updated to develop better tools, as stated in many of the strategic documents mentioned already, not least The Hague Programme. The future EU crime statistics system should collect information from law enforcement agencies and also quantitative information based on citizen and business surveys, as well as measuring crime and victimisation in specific groups to aid decision-making in different policy areas. This crime statistics system will be developed in collaboration with Member States, using, as needed, the Community Statistical Programme. Further development, testing and dissemination of a methodology for studies of economic sectors' vulnerability to OC are also needed. On this basis the Commission intends to produce

an annual or biennial EU crime report in the future.

8. The Hague Programme highlighted the need to develop an EU intelligence-led law enforcement mechanism to enable decision makers to define European law enforcement strategies based on thorough assessments. Availability of and access to information (cf. section 2.3.3.), production of European criminal intelligence and enhanced trust between law enforcement authorities at European and international level are its core elements. The Commission will present a Communication on an EU intelligence-led law enforcement policy in 2005.

9. Within this policy, a 'European Criminal Intelligence Model' should be developed to address issues such as coherent intelligence actions products and services of national and EU bodies active in the domain of Justice, Freedom and Security, the synchronisation of national threat assessments based on a common methodology, underpinned by sectoral vulnerability studies, the production of quantitative and qualitative information by the private sector and other relevant data from evolving European crime statistics. A key element of the Model will be a European OC threat assessment by Europol as requested in The Hague Programme based on synchronised national assessments.

10. OC-related research is currently funded under the 6th Research Framework Programme (RFP) and the Preparatory Action for Security Research. It is envisaged that OC-related research would be part of the new Security Research Programme and of other related areas in the proposed 7th RFP. Specific research projects to support policy development will also be possible through the AGIS programme, any successor under the Financial Perspectives (2007–2013), and studies funds.

Strengthen OC Prevention

11. An effective crime prevention policy goes beyond classical law enforcement cooperation to include good governance, transparency, accountability and social responsibility standards for the public and private sector to reduce crime opportunities. Some EU Member States have been innovative in using an administrative approach to prevent the penetration of legal markets by criminal organisations. The Council recently adopted recommendations that this approach merits further research and dissemination across the EU. At EU level, the Commission intends to develop a model for crime proofing legislation and new products and services which could be widely disseminated to avoid inadvertently creating new opportunities for OC.

12. One key tool by which OC infiltrates licit markets is corruption. Therefore further development and implementation of a comprehensive EU anti-corruption policy including criminal law measures, promotion of ethics and integrity in public administration and improved monitoring of national anti-corruption policies in the context of EU and international obligations and other standards is essential and also timely in order to effectively implement the UN Convention Against Corruption. Fostering public sector transparency is one of the Commission's strategic objectives 2005–2009 and a White Paper on a European Transparency Initiative will follow.

13. The Dublin Declaration recognised Public Private Partnerships as an effective tool for preventing crime in general, and OC in particular. The preparation and implementation of an EU Action Plan on Public Private Partnerships is a priority for the Commission in 2006, under The Hague Programme.

14. The prevention of human trafficking, a particularly serious crime involving severe human rights violations, is a primary aim. The Commission will submit a dedicated Communication on combating trafficking in human beings in 2005 which will take

an integrated, human-rights oriented and victim-centred approach.

15. Under the Structural Funds financial support for preventive measures has been available but was rarely used by Member States, contributing to the Commission's proposal to set up a distinct Security and Safeguarding Liberties Framework Programme under the Financial Perspectives 2007–2013 to finance such measures.

Strengthen Tools and Improve Cooperation

Strengthen Investigation of OC
16. Special investigation techniques have proven effective in police, customs' and judicial investigation of cross-border OC. The 2000 Mutual Legal Assistance (MLA) Convention and 2001 Protocol provide for these techniques although neither instrument has yet entered into force, hence the separate Framework Decision (FD) on the use of Joint Investigation Teams (JIT). Further work is needed to improve the use of JITs and other special investigation techniques.

17. To speed up and simplify the obtaining of evidence across borders, the Commission has proposed the European Evidence Warrant which would for certain types of evidence replace mutual legal assistance. In the medium term the principle of mutual recognition should be extended to cover all types of evidence. The Commission plans several initiatives on admissibility of evidence as explained in its Communication on the principle of mutual recognition in criminal matters. These initiatives would enhance mutual trust by ensuring a fair balance between efficient prosecution and defence rights. The cross border use of intelligence as evidence is an additional theme requiring further study.

18. As well as the collection of evidence in the context of financial investigations (cf. section 2.3.2.), capturing, safeguarding and exchanging electronic evidence is an increasingly relevant issue to be

addressed shortly by the Commission as requested by the European Council of 16/17.12.2004.

19. Data retention for electronic communication services is an important element in the investigation of criminal offences involving the use of information technology. It requires a balance between effective law enforcement, the protection of fundamental rights and the financial burden which resulting obligations cause to service providers. To meet legal considerations the Commission will submit in 2005 a proposal for a directive as appropriate legal instrument.

20. It is often essential to rely on witnesses or collaborators of justice in order to bring key figures of OC groups to justice. Building on two Council Resolutions, the Millennium Strategy suggested further work be done. The Council invited the Commission to work on a witness protection programme for terrorism. Europol developed two useful documents and the Commission is preparing a legal instrument on this.

21. Some EU Member States have created specialised investigation or prosecutorial services to deal with OC related offences. Such services are made up of multi-disciplinary expert teams for complex crime investigations. The Commission encourages all Member States to consider this approach.

Strengthen Tools to Address Financial Aspects of OC
22. Financial gain drives OC. Removing the ability to launder criminal proceeds or to finance criminal activity would significantly impede the motivation and capacity of OC groups. Therefore an enhanced ability to freeze and confiscate the proceeds of crime is key to fighting and preventing such criminal activity. The Commission will therefore promote stronger financial investigation skills and appropriate legal instruments aiding rapid identification and tracing of illicit financial transfers and other transactions.

23. Three FDs dealing with the freezing and confiscation of assets, including extended confiscatory powers have been agreed with one still subject to reservations. The FD on confiscation of crime-related proceeds provides that in using extended confiscation powers, Member States may use non-criminal procedures. Its recitals also refer to the UN Convention on Transnational OC where State Parties may consider the possibility of requiring an offender to show the lawful origin of alleged proceeds of crime, including by reversing the onus and/or lightening the standard of proof. The Commission will review EU legislation on confiscation of criminal assets in this light. In addition, the Commission will explore standards on the return of confiscated or forfeited assets as compensation or restitution to identifiable victims of crime or charitable organisations.

24. The proposed third money laundering Directive strengthens existing Community anti-money laundering legislation by e.g. widening the definition of predicate offences and adding new categories of persons subject to reporting obligations. Yet, to ensure future commitment of financial institutions and others, it should be shown that anti-money laundering reporting generates worthwhile results. For this purpose, financial intelligence units must provide adequate feedback.

25. Organised criminals use the financial system of a Member State to integrate money from criminal activity carried out in another Member State. Europol seeks to identify links between such criminal activity and related transactions within the framework of the Analysis Work Files, e.g. the "SUSTRANS" project. All Member States should actively support this work, by providing high quality data to Europol.

26. The Protocol to the 2000 MLA Convention aims at facilitating cooperation in cross-border financial investigations. Due to the low rate of ratification of this Protocol its date of entry into force is uncertain. As the principle of mutual recognition should progressively replace mutual legal assistance the Commission will need to consider new legislative proposals.

Strengthen the Access to and Exchange of Information and Intelligence between Law Enforcement Authorities
27. The European Council stressed in The Hague Programme that strengthening freedom, security and justice requires an innovative approach to the cross-border exchange of law enforcement information. The action plan implementing The Hague Programme will further develop the Commission's initiatives to implement the principle of availability for the exchange of law enforcement information, common standards for access to databases and interoperability of national and EU databases. National and EU databases should progressively use the same standards and compatible technologies to ensure the selective exchange of law enforcement data while taking into account the appropriate inter-linkages with international databases. Personal data protection and data security measures such as proportionality, integrity and confidentiality of data and effective legal remedies must proceed along with these extended possibilities. The Commission will submit a legislative proposal on this in 2005.

28. Intensive cooperation between national law enforcement authorities and with relevant EU bodies is necessary to the building of trust. Established information channels e.g. Europol's Virtual Private Network or its Information System should be used and, where appropriate, supplemented by expert networks (cf. section 2.4.).

Strengthen Inter-Institutional and Cross-Jurisdictional Cooperation
29. The Hague Programme stresses the need for intensified practical cooperation between police and customs authorities of Member States and with Europol and Eurojust. Prosecutors/judiciary and Eurojust must be involved at an early stage e.g. for wire-tapping or arrest warrants. Joint cus-

toms, police and/or judicial operations should become a frequent tool of practical cooperation. Common structures of cooperation in internal border regions of the Union should be fostered. In addition, the Commission proposes funding joint EU operations systematically in the future under financial perspectives 2007–2013. The Committee on Internal Security envisaged in Article III-261, Constitutional Treaty, should facilitate the coordination of the action of Member States' competent authorities, focusing on operational cooperation.

30. As a follow-up to the relevant Green Paper, the Commission will undertake an impact assessment and submit a White Paper on a legislative proposal to establish the European Public Prosecutor's (EPP) Office from Eurojust, with responsibility for investigating, prosecuting and bringing to judgement offences against the Union's financial interests under the future Constitutional Treaty and also for the possibility to extend the EPP's powers to serious crime with a cross-border dimension.

Improve Use of, and Strengthen, Existing Bodies
31. It is important to ratify and implement the relevant legal instruments regarding Europol and Eurojust, including the three protocols to the Europol Convention. The report on the implementation of the Eurojust Decision identified shortcomings, e.g. differences in the judicial powers of national members which hamper its effectiveness.

32. The potential of Eurojust and Europol in the fight against OC has yet to be fully exploited by Member States. Significant multilateral cases should be referred, and serious cross-border crime reported, to Eurojust. The flow of information to Europol is still insufficient. Ways of increasing the systematic forwarding of high quality, live investigative data by Member States must be developed. Implementation of the Europol Information System in all Member States will facilitate Europol's access to information on OC.

33. Europol and Eurojust should be more closely involved in the investigation phase of cross-border OC cases and in JITs. The opportunities opened by existing legislation and the Constitutional Treaty with regard to their tasks should be used. More specifically, consideration should be given to enhanced coordination by Europol and Eurojust for complex cross-border operations and criminal investigations of serious and OC, providing logistical support, expertise and knowledge of best practice and enhanced use of the Europol/Eurojust agreement.

34. Training and systematic exchange programmes should be promoted via CEPOL with funding under the Community budget. The Commission has proposed that these activities grow in size and impact.

35. The Border Management Agency, though primarily tasked with improving the implementation of the Schengen acquis on control of persons at the external borders, should provide intelligence and play a role in the coordination of operations on illegal immigration-related OC in cooperation with Member States and Europol, and develop an integrated risk analysis model.

Improve Legislation Where Needed
36. Offences related to transborder OC justify by their nature and potential impact consideration of a common basis in the Union to combat them. The most recent example is the proposal for a FD on the fight against OC to provide a harmonised definition of offences and penalties of different forms of participation in a criminal organisation. In the Commission's view approximation of legislation should complement the mutual recognition of judicial decisions in criminal matters. When adopting the FD on the European Arrest Warrant the Council agreed "to continue, in accordance with Article 31(e) TEU, the work on approximation of the offences contained in Article 2(2)" thereof with a view to arriving at a mutual legal understanding among Member States. The Commission will

therefore study the scope for further approximation of legislation in criminal matters e.g. in the fields of counterfeiting, illicit arms trafficking, fraud, especially tax fraud and identity theft, environmental crime, racketeering and extortion.

Improve Monitoring and Evaluation
37. Several instruments currently provide evaluation of OC policy or contribute to it. They need refinement since The Hague Programme's call for evaluation of the implementation, as well as of the effects of Union policies in the area of freedom, security and justice. The Commission regards this as of crucial importance and will present its views on evaluation, bearing in mind Article III-260 of the Constitutional Treaty in 2006. In the OC context, the future EU crime report and the EU OC Threat Assessments (cf. section 2.1.) will be important tools for an evaluation mechanism on OC-related matters. Evaluations of customs cooperation, anti-corruption policies and fight against financial crime, already announced in respective Communications, should be given priority due to their horizontal impact.

Strengthen Co-operation with Non-EU Countries and International Organisations
38. In this era of open borders and global integration and inter-dependence, the internal security of the EU is inseparably linked to external aspects of security. The external dimension of the EU's response to OC, and other security threats, has developed considerably over recent years. Bi-lateral, regional and international initiatives need to be further refined.

39. Co-operation to tackle OC should be developed further with priority third countries through agreements and other instruments. Such cooperation should include the promotion of relevant EU benchmarks and international standards.

40. The EU should promote and support the development of regional approaches and cooperation to combat OC, particularly in those regions bordering the EU.

41. The EU should also fully support the development of multilateral approaches to combat OC, to ensure comprehensive ratification and implementation of international instruments, such as the UN Conventions on Transnational OC and Corruption, and the development of international standards and provisions in other fora such as the Council of Europe, G8, FATF, OSCE and OECD.

42. Direct cooperation between Europol, Eurojust on the one hand, and non-EU countries/bodies on the other, is essential for developing a European dimension to law enforcement and judicial cooperation beyond EU borders. Europol's strategy on external relations 2004–2006 should be pursued further and Eurojust should develop its own external relations strategy.

Setting Priorities for Tackling Specific Forms of OC at EU-Level and for Follow-up
43. Consensus was reached in the Council's Multidisciplinary Group to analyse Europol's OC Report, consult with Eurojust and Europol, and then forward the result to the relevant bodies of the Council with a view to identifying a limited number of yearly strategic priorities in the fight against OC.

44. The Hague Programme establishes that the Council should use the yearly OC threat assessments by Europol to establish such priorities as of 2006. In order to make it possible for Europol to fulfil this requirement, work on intelligence-led law enforcement must be taken further without delay. This will require significant efforts not only from Europol, but equally from Member States and competent EU bodies (cf. section 2.1.)

Summary of Follow-up to the Conclusions of the Mid-Term Evaluation Report on the Millennium Strategy

45. The conclusions of the mid-term evaluation of the Millennium Strategy identified six recommendations for further action. Dealing with drugs trafficking has been met with the Council's adoption of a FD approximating legislation in the field of drug trafficking in October 2004. Follow-up work on the other five recommendations is underway. The Commission proposed legislation and adopted a White Paper on the exchange of information on convictions; a Communication on disqualifications will follow later in 2005. The proposal for a Third Money Laundering Directive includes a provision to prevent the use of large-scale cash payments for money laundering purposes. The development of comparable crime statistics is a long term project on which the Commission is engaged along with other stakeholders. It will present an Action Plan on EU Crime Statistics during 2005. A study has been launched on fiscal fraud. Its results are expected in July 2005. The Commission (OLAF) and Europol, within their respective legal frameworks will provide assistance to Member States in the format of a service platform for joint customs operations in 2005. Finally, the Commission is currently working on a proposal on the protection of witnesses and collaborators of justice.

The Way Forward

46. This Communication spells out the strategic concept on tackling OC in terms of objectives. Annex 1 comprises a list of implementing actions within a 5 year perspective. Once adopted by the Council, the strategic concept on tackling OC should complement the action plan implementing The Hague Programme as it contributes to strengthening freedom, security and justice in the Union. Building and integrating the different elements for a European criminal intelligence model is the most important task ahead, and will require a shared effort by Member States and EU institutions and bodies.

47. The strategic concept should be considered a living document. The Commission is invited to present to the Council a yearly report on the implementation of The Hague programme (scoreboard) which would incorporate a progress report on the strategic concept. Alternatively, it could be evaluated separately in order for this evaluation to be tuned to the process of annually identifying strategic priorities in the fight against OC at EU level.

48. A specific evaluation of the strategic concept is recommended at the end of 2006 to provide a benchmark before implementation of the financial perspectives 2007–2013 and in view of the entry into force of the Constitutional Treaty.

25.
Racketeer Influenced and Corrupt Organizations Act

The Racketeer Influenced and Corrupt Organizations Act (RICO) was passed by the U.S. Congress and became law in October 1970. RICO was originally legislated to go after the Mafia and other organized criminal entities. The statute was designed to undermine and reduce the economic muscle of these groups. The purpose of this act was to protect organizations engaged in interstate commerce from being infiltrated by career criminals as well as organized criminal enterprises. Section 1962 (c) states, "It shall be unlawful for any person employed by or associated with any enterprise engaged in, or the activities of which affect, interstate or foreign commerce, to conduct or participate, directly or indirectly, in the conduct of such enterprise's affairs through a pattern of racketeering activity or collection of unlawful debt." RICO has been successfully applied in criminal prosecutions as well as civil litigation. Persons convicted under this statute are subject to a fine, imprisonment, and forfeiture of assets.

Source
FindLaw, http://caselaw.lp.findlaw.com/casecode/uscodes/
18/parts/i/chapters/96/toc.html.

Title 18—Crimes and Criminal Procedure

Part I—Crimes

Chapter 96—Racketeer Influenced and Corrupt Organizations

Section 1961. Definitions
As used in this chapter—

(1) "racketeering activity" means (A) any act or threat involving murder, kidnapping, gambling, arson, robbery, bribery, extortion, dealing in obscene matter, or dealing in a controlled substance or listed chemical (as defined in section 102 of the Controlled Substances Act), which is chargeable under State law and punishable by imprisonment for more than one year; (B) any act which is indictable under any of the following provisions of title 18, United States Code: Section 201 (relating to bribery), section 224 (relating to sports bribery), sections 471, 472, and 473 (relating to counterfeiting), section 659 (relating to theft from interstate shipment) if the act indictable under section 659 is felonious, section 664 (relating to embezzlement from pension and welfare funds), sections 891–894 (relating to extortionate credit transactions), section 1028 (relating to fraud and related activity in connection with identification documents), section 1029 (relating to fraud and related activity in connection with access devices), section 1084 (relating to the transmission of gambling information), section 1341 (relating to mail fraud), section 1343 (relating to wire fraud), section 1344 (relating to financial institution fraud), section 1425 (relating to the procurement of citizenship or naturalization unlawfully), section 1426 (relating to the reproduction of naturalization or citizenship papers), section 1427 (relating to the sale of naturalization or citizenship papers), sections 1461– 1465 (relating to obscene matter), section 1503 (relating to obstruction of justice), section 1510 (relating to obstruction of criminal investigations), section 1511 (relating to the obstruction of State or local law enforcement), section 1512 (relating to tampering with a witness, victim, or an informant), section 1513 (relating to retaliating against a witness, victim, or an informant), section 1542 (relating to false statement in application and use of passport), section 1543 (relating to forgery or false use of passport), section 1544 (relating to misuse of passport), section 1546 (relating to fraud and misuse of visas, permits, and other documents), sections 1581–1591 (relating to peonage, slavery, and trafficking in persons), section 1951 (relating to interference with commerce, robbery, or extortion), section 1952 (relating to racketeering), section 1953 (relating to interstate transportation of wagering paraphernalia), section 1954 (relating to unlawful welfare fund payments), section 1955 (relating to the prohibition of illegal gambling businesses), section 1956 (relating to the laundering of monetary instruments), section 1957 (relating to engaging in monetary transactions in property derived from specified unlawful activity), section 1958 (relating to use of interstate commerce facilities in the commission of murder-for-hire), sections 2251, 2251A, 2252, and 2260 (relating to sexual exploitation of children), sections 2312 and 2313 (relating to interstate transportation of stolen motor vehicles), sections 2314 and 2315 (relating to interstate transportation of stolen property), section 2318 (relating to trafficking in counterfeit labels for phonorecords, computer programs or computer program documentation or packaging and copies of motion pictures or other audiovisual works), section 2319 (relating to criminal infringement of a copyright), section 2319A (relating to unauthorized fixation of and trafficking in sound recordings and music videos of live musical performances), section 2320 (relating to trafficking in goods or services bearing counterfeit marks), section 2321 (relating to trafficking in certain motor vehicles or motor vehicle parts),

sections 2341–2346 (relating to trafficking in contraband cigarettes), sections 2421–24 (relating to white slave traffic), (C) any act which is indictable under title 29, United States Code, section 186 (dealing with restrictions on payments and loans to labor organizations) or section 501(c) (relating to embezzlement from union funds), (D) any offense involving fraud connected with a case under title 11 (except a case under section 157 of this title), fraud in the sale of securities, or the felonious manufacture, importation, receiving, concealment, buying, selling, or otherwise dealing in a controlled substance or listed chemical (as defined in section 102 of the Controlled Substances Act), punishable under any law of the United States, (E) any act which is indictable under the Currency and Foreign Transactions Reporting Act, (F) any act which is indictable under the Immigration and Nationality Act, section 274 (relating to bringing in and harboring certain aliens), section 277 (relating to aiding or assisting certain aliens to enter the United States), or section 278 (relating to importation of alien for immoral purpose) if the act indictable under such section of such Act was committed for the purpose of financial gain, or (G) any act that is indictable under any provision listed in section 2332b(g)(5)(B);

(2) "State" means any State of the United States, the District of Columbia, the Commonwealth of Puerto Rico, any territory or possession of the United States, any political subdivision, or any department, agency, or instrumentality thereof;

(3) "person" includes any individual or entity capable of holding a legal or beneficial interest in property;

(4) "enterprise" includes any individual, partnership, corporation, association, or other legal entity, and any union or group of individuals associated in fact although not a legal entity;

(5) "pattern of racketeering activity" requires at least two acts of racketeering activity, one of which occurred after the effective date of this chapter and the last of which occurred within ten years (excluding any period of imprisonment) after the commission of a prior act of racketeering activity;

(6) "unlawful debt" means a debt (A) incurred or contracted in gambling activity which was in violation of the law of the United States, a State or political subdivision thereof, or which is unenforceable under State or Federal law in whole or in part as to principal or interest because of the laws relating to usury, and (B) which was incurred in connection with the business of gambling in violation of the law of the United States, a State or political subdivision thereof, or the business of lending money or a thing of value at a rate usurious under State or Federal law, where the usurious rate is at least twice the enforceable rate;

(7) "racketeering investigator" means any attorney or investigator so designated by the Attorney General and charged with the duty of enforcing or carrying into effect this chapter;

(8) "racketeering investigation" means any inquiry conducted by any racketeering investigator for the purpose of ascertaining whether any person has been involved in any violation of this chapter or of any final order, judgment, or decree of any court of the United States, duly entered in any case or proceeding arising under this chapter;

(9) "documentary material" includes any book, paper, document, record, recording, or other material; and

(10) "Attorney General" includes the Attorney General of the United States, the Deputy Attorney General of the United States, the Associate Attorney General of the United States, any Assistant Attorney General of the United States, or any employee of the Department of Justice or any employee of any department or agency of the United States so designated by the Attorney General to carry out the powers conferred on the Attorney General by this chapter. Any department or agency so designated may use in investigations authorized by this chapter either the investigative provisions of this chapter or the investigative power of such department or agency otherwise conferred by law.

Section 1962. Prohibited Activities

(a) It shall be unlawful for any person who has received any income derived, directly or indirectly, from a pattern of racketeering activity or through collection of an unlawful debt in which such person has participated as a principal within the meaning of section 2, title 18, United States Code, to use or invest, directly or indirectly, any part of such income, or the proceeds of such income, in acquisition of any interest in, or the establishment or operation of, any enterprise which is engaged in, or the activities of which affect, interstate or foreign commerce. A purchase of securities on the open market for purposes of investment, and without the intention of controlling or participating in the control of the issuer, or of assisting another to do so, shall not be unlawful under this subsection if the securities of the issuer held by the purchaser, the members of his immediate family, and his or their accomplices in any pattern or racketeering activity or the collection of an unlawful debt after such purchase do not amount in the aggregate to one percent of the outstanding securities of any one class, and do not confer, either in law or in fact, the power to elect one or more directors of the issuer.

(b) It shall be unlawful for any person through a pattern of racketeering activity or through collection of an unlawful debt to acquire or maintain, directly or indirectly, any interest in or control of any enterprise which is engaged in, or the activities of which affect, interstate or foreign commerce.

(c) It shall be unlawful for any person employed by or associated with any enterprise engaged in, or the activities of which affect, interstate or foreign commerce, to conduct or participate, directly or indirectly, in the conduct of such enterprise's affairs through a pattern of racketeering activity or collection of unlawful debt.

(d) It shall be unlawful for any person to conspire to violate any of the provisions of subsection (a), (b), or (c) of this section.

Section 1963. Criminal Penalties

(a) Whoever violates any provision of section 1962 of this chapter shall be fined under this title or imprisoned not more than 20 years (or for life if the violation is based on a racketeering activity for which the maximum penalty includes life imprisonment), or both, and shall forfeit to the United States, irrespective of any provision of State law—

  (1) any interest the person has acquired or maintained in violation of section 1962;

  (2) any—

    (A) interest in;

    (B) security of;

    (C) claim against; or

    (D) property or contractual right of any kind affording a source of influence over; any enterprise which the person has established, operated, controlled, conducted, or participated in the conduct of, in violation of section 1962; and

  (3) any property constituting, or derived from, any proceeds which the person obtained, directly or indirectly, from racketeering activity or unlawful debt collection in violation of section 1962.

The court, in imposing sentence on such person shall order, in addition to any other sentence imposed pursuant to this section, that the person forfeit to the United States all property described in this subsection. In lieu of a fine otherwise authorized by this section, a defendant who derives profits or other proceeds from an offense may be fined not more than twice the gross profits or other proceeds.

(b) Property subject to criminal forfeiture under this section includes—

  (1) real property, including things growing on, affixed to, and found in land; and

(2) tangible and intangible personal property, including rights, privileges, interests, claims, and securities.

(c) All right, title, and interest in property described in subsection (a) vests in the United States upon the commission of the act giving rise to forfeiture under this section. Any such property that is subsequently transferred to a person other than the defendant may be the subject of a special verdict of forfeiture and thereafter shall be ordered forfeited to the United States, unless the transferee establishes in a hearing pursuant to subsection (1) that he is a bona fide purchaser for value of such property who at the time of purchase was reasonably without cause to believe that the property was subject to forfeiture under this section.

(d)(1) Upon application of the United States, the court may enter a restraining order or injunction, require the execution of a satisfactory performance bond, or take any other action to preserve the availability of property described in subsection (a) for forfeiture under this section—

(A) upon the filing of an indictment or information charging a violation of section 1962 of this chapter and alleging that the property with respect to which the order is sought would, in the event of conviction, be subject to forfeiture under this section; or

(B) prior to the filing of such an indictment or information, if, after notice to persons appearing to have an interest in the property and opportunity for a hearing, the court determines that—

(i) there is a substantial probability that the United States will prevail on the issue of forfeiture and that failure to enter the order will result in the property being destroyed, removed from the jurisdiction of the court, or otherwise made unavailable for forfeiture; and

(ii) the need to preserve the availability of the property through the entry of the requested order outweighs the hardship on any party against whom the order is to be entered:

Provided, however, That an order entered pursuant to subparagraph (B) shall be effective for not more than ninety days, unless extended by the court for good cause shown or unless an indictment or information described in subparagraph (A) has been filed.

(2) A temporary restraining order under this subsection may be entered upon application of the United States without notice or opportunity for a hearing when an information or indictment has not yet been filed with respect to the property, if the United States demonstrates that there is probable cause to believe that the property with respect to which the order is sought would, in the event of conviction, be subject to forfeiture under this section and that provision of notice will jeopardize the availability of the property for forfeiture. Such a temporary order shall expire not more than ten days after the date on which it is entered, unless extended for good cause shown or unless the party against whom it is entered consents to an extension for a longer period. A hearing requested concerning an order entered under this paragraph shall be held at the earliest possible time, and prior to the expiration of the temporary order.

(3) The court may receive and consider, at a hearing held pursuant to this subsection, evidence and information that would be inadmissible under the Federal Rules of Evidence.

(e) Upon conviction of a person under this section, the court shall enter a judgment of forfeiture of the property to the United States and shall also authorize the Attorney General to seize all property ordered forfeited upon such terms and conditions as the court shall deem proper. Following the entry of an order declaring the property forfeited, the court may, upon application of the United States, enter such appropriate restraining orders or injunctions, require the execution of satisfactory performance bonds, appoint receivers, conservators, appraisers, accountants, or trustees, or take any other action to protect the interest of the United States in the property ordered forfeited. Any income accruing to, or derived from, an enterprise or an interest in an enterprise which has been ordered forfeited under this section may be used to offset ordinary and necessary expenses to the enterprise which are required by law, or which are necessary to protect the interests of the United States or third parties.

(f) Following the seizure of property ordered forfeited under this section, the Attorney General shall direct the disposition of the property by sale or any other commercially feasible means, making due provision for the rights of any innocent persons. Any property right or interest not exercisable by, or transferable for value to, the United States shall expire and shall not revert to the defendant, nor shall the defendant or any person acting in concert with or on behalf of the defendant be eligible to purchase forfeited property at any sale held by the United States. Upon application of a person, other than the defendant or a person acting in concert with or on behalf of the defendant, the court may restrain or stay the sale or disposition of the property pending the conclusion of any appeal of the criminal case giving rise to the forfeiture, if the applicant demonstrates that proceeding with the sale or disposition of the property will result in irreparable injury, harm or loss to him. Notwithstanding 31 U.S.C. 3302(b), the proceeds of any sale or other disposition of property forfeited under this section and any moneys forfeited shall be used to pay all proper expenses for the forfeiture and the sale, including expenses of seizure, maintenance and custody of the property pending its disposition, advertising and court costs. The Attorney General shall deposit in the Treasury any amounts of such proceeds or moneys remaining after the payment of such expenses.

(g) With respect to property ordered forfeited under this section, the Attorney General is authorized to—

(1) grant petitions for mitigation or remission of forfeiture, restore forfeited property to victims of a violation of this chapter, or take any other action to protect the rights of innocent persons which is in the interest of justice and which is not inconsistent with the provisions of this chapter;

(2) compromise claims arising under this section;

(3) award compensation to persons providing information resulting in a forfeiture under this section;

(4) direct the disposition by the United States of all property ordered forfeited under this section by public sale or any other commercially feasible means, making due provision for the rights of innocent persons; and

(5) take appropriate measures necessary to safeguard and maintain property ordered forfeited under this section pending its disposition.

(h) The Attorney General may promulgate regulations with respect to—

(1) making reasonable efforts to provide notice to persons who may have an interest in property ordered forfeited under this section;

(2) granting petitions for remission or mitigation of forfeiture;

(3) the restitution of property to victims of an offense petitioning for remission or mitigation of forfeiture under this chapter;

(4) the disposition by the United States of forfeited property by public sale or other commercially feasible means;

(5) the maintenance and safekeeping of any property forfeited under this section pending its disposition; and

(6) the compromise of claims arising under this chapter.

Pending the promulgation of such regulations, all provisions of law relating to the disposition of property, or the proceeds from the sale thereof, or the remission or mitigation of forfeitures for violation of the customs laws, and the compromise of claims and the award of compensation to informers in respect of such forfeitures shall apply to forfeitures incurred, or alleged to have been incurred, under the provisions of this section, insofar as applicable and not inconsistent with the provisions hereof. Such duties as are imposed upon the Customs Service or any person with respect to the disposition of property under the customs law shall be performed under this chapter by the Attorney General.

(i) Except as provided in subsection (l), no party claiming an interest in property subject to forfeiture under this section may—

    (1) intervene in a trial or appeal of a criminal case involving the forfeiture of such property under this section; or

    (2) commence an action at law or equity against the United States concerning the validity of his alleged interest in the property subsequent to the filing of an indictment or information alleging that the property is subject to forfeiture under this section.

(j) The district courts of the United States shall have jurisdiction to enter orders as provided in this section without regard to the location of any property which may be subject to forfeiture under this section or which has been ordered forfeited under this section.

(k) In order to facilitate the identification or location of property declared forfeited and to facilitate the disposition of petitions for remission or mitigation of forfeiture, after the entry of an order declaring property forfeited to the United States the court may, upon application of the United States, order that the testimony of any witness relating to the property forfeited be taken by deposition and that any designated book, paper, document, record, recording, or other material not privileged be produced at the same time and place, in the same manner as provided for the taking of depositions under Rule 15 of the Federal Rules of Criminal Procedure.

(l)(1) Following the entry of an order of forfeiture under this section, the United States shall publish notice of the order and of its intent to dispose of the property in such manner as the Attorney General may direct. The Government may also, to the extent practicable, provide direct written notice to any person known to have alleged an interest in the property that is the subject of the order of forfeiture as a substitute for published notice as to those persons so notified.

(2) Any person, other than the defendant, asserting a legal interest in property which has been ordered forfeited to the United States pursuant to this section may, within thirty days of the final publication of notice or his receipt of notice under paragraph (1), whichever is earlier, petition the court for a hearing to adjudicate the validity of his alleged interest in the property. The hearing shall be held before the court alone, without a jury.

(3) The petition shall be signed by the petitioner under penalty of perjury and shall set forth the nature and extent of the petitioner's right, title, or interest in the property, the time and circumstances of the petitioner's acquisition of the right, title, or interest in the property, any additional facts supporting the petitioner's claim, and the relief sought.

(4) The hearing on the petition shall, to the extent practicable and consistent with the interests of justice, be held within thirty days of the filing of the petition. The court may consolidate the hearing on the petition with a hearing on any other petition filed by a person other than the defendant under this subsection.

(5) At the hearing, the petitioner may testify and present evidence and witnesses on his own behalf, and cross-examine witnesses who appear at the hearing. The United States may present evidence and witnesses in rebuttal and in defense of its claim to the property and cross-examine witnesses who appear at the hearing. In addition to testimony and evidence presented at the hearing, the court shall consider the relevant portions of the record of the criminal case which resulted in the order of forfeiture.

(6) If, after the hearing, the court determines that the petitioner has established by a preponderance of the evidence that—

(A) the petitioner has a legal right, title, or interest in the property, and such right, title, or interest renders the order of forfeiture invalid in whole or in part because the right, title, or interest was vested in the petitioner rather than the defendant or was superior to any right, title, or interest of the defendant at the time of the commission of the acts which gave rise to the forfeiture of the property under this section; or

(B) the petitioner is a bona fide purchaser for value of the right, title, or interest in the property and was at the time of purchase reasonably without cause to believe that the property was subject to forfeiture under this section; the court shall amend the order of forfeiture in accordance with its determination.

(7) Following the court's disposition of all petitions filed under this subsection, or if no such petitions are filed following the expiration of the period provided in paragraph (2) for the filing of such petitions, the United States shall have clear title to property that is the subject of the order of forfeiture and may warrant good title to any subsequent purchaser or transferee.

(m) If any of the property described in subsection (a), as a result of any act or omission of the defendant—

(1) cannot be located upon the exercise of due diligence;

(2) has been transferred or sold to, or deposited with, a third party;

(3) has been placed beyond the jurisdiction of the court;

(4) has been substantially diminished in value; or

(5) has been commingled with other property which cannot be divided without difficulty; the court shall order the forfeiture of any other property of the defendant up to the value of any property described in paragraphs (1) through (5).

Section 1964. Civil Remedies

(a) The district courts of the United States shall have jurisdiction to prevent and restrain violations of section 1962 of this chapter by issuing appropriate orders, including, but not limited to:

ordering any person to divest himself of any interest, direct or indirect, in any enterprise; imposing reasonable restrictions on the future activities or investments of any person, including, but not limited to, prohibiting any person from engaging in the same type of endeavor as the enterprise engaged in, the activities of which affect interstate or foreign commerce; or ordering dissolution or reorganization of any enterprise, making due provision for the rights of innocent persons.

(b) The Attorney General may institute proceedings under this section. Pending final determination thereof, the court may at any time enter such restraining orders or prohibitions, or take such other actions, including the acceptance of satisfactory performance bonds, as it shall deem proper.

(c) Any person injured in his business or property by reason of a violation of section 1962 of this chapter may sue therefore in any appropriate United States district court and shall recover threefold the damages he sustains and the cost of the suit, including a reasonable attorney's fee, except that no person may rely upon any conduct that would have been actionable as fraud in the purchase or sale of securities to establish a violation of section 1962. The exception contained in the preceding sentence does not apply to an action against any person that is criminally convicted in connection with the fraud, in which case the statute of limitations shall start to run on the date on which the conviction becomes final.

(d) A final judgment or decree rendered in favor of the United States in any criminal proceeding brought by the United States under this chapter shall estop the defendant from denying the essential allegations of the criminal offense in any subsequent civil proceeding brought by the United States.

Section 1965. Venue and Process

(a) Any civil action or proceeding under this chapter against any person may be instituted in the district court of the United States for any district in which such person resides, is found, has an agent, or transacts his affairs.

(b) In any action under section 1964 of this chapter in any district court of the United States in which it is shown that the ends of justice require that other parties residing in any other district be brought before the court, the court may cause such parties to be summoned, and process for that purpose may be served in any judicial district of the United States by the marshal thereof.

(c) In any civil or criminal action or proceeding instituted by the United States under this chapter in the district court of the United States for any judicial district, subpenas issued by such court to compel the attendance of witnesses may be served in any other judicial district, except that in any civil action or proceeding no such subpena shall be issued for service upon any individual who resides in another district at a place more than one hundred miles from the place at which such court is held without approval given by a judge of such court upon a showing of good cause.

(d) All other process in any action or proceeding under this chapter may be served on any person in any judicial district in which such person resides, is found, has an agent, or transacts his affairs.

Section 1966. Expedition of Actions

In any civil action instituted under this chapter by the United States in any district court of the United States, the Attorney General may file with the clerk of such court a certificate stating that in his opinion the case is of general public importance. A copy of that certificate shall be furnished immediately by such clerk to the chief judge or in his absence to the presiding district judge of the district in which such action is pending. Upon receipt of such copy, such judge shall designate immediately a judge of that district to hear and determine action.

Section 1967. Evidence

In any proceeding ancillary to or in any civil action instituted by the United States under this chapter the proceedings may be open or closed to the public at the discretion of the court after consideration of the rights of affected persons.

Section 1968. Civil Investigative Demand

(a) Whenever the Attorney General has reason to believe that any person or enterprise may be in possession, custody, or control of any documentary materials relevant to a racketeering investigation, he may, prior to the institution of a civil or criminal proceeding thereon, issue in writing, and cause to be served upon such person, a civil investigative demand requiring such person to produce such material for examination.

(b) Each such demand shall—

(1) state the nature of the conduct constituting the alleged racketeering violation which is under investigation and the provision of law applicable thereto;

(2) describe the class or classes of documentary material produced thereunder with such definiteness and certainty as to permit such material to be fairly identified;

(3) state that the demand is returnable forthwith or prescribe a return date which will provide a reasonable period of time within which the material so demanded may be assembled and made available for inspection and copying or reproduction; and

(4) identify the custodian to whom such material shall be made available.

(c) No such demand shall—

(1) contain any requirement which would be held to be unreasonable if contained in a subpena duces tecum issued by a court of the United States in

aid of a grand jury investigation of such alleged racketeering violation; or

(2) require the production of any documentary evidence which would be privileged from disclosure if demanded by a subpena duces tecum issued by a court of the United States in aid of a grand jury investigation of such alleged racketeering violation.

(d) Service of any such demand or any petition filed under this section may be made upon a person by—

(1) delivering a duly executed copy thereof to any partner, executive officer, managing agent, or general agent thereof, or to any agent thereof authorized by appointment or by law to receive service of process on behalf of such person, or upon any individual person;

(2) delivering a duly executed copy thereof to the principal office or place of business of the person to be served; or

(3) depositing such copy in the United States mail, by registered or certified mail duly addressed to such person at its principal office or place of business.

(e) A verified return by the individual serving any such demand or petition setting forth the manner of such service shall be prima facie proof of such service. In the case of service by registered or certified mail, such return shall be accompanied by the return post office receipt of delivery of such demand.

(f)(1) The Attorney General shall designate a racketeering investigator to serve as racketeer document custodian, and such additional racketeering investigators as he shall determine from time to time to be necessary to serve as deputies to such officer.

(2) Any person upon whom any demand issued under this section has been duly served shall make such material available for inspection and copying or reproduction to the custodian desig-

nated therein at the principal place of business of such person, or at such other place as such custodian and such person thereafter may agree and prescribe in writing or as the court may direct, pursuant to this section on the return date specified in such demand, or on such later date as such custodian may prescribe in writing. Such person may upon written agreement between such person and the custodian substitute for copies of all or any part of such material originals thereof.

(3) The custodian to whom any documentary material is so delivered shall take physical possession thereof, and shall be responsible for the use made thereof and for the return thereof pursuant to this chapter. The custodian may cause the preparation of such copies of such documentary material as may be required for official use under regulations which shall be promulgated by the Attorney General. While in the possession of the custodian, no material so produced shall be available for examination, without the consent of the person who produced such material, by any individual other than the Attorney General. Under such reasonable terms and conditions as the Attorney General shall prescribe, documentary material while in the possession of the custodian shall be available for examination by the person who produced such material or any duly authorized representatives of such person.

(4) Whenever any attorney has been designated to appear on behalf of the United States before any court or grand jury in any case or proceeding involving any alleged violation of this chapter, the custodian may deliver to such attorney such documentary material in the possession of the custodian as such attorney determines to be required for use in the presentation of such case or proceeding on behalf of the United States. Upon the conclusion of any such case or proceeding, such attorney shall return to the custodian any documentary material so withdrawn which has not passed into the control of such court or grand jury through the introduction thereof into the record of such case or proceeding.

(5) Upon the completion of—

    (i) the racketeering investigation for which any documentary material was produced under this chapter, and

    (ii) any case or proceeding arising from such investigation, the custodian shall return to the person who produced such material all such material other than copies thereof made by the Attorney General pursuant to this subsection which has not passed into the control of any court or grand jury through the introduction thereof into the record of such case or proceeding.

(6) When any documentary material has been produced by any person under this section for use in any racketeering investigation, and no such case or proceeding arising therefrom has been instituted within a reasonable time after completion of the examination and analysis of all evidence assembled in the course of such investigation, such person shall be entitled, upon written demand made upon the Attorney General, to the return of all documentary material other than copies thereof made pursuant to this subsection so produced by such person.

(7) In the event of the death, disability, or separation from service of the custodian of any documentary material produced under any demand issued under this section or the official relief of such custodian from responsibility for the custody and control of such material, the Attorney General shall promptly—

    (i) designate another racketeering investigator to serve as custodian thereof, and

    (ii) transmit notice in writing to the person who produced such material as to the identity and address of the successor so designated.

Any successor so designated shall have with regard to such materials all duties and responsibilities imposed by this section upon his predecessor in office with regard thereto, except that he shall not be held responsible for any default or dereliction which occurred before his designation as custodian.

(g) Whenever any person fails to comply with any civil investigative demand duly served upon him under this section or whenever satisfactory copying or reproduction of any such material cannot be done and such person refuses to surrender such material, the Attorney General may file, in the district court of the United States for any judicial district in which such person resides, is found, or transacts business, and serve upon such person a petition for an order of such court for the enforcement of this section, except that if such person transacts business in more than one such district such petition shall be filed in the district in which such person maintains his principal place of business, or in such other district in which such person transacts business as may be agreed upon by the parties to such petition.

(h) Within twenty days after the service of any such demand upon any person, or at any time before the return date specified in the demand, whichever period is shorter, such person may file, in the district court of the United States for the judicial district within which such person resides, is found, or transacts business, and serve upon such custodian a petition for an order of such court modifying or setting aside such demand. The time allowed for compliance with the demand in whole or in part as deemed proper and ordered by the court shall not run during the pendency of such petition in the court. Such petition shall specify each ground upon which the petitioner relies in seeking such relief, and may be based upon any failure of such demand to comply with the provisions of this section or upon any constitutional or other legal right or privilege of such person.

(i) At any time during which any custodian is in custody or control of any documentary material delivered by any person in compliance with any such demand, such person may file, in the district court of the United States for the judicial district within which the office of such custodian is situated, and serve upon such custodian a petition for an order of such court requiring the performance by such custodian of any duty imposed upon him by this section.

(j) Whenever any petition is filed in any district court of the United States under this section, such court shall have jurisdiction to hear and determine the matter so presented, and to enter such order or orders as may be required to carry into effect the provisions of this section.

26.
South Africa Crime Act 1996

Between $2 billion and $8 billion are laundered every year through South African organizations, with the money coming from narcotics, kidnapping, fraud, stolen vehicles, human trafficking, diamonds, etc. There is a close nexus between terrorist groups and criminal gangs. Money laundering became a criminal offense under the Proceeds of Crime Act, passed on 6 November 1996. According to Chapter V, Article 33, the penalties for illegal financial transactions are maximum imprisonment of thirty years and a fine, depending on the seriousness of the offense. The government passed subsequent amendments and acts to tackle the problem more effectively. There were also court cases challenging the provisions of earlier acts.

Source
United Nations Office on Drugs and Crime, http://www.unodc.org/unodc/en/legal_library/za/legal _library_1998-09-27_1998-68.html.

Chapter 1—Application of Act

1. Definitions
(1) In this Act, unless the context indicates otherwise—

"*affected gift*"

means any gift—

(a) made by the defendant concerned not more than seven years before the fixed date; or
(b) made by the defendant concerned at any time, if it was a gift—
   (i) of property received by that defendant in connection with an offence committed by him or her or any other person; or
   (ii) of property, or any part thereof, which directly or indirectly represented in that defendant's hands property received by him or her in that connection, whether any such gift was made before or after the commencement of this Act;

"*confiscation order*"

means an order referred to in section 8 (1);

"*defendant*"

means a person against whom a prosecution for an offence has been instituted, irrespective of whether he or she has been convicted or not, and includes a person referred to in section 15 (1) (b);

"*fixed date*"

in relation to a defendant

(a) if a prosecution for an offence has been instituted against the defendant, means the date on which such prosecution has been instituted; or
(b) if a restraint order has been made against the defendant, means the date of such restraint order, whichever is the earlier date;

"*interest*"

includes any right;

"*Minister*"

means the Minister of Justice;

"*proceeds*"

in relation to an offence, means any property or part thereof which was derived directly or indirectly as a result of

(a) the commission in the Republic of such offence; or

(b) any act or omission outside the Republic which, if it had occurred in the Republic, would have constituted such an offence, and includes any property representing property so derived;

"property"

means money or any other movable, immovable, corporeal or incorporeal thing and includes any interest therein and all proceeds thereof;

"realizable property"

means property referred to in section 4;

"restraint order"

means an order referred to in section 16 (1);

"superior court"

means a provincial or local division of the Supreme Court of South Africa, and includes, for the purpose of sections 14 to 18, any judge thereof.

(2) In this Act, except where it is inconsistent with the context or clearly inappropriate, any reference

(a) to a person who holds property shall be construed as a reference to a person who has any interest in the property, and—

(i) if the estate of such person has been sequestrated, also to the executor of his or her insolvent estate; or

(ii) if such person is a company or other juristic person which is being wound up, also to the liquidator thereof;

(b) to a person who transfers property to any other person shall be construed as a reference to a per-

son who transfers or grants to any other person any interest in the property;

(c) to anything received in connection with an offence shall be construed as a reference also to anything received both in that connection and in some other connection.

2. *Persons Who Have Benefited from Crime*

For the purposes of this Act, a person has benefited from crime if he or she has at any time, whether before or after the commencement of this Act, received any payment or other reward in connection with any criminal activity carried on by him or her or by any other person.

3. *Proceeds of Crime*

For the purposes of this Act, any payment or other reward received or held by the defendant or over which the defendant has effective control at any time, whether before or after the commencement of this Act, in connection with any criminal activity carried on by him or her or any other person, shall be his or her proceeds of crime.

4. *Realizable Property*

(1) Subject to the provisions of subsection (2), the following property shall be realizable in terms of this Act, namely—

(a) any property held by the defendant concerned; and

(b) any property held by a person to whom that defendant has directly or indirectly made any affected gift.

(2) Property shall not be realizable property if a declaration of forfeiture is in force in respect thereof.

5. *Value of Property*

(1) For the purposes of this Act, the value of property, other than money, in relation to any person holding the property, shall be

(a) where any other person holds an interest in the property

(i) the market value of the property; less

(ii) the amount required to discharge any encumbrance on the property; and

(b) where no other person holds an interest in the property, the market value of the property.

(2) Notwithstanding the provisions of subsection (1), any reference in this Act to the value at a particular time of a payment or reward, shall be construed as a reference to

(a) the value of the payment or reward at the time when the recipient received it, as adjusted to take into account subsequent fluctuations in the value of money; or

(b) where subsection (3) applies, the value mentioned in that subsection, whichever is the greater value.

(3) If at the particular time the recipient holds

(a) the property, other than cash, which he or she received, the value concerned shall be the value of the property at the particular time; or

(b) property, or any part thereof, which directly or indirectly represents in his or her hands the property which he or she received, the value concerned shall be the value of the property, in so far as it represents the property which he or she received, at the relevant time.

6. Gifts

(1) For the purposes of this Act, a defendant shall be deemed to have made a gift if he or she has transferred any property to any other person directly or indirectly for a consideration the value of which is significantly less than the value of the consideration supplied by the defendant.

(2) For the purposes of section 10 (2) the gift which a defendant is deemed to have made shall consist of that share in the property transferred by the defendant which is equal to the difference between the value of that property as a whole and the consideration received by the defendant in return.

7. Conclusion of Proceedings against Defendant

For the purposes of this Act, the proceedings contemplated in terms of this Act against a defendant shall be concluded when—

(a) the defendant is acquitted or found not guilty of an offence;

(b) subject to section 8 (2), the court convicting the defendant of an offence, sentences the defendant without making a confiscation order against him or her;

(c) the conviction in respect of an offence is set aside on review or appeal; or

(d) the defendant satisfies the confiscation order made against him or her.

Chapter 2—Confiscation Orders

8. Confiscation Orders

(1) Whenever a defendant is convicted of an offence the court convicting the defendant may, on the application of the public prosecutor, enquire into any benefit which the defendant may have derived from such offence or any related criminal activity and, if the court finds that the defendant has so benefited, the court may, in addition to any punishment which it may impose in respect of the offence, make an order against the defendant for the payment to the State of such amount as it may consider appropriate, which amount—

(a) shall not exceed the value of the defendant's proceeds of such offence or any related criminal activity as determined by the court in accordance with the provisions of this Act; or

(b) if the court is satisfied that the amount which might be realized as contemplated in section 10

(1) is less than the value referred to in paragraph (a), shall not exceed an amount which in the opinion of the court might be so realized.

(2) A court convicting a defendant may, when passing sentence, indicate that it will hold an enquiry contemplated in subsection (1) at a later stage if

(a) it is satisfied that such enquiry will unreasonably delay the proceedings in sentencing the defendant; or

(b) the public prosecutor applies to the court to first sentence the defendant and the court is satisfied that it is reasonable and justifiable to do so in the circumstances.

(3) If the judicial officer who convicted the defendant is absent or for any other reason not available, any judicial officer of the same court may consider an application referred to in subsection (1) and hold an enquiry referred to in that subsection and he or she may in such proceedings take such steps as the judicial officer who is absent or not available could lawfully have taken.

(4) No application referred to in subsection (1) shall be made without the written authority of the attorney-general concerned.

(5) A court before which proceedings under this section are pending, may

(a) in order to make a confiscation order
  (i) refer to the evidence and proceedings at the trial;
  (ii) hear such further oral evidence as the court may deem fit;
  (iii) direct the public prosecutor to tender to the court a statement referred to in section 11 (1) (a); and
  (iv) direct a defendant to tender to the court a statement referred to in subsection (3) (a) of that section;

(b) subject to subsection (1) (b) or (3) (b) of section 11, adjourn such proceedings to any day on such conditions not inconsistent with a provision of the Criminal Procedure Act, 1977 (Act No. 51 of 1977), as the court may deem fit.

9. Value of Proceeds of Crime

(1) Subject to the provisions of subsection (2), the value of a defendant's proceeds of crime shall be the sum of the values of the payments or other rewards received by him or her at any time, whether before or after the commencement of this Act, in connection with the criminal activity carried on by him or her or any other person.

(2) In determining the value of a defendant's proceeds of crime the court shall

(a) where it has made a declaration of forfeiture or where a declaration of forfeiture has previously been made in respect of property which is proved to the satisfaction of the court—
  (i) to have been the property which the defendant received in connection with the criminal activity carried on by him or her or any other person; or
  (ii) to have been property, or any part thereof, which directly or indirectly represented in the defendant's hands the property which he or she received in that connection, leave the property out of account;

(b) where a confiscation order has previously been made against the defendant leave out of account those proceeds of crime which are proved to the satisfaction of the court to have been taken into account in determining the amount to be recovered under that confiscation order.

10. Amounts Which Might Be Realized

(1) For the purpose of section 8 (1) (b) or 11 (3) (a), the amount which might be realized at the time of the making of a confiscation order against a defendant shall be the amount equal to the sum of

(a) the values at that time of all realizable property held by the defendant; and

(b) the values at that time of all affected gifts made by the defendant, less the sum of all obligations (if any) of the defendant having priority and which the court may recognize for this purpose.

(2) Notwithstanding the provisions of section 5 (1) but subject to the provisions of section 6 (2), the value of an affected gift at the time of the making of the relevant confiscation order shall be

(a) the value of the affected gift at the time when the recipient received it, as adjusted to take into account subsequent fluctuations in the value of money; or

(b) here subsection (3) applies, the value mentioned in that subsection, whichever is the greater value.

(3) If at the time of the making of the relevant confiscation order the recipient holds

(a) the property, other than cash, which he or she received, the value concerned shall be the value of the property at that time; or

(b) the property, or any part thereof, which directly or indirectly represents in his or her hands the property which he or she received, the value concerned shall be the value of the property, in so far as it represents the property which he or she received, at the time.

(4) For the purposes of subsection (1), an obligation has priority at the time of the making of the relevant confiscation order

(a) if it is an obligation of the defendant, where he or she has been convicted by a court of any offence
  (i) to pay a fine imposed before that time by the court; or
  (ii) to pay any other amount under any resultant order made before that time by the court;

(b) if it is an obligation which
  (i) if the estate of the defendant had at that time been sequestrated; or
  (ii) where the defendant is a company or other juristic person, if such company or juristic person is at that time being wound up, would be payable in pursuance of any secured or preferment claim against the insolvent estate or against such company or juristic person, as the case may be.

(5) A court shall not determine the amounts which might be realized as contemplated in subsection (1) unless it has afforded all persons holding any interest in the property concerned an opportunity to make representations to it in connection with the realization of that property.

11. Statements Relating to Proceeds of Crime

(1) (a) The public prosecutor may or, if so directed by the court, shall tender to the court a statement in writing under oath or affirmation by him or her or any other person in connection with any matter which is being enquired into by the court under section 8 (1), or which relates to the determination of the value of a defendant's proceeds of crime.

(b) A copy of such statement shall be served on the defendant at least 14 days before the date on which that statement is to be tendered to the court.

(2) (a) The defendant may dispute the correctness of any allegation contained in a statement referred to in subsection (1) (a), and if the defendant does so dispute the correctness of any such allegation, he or she shall state the grounds on which he or she relies.

(b) In so far as the defendant does not dispute the correctness of any allegation contained in such statement, that allegation shall be deemed to be conclusive proof of the matter to which it relates.

(3) (a) A defendant may or, if so directed by the court, shall tender to the court a statement in writing under oath or affirmation by him or her or by any other person in connection with any matter which relates to the determination of the amount which might be realized as contemplated in section 10 (1).

(b) A copy of such statement shall be served on the public prosecutor at least 14 days before the date on which that statement is to be tendered to the court.

(4) (a) The public prosecutor may admit the correctness of any allegation contained in a statement referred to in subsection (3) (a).

(b) In so far as the public prosecutor admits the correctness of any allegation contained in such statement, that allegation shall be deemed to be conclusive proof of the matter to which it relates.

12. Presumptions Relating to Proceeds of Crime
(1) For the purposes of an enquiry under section 8 (1) and, if it is found that the defendant did not at the fixed date, or since the beginning of a period of seven years before the fixed date, have legitimate sources of income sufficient to justify the interests in any property that the defendant holds, in determining whether the defendant has derived a benefit from an offence or related criminal activity, it shall be presumed, in the absence of evidence to the contrary, that such interests form part of such a benefit.

(2) For the purposes of an enquiry under section 8 (1) and, if it is found that a court had ordered the defendant to disclose any facts under section 16 (7) and that the defendant had without sufficient cause failed to disclose such facts or had, after being so ordered, furnished false information, knowing such information to be false or not believing it to be true, it shall be presumed, in the absence of evidence to the contrary, in determining

(a) whether the defendant has derived a benefit from an offence, that any property to which the information relates, forms part of such a benefit; and

(b) the value of his or her proceeds of crime, that any property to which the information relates, is held by the defendant as a payment or reward in connection with the offence or related criminal activity.

(3) For the purposes of an enquiry under section 8 (1) and, if it is found that a defendant has benefited from an offence in determining the value of his or her proceeds of crime, it shall be presumed, in the absence of evidence to the contrary that

(a) any property
  (i) held by him or her at any time at, or since, his or her conviction; or
  (ii) transferred to him or her at any time since the beginning of a period of seven years before the

fixed date, was received by him or her at the earliest time at which he or she held it, as a payment or other reward in connection with the offence or any related criminal activity committed by him or her;

(b) any expenditure incurred by him or her since the beginning of the period contemplated in paragraph (a) was met out of payments received by him or her in connection with the offence or any related criminal activity committed by him or her; and

(c) for the purpose of determining the value of any property
  (i) received by him or her at any time as a reward in connection with the offence or any related criminal activity committed by him or her or by any other person; or
  (ii) presumed in terms of paragraph (a) to have been received by him or her as a reward in connection with the offence or any related criminal activity committed by him or her, he or she received that property free of any other interest therein.

13. Effect of Confiscation Orders
(1) A confiscation order made

(a) by a magistrate's court, other than a regional court, shall have the effect of a civil judgment of that court;

(b) by a regional court shall have the effect of a civil judgment of the magistrate's court of the district in which the relevant trial took place.

(2) Where a superior court makes a confiscation order—

(a) the confiscation order shall have the effect of a civil judgment of that court; or

(b) the presiding judge may direct the registrar of that court to forward a certified copy of the confiscation order to the clerk of the magistrate's court designated by the presiding judge or, if no such court is designated, to the clerk of the magistrate's court within the area of jurisdiction of which the offence concerned was committed, and, on receipt of the said copy of the confiscation order the clerk of the magistrate's court concerned shall register the confiscation order whereupon it shall have the effect of a civil judgment of that magistrate's court.

14. *Procedure Where Person Absconds*

(1) If a person has absconded and the proceedings against him or her cannot be resumed within a period of six months due to his or her continued absence and the court is satisfied that

   (a) the person had been charged with an offence, that a restraint order had been made against him or her or that there would have been sufficient evidence for putting him or her on trial for an offence were it not for his or her absence; and

   (b) there are reasonable grounds to believe that a confiscation order would have been made against him or her, the court may, on the application by the Attorney-General or any public prosecutor authorized thereto in writing by him or her, enquire into any benefit the person may have derived from that offence or any related criminal activity.

(2) The court conducting an enquiry contemplated in subsection (1) may

   (a) if the court finds that the person referred to in that subsection has so benefited, make a confiscation order and the provisions of this Chapter shall, with the necessary changes, apply to the making of such order;

   (b) if a *curator bonis* has not been appointed in respect of any of the property concerned, appoint a *curator bonis* in respect of realizable property; and

   (c) authorize the realization of the property concerned in terms of Chapter 4.

(3) A court shall not exercise its powers under subsection (2) (a) and (c) unless it has afforded all persons having any interest in the property

concerned an opportunity to make representations to it in connection with the making of such orders.

[. . .]

Chapter 5—Offences

28. *Money Laundering*

Any person who, knowing or having reasonable grounds to believe that property is or forms part of the proceeds of crime

   (a) enters into any agreement or engages in any arrangement or transaction with anyone in connection with that property, whether such agreement, arrangement or transaction is legally enforceable or not; or

   (b) performs any other act in connection with such property, whether it is performed independently or in concert with any other person, which has or is likely to have the effect

      (i) of concealing or disguising the nature, source, location, disposition or movement of the said property or its ownership or any interest which anyone may have in respect thereof; or

      (ii) of enabling or assisting any person who has committed or commits an offence, whether in the Republic or elsewhere—
      (aa) to avoid prosecution; or
      (bb) to remove or diminish any property acquired directly or indirectly as a result of the commission of an offence, shall be guilty of an offence.

29. *Assisting Another to Benefit from Proceeds of Crime*

Any person who knowing, or having reasonable grounds to believe, that another person has obtained the proceeds of crime, enters into any agreement with anyone or engages in any arrangement whereby

   (a) the retention or the control by or on behalf of the said other person of the proceeds of crime is facilitated; or

   (b) the said proceeds of crime are used to make funds available to the said other person or to acquire property on his or her behalf or to benefit him or her in any other way, shall be guilty of an offence.

30. Acquisition, Possession or Use of Proceeds of Crime

Any person who acquires or uses or has possession of property knowing, or having reasonable grounds to believe, that it is or forms part of the proceeds of crime of another person, shall be guilty of an offence, unless such a person reports his or her suspicion or knowledge as contemplated in section 31.

31. Failure to Report Suspicion Regarding Proceeds of Crime

(1) Any person who carries on a business or is in charge of a business undertaking who has reason to suspect that any property which comes into his or her possession or the possession of the said business undertaking forms the proceeds of crime, shall be obliged to report his or her suspicion and the grounds on which it rests, within a reasonable time to a person designated by the Minister and shall take all reasonable steps to discharge such obligation: Provided that nothing in this section shall be construed so as to infringe upon the common law right to professional privilege between an attorney and his or her client in respect of information communicated to the attorney so as to enable him or her to provide advice, to defend or to render other legal assistance to the client in connection with an offence under any law, of which he or she is charged, in respect of which he or she has been arrested or summoned to appear in court or in respect of which an investigation with a view to instituting criminal proceedings is being conducted against him or her.

(2) Any person who fails to comply with an obligation contemplated in subsection (I) shall be guilty of an offence.

(3) (a) No obligation as to secrecy and no other restriction on the disclosure of information, whether imposed by any law, the common law or any agreement, shall affect any obligation imposed by subsection (1).

(b) No liability based on a breach of an obligation as to secrecy or any restriction on the disclosure of information, whether imposed by any law, the common law or any agreement, shall arise from a disclosure of any information in compliance with any obligation imposed by subsection (1).

32. Misuse of Information, Failure to Comply with Order of Court, and Hindering Person in Performance of Functions

(1) Any person who, knowing or having reasonable grounds to believe

(a) that information has been disclosed under the provisions of this Act; or

(b) that an investigation is being, or may be, conducted as a result of such a disclosure, directly or indirectly alerts another or brings information to the attention of another which will or is likely to prejudice such an investigation, shall be guilty of an offence.

(2) Any person who intentionally refuses or fails to comply with an order of court made in terms of this Act, shall be guilty of an offence.

(3) Any person who hinders a *curator bonis,* a police officer or any other person in the exercise, performance or carrying out of his or her powers, functions or duties under this Act, shall be guilty of an offence.

33. Penalties

(1) Any person convicted of an offence contemplated in section 28, 29 or 30 shall be liable to a fine, or to imprisonment for a period not exceeding 30 years.

(2) Any person convicted of an offence contemplated in

(*a*) section 31, 32 (1) or (2) shall be liable to a fine, or to imprisonment for a period not exceeding 15 years;

(*b*) section 32 (3) shall be liable to a fine, or to imprisonment for a period not exceeding two years.

[. . .]

27.
United States Code, Title 18—Crimes and Criminal Procedure

Title 18, Part I, Chapter 47, of the United States Code addresses fraud and false statements. Sections 1028, 1030, and 1037 address various aspects of fraud. Section 1028 deals with fraud in reference to the production, possession, use, or transfer of false identification documents. This section also covers the material, equipment, or device used to produce such documents. Also addressed in this section is the use of another person's identification with the intent to commit a criminal act. Sections 1030 and 1037 address computer-related fraud and applies to individuals who "having knowingly accessed a computer without authorization or exceeding authorized access" or an individual who "accesses a protected computer without authorization."

Source
FindLaw, http://caselaw.lp.findlaw.com/casecode/uscodes/ 18/toc.html.

Part I—Crimes

Chapter 47—Fraud and False Statements

Section 1028. Fraud and Related Activity in Connection with Identification Documents, Authentication Features, and Information
(a) Whoever, in a circumstance described in subsection (c) of this section—

(1) knowingly and without lawful authority produces an identification document, authentication feature, or a false identification document;

(2) knowingly transfers an identification document, authentication feature, or a false identification document knowing that such document or feature was stolen or produced without lawful authority;

(3) knowingly possesses with intent to use unlawfully or transfer unlawfully five or more identification documents (other than those issued lawfully for the use of the possessor), authentication features, or false identification documents;

(4) knowingly possesses an identification document (other than one issued lawfully for the use of the possessor), authentication feature, or a false identification document, with the intent such document or feature be used to defraud the United States;

(5) knowingly produces, transfers, or possesses a document-making implement or authentication feature with the intent such document-making implement or authentication feature will be used in the production of a false identification document or another document-making implement or authentication feature which will be so used;

(6) knowingly possesses an identification document or authentication feature that is or appears to be an identification document or authentication feature of the United States which is stolen or produced without lawful authority knowing that such document or feature was stolen or produced without such authority;

(7) knowingly transfers or uses, without lawful authority, a means of identification of another person with the intent to commit, or to aid or abet, any unlawful activity that constitutes a violation of Federal law, or that constitutes a felony under any applicable State or local law; or

(8) knowingly traffics in false authentication features for use in false identification documents, document-making implements, or means of identification; shall be punished as provided in subsection (b) of this section.

(b) The punishment for an offense under subsection (a) of this section is—

(1) except as provided in paragraphs (3) and (4), a fine under this title or imprisonment for not more than 15 years, or both, if the offense is—

  (A) the production or transfer of an identification document, authentication feature, or false identification document that is or appears to be—

    (i) an identification document or authentication feature issued by or under the authority of the United States; or

    (ii) a birth certificate, or a driver's license or personal identification card;

  (B) the production or transfer of more than five identification documents, authentication features, or false identification documents;

  (C) an offense under paragraph (5) of such subsection; or

  (D) an offense under paragraph (7) of such subsection that involves the transfer or use of 1 or more means of identification if, as a result of the offense, any individual committing the offense obtains anything of value aggregating $1,000 or more during any 1-year period;

(2) except as provided in paragraphs (3) and (4), a fine under this title or imprisonment for not more than three years, or both, if the offense is—

  (A) any other production, transfer, or use of a means of identification, an identification document, authentication feature, or a false identification document; or

  (B) an offense under paragraph (3) or (7) of such subsection;

(3) a fine under this title or imprisonment for not more than 20 years, or both, if the offense is committed—

  (A) to facilitate a drug trafficking crime (as defined in section 929(a)(2));

  (B) in connection with a crime of violence (as defined in section 924(c)(3)); or

  (C) after a prior conviction under this section becomes final;

(4) a fine under this title or imprisonment for not more than 25 years, or both, if the offense is committed to facilitate an act of international terrorism (as defined in section 2331(1) of this title);

(5) in the case of any offense under subsection (a), forfeiture to the United States of any personal property used or intended to be used to commit the offense; and

(6) a fine under this title or imprisonment for not more than one year, or both, in any other case.

(c) The circumstance referred to in subsection (a) of this section is that—

(1) the identification document, authentication feature, or false identification document is or appears to be issued by or under the authority of the United States or the document-making implement is designed or suited for making such an identification document, authentication feature, or false identification document;

(2) the offense is an offense under subsection (a)(4) of this section; or

(3) either—

  (A) the production, transfer, possession, or use prohibited by this section is in or affects interstate or foreign commerce, including the transfer of a document by electronic means; or

  (B) the means of identification, identification document, false identification document, or document-making implement is transported in the mail in the course of the production, transfer, possession, or use prohibited by this section.

(d) In this section—

(1) the term "authentication feature" means any hologram, watermark, certification, symbol, code, image, sequence of numbers or letters, or other feature that either individually or in combination with another feature is used by the issuing authority on an identification document, document-making implement, or means of identification to determine if the document is counterfeit, altered, or otherwise falsified;

(2) the term "document-making implement" means any implement, impression, template, computer

file, computer disc, electronic device, or computer hardware or software, that is specifically configured or primarily used for making an identification document, a false identification document, or another document-making implement;

(3) the term "identification document" means a document made or issued by or under the authority of the United States Government, a State, political subdivision of a State, a foreign government, political subdivision of a foreign government, an international governmental or an international quasi-governmental organization which, when completed with information concerning a particular individual, is of a type intended or commonly accepted for the purpose of identification of individuals;

(4) the term "false identification document" means a document of a type intended or commonly accepted for the purposes of identification of individuals that—

    (A) is not issued by or under the authority of a governmental entity or was issued under the authority of a governmental entity but was subsequently altered for purposes of deceit; and

    (B) appears to be issued by or under the authority of the United States Government, a State, a political subdivision of a State, a foreign government, a political subdivision of a foreign government, or an international governmental or quasi-governmental organization;

(5) the term "false authentication feature" means an authentication feature that—

    (A) is genuine in origin, but, without the authorization of the issuing authority, has been tampered with or altered for purposes of deceit;

    (B) is genuine, but has been distributed, or is intended for distribution, without the authorization of the issuing authority and not in connection with a lawfully made identification document, document-making implement, or means of identification to which such authentication feature is intended to be affixed or embedded by the respective issuing authority; or

    (C) appears to be genuine, but is not;

(6) the term "issuing authority"—

    (A) means any governmental entity or agency that is authorized to issue identification documents, means of identification, or authentication features; and

    (B) includes the United States Government, a State, a political subdivision of a State, a foreign government, a political subdivision of a foreign government, or an international government or quasi-governmental organization;

(7) the term "means of identification" means any name or number that may be used, alone or in conjunction with any other information, to identify a specific individual, including any—

    (A) name, social security number, date of birth, official State or government issued driver's license or identification number, alien registration number, government passport number, employer or taxpayer identification number;

    (B) unique biometric data, such as fingerprint, voice print, retina or iris image, or other unique physical representation;

    (C) unique electronic identification number, address, or routing code; or

    (D) telecommunication identifying information or access device (as defined in section 1029(e));

(8) the term "personal identification card" means an identification document issued by a State or local government solely for the purpose of identification;

(9) the term "produce" includes alter, authenticate, or assemble;

(10) the term "transfer" includes selecting an identification document, false identification document, or document-making implement and placing or directing the placement of such identification document, false identification document, or document-making implement on an online location where it is available to others;

(11) the term "State" includes any State of the United States, the District of Columbia, the Commonwealth of Puerto Rico, and any other commonwealth, possession, or territory of the United States; and

(12) the term "traffic" means—

    (A) to transport, transfer, or otherwise dispose of, to another, as consideration for anything of value; or

    (B) to make or obtain control of with intent to so transport, transfer, or otherwise dispose of.

(e) This section does not prohibit any lawfully authorized investigative, protective, or intelligence activity of a law enforcement agency of the United States, a State, or a political subdivision of a State, or of an intelligence agency of the United States, or any activity authorized under chapter 224 of this title.

(f) Attempt and Conspiracy.—Any person who attempts or conspires to commit any offense under this section shall be subject to the same penalties as those prescribed for the offense, the commission of which was the object of the attempt or conspiracy.

(g) Forfeiture Procedures.—The forfeiture of property under this section, including any seizure and disposition of the property and any related judicial or administrative proceeding, shall be governed by the provisions of section 413 (other than subsection (d) of that section) of the Comprehensive Drug Abuse Prevention and Control Act of 1970 (21 U.S.C. 853).

(h) Forfeiture; Disposition.—In the circumstance in which any person is convicted of a violation of subsection (a), the court shall order, in addition to the penalty prescribed, the forfeiture and destruction or other disposition of all illicit authentication features, identification documents, document-making implements, or means of identification.

(i) Rule of Construction.—For purpose of subsection (a)(7), a single identification document or false identification document that contains 1 or more means of identification shall be construed to be 1 means of identification.

Section 1030. Fraud and Related Activity in Connection with Computers

(a) Whoever—

    (1) having knowingly accessed a computer without authorization or exceeding authorized access, and by means of such conduct having obtained information that has been determined by the United States Government pursuant to an Executive order or statute to require protection against unauthorized disclosure for reasons of national defense or foreign relations, or any restricted data, as defined in paragraph y. of section 11 of the Atomic Energy Act of 1954, with reason to believe that such information so obtained could be used to the injury of the United States, or to the advantage of any foreign nation willfully communicates, delivers, transmits, or causes to be communicated, delivered, or transmitted, or attempts to communicate, deliver, transmit or cause to be communicated, delivered, or transmitted the same to any person not entitled to receive it, or willfully retains the same and fails to deliver it to the officer or employee of the United States entitled to receive it;

    (2) intentionally accesses a computer without authorization or exceeds authorized access, and thereby obtains—

        (A) information contained in a financial record of a financial institution, or of a card issuer as defined in section 1602(n) of title 15, or contained in a file of a consumer reporting agency on a consumer, as such terms are defined in the Fair Credit Reporting Act (15 U.S.C. 1681 et seq.);

        (B) information from any department or agency of the United States; or

        (C) information from any protected computer if the conduct involved an interstate or foreign communication;

    (3) intentionally, without authorization to access any nonpublic computer of a department or agency of the United States, accesses such a computer of that department or agency that is exclusively for the use of the Government of the United States

or, in the case of a computer not exclusively for such use, is used by or for the Government of the United States and such conduct affects that use by or for the Government of the United States;

(4) knowingly and with intent to defraud, accesses a protected computer without authorization, or exceeds authorized access, and by means of such conduct furthers the intended fraud and obtains anything of value, unless the object of the fraud and the thing obtained consists only of the use of the computer and the value of such use is not more than $5,000 in any 1-year period;

(5)(A)(i) knowingly causes the transmission of a program, information, code, or command, and as a result of such conduct, intentionally causes damage without authorization, to a protected computer;

(ii) intentionally accesses a protected computer without authorization, and as a result of such conduct, recklessly causes damage; or

(iii) intentionally accesses a protected computer without authorization, and as a result of such conduct, causes damage; and

(B) by conduct described in clause (i), (ii), or (iii) of subparagraph (A), caused (or, in the case of an attempted offense, would, if completed, have caused)—

(i) loss to 1 or more persons during any 1-year period (and, for purposes of an investigation, prosecution, or other proceeding brought by the United States only, loss resulting from a related course of conduct affecting 1 or more other protected computers) aggregating at least $5,000 in value;

(ii) the modification or impairment, or potential modification or impairment, of the medical examination, diagnosis, treatment, or care of 1 or more individuals;

(iii) physical injury to any person;

(iv) a threat to public health or safety; or

(v) damage affecting a computer system used by or for a government entity in furtherance of the administration of justice, national defense, or national security;

(6) knowingly and with intent to defraud traffics (as defined in section 1029) in any password or similar information through which a computer may be accessed without authorization, if—

(A) such trafficking affects interstate or foreign commerce; or

(B) such computer is used by or for the Government of the United States;

(7) with intent to extort from any person any money or other thing of value, transmits in interstate or foreign commerce any communication containing any threat to cause damage to a protected computer; shall be punished as provided in subsection (c) of this section.

(b) Whoever attempts to commit an offense under subsection (a) of this section shall be punished as provided in subsection (c) of this section.

(c) The punishment for an offense under subsection (a) or (b) of this section is—

(1)(A) a fine under this title or imprisonment for not more than ten years, or both, in the case of an offense under subsection (a)(1) of this section which does not occur after a conviction for another offense under this section, or an attempt to commit an offense punishable under this subparagraph; and

(B) a fine under this title or imprisonment for not more than twenty years, or both, in the case of an offense under subsection (a)(1) of this section which occurs after a conviction for another offense under this section, or an attempt to commit an offense punishable under this subparagraph;

(2)(A) except as provided in subparagraph (B), a fine under this title or imprisonment for not more than one year, or both, in the case of an offense under subsection (a)(2), (a)(3), (a)(5)(A)(iii), or (a)(6) of this section which does not occur after a conviction for another offense under this section, or an attempt to commit an offense punishable under this subparagraph;

(B) a fine under this title or imprisonment for not more than 5 years, or both, in the case of an offense under subsection (a)(2), or an attempt to commit an offense punishable under this subparagraph, if—

(i) the offense was committed for purposes of commercial advantage or private financial gain;

    (ii) the offense was committed in furtherance of any criminal or tortious act in violation of the Constitution or laws of the United States or of any State; or

    (iii) the value of the information obtained exceeds $5,000; and

(C) a fine under this title or imprisonment for not more than ten years, or both, in the case of an offense under subsection (a)(2), (a)(3) or (a)(6) of this section which occurs after a conviction for another offense under this section, or an attempt to commit an offense punishable under this subparagraph;

(3)(A) a fine under this title or imprisonment for not more than five years, or both, in the case of an offense under subsection (a)(4) or (a)(7) of this section which does not occur after a conviction for another offense under this section, or an attempt to commit an offense punishable under this subparagraph; and

(B) a fine under this title or imprisonment for not more than ten years, or both, in the case of an offense under subsection (a)(4), (a)(5)(A)(iii), or (a)(7) of this section which occurs after a conviction for another offense under this section, or an attempt to commit an offense punishable under this subparagraph;

(4)(A) except as provided in paragraph (5), a fine under this title, imprisonment for not more than 10 years, or both, in the case of an offense under subsection (a)(5)(A)(i), or an attempt to commit an offense punishable under that subsection;

(B) a fine under this title, imprisonment for not more than 5 years, or both, in the case of an offense under subsection (a)(5)(A)(ii), or an attempt to commit an offense punishable under that subsection;

(C) except as provided in paragraph (5), a fine under this title, imprisonment for not more than 20 years, or both, in the case of an offense under subsection (a)(5)(A)(i) or (a)(5)(A)(ii), or an attempt to commit an offense punishable under either subsection, that occurs after a conviction for another offense under this section; and

(5)(A) if the offender knowingly or recklessly causes or attempts to cause serious bodily injury from conduct in violation of subsection (a)(5)(A)(i), a fine under this title or imprisonment for not more than 20 years, or both; and

(B) if the offender knowingly or recklessly causes or attempts to cause death from conduct in violation of subsection (a)(5)(A)(i), a fine under this title or imprisonment for any term of years or for life, or both.

(d)(1) The United States Secret Service shall, in addition to any other agency having such authority, have the authority to investigate offenses under this section.

(2) The Federal Bureau of Investigation shall have primary authority to investigate offenses under subsection (a)(1) for any cases involving espionage, foreign counterintelligence, information protected against unauthorized disclosure for reasons of national defense or foreign relations, or Restricted Data (as that term is defined in section 11y of the Atomic Energy Act of 1954 (42 U.S.C. 2014(y)), except for offenses affecting the duties of the United States Secret Service pursuant to section 3056(a) of this title.

(3) Such authority shall be exercised in accordance with an agreement which shall be entered into by the Secretary of the Treasury and the Attorney General.

(e) As used in this section—

(1) the term "computer" means an electronic, magnetic, optical, electrochemical, or other high speed data processing device performing logical, arithmetic, or storage functions, and includes any data storage facility or communications facility directly related to or operating in conjunction with such device, but such term does not include an automated typewriter or typesetter, a portable hand held calculator, or other similar device;

(2) the term "protected computer" means a computer—

(A) exclusively for the use of a financial institution or the United States Government, or, in the case of a computer not exclusively for such use, used by or for a financial institution or the United States Government and the conduct constituting the offense affects that use by or for the financial institution or the Government; or

(B) which is used in interstate or foreign commerce or communication, including a computer located outside the United States that is used in a manner that affects interstate or foreign commerce or communication of the United States;

(3) the term "State" includes the District of Columbia, the Commonwealth of Puerto Rico, and any other commonwealth, possession or territory of the United States;

(4) the term "financial institution" means—

(A) an institution, with deposits insured by the Federal Deposit Insurance Corporation;

(B) the Federal Reserve or a member of the Federal Reserve including any Federal Reserve Bank;

(C) a credit union with accounts insured by the National Credit Union Administration;

(D) a member of the Federal home loan bank system and any home loan bank;

(E) any institution of the Farm Credit System under the Farm Credit Act of 1971;

(F) a broker-dealer registered with the Securities and Exchange Commission pursuant to section 15 of the Securities Exchange Act of 1934;

(G) the Securities Investor Protection Corporation;

(H) a branch or agency of a foreign bank (as such terms are defined in paragraphs (1) and (3) of section 1(b) of the International Banking Act of 1978); and

(I) an organization operating under section 25 or section 25(a) of the Federal Reserve Act;

(5) the term "financial record" means information derived from any record held by a financial institution pertaining to a customer's relationship with the financial institution;

(6) the term "exceeds authorized access" means to access a computer with authorization and to use such access to obtain or alter information in the computer that the accesser is not entitled so to obtain or alter;

(7) the term "department of the United States" means the legislative or judicial branch of the Government or one of the executive departments enumerated in section 101 of title 5;

(8) the term "damage" means any impairment to the integrity or availability of data, a program, a system, or information;

(9) the term "government entity" includes the Government of the United States, any State or political subdivision of the United States, any foreign country, and any state, province, municipality, or other political subdivision of a foreign country;

(10) the term "conviction" shall include a conviction under the law of any State for a crime punishable by imprisonment for more than 1 year, an element of which is unauthorized access, or exceeding authorized access, to a computer;

(11) the term "loss" means any reasonable cost to any victim, including the cost of responding to an offense, conducting a damage assessment, and restoring the data, program, system, or information to its condition prior to the offense, and any revenue lost, cost incurred, or other consequential damages incurred because of interruption of service; and

(12) the term "person" means any individual, firm, corporation, educational institution, financial institution, governmental entity, or legal or other entity.

(f) This section does not prohibit any lawfully authorized investigative, protective, or intelligence activity of a law enforcement agency of the United States, a State, or a political subdivision of a State, or of an intelligence agency of the United States.

(g) Any person who suffers damage or loss by reason of a violation of this section may maintain a civil action against the violator to obtain compensatory damages and injunctive relief or other equitable relief. A civil action for a violation of this section may be brought only if the conduct involves 1 of the factors set forth in clause (i), (ii), (iii), (iv), or (v) of subsection (a)(5)(B). Damages for a violation involving only conduct described in subsection (a)(5)(B)(i) are limited to economic damages. No action may be brought under this subsection unless such action is begun within 2 years of the date of the act complained of or the date of the discovery of the damage. No action may be brought under this subsection for the negligent design or manufacture of computer hardware, computer software, or firmware.

(h) The Attorney General and the Secretary of the Treasury shall report to the Congress annually, during the first 3 years following the date of the enactment of this subsection, concerning investigations and prosecutions under subsection (a)(5).

Section 1037. Fraud and Related Activity in Connection with Electronic Mail

(a) In General.—Whoever, in or affecting interstate or foreign commerce, knowingly—

(1) accesses a protected computer without authorization, and intentionally initiates the transmission of multiple commercial electronic mail messages from or through such computer,

(2) uses a protected computer to relay or retransmit multiple commercial electronic mail messages, with the intent to deceive or mislead recipients, or any Internet access service, as to the origin of such messages,

(3) materially falsifies header information in multiple commercial electronic mail messages and intentionally initiates the transmission of such messages,

(4) registers, using information that materially falsifies the identity of the actual registrant, for five or more electronic mail accounts or online user accounts or two or more domain names, and intentionally initiates the transmission of multiple commercial electronic mail messages from any

combination of such accounts or domain names, or

(5) falsely represents oneself to be the registrant or the legitimate successor in interest to the registrant of 5 or more Internet Protocol addresses, and intentionally initiates the transmission of multiple commercial electronic mail messages from such addresses, or conspires to do so, shall be punished as provided in subsection (b).

(b) Penalties.—The punishment for an offense under subsection (a) is—

(1) a fine under this title, imprisonment for not more than 5 years, or both, if—

(A) the offense is committed in furtherance of any felony under the laws of the United States or of any State; or

(B) the defendant has previously been convicted under this section or section 1030, or under the law of any State for conduct involving the transmission of multiple commercial electronic mail messages or unauthorized access to a computer system;

(2) a fine under this title, imprisonment for not more than 3 years, or both, if—

(A) the offense is an offense under subsection (a)(1);

(B) the offense is an offense under subsection (a)(4) and involved 20 or more falsified electronic mail or online user account registrations, or 10 or more falsified domain name registrations;

(C) the volume of electronic mail messages transmitted in furtherance of the offense exceeded 2,500 during any 24-hour period, 25,000 during any 30-day period, or 250,000 during any 1-year period;

(D) the offense caused loss to one or more persons aggregating $5,000 or more in value during any 1-year period;

(E) as a result of the offense any individual committing the offense obtained anything of value aggregating $5,000 or more during any 1-year period; or

(F) the offense was undertaken by the defendant in concert with three or more other persons with respect to whom the defendant occupied a position of organizer or leader; and

(3) a fine under this title or imprisonment for not more than 1 year, or both, in any other case.

(c) Forfeiture.—

(1) In general.—The court, in imposing sentence on a person who is convicted of an offense under this section, shall order that the defendant forfeit to the United States—

(A) any property, real or personal, constituting or traceable to gross proceeds obtained from such offense; and

(B) any equipment, software, or other technology used or intended to be used to commit or to facilitate the commission of such offense.

(2) Procedures.—The procedures set forth in section 413 of the Controlled Substances Act (21 U.S.C. 853), other than subsection (d) of that section, and in Rule 32.2 of the Federal Rules of Criminal Procedure, shall apply to all stages of a criminal forfeiture proceeding under this section.

(d) Definitions.—In this section:

(1) Loss.—The term "loss" has the meaning given that term in section 1030(e) of this title.

(2) Materially.—For purposes of paragraphs (3) and (4) of subsection (a), header information or registration information is materially falsified if it is altered or concealed in a manner that would impair the ability of a recipient of the message, an Internet access service processing the message on behalf of a recipient, a person alleging a violation of this section, or a law enforcement agency to identify, locate, or respond to a person who initiated the electronic mail message or to investigate the alleged violation.

(3) Multiple.—The term "multiple" means more than 100 electronic mail messages during a 24-hour period, more than 1,000 electronic mail messages during a 30-day period, or more than 10,000 electronic mail messages during a 1-year period.

(4) Other terms.—Any other term has the meaning given that term by section 3 of the CAN-SPAM Act of 2003.

28.
United Nations Convention against Transnational Organized Crime 2000

The United Nations (UN) has been a vanguard in taking steps toward preventing organized crime. On 29 September 2003, the UN convention took a measured step in this direction. The convention was adopted by a resolution of the General Assembly on 15 November 2000. Signed by 147 members, the convention became operational in 2003. The majority of the members had signed it by December 2000. The reservation of some members was duly noted. The purpose of the convention, "to promote cooperation to prevent and combat transnational organized crime," is specified in Article 1,

Source
United Nations Office on Drugs and Crime, http://www.uncjin.org/Documents/Conventions/dcatoc/final_documents_2/convention_eng.pdf.

Article 1

Statement of Purpose
The purpose of this Convention is to promote cooperation to prevent and combat transnational organized crime more effectively.

Article 2

Use of Terms
For the purposes of this Convention:

(a) "Organized criminal group" shall mean a structured group of three or more persons, existing for a period of time and acting in concert with the aim of committing one or more serious crimes or offences established in accordance with this

Convention, in order to obtain, directly or indirectly, a financial or other material benefit;

(b) "Serious crime" shall mean conduct constituting an offence punishable by a maximum deprivation of liberty of at least four years or a more serious penalty;

(c) "Structured group" shall mean a group that is not randomly formed for the immediate commission of an offence and that does not need to have formally defined roles for its members, continuity of its membership or a developed structure;

(d) "Property" shall mean assets of every kind, whether corporeal or incorporeal, movable or immovable, tangible or intangible, and legal documents or instruments evidencing title to, or interest in, such assets;

(e) "Proceeds of crime" shall mean any property derived from or obtained, directly or indirectly, through the commission of an offence;

(f) "Freezing" or "seizure" shall mean temporarily prohibiting the transfer, conversion, disposition or movement of property or temporarily assuming custody or control of property on the basis of an order issued by a court or other competent authority;

(g) "Confiscation", which includes forfeiture where applicable, shall mean the permanent deprivation of property by order of a court or other competent authority;

(h) "Predicate offence" shall mean any offence as a result of which proceeds have been generated that may become the subject of an offence as defined in article 6 of this Convention;

(i) "Controlled delivery" shall mean the technique of allowing illicit or suspect consignments to pass out of, through or into the territory of one or more States, with the knowledge and under the supervision of their competent authorities, with a view to the investigation of an offence and the identification of persons involved in the commission of the offence;

(j) "Regional economic integration organization" shall mean an organization constituted by sovereign States of a given region, to which its member States have transferred competence in respect of

matters governed by this Convention and which has been duly authorized, in accordance with its internal procedures, to sign, ratify, accept, approve or accede to it; references to "States Parties" under this Convention shall apply to such organizations within the limits of their competence.

Article 3

Scope of Application

1. This Convention shall apply, except as otherwise stated herein, to the prevention, investigation and prosecution of:

(a) The offences established in accordance with articles 5, 6, 8 and 23 of this Convention; and

(b) Serious crime as defined in article 2 of this Convention; where the offence is transnational in nature and involves an organized criminal group.

2. For the purpose of paragraph 1 of this article, an offence is transnational in nature if:

(a) It is committed in more than one State;

(b) It is committed in one State but a substantial part of its preparation, planning, direction or control takes place in another State;

(c) It is committed in one State but involves an organized criminal group that engages in criminal activities in more than one State; or

(d) It is committed in one State but has substantial effects in another State.

Article 4

Protection of Sovereignty

1. States Parties shall carry out their obligations under this Convention in a manner consistent with the principles of sovereign equality and territorial integrity of States and that of non-intervention in the domestic affairs of other States.

2. Nothing in this Convention entitles a State Party to undertake in the territory of another State the exercise of jurisdiction and performance of functions that are reserved exclusively for the authorities of that other State by its domestic law.

Article 5

Criminalization of Participation in an Organized Criminal Group

1. Each State Party shall adopt such legislative and other measures as may be necessary to establish as criminal offences, when committed intentionally:

(a) Either or both of the following as criminal offences distinct from those involving the attempt or completion of the criminal activity:

(i) Agreeing with one or more other persons to commit a serious crime for a purpose relating directly or indirectly to the obtaining of a financial or other material benefit and, where required by domestic law, involving an act undertaken by one of the participants in furtherance of the agreement or involving an organized criminal group;

(ii) Conduct by a person who, with knowledge of either the aim and general criminal activity of an organized criminal group or its intention to commit the crimes in question, takes an active part in:
a. Criminal activities of the organized criminal group;
b. Other activities of the organized criminal group in the knowledge that his or her participation will contribute to the achievement of the above-described criminal aim;

(b) Organizing, directing, aiding, abetting, facilitating or counselling the commission of serious crime involving an organized criminal group.

2. The knowledge, intent, aim, purpose or agreement referred to in paragraph 1 of this article may be inferred from objective factual circumstances.

3. States Parties whose domestic law requires involvement of an organized criminal group for purposes of the offences established in accordance with paragraph 1 (a) (i) of this article shall ensure that their domestic law covers all serious crimes involving organized criminal groups. Such States Parties, as well as States Parties whose domestic law requires an act in furtherance of the agreement for purposes of the offences established in accordance with paragraph 1 (a) (i) of this article, shall so inform the Secretary-General of the United Nations at the time of their signature or of deposit of their instrument of ratification, acceptance or approval of or accession to this Convention.

Article 6

Criminalization of the Laundering of Proceeds of Crime

1. Each State Party shall adopt, in accordance with fundamental principles of its domestic law, such legislative and other measures as may be necessary to establish as criminal offences, when committed intentionally:

(a) (i) The conversion or transfer of property, knowing that such property is the proceeds of crime, for the purpose of concealing or disguising the illicit origin of the property or of helping any person who is involved in the commission of the predicate offence to evade the legal consequences of his or her action;

(ii) The concealment or disguise of the true nature, source, location, disposition, movement or ownership of or rights with respect to property, knowing that such property is the proceeds of crime;

(b) Subject to the basic concepts of its legal system:

(i) The acquisition, possession or use of property, knowing, at the time of receipt, that such property is the proceeds of crime;

(ii) Participation in, association with or conspiracy to commit, attempts to commit and aiding, abetting, facilitating and counselling the commission of any of the offences established in accordance with this article.

2. For purposes of implementing or applying paragraph 1 of this article:

(a) Each State Party shall seek to apply paragraph 1 of this article to the widest range of predicate offences;

(b) Each State Party shall include as predicate offences all serious crime as defined in article 2 of this Convention and the offences established in accordance with articles 5, 8 and 23 of this Convention. In the case of States Parties whose legislation sets out a list of specific predicate offences, they shall, at a minimum, include in such list a comprehensive range of offences associated with organized criminal groups;

(c) For the purposes of subparagraph (b), predicate offences shall include offences committed both within and outside the jurisdiction of the State Party in question. However, offences committed outside the jurisdiction of a State Party shall constitute predicate offences only when the relevant conduct is a criminal offence under the domestic law of the State where it is committed and would be a criminal offence under the domestic law of the State Party implementing or applying this article had it been committed there;

(d) Each State Party shall furnish copies of its laws that give effect to this article and of any subsequent changes to such laws or a description thereof to the Secretary-General of the United Nations;

(e) If required by fundamental principles of the domestic law of a State Party, it may be provided that the offences set forth in paragraph 1 of this article do not apply to the persons who committed the predicate offence;

(f) Knowledge, intent or purpose required as an element of an offence set forth in paragraph 1 of this article may be inferred from objective factual circumstances.

Article 7

Measures to Combat Money-Laundering
1. Each State Party:

(a) Shall institute a comprehensive domestic regulatory and supervisory regime for banks and non-bank financial institutions and, where appropriate, other bodies particularly susceptible to money laundering, within its competence, in order to deter and detect all forms of money laundering, which regime shall emphasize requirements for customer identification, record-keeping and the reporting of suspicious transactions;

(b) Shall, without prejudice to articles 18 and 27 of this Convention, ensure that administrative, regulatory, law enforcement and other authorities dedicated to combating money-laundering (including, where appropriate under domestic law, judicial authorities) have the ability to cooperate and exchange information at the national and international levels within the conditions prescribed by its domestic law and, to that end, shall consider the establishment of a financial intelligence unit to serve as a national centre for the collection, analysis and dissemination of information regarding potential money-laundering.

2. States Parties shall consider implementing feasible measures to detect and monitor the movement of cash and appropriate negotiable instruments across their borders, subject to safeguards to ensure proper use of information and without impeding in any way the movement of legitimate capital. Such measures may include a requirement that individuals and businesses report the cross-border transfer of substantial quantities of cash and appropriate negotiable instruments.

3. In establishing a domestic regulatory and supervisory regime under the terms of this article, and without prejudice to any other article of this Convention, States Parties are called upon to use as a guideline the relevant initiatives of regional, interregional and multilateral organizations against money-laundering.

4. States Parties shall endeavour to develop and promote global, regional, subregional and bilateral cooperation among judicial, law enforcement and financial regulatory authorities in order to combat moneylaundering.

Article 8

Criminalization of Corruption

1. Each State Party shall adopt such legislative and other measures as may be necessary to establish as criminal offences, when committed intentionally:

   (a) The promise, offering or giving to a public official, directly or indirectly, of an undue advantage, for the official himself or herself or another person or entity, in order that the official act or refrain from acting in the exercise of his or her official duties;

   (b) The solicitation or acceptance by a public official, directly or indirectly, of an undue advantage, for the official himself or herself or another person or entity, in order that the official act or refrain from acting in the exercise of his or her official duties.

2. Each State Party shall consider adopting such legislative and other measures as may be necessary to establish as criminal offences conduct referred to in paragraph 1 of this article involving a foreign public official or international civil servant. Likewise, each State Party shall consider establishing as criminal offences other forms of corruption.

3. Each State Party shall also adopt such measures as may be necessary to establish as a criminal offence participation as an accomplice in an offence established in accordance with this article.

4. For the purposes of paragraph 1 of this article and article 9 of this Convention, "public official" shall mean a public official or a person who provides a public service as defined in the domestic law and as applied in the criminal law of the State Party in which the person in question performs that function.

Article 9

Measures against Corruption

1. In addition to the measures set forth in article 8 of this Convention, each State Party shall, to the extent appropriate and consistent with its legal system, adopt legislative, administrative or other effective measures to promote integrity and to prevent, detect and punish the corruption of public officials.

2. Each State Party shall take measures to ensure effective action by its authorities in the prevention, detection and punishment of the corruption of public officials, including providing such authorities with adequate independence to deter the exertion of inappropriate influence on their actions.

Article 10

Liability of Legal Persons

1. Each State Party shall adopt such measures as may be necessary, consistent with its legal principles, to establish the liability of legal persons for participation in serious crimes involving an organized criminal group and for the offences established in accordance with articles 5, 6, 8 and 23 of this Convention.

2. Subject to the legal principles of the State Party, the liability of legal persons may be criminal, civil or administrative.

3. Such liability shall be without prejudice to the criminal liability of the natural persons who have committed the offences.

4. Each State Party shall, in particular, ensure that legal persons held liable in accordance with this article are subject to effective, proportionate and dissuasive criminal or non-criminal sanctions, including monetary sanctions.

Article 11

Prosecution, Adjudication and Sanctions
1. Each State Party shall make the commission of an offence established in accordance with articles 5, 6, 8 and 23 of this Convention liable to sanctions that take into account the gravity of that offence.

2. Each State Party shall endeavour to ensure that any discretionary legal powers under its domestic law relating to the prosecution of persons for offences covered by this Convention are exercised to maximize the effectiveness of law enforcement measures in respect of those offences and with due regard to the need to deter the commission of such offences.

3. In the case of offences established in accordance with articles 5, 6, 8 and 23 of this Convention, each State Party shall take appropriate measures, in accordance with its domestic law and with due regard to the rights of the defence, to seek to ensure that conditions imposed in connection with decisions on release pending trial or appeal take into consideration the need to ensure the presence of the defendant at subsequent criminal proceedings.

4. Each State Party shall ensure that its courts or other competent authorities bear in mind the grave nature of the offences covered by this Convention when considering the eventuality of early release or parole of persons convicted of such offences.

5. Each State Party shall, where appropriate, establish under its domestic law a long statute of limitations period in which to commence proceedings for any offence covered by this Convention and a longer period where the alleged offender has evaded the administration of justice.

6. Nothing contained in this Convention shall affect the principle that the description of the offences established in accordance with this Convention and of the applicable legal defences or other legal principles controlling the lawfulness of conduct is reserved to the domestic law of a State Party and that such offences shall be prosecuted and punished in accordance with that law.

Article 12

Confiscation and Seizure
1. States Parties shall adopt, to the greatest extent possible within their domestic legal systems, such measures as may be necessary to enable confiscation of:

(a) Proceeds of crime derived from offences covered by this Convention or property the value of which corresponds to that of such proceeds;
(b) Property, equipment or other instrumentalities used in or destined for use in offences covered by this Convention.

2. States Parties shall adopt such measures as may be necessary to enable the identification, tracing, freezing or seizure of any item referred to in paragraph 1 of this article for the purpose of eventual confiscation.

3. If proceeds of crime have been transformed or converted, in part or in full, into other property, such property shall be liable to the measures referred to in this article instead of the proceeds.

4. If proceeds of crime have been intermingled with property acquired from legitimate sources, such property shall, without prejudice to any powers relating to freezing or seizure, be liable to confiscation up to the assessed value of the intermingled proceeds.

5. Income or other benefits derived from proceeds of crime, from property into which proceeds of crime have been transformed or converted or from property with which proceeds of crime have been intermingled shall also be liable to the measures referred to in this article, in the same manner and to the same extent as proceeds of crime.

6. For the purposes of this article and article 13 of this Convention, each State Party shall empower its courts or other competent authorities to order that bank, financial or commercial records be made available or be seized. States Parties shall not decline to act under the provisions of this paragraph on the ground of bank secrecy.

7. States Parties may consider the possibility of requiring that an offender demonstrate the lawful origin of alleged proceeds of crime or other property liable to confiscation, to the extent that such a requirement is consistent with the principles of their domestic law and with the nature of the judicial and other proceedings.

8. The provisions of this article shall not be construed to prejudice the rights of bona fide third parties.

9. Nothing contained in this article shall affect the principle that the measures to which it refers shall be defined and implemented in accordance with and subject to the provisions of the domestic law of a State Party.

Article 13

International Cooperation for Purposes of Confiscation
1. A State Party that has received a request from another State Party having jurisdiction over an offence covered by this Convention for confiscation of proceeds of crime, property, equipment or other instrumentalities referred to in article 12, paragraph 1, of this Convention situated in its territory shall, to the greatest extent possible within its domestic legal system:

   (a) Submit the request to its competent authorities for the purpose of obtaining an order of confiscation and, if such an order is granted, give effect to it; or

   (b) Submit to its competent authorities, with a view to giving effect to it to the extent requested, an

order of confiscation issued by a court in the territory of the requesting State Party in accordance with article 12, paragraph 1, of this Convention insofar as it relates to proceeds of crime, property, equipment or other instrumentalities referred to in article 12, paragraph 1, situated in the territory of the requested State Party.

2. Following a request made by another State Party having jurisdiction over an offence covered by this Convention, the requested State Party shall take measures to identify, trace and freeze or seize proceeds of crime, property, equipment or other instrumentalities referred to in article 12, paragraph 1, of this Convention for the purpose of eventual confiscation to be ordered either by the requesting State Party or, pursuant to a request under paragraph 1 of this article, by the requested State Party.

3. The provisions of article 18 of this Convention are applicable, mutatis mutandis, to this article. In addition to the information specified in article 18, paragraph 15, requests made pursuant to this article shall contain:

   (a) In the case of a request pertaining to paragraph 1 (a) of this article, a description of the property to be confiscated and a statement of the facts relied upon by the requesting State Party sufficient to enable the requested State Party to seek the order under its domestic law;

   (b) In the case of a request pertaining to paragraph 1 (b) of this article, a legally admissible copy of an order of confiscation upon which the request is based issued by the requesting State Party, a statement of the facts and information as to the extent to which execution of the order is requested;

   (c) In the case of a request pertaining to paragraph 2 of this article, a statement of the facts relied upon by the requesting State Party and a description of the actions requested.

4. The decisions or actions provided for in paragraphs 1 and 2 of this article shall be taken by the requested State Party in accordance with and subject to the provisions of its domestic law and its procedural rules or any bilateral or multilateral treaty, agreement or arrangement to which it may be bound in relation to the requesting State Party.

5. Each State Party shall furnish copies of its laws and regulations that give effect to this article and of any subsequent changes to such laws and regulations or a description thereof to the Secretary-General of the United Nations.

6. If a State Party elects to make the taking of the measures referred to in paragraphs 1 and 2 of this article conditional on the existence of a relevant treaty, that State Party shall consider this Convention the necessary and sufficient treaty basis.

7. Cooperation under this article may be refused by a State Party if the offence to which the request relates is not an offence covered by this Convention.

8. The provisions of this article shall not be construed to prejudice the rights of bona fide third parties.

9. States Parties shall consider concluding bilateral or multilateral treaties, agreements or arrangements to enhance the effectiveness of international cooperation undertaken pursuant to this article.

Article 14

Disposal of Confiscated Proceeds of Crime or Property

1. Proceeds of crime or property confiscated by a State Party pursuant to articles 12 or 13, paragraph 1, of this Convention shall be disposed of by that State Party in accordance with its domestic law and administrative procedures.

2. When acting on the request made by another State Party in accordance with article 13 of this Convention, States Parties shall, to the extent permitted by domestic law and if so requested, give priority consideration to returning the confiscated proceeds of crime or property to the requesting State Party so that it can give compensation to the victims of the crime or return such proceeds of crime or property to their legitimate owners.

3. When acting on the request made by another State Party in accordance with articles 12 and 13 of this Convention, a State Party may give special consideration to concluding agreements or arrangements on:

(a) Contributing the value of such proceeds of crime or property or funds derived from the sale of such proceeds of crime or property or a part thereof to the account designated in accordance with article 30, paragraph 2 (c), of this Convention and to intergovernmental bodies specializing in the fight against organized crime;

(b) Sharing with other States Parties, on a regular or case-by-case basis, such proceeds of crime or property, or funds derived from the sale of such proceeds of crime or property, in accordance with its domestic law or administrative procedures.

Article 15

Jurisdiction

1. Each State Party shall adopt such measures as may be necessary to establish its jurisdiction over the offences established in accordance with articles 5, 6, 8 and 23 of this Convention when:

(a) The offence is committed in the territory of that State Party; or

(b) The offence is committed on board a vessel that is flying the flag of that State Party or an aircraft that is registered under the laws of that State Party at the time that the offence is committed.

2. Subject to article 4 of this Convention, a State Party may also establish its jurisdiction over any such offence when:

(a) The offence is committed against a national of that State Party;

(b) The offence is committed by a national of that State Party or a stateless person who has his or her habitual residence in its territory; or

(c) The offence is:

(i) One of those established in accordance with article 5, paragraph 1, of this Convention and is committed outside its territory with a view to the commission of a serious crime within its territory;

(ii) One of those established in accordance with article 6, paragraph 1 (b) (ii), of this Convention and is committed outside its territory with a view to the commission of an offence established in accordance with article 6, paragraph 1 (a) (i) or (ii) or (b) (i), of this Convention within its territory.

3. For the purposes of article 16, paragraph 10, of this Convention, each State Party shall adopt such measures as may be necessary to establish its jurisdiction over the offences covered by this Convention when the alleged offender is present in its territory and it does not extradite such person solely on the ground that he or she is one of its nationals.

4. Each State Party may also adopt such measures as may be necessary to establish its jurisdiction over the offences covered by this Convention when the alleged offender is present in its territory and it does not extradite him or her.

5. If a State Party exercising its jurisdiction under paragraph 1 or 2 of this article has been notified, or has otherwise learned, that one or more other States Parties are conducting an investigation, prosecution or judicial proceeding in respect of the same conduct, the competent authorities of those States Parties shall, as appropriate, consult one another with a view to coordinating their actions.

6. Without prejudice to norms of general international law, this Convention does not exclude the exercise of any criminal jurisdiction established by a State Party in accordance with its domestic law.

Article 16

Extradition

1. This article shall apply to the offences covered by this Convention or in cases where an offence referred to in article 3, paragraph 1 (a) or (b), involves an organized criminal group and the person who is the subject of the request for extradition is located in the territory of the requested State Party, provided that the offence for which extradition is sought is punishable under the domestic law of both the requesting State Party and the requested State Party.

2. If the request for extradition includes several separate serious crimes, some of which are not covered by this article, the requested State Party may apply this article also in respect of the latter offences.

3. Each of the offences to which this article applies shall be deemed to be included as an extraditable offence in any extradition treaty existing between States Parties. States Parties undertake to include such offences as extraditable offences in every extradition treaty to be concluded between them.

4. If a State Party that makes extradition conditional on the existence of a treaty receives a request for extradition from another State Party with which it has no extradition treaty, it may consider this Convention the legal basis for extradition in respect of any offence to which this article applies.

5. States Parties that make extradition conditional on the existence of a treaty shall:

    (a) At the time of deposit of their instrument of ratification, acceptance, approval of or accession to this Convention, inform the Secretary-General of the United Nations whether they will take this Convention as the legal basis for cooperation on extradition with other States Parties to this Convention; and

    (b) If they do not take this Convention as the legal basis for cooperation on extradition, seek, where appropriate, to conclude treaties on extradition with other States Parties to this Convention in order to implement this article.

6. States Parties that do not make extradition conditional on the existence of a treaty shall recognize offences to which this article applies as extraditable offences between themselves.

7. Extradition shall be subject to the conditions provided for by the domestic law of the requested State Party or by applicable extradition treaties, including, inter alia, conditions in relation to the minimum penalty requirement for extradition and the grounds upon which the requested State Party may refuse extradition.

8. States Parties shall, subject to their domestic law, endeavour to expedite extradition procedures and to simplify evidentiary requirements relating thereto in respect of any offence to which this article applies.

9. Subject to the provisions of its domestic law and its extradition treaties, the requested State Party may, upon being satisfied that the circumstances so warrant and are urgent and at the request of the requesting State Party, take a person whose extradition is sought and who is present in its territory into custody or take other appropriate measures to ensure his or her presence at extradition proceedings.

10. A State Party in whose territory an alleged offender is found, if it does not extradite such person in respect of an offence to which this article applies solely on the ground that he or she is one of its nationals, shall, at the request of the State Party seeking extradition, be obliged to submit the case without undue delay to its competent authorities for the purpose of prosecution. Those authorities shall take their decision and conduct their proceedings in the same manner as in the case of any other offence of a grave nature under the domestic law of that State Party. The States Parties concerned shall cooperate with each other, in particular on procedural and evidentiary aspects, to ensure the efficiency of such prosecution.

11. Whenever a State Party is permitted under its domestic law to extradite or otherwise surrender one of its nationals only upon the condition that the person will be returned to that State Party to serve the sentence imposed as a result of the trial or proceedings for which the extradition or surrender of the person was sought and that State Party and the State Party seeking the extradition of the person agree with this option and other terms that they may deem appropriate, such conditional extradition or surrender shall be sufficient to discharge the obligation set forth in paragraph 10 of this article.

12. If extradition, sought for purposes of enforcing a sentence, is refused because the person sought is a national of the requested State Party, the requested Party shall, if its domestic law so permits and in conformity with the requirements of such law, upon application of the requesting Party, consider the enforcement of the sentence that has been imposed under the domestic law of the requesting Party or the remainder thereof.

13. Any person regarding whom proceedings are being carried out in connection with any of the offences to which this article applies shall be guaranteed fair treatment at all stages of the proceedings, including enjoyment of all the rights

and guarantees provided by the domestic law of the State Party in the territory of which that person is present.

14. Nothing in this Convention shall be interpreted as imposing an obligation to extradite if the requested State Party has substantial grounds for believing that the request has been made for the purpose of prosecuting or punishing a person on account of that person's sex, race, religion, nationality, ethnic origin or political opinions or that compliance with the request would cause prejudice to that person's position for any one of these reasons.

15. States Parties may not refuse a request for extradition on the sole ground that the offence is also considered to involve fiscal matters.

16. Before refusing extradition, the requested State Party shall, where appropriate, consult with the requesting State Party to provide it with ample opportunity to present its opinions and to provide information relevant to its allegation.

17. States Parties shall seek to conclude bilateral and multilateral agreements or arrangements to carry out or to enhance the effectiveness of extradition.

Article 17

Transfer of Sentenced Persons
States Parties may consider entering into bilateral or multilateral agreements or arrangements on the transfer to their territory of persons sentenced to imprisonment or other forms of deprivation of liberty for offences covered by this Convention, in order that they may complete their sentences there.

Article 18

Mutual Legal Assistance
1. States Parties shall afford one another the widest measure of mutual legal assistance in investigations, prosecutions and judicial proceedings in relation to the offences covered by this Convention as provided for in article 3 and shall reciprocally extend to one another similar assistance where the requesting State Party has reasonable grounds to suspect that the offence referred to in article 3, paragraph 1 (a) or (b), is transnational in nature, including that victims, witnesses, proceeds, instrumentalities or evidence of such offences are located in the requested State Party and that the offence involves an organized criminal group.

2. Mutual legal assistance shall be afforded to the fullest extent possible under relevant laws, treaties, agreements and arrangements of the requested State Party with respect to investigations, prosecutions and judicial proceedings in relation to the offences for which a legal person may be held liable in accordance with article 10 of this Convention in the requesting State Party.

3. Mutual legal assistance to be afforded in accordance with this article may be requested for any of the following purposes:

(a) Taking evidence or statements from persons;
(b) Effecting service of judicial documents;
(c) Executing searches and seizures, and freezing;
(d) Examining objects and sites;
(e) Providing information, evidentiary items and expert evaluations;
(f) Providing originals or certified copies of relevant documents and records, including government, bank, financial, corporate or business records;
(g) Identifying or tracing proceeds of crime, property, instrumentalities or other things for evidentiary purposes;
(h) Facilitating the voluntary appearance of persons in the requesting State Party;

(i) Any other type of assistance that is not contrary to the domestic law of the requested State Party.

4. Without prejudice to domestic law, the competent authorities of a State Party may, without prior request, transmit information relating to criminal matters to a competent authority in another State Party where they believe that such information could assist the authority in undertaking or successfully concluding inquiries and criminal proceedings or could result in a request formulated by the latter State Party pursuant to this Convention.

5. The transmission of information pursuant to paragraph 4 of this article shall be without prejudice to inquiries and criminal proceedings in the State of the competent authorities providing the information. The competent authorities receiving the information shall comply with a request that said information remain confidential, even temporarily, or with restrictions on its use. However, this shall not prevent the receiving State Party from disclosing in its proceedings information that is exculpatory to an accused person. In such a case, the receiving State Party shall notify the transmitting State Party prior to the disclosure and, if so requested, consult with the transmitting State Party. If, in an exceptional case, advance notice is not possible, the receiving State Party shall inform the transmitting State Party of the disclosure without delay.

6. The provisions of this article shall not affect the obligations under any other treaty, bilateral or multilateral, that governs or will govern, in whole or in part, mutual legal assistance.

7. Paragraphs 9 to 29 of this article shall apply to requests made pursuant to this article if the States Parties in question are not bound by a treaty of mutual legal assistance. If those States Parties are bound by such a treaty, the corresponding provisions of that treaty shall apply unless the States Parties agree to apply paragraphs 9 to 29 of

this article in lieu thereof. States Parties are strongly encouraged to apply these paragraphs if they facilitate cooperation.

8. States Parties shall not decline to render mutual legal assistance pursuant to this article on the ground of bank secrecy.

9. States Parties may decline to render mutual legal assistance pursuant to this article on the ground of absence of dual criminality. However, the requested State Party may, when it deems appropriate, provide assistance, to the extent it decides at its discretion, irrespective of whether the conduct would constitute an offence under the domestic law of the requested State Party.

10. A person who is being detained or is serving a sentence in the territory of one State Party whose presence in another State Party is requested for purposes of identification, testimony or otherwise providing assistance in obtaining evidence for investigations, prosecutions or judicial proceedings in relation to offences covered by this Convention may be transferred if the following conditions are met:

(a) The person freely gives his or her informed consent;

(b) The competent authorities of both States Parties agree, subject to such conditions as those States Parties may deem appropriate.

11. For the purposes of paragraph 10 of this article:

(a) The State Party to which the person is transferred shall have the authority and obligation to keep the person transferred in custody, unless otherwise requested or authorized by the State Party from which the person was transferred;

(b) The State Party to which the person is transferred shall without delay implement its obligation to return the person to the custody of the State Party from which the person was transferred as agreed beforehand, or as otherwise agreed, by the competent authorities of both States Parties;

(c) The State Party to which the person is transferred shall not require the State Party from which the person was transferred to initiate extradition proceedings for the return of the person;

(d) The person transferred shall receive credit for service of the sentence being served in the State from which he or she was transferred for time spent in the custody of the State Party to which he or she was transferred.

12. Unless the State Party from which a person is to be transferred in accordance with paragraphs 10 and 11 of this article so agrees, that person, whatever his or her nationality, shall not be prosecuted, detained, punished or subjected to any other restriction of his or her personal liberty in the territory of the State to which that person is transferred in respect of acts, omissions or convictions prior to his or her departure from the territory of the State from which he or she was transferred.

13. Each State Party shall designate a central authority that shall have the responsibility and power to receive requests for mutual legal assistance and either to execute them or to transmit them to the competent authorities for execution. Where a State Party has a special region or territory with a separate system of mutual legal assistance, it may designate a distinct central authority that shall have the same function for that region or territory. Central authorities shall ensure the speedy and proper execution or transmission of the requests received. Where the central authority transmits the request to a competent authority for execution, it shall encourage the speedy and proper execution of the request by the competent authority. The Secretary-General of the United Nations shall be notified of the central authority designated for this purpose at the time each State Party deposits its instrument of ratification, acceptance or approval of or accession to this Convention. Requests for mutual legal assistance and any communication related thereto shall be transmitted to the central authorities designated by the States Parties. This requirement shall be without prejudice to the right of a State Party to require that such requests and communications be addressed to it through diplomatic channels and, in urgent circumstances, where the States Parties agree, through the International Criminal Police Organization, if possible.

14. Requests shall be made in writing or, where possible, by any means capable of producing a written record, in a language acceptable to the requested State Party, under conditions allowing that State Party to establish authenticity. The Secretary-General of the United Nations shall be notified of the language or languages acceptable to each State Party at the time it deposits its instrument of ratification, acceptance or approval of or accession to this Convention. In urgent circumstances and where agreed by the States Parties, requests may be made orally, but shall be confirmed in writing forthwith.

15. A request for mutual legal assistance shall contain:

(a) The identity of the authority making the request;

(b) The subject matter and nature of the investigation, prosecution or judicial proceeding to which the request relates and the name and functions of the authority conducting the investigation, prosecution or judicial proceeding;

(c) A summary of the relevant facts, except in relation to requests for the purpose of service of judicial documents;

(d) A description of the assistance sought and details of any particular procedure that the requesting State Party wishes to be followed;

(e) Where possible, the identity, location and nationality of any person concerned; and

(f) The purpose for which the evidence, information or action is sought.

16. The requested State Party may request additional information when it appears necessary for the execution of the request in accordance with

its domestic law or when it can facilitate such execution.

17. A request shall be executed in accordance with the domestic law of the requested State Party and, to the extent not contrary to the domestic law of the requested State Party and where possible, in accordance with the procedures specified in the request.

18. Wherever possible and consistent with fundamental principles of domestic law, when an individual is in the territory of a State Party and has to be heard as a witness or expert by the judicial authorities of another State Party, the first State Party may, at the request of the other, permit the hearing to take place by video conference if it is not possible or desirable for the individual in question to appear in person in the territory of the requesting State Party. States Parties may agree that the hearing shall be conducted by a judicial authority of the requesting State Party and attended by a judicial authority of the requested State Party.

19. The requesting State Party shall not transmit or use information or evidence furnished by the requested State Party for investigations, prosecutions or judicial proceedings other than those stated in the request without the prior consent of the requested State Party. Nothing in this paragraph shall prevent the requesting State Party from disclosing in its proceedings information or evidence that is exculpatory to an accused person. In the latter case, the requesting State Party shall notify the requested State Party prior to the disclosure and, if so requested, consult with the requested State Party. If, in an exceptional case, advance notice is not possible, the requesting State Party shall inform the requested State Party of the disclosure without delay.

20. The requesting State Party may require that the requested State Party keep confidential the fact and substance of the request, except to the extent necessary to execute the request. If the requested State Party cannot comply with the requirement of confidentiality, it shall promptly inform the requesting State Party.

21. Mutual legal assistance may be refused:

    (a) If the request is not made in conformity with the provisions of this article;

    (b) If the requested State Party considers that execution of the request is likely to prejudice its sovereignty, security, order, public or other essential interests;

    (c) If the authorities of the requested State Party would be prohibited by its domestic law from carrying out the action requested with regard to any similar offence, had it been subject to investigation, prosecution or judicial proceedings under their own jurisdiction;

    (d) If it would be contrary to the legal system of the requested State Party relating to mutual legal assistance for the request to be granted.

22. States Parties may not refuse a request for mutual legal assistance on the sole ground that the offence is also considered to involve fiscal matters.

23. Reasons shall be given for any refusal of mutual legal assistance.

24. The requested State Party shall execute the request for mutual legal assistance as soon as possible and shall take as full account as possible of any deadlines suggested by the requesting State Party and for which reasons are given, preferably in the request. The requested State Party shall respond to reasonable requests by the requesting State Party on progress of its handling of the request. The requesting State Party shall promptly inform the requested State Party when the assistance sought is no longer required.

25. Mutual legal assistance may be postponed by the requested State Party on the ground that it

interferes with an ongoing investigation, prosecution or judicial proceeding.

26. Before refusing a request pursuant to paragraph 21 of this article or postponing its execution pursuant to paragraph 25 of this article, the requested State Party shall consult with the requesting State Party to consider whether assistance may be granted subject to such terms and conditions as it deems necessary. If the requesting State Party accepts assistance subject to those conditions, it shall comply with the conditions.

27. Without prejudice to the application of paragraph 12 of this article, a witness, expert or other person who, at the request of the requesting State Party, consents to give evidence in a proceeding or to assist in an investigation, prosecution or judicial proceeding in the territory of the requesting State Party shall not be prosecuted, detained, punished or subjected to any other restriction of his or her personal liberty in that territory in respect of acts, omissions or convictions prior to his or her departure from the territory of the requested State Party. Such safe conduct shall cease when the witness, expert or other person having had, for a period of fifteen consecutive days or for any period agreed upon by the States Parties from the date on which he or she has been officially informed that his or her presence is no longer required by the judicial authorities, an opportunity of leaving, has nevertheless remained voluntarily in the territory of the requesting State Party or, having left it, has returned of his or her own free will.

28. The ordinary costs of executing a request shall be borne by the requested State Party, unless otherwise agreed by the States Parties concerned. If expenses of a substantial or extraordinary nature are or will be required to fulfil the request, the States Parties shall consult to determine the terms and conditions under which the request will be executed, as well as the manner in which the costs shall be borne.

29. The requested State Party:

(a) Shall provide to the requesting State Party copies of government records, documents or information in its possession that under its domestic law are available to the general public;

(b) May, at its discretion, provide to the requesting State Party in whole, in part or subject to such conditions as it deems appropriate, copies of any government records, documents or information in its possession that under its domestic law are not available to the general public.

30. States Parties shall consider, as may be necessary, the possibility of concluding bilateral or multilateral agreements or arrangements that would serve the purposes of, give practical effect to or enhance the provisions of this article.

Article 19

Joint Investigations
States Parties shall consider concluding bilateral or multilateral agreements or arrangements whereby, in relation to matters that are the subject of investigations, prosecutions or judicial proceedings in one or more States, the competent authorities concerned may establish joint investigative bodies. In the absence of such agreements or arrangements, joint investigations may be undertaken by agreement on a case-by-case basis. The States Parties involved shall ensure that the sovereignty of the State Party in whose territory such investigation is to take place is fully respected.

Article 20

Special Investigative Techniques
1. If permitted by the basic principles of its domestic legal system, each State Party shall, within its possibilities and under the conditions prescribed by its domestic law, take the necessary

measures to allow for the appropriate use of controlled delivery and, where it deems appropriate, for the use of other special investigative techniques, such as electronic or other forms of surveillance and undercover operations, by its competent authorities in its territory for the purpose of effectively combating organized crime.

2. For the purpose of investigating the offences covered by this Convention, States Parties are encouraged to conclude, when necessary, appropriate bilateral or multilateral agreements or arrangements for using such special investigative techniques in the context of cooperation at the international level. Such agreements or arrangements shall be concluded and implemented in full compliance with the principle of sovereign equality of States and shall be carried out strictly in accordance with the terms of those agreements or arrangements.

3. In the absence of an agreement or arrangement as set forth in paragraph 2 of this article, decisions to use such special investigative techniques at the international level shall be made on a case-by-case basis and may, when necessary, take into consideration financial arrangements and understandings with respect to the exercise of jurisdiction by the States Parties concerned.

4. Decisions to use controlled delivery at the international level may, with the consent of the States Parties concerned, include methods such as intercepting and allowing the goods to continue intact or be removed or replaced in whole or in part.

Article 21

Transfer of Criminal Proceedings
States Parties shall consider the possibility of transferring to one another proceedings for the prosecution of an offence covered by this Convention in cases where such transfer is considered to be in the interests of the proper administration of justice, in particular in cases where several jurisdictions are involved, with a view to concentrating the prosecution.

Article 22

Establishment of Criminal Record
Each State Party may adopt such legislative or other measures as may be necessary to take into consideration, under such terms as and for the purpose that it deems appropriate, any previous conviction in another State of an alleged offender for the purpose of using such information in criminal proceedings relating to an offence covered by this Convention.

Article 23

Criminalization of Obstruction of Justice
Each State Party shall adopt such legislative and other measures as may be necessary to establish as criminal offences, when committed intentionally:

(a) The use of physical force, threats or intimidation or the promise, offering or giving of an undue advantage to induce false testimony or to interfere in the giving of testimony or the production of evidence in a proceeding in relation to the commission of offences covered by this Convention;

(b) The use of physical force, threats or intimidation to interfere with the exercise of official duties by a justice or law enforcement official in relation to the commission of offences covered by this Convention. Nothing in this subparagraph shall prejudice the right of States Parties to have legislation that protects other categories of public officials.

Article 24

Protection of Witnesses
1. Each State Party shall take appropriate measures within its means to provide effective protection from potential retaliation or intimidation for

witnesses in criminal proceedings who give testimony concerning offences covered by this Convention and, as appropriate, for their relatives and other persons close to them.

2. The measures envisaged in paragraph 1 of this article may include, inter alia, without prejudice to the rights of the defendant, including the right to due process:

    (a) Establishing procedures for the physical protection of such persons, such as, to the extent necessary and feasible, relocating them and permitting, where appropriate, non-disclosure or limitations on the disclosure of information concerning the identity and whereabouts of such persons;

    (b) Providing evidentiary rules to permit witness testimony to be given in a manner that ensures the safety of the witness, such as permitting testimony to be given through the use of communications technology such as video links or other adequate means.

3. States Parties shall consider entering into agreements or arrangements with other States for the relocation of persons referred to in paragraph 1 of this article.

4. The provisions of this article shall also apply to victims insofar as they are witnesses.

Article 25

Assistance to and Protection of Victims
1. Each State Party shall take appropriate measures within its means to provide assistance and protection to victims of offences covered by this Convention, in particular in cases of threat of retaliation or intimidation.

2. Each State Party shall establish appropriate procedures to provide access to compensation and restitution for victims of offences covered by this Convention.

3. Each State Party shall, subject to its domestic law, enable views and concerns of victims to be presented and considered at appropriate stages of criminal proceedings against offenders in a manner not prejudicial to the rights of the defence.

Article 26

Measures to Enhance Cooperation with Law Enforcement Authorities
1. Each State Party shall take appropriate measures to encourage persons who participate or who have participated in organized criminal groups:

    (a) To supply information useful to competent authorities for investigative and evidentiary purposes on such matters as:
        (i) The identity, nature, composition, structure, location or activities of organized criminal groups;
        (ii) Links, including international links, with other organized criminal groups;
        (iii) Offences that organized criminal groups have committed or may commit;

    (b) To provide factual, concrete help to competent authorities that may contribute to depriving organized criminal groups of their resources or of the proceeds of crime.

2. Each State Party shall consider providing for the possibility, in appropriate cases, of mitigating punishment of an accused person who provides substantial cooperation in the investigation or prosecution of an offence covered by this Convention.

3. Each State Party shall consider providing for the possibility, in accordance with fundamental principles of its domestic law, of granting immunity from prosecution to a person who provides substantial cooperation in the investigation or prosecution of an offence covered by this Convention.

4. Protection of such persons shall be as provided for in article 24 of this Convention.

5. Where a person referred to in paragraph 1 of this article located in one State Party can provide substantial cooperation to the competent authorities of another State Party, the States Parties concerned may consider entering into agreements or arrangements, in accordance with their domestic law, concerning the potential provision by the other State Party of the treatment set forth in paragraphs 2 and 3 of this article.

Article 27

Law Enforcement Cooperation

1. States Parties shall cooperate closely with one another, consistent with their respective domestic legal and administrative systems, to enhance the effectiveness of law enforcement action to combat the offences covered by this Convention. Each State Party shall, in particular, adopt effective measures:

   (a) To enhance and, where necessary, to establish channels of communication between their competent authorities, agencies and services in order to facilitate the secure and rapid exchange of information concerning all aspects of the offences covered by this Convention, including, if the States Parties concerned deem it appropriate, links with other criminal activities;

   (b) To cooperate with other States Parties in conducting inquiries with respect to offences covered by this Convention concerning:

      (i) The identity, whereabouts and activities of persons suspected of involvement in such offences or the location of other persons concerned;

      (ii) The movement of proceeds of crime or property derived from the commission of such offences;

      (iii) The movement of property, equipment or other instrumentalities used or intended for use in the commission of such offences;

   (c) To provide, when appropriate, necessary items or quantities of substances for analytical or investigative purposes;

   (d) To facilitate effective coordination between their competent authorities, agencies and services and to promote the exchange of personnel and other experts, including, subject to bilateral agreements or arrangements between the States Parties concerned, the posting of liaison officers;

   (e) To exchange information with other States Parties on specific means and methods used by organized criminal groups, including, where applicable, routes and conveyances and the use of false identities, altered or false documents or other means of concealing their activities;

   (f) To exchange information and coordinate administrative and other measures taken as appropriate for the purpose of early identification of the offences covered by this Convention.

2. With a view to giving effect to this Convention, States Parties shall consider entering into bilateral or multilateral agreements or arrangements on direct cooperation between their law enforcement agencies and, where such agreements or arrangements already exist, amending them. In the absence of such agreements or arrangements between the States Parties concerned, the Parties may consider this Convention as the basis for mutual law enforcement cooperation in respect of the offences covered by this Convention. Whenever appropriate, States Parties shall make full use of agreements or arrangements, including international or regional organizations, to enhance the cooperation between their law enforcement agencies.

3. States Parties shall endeavour to cooperate within their means to respond to transnational organized crime committed through the use of modern technology.

Article 28

Collection, Exchange and Analysis of Information on the Nature of Organized Crime
1. Each State Party shall consider analysing, in consultation with the scientific and academic communities, trends in organized crime in its territory, the circumstances in which organized crime operates, as well as the professional groups and technologies involved.

2. States Parties shall consider developing and sharing analytical expertise concerning organized criminal activities with each other and through international and regional organizations. For that purpose, common definitions, standards and methodologies should be developed and applied as appropriate.

3. Each State Party shall consider monitoring its policies and actual measures to combat organized crime and making assessments of their effectiveness and efficiency.

Article 29

Training and Technical Assistance
1. Each State Party shall, to the extent necessary, initiate, develop or improve specific training programmes for its law enforcement personnel, including prosecutors, investigating magistrates and customs personnel, and other personnel charged with the prevention, detection and control of the offences covered by this Convention. Such programmes may include secondments and exchanges of staff. Such programmes shall deal, in particular and to the extent permitted by domestic law, with the following:

(a) Methods used in the prevention, detection and control of the offences covered by this Convention;

(b) Routes and techniques used by persons suspected of involvement in offences covered by this Convention, including in transit States, and appropriate countermeasures;

(c) Monitoring of the movement of contraband;

(d) Detection and monitoring of the movements of proceeds of crime, property, equipment or other instrumentalities and methods used for the transfer, concealment or disguise of such proceeds, property, equipment or other instrumentalities, as well as methods used in combating moneylaundering and other financial crimes;

(e) Collection of evidence;

(f) Control techniques in free trade zones and free ports;

(g) Modern law enforcement equipment and techniques, including electronic surveillance, controlled deliveries and undercover operations;

(h) Methods used in combating transnational organized crime committed through the use of computers, telecommunications networks or other forms of modern technology; and

(i) Methods used in the protection of victims and witnesses.

2. States Parties shall assist one another in planning and implementing research and training programmes designed to share expertise in the areas referred to in paragraph 1 of this article and to that end shall also, when appropriate, use regional and international conferences and seminars to promote cooperation and to stimulate discussion on problems of mutual concern, including the special problems and needs of transit States.

3. States Parties shall promote training and technical assistance that will facilitate extradition and mutual legal assistance. Such training and technical assistance may include language training, secondments and exchanges between personnel in central authorities or agencies with relevant responsibilities.

4. In the case of existing bilateral and multilateral agreements or arrangements, States Parties shall strengthen, to the extent necessary, efforts to

maximize operational and training activities within international and regional organizations and within other relevant bilateral and multilateral agreements or arrangements.

Article 30

Other Measures: Implementation of the Convention through Economic Development and Technical Assistance

1. States Parties shall take measures conducive to the optimal implementation of this Convention to the extent possible, through international cooperation, taking into account the negative effects of organized crime on society in general, in particular on sustainable development.

2. States Parties shall make concrete efforts to the extent possible and in coordination with each other, as well as with international and regional organizations:

(a) To enhance their cooperation at various levels with developing countries, with a view to strengthening the capacity of the latter to prevent and combat transnational organized crime;

(b) To enhance financial and material assistance to support the efforts of developing countries to fight transnational organized crime effectively and to help them implement this Convention successfully;

(c) To provide technical assistance to developing countries and countries with economies in transition to assist them in meeting their needs for the implementation of this Convention. To that end, States Parties shall endeavour to make adequate and regular voluntary contributions to an account specifically designated for that purpose in a United Nations funding mechanism. States Parties may also give special consideration, in accordance with their domestic law and the provisions of this Convention, to contributing to the aforementioned account a percentage of the money or of the corresponding value of proceeds

of crime or property confiscated in accordance with the provisions of this Convention;

(d) To encourage and persuade other States and financial institutions as appropriate to join them in efforts in accordance with this article, in particular by providing more training programmes and modern equipment to developing countries in order to assist them in achieving the objectives of this Convention.

3. To the extent possible, these measures shall be without prejudice to existing foreign assistance commitments or to other financial cooperation arrangements at the bilateral, regional or international level.

4. States Parties may conclude bilateral or multilateral agreements or arrangements on material and logistical assistance, taking into consideration the financial arrangements necessary for the means of international cooperation provided for by this Convention to be effective and for the prevention, detection and control of transnational organized crime.

Article 31

Prevention

1. States Parties shall endeavour to develop and evaluate national projects and to establish and promote best practices and policies aimed at the prevention of transnational organized crime.

2. States Parties shall endeavour, in accordance with fundamental principles of their domestic law, to reduce existing or future opportunities for organized criminal groups to participate in lawful markets with proceeds of crime, through appropriate legislative, administrative or other measures. These measures should focus on:

(a) The strengthening of cooperation between law enforcement agencies or prosecutors and relevant private entities, including industry;

(b) The promotion of the development of standards and procedures designed to safeguard the integrity of public and relevant private entities, as well as codes of conduct for relevant professions, in particular lawyers, notaries public, tax consultants and accountants;

(c) The prevention of the misuse by organized criminal groups of tender procedures conducted by public authorities and of subsidies and licences granted by public authorities for commercial activity;

(d) The prevention of the misuse of legal persons by organized criminal groups; such measures could include:

   (i) The establishment of public records on legal and natural persons involved in the establishment, management and funding of legal persons;

   (ii) The introduction of the possibility of disqualifying by court order or any appropriate means for a reasonable period of time persons convicted of offences covered by this Convention from acting as directors of legal persons incorporated within their jurisdiction;

   (iii) The establishment of national records of persons disqualified from acting as directors of legal persons; and

   (iv) The exchange of information contained in the records referred to in subparagraphs (d) (i) and (iii) of this paragraph with the competent authorities of other States Parties.

3. States Parties shall endeavour to promote the reintegration into society of persons convicted of offences covered by this Convention.

4. States Parties shall endeavour to evaluate periodically existing relevant legal instruments and administrative practices with a view to detecting their vulnerability to misuse by organized criminal groups.

5. States Parties shall endeavour to promote public awareness regarding the existence, causes and gravity of and the threat posed by transnational organized crime. Information may be disseminated where appropriate through the mass media and shall include measures to promote public participation in preventing and combating such crime.

6. Each State Party shall inform the Secretary-General of the United Nations of the name and address of the authority or authorities that can assist other States Parties in developing measures to prevent transnational organized crime.

7. States Parties shall, as appropriate, collaborate with each other and relevant international and regional organizations in promoting and developing the measures referred to in this article. This includes participation in international projects aimed at the prevention of transnational organized crime, for example by alleviating the circumstances that render socially marginalized groups vulnerable to the action of transnational organized crime.

29.
Treaty on Cooperation among the States Members of the Commonwealth of Independent States in Combating Terrorism 1999

The Commonwealth of Independent States (CIS), formed after the breakup of the Soviet Union, faced various forms of terrorism that posed a danger to its stability and security. The member states met at the Belarus capital, Minsk, on 4 June 1999 to tackle the problem. Apart from defining terrorism in general terms, the convention used the term "technological terrorism" for nuclear and biological weapons. Antiterrorist units were to be formed. The member states agreed to cooperate and take necessary steps to combat terrorism.

Source
United Nations Treaty Collection,
http://untreaty.un.org/English/Terrorism/csi_e.pdf.

The States parties to this Treaty, in the person of their Governments, hereinafter referred to as the Parties,

Aware of the danger posed by acts of terrorism,

Bearing in mind the instruments adopted within the United Nations and the Commonwealth of Independent States, as well as other international instruments, relating to combating the various manifestations of terrorism,

Wishing to render one another the broadest possible assistance in increasing the effectiveness of cooperation in this field,

Have agreed as follows:

Article 1
For purposes of this Treaty, the terms used in it mean:

"Terrorism"—an illegal act punishable under criminal law committed for the purpose of undermining public safety, influencing decision-making by the authorities or terrorizing the population, and taking the form of:

Violence or the threat of violence against natural or juridical persons;

Destroying (damaging) or threatening to destroy (damage) property and other material objects so as to endanger people's lives;

Causing substantial harm to property or the occurrence of other consequences dangerous to society;

Threatening the life of a statesman or public figure for the purpose of putting an end to his State or other public activity or in revenge for such activity;

Attacking a representative of a foreign State or an internationally protected staff member of an international organization, as well as the business premises or vehicles of internationally protected persons;

Other acts classified as terrorist under the national legislation of the Parties or under universally recognized international legal instruments aimed at combating terrorism;

"Technological terrorism"—the use or threat of the use of nuclear, radiological, chemical or bacteriological (biological) weapons or their components, pathogenic micro-organisms, radioactive substances or other substances harmful to human health, including the seizure, putting out of operation or destruction of nuclear, chemical or other facilities posing an increased technological and environmental danger and the utility systems of towns and other inhabited localities, if these acts are committed for the purpose of undermining public safety, terrorizing the population or influencing the decisions of the authorities in order to achieve political, mercenary or any other ends, as well as attempts to commit one of the crimes listed above for the same purposes and leading, financing or acting as the instigator, accessory or accomplice of a person who commits or attempts to commit such a crime;

"Facilities posing an increased technological and environmental danger"—enterprises, installations, plant and other facilities whose inoperability may lead to loss of human life, the impairment of human health, pollution of the environment or destabilization of the situation in a given region or a given State as a whole;

"Special anti-terrorist units"—groups of specialists formed by the Parties in accordance with their national legislation to combat acts of terrorism;

"Special items and supplies"—materials, machinery and vehicles, personal equipment for members of special anti-terrorist units including weapons and ammunition, and special items and equipment.

Article 2

The Parties shall cooperate in preventing, uncovering, halting and investigating acts of terrorism in accordance with this Treaty, their national legislation and their international obligations.

Article 3

1. Each of the Parties shall, on signing this Treaty or carrying out the domestic procedures required for its entry into force, indicate its competent authorities responsible for implementing the provisions of this Treaty.

The Parties shall immediately notify the depositary of any changes with regard to their competent authority.

2. In implementing the provisions of this Treaty, the competent authorities of the Parties shall maintain direct relations with one another.

Article 4

1. In cooperating in combating acts of terrorism, including in relation to the extradition of persons committing them, the Parties shall not regard the acts involved as other than criminal.

2. The nationality of a person accused of an act of terrorism shall be deemed to be his nationality at the time of commission of the act.

Article 5

1. The competent authorities of the Party shall, in accordance with this Treaty, other international agreements and national legislation, cooperate and assist one another by:

(a) Exchanging information;
(b) Responding to enquiries regarding the conduct of investigations;
(c) Developing and adopting agreed measures for preventing, uncovering, halting or investigating acts of terrorism, and informing one another about such measures;

(d) Adopting measures to prevent and halt preparations in their territory for the commission of acts of terrorism in the territory of another Party;
(e) Assisting in assessing the condition of the system for physical protection of facilities posing an increased technological and environmental danger, and developing and implementing measures to improve that system;
(f) Exchanging legislative texts and materials on the practice with respect to their application;
(g) Sending, by agreement between interested Parties, special anti-terrorist units to render practical assistance in halting acts of terrorism and combating their consequences;
(h) Exchanging experience on the prevention and combating of terrorist acts, including the holding of training courses, seminars, consultations and workshops;
(i) Training and further specialized training of personnel;
(j) Joint financing, by agreement between Parties, and conduct of research and development work on systems for and means of physically protecting facilities posing an increased technological and environmental danger;
(k) Implementation on a contractual basis of deliveries of special items, technology and equipment for anti-terrorist activity.

2. The procedure for sending and executing requests for extradition, for the provision of legal aid in criminal cases and for the institution of criminal proceedings shall be determined by the international agreements to which the Parties concerned are parties.

Article 6

The Parties shall, through joint consultations, jointly draw up recommendations for achieving concerted approaches to the legal regulation of issues relating to the prevention and combating of terrorist acts.

Article 7

1. Cooperation under this Treaty shall be conducted on the basis of requests by an interested Party for assistance to be rendered, or on the initiative of a Party which believes such assistance to be of interest to another Party.

2. The request for the rendering of assistance shall be made in writing. In urgent cases requests may be transmitted orally, but must be confirmed in writing not later than 72 hours thereafter, including through the use of technical text transmission facilities.

If doubt arises as to the genuineness or content of a request, additional confirmation may be requested.

Requests shall contain:

(a) The name of the competent authority requesting assistance and of the authority requested; a statement of the substance of the matter; the purpose of and justification for the request; and a description of the nature of the assistance requested;

(b) Any other information that may be useful for the proper fulfilment of the request.

3. A request for the rendering of assistance transmitted or confirmed in writing shall be signed by the head of the requesting competent authority or his deputy and shall be certified by the seal of the competent authority.

Article 8

1. The requested Party shall take all necessary measures to ensure the prompt and fullest possible fulfilment of the request.

The requesting Party shall be immediately notified of circumstances that prevent or will substantially delay the fulfilment of the request.

2. If the fulfilment of the request does not fall within the competence of the requested competent authority, it shall transmit the request to an authority of its State which is competent to fulfil it, and shall immediately so inform the requesting competent authority.

3. The requested Party shall be entitled to request additional information that is in its view needed for the proper fulfilment of the request.

4. In fulfilling a request, the legislation of the requested Party shall be applied; however, at the request of the requesting Party, its legislation may be applied if that does not contradict fundamental principles of the legislation of the requested Party or its international obligations.

5. If the requested Party considers that immediate fulfilment of the request may impede a criminal prosecution or other proceedings taking place on its territory, it may postpone fulfilment of the request or tie its fulfilment to compliance with conditions determined to be necessary following consultations with the requesting Party. If the requesting Party agrees that assistance shall be rendered to it on the proposed terms, it shall comply with those terms.

6. The requested Party shall at the request of the requesting Party take the necessary measures to ensure confidentiality of the fact that the request has been received, the content of the request and accompanying documents, and the rendering of assistance.

If it is impossible to fulfil the request without maintaining confidentiality, the requested Party shall so inform the requesting Party, which shall decide whether the request should be fulfilled under those conditions.

7. The requested Party shall inform the requesting Party as soon as possible about the results of the fulfilment of the request.

Article 9

1. The rendering of assistance under this Treaty shall be denied in whole or in part if the requested Party believes that fulfilment of the request may impair its sovereignty, security, social order or other vital interests or is in contravention of its legislation or international obligations.

2. The rendering of assistance may be denied if the act in relation to which the request was made is not a crime under the legislation of the requested Party.

3. The requesting Party shall be notified in writing of a refusal to fulfil a request in whole or in part, with an indication of the reasons for refusal listed in paragraph 1 of this Article.

Article 10

1. Each Party shall ensure confidentiality of information and documents received from another Party if they are classified as restricted or the transmitting Party considers it undesirable that they should be made public. The level of security classification of such information and documents shall be determined by the transmitting Party.

2. Results of the fulfilment of a request obtained on the basis of this Treaty may not without the consent of the Party providing them be used for purposes other than those for which they were requested and provided.

3. Transmission to a third party of information obtained by one Party on the basis of this Treaty shall require the prior consent of the Party providing the information.

Article 11

The competent authorities of the Parties shall exchange information on issues of mutual interest, including:

(a) Materials distributed in the territory of their States containing information on terrorist threats, terrorist acts in the course of preparation or committed and the identified intentions of given persons, groups of persons or organizations to commit acts of terrorism;

(b) Acts of terrorism in the course of preparation that are directed against heads of State, internationally protected persons, staff of diplomatic missions, consular institutions and international organizations of the Parties and participants in State visits and international and national political, sporting and other activities;

(c) Instances of illegal circulation of nuclear materials, chemical, bacteriological (biological) weapons or their components, highly toxic chemicals and pathogenic micro-organisms;

(d) Terrorist organizations, groups and individuals that present a threat to the State security of the Parties and the establishment of contacts between terrorist organizations, groups or individuals;

(e) Illegal armed formations employing methods of terrorist activity, their structure, members, aims and objectives;

(f) Ways, means and methods of terrorist action they have identified;

(g) Supplies and equipment that may be provided by the Parties to one another to the extent of their ability;

(h) Practice with respect to the legal and other regulatory settlement of issues related to the subject of this Treaty;

(i) Identified and presumed channels for the financing and illegal delivery to the territory of their States of weapons and other means of committing terrorist acts;

(j) Terrorist encroachments aimed at violating the sovereignty and territorial integrity of Parties;

Other issues of interest to the Parties.

Article 12

1. The Parties may, at the request or with the consent of the Party concerned, send representatives of their competent authorities, including special anti-terrorist units, to provide

procedural, advisory or practical aid in accordance with this Treaty.

In such cases, the receiving Party shall notify the other Party in writing of the place and time of and procedure for crossing its State border and the nature of the problems to be dealt with, and shall promote and facilitate the necessary conditions for their effective solution, including unimpeded carriage of persons and special items and supplies and cost-free accommodation, food and use of the transport infrastructure of the receiving Party.

Any movement of a special anti-terrorist unit or of individual members of such a unit within the territory of the receiving Party shall be possible only with special permission from and under the control of the head of the competent authority of the receiving Party.

2. The procedure for the use of air, road, rail, river and maritime transport to provide aid shall be determined by the competent authorities of the Parties in agreement with the relevant ministries and departments of the receiving Party.

Article 13
1. For purposes of the effective and timely provision of aid, the Parties shall, when special anti-terrorist units cross the State border, ensure accelerated conduct of the formalities established by national legislation.

2. At the border crossing point, the commanding officer of a special anti-terrorist unit shall present the nominal role of members of the group and list of special items and supplies certified by the competent authorities of the sending Party, together with an indication of the purposes of the Unit's arrival in the territory of the receiving Party, while all members of the group shall present their national passports and documents confirming that they belong to competent authorities for combating terrorism.

3. Special items and supplies shall be exempt from customs duties and payments and must be either used during the operation for the provision of aid or removed from the territory of the receiving Party upon its conclusion.

If special circumstances make it impossible to remove the special items and supplies, the competent authorities of the sending Party shall hand them over to the competent authorities of the receiving Party.

Article 14
The decision on the procedure for conducting special measures under this Treaty shall be taken by the competent authority of the receiving Party, taking into account the views of the commanding officer of the incoming anti-terrorist unit of the other Party. If these views are not taken into account, the commanding officer shall be entitled to refuse to participate in the conduct of the special measure.

Article 15
1. The receiving Party shall refrain from any claims against a Party providing aid, including with regard to compensation for damages arising out of death, bodily injury or any other harm caused to the lives, health and property of natural persons located in the territory of the receiving Party, and also to juridical persons and the receiving Party itself, if such harm was inflicted during the performance of activities associated with the implementation of this Treaty.

2. If a participant in the special anti-terrorist unit of the sending Party inflicts harm on some person or organization while performing activities associated with the implementation of this Treaty in the territory of the receiving Party, the receiving Party shall make compensation for the harm in accordance with the provisions of national legislation which would be applied in the case of harm being inflicted by members of anti-terrorist

units of the receiving Party in similar circumstances.

3. The procedure for repayment of expenses incurred by the sending Party, including expenses associated with the loss or complete or partial destruction of imported special items and supplies, shall be established by agreement between the Parties concerned.

4. If one of the Parties considers the damage caused by the actions of the special anti-terrorist unit to be disproportionate to the purposes of the operation, the differences of opinion that arise shall be settled at the bilateral level by the Parties concerned.

Article 16

For purposes of the implementation of this Treaty, the competent authorities of the Parties may where necessary hold consultations and working meetings.

Article 17

The Parties may, by mutual agreement and on the basis of separate agreements, conduct joint exercises of special anti-terrorist units and, on a reciprocal basis, organize training for representatives of another Party in their national anti-terrorist detachments.

Article 18

1. Materials, special items, technology and equipment received by the competent authorities of the Parties pursuant to this Agreement may be transferred to a third party only with the consent of and on the terms specified by the competent authority which provided such materials, special items, technology and equipment.

2. Information on the investigation methods of special anti-terrorist units and on the characteristics of special forces and of items and supplies used in providing aid under this Agreement may not be disclosed.

Article 19

The Parties concerned shall where necessary agree on the financial, organizational and technical and other conditions for the provision of assistance under this Agreement.

Article 20

1. This Treaty shall not limit the right of the Parties to conclude bilateral international agreements on issues which are the subject of this Treaty, and shall not affect the rights and obligations of Parties arising out of other international agreements to which they are parties.

2. The competent authorities of the Parties may conclude with one another agreements that regulate in more detail the procedure for implementation of this Treaty.

Article 21

Disputes arising out of the interpretation or application of this Treaty shall be resolved through consultations and negotiations between the Parties.

30.
Council of Europe Convention on the Prevention of Terrorism

The Council of Europe Convention on the Prevention of Terrorism supplements existing treaties that focus on criminal and terrorist issues. The recent terrorist attacks in the United States, United Kingdom, and Spain have made it clear that stronger initiatives need to be taken to respond to this growing threat to international security. This convention calls for an increased emphasis on measures such as civil preparedness, protection of vulnerable facilities, and enhancing states' cooperation with each other and internationally. Articles 5, 7, and 9 cover the offenses addressed in this instrument. Article 13 addresses support actions for the victims of terrorism.

Source
Council of Europe, http://conventions.coe.int/Treaty/EN/
Treaties/Html/196.htm.

The member States of the Council of Europe and the other Signatories hereto,

Considering that the aim of the Council of Europe is to achieve greater unity between its members;

Recognising the value of reinforcing co-operation with the other Parties to this Convention;

Wishing to take effective measures to prevent terrorism and to counter, in particular, public provocation to commit terrorist offences and recruitment and training for terrorism;

Aware of the grave concern caused by the increase in terrorist offences and the growing terrorist threat;

Aware of the precarious situation faced by those who suffer from terrorism, and in this connection reaffirming their profound solidarity with the victims of terrorism and their families;

Recognising that terrorist offences and the offences set forth in this Convention, by whoever perpetrated, are under no circumstances justifiable by considerations of a political, philosophical, ideological, racial, ethnic, religious or other similar nature, and recalling the obligation of all Parties to prevent such offences and, if not prevented, to prosecute and ensure that they are punishable by penalties which take into account their grave nature;

Recalling the need to strengthen the fight against terrorism and reaffirming that all measures taken to prevent or suppress terrorist offences have to respect the rule of law and democratic values, human rights and fundamental freedoms as well as other provisions of international law, including, where applicable, international humanitarian law;

Recognising that this Convention is not intended to affect established principles relating to freedom of expression and freedom of association;

Recalling that acts of terrorism have the purpose by their nature or context to seriously intimidate a population or unduly compel a government or an international organisation to perform or abstain from performing any act or seriously destabilise or destroy the fundamental political, constitutional, economic or social structures of a country or an international organisation;

Have agreed as follows:

Article 1—Terminology
1 For the purposes of this Convention, "terrorist offence" means any of the offences within the scope of and as defined in one of the treaties listed in the Appendix.

2 On depositing its instrument of ratification, acceptance, approval or accession, a State or the European Community which is not a party to a treaty listed in the Appendix may declare that, in the application of this Convention to the Party concerned, that treaty shall be deemed not to be included in the Appendix. This declaration shall cease to have effect as soon as the treaty enters into force for the Party having made such a declaration, which shall notify the Secretary General of the Council of Europe of this entry into force.

Article 2—Purpose
The purpose of the present Convention is to enhance the efforts of Parties in preventing terrorism and its negative effects on the full enjoyment of human rights, in particular the right to life, both by measures to be taken at national level and through international co-operation, with due regard to the existing applicable multilateral or bilateral treaties or agreements between the Parties.

Article 3—National Prevention Policies
1. Each Party shall take appropriate measures, particularly in the field of training of law enforcement authorities and other bodies, and in the fields of education, culture, information, media and public awareness raising, with a view to preventing terrorist offences and their negative effects while respecting human rights obligations as set forth in, where applicable to that Party, the Convention for the Protection of Human Rights and Fundamental Freedoms, the International Covenant on Civil and Political Rights, and other obligations under international law.

2. Each Party shall take such measures as may be necessary to improve and develop the co-operation among national authorities with a view to preventing terrorist offences and their negative effects by, *inter alia:*

   a. exchanging information;
   b. improving the physical protection of persons and facilities;
   c. enhancing training and coordination plans for civil emergencies.

3. Each Party shall promote tolerance by encouraging inter-religious and cross-cultural dialogue involving, where appropriate, non-governmental organisations and other elements of civil society with a view to preventing tensions that might contribute to the commission of terrorist offences.

4. Each Party shall endeavour to promote public awareness regarding the existence, causes and gravity of and the threat posed by terrorist offences and the offences set forth in this Convention and consider encouraging the public to provide factual, specific help to its competent authorities that may contribute to preventing terrorist offences and offences set forth in this Convention.

Article 4—International Co-operation on Prevention
Parties shall, as appropriate and with due regard to their capabilities, assist and support each other with a view to enhancing their capacity to prevent the commission of terrorist offences, including through exchange of information and best practices, as well as through training and other joint efforts of a preventive character.

Article 5—Public Provocation to Commit a Terrorist Offence
1. For the purposes of this Convention, "public provocation to commit a terrorist offence" means the distribution, or otherwise making available, of a message to the public, with the intent to incite the commission of a terrorist offence, where such conduct, whether or not directly advocating terrorist offences, causes a danger that one or more such offences may be committed.

2. Each Party shall adopt such measures as may be necessary to establish public provocation to commit a terrorist offence, as defined in paragraph 1, when committed unlawfully and intentionally, as a criminal offence under its domestic law.

Article 6—Recruitment for Terrorism
1. For the purposes of this Convention, "recruitment for terrorism" means to solicit another person to commit or participate in the commission of a terrorist offence, or to join an association or group, for the purpose of contributing to the commission of one or more terrorist offences by the association or the group.

2. Each Party shall adopt such measures as may be necessary to establish recruitment for terrorism, as defined in paragraph 1, when committed unlawfully and intentionally, as a criminal offence under its domestic law.

Article 7—Training for Terrorism
1. For the purposes of this Convention, "training for terrorism" means to provide instruction in the

making or use of explosives, firearms or other weapons or noxious or hazardous substances, or in other specific methods or techniques, for the purpose of carrying out or contributing to the commission of a terrorist offence, knowing that the skills provided are intended to be used for this purpose.

2. Each Party shall adopt such measures as may be necessary to establish training for terrorism, as defined in paragraph 1, when committed unlawfully and intentionally, as a criminal offence under its domestic law.

Article 8—Irrelevance of the Commission of a Terrorist Offence
For an act to constitute an offence as set forth in Articles 5 to 7 of this Convention, it shall not be necessary that a terrorist offence be actually committed.

Article 9—Ancillary Offences
1. Each Party shall adopt such measures as may be necessary to establish as a criminal offence under its domestic law:

  a. Participating as an accomplice in an offence as set forth in Articles 5 to 7 of this Convention;
  b. Organising or directing others to commit an offence as set forth in Articles 5 to 7 of this Convention;
  c. Contributing to the commission of one or more offences as set forth in Articles 5 to 7 of this Convention by a group of persons acting with a common purpose. Such contribution shall be intentional and shall either:
    i. be made with the aim of furthering the criminal activity or criminal purpose of the group, where such activity or purpose involves the commission of an offence as set forth in Articles 5 to 7 of this Convention; or
    ii. be made in the knowledge of the intention of the group to commit an offence as set forth in Articles 5 to 7 of this Convention.

2. Each Party shall also adopt such measures as may be necessary to establish as a criminal offence under, and in accordance with, its domestic law the attempt to commit an offence as set forth in Articles 6 and 7 of this Convention.

[. . .]

Article 11—Sanctions and Measures
1. Each Party shall adopt such measures as may be necessary to make the offences set forth in Articles 5 to 7 and 9 of this Convention punishable by effective, proportionate and dissuasive penalties.

2. Previous final convictions pronounced in foreign States for offences set forth in the present Convention may, to the extent permitted by domestic law, be taken into account for the purpose of determining the sentence in accordance with domestic law.

3. Each Party shall ensure that legal entities held liable in accordance with Article 10 are subject to effective, proportionate and dissuasive criminal or non-criminal sanctions, including monetary sanctions.

[. . .]

Article 13—Protection, Compensation and Support for Victims of Terrorism
Each Party shall adopt such measures as may be necessary to protect and support the victims of terrorism that has been committed within its own territory. These measures may include, through the appropriate national schemes and subject to domestic legislation, *inter alia,* financial assistance and compensation for victims of terrorism and their close family members.

Article 14—Jurisdiction
1. Each Party shall take such measures as may be necessary to establish its jurisdiction over the offences set forth in this Convention:

a. when the offence is committed in the territory of that Party;

b. when the offence is committed on board a ship flying the flag of that Party, or on board an aircraft registered under the laws of that Party;

c. when the offence is committed by a national of that Party.

2. Each Party may also establish its jurisdiction over the offences set forth in this Convention:

a. when the offence was directed towards or resulted in the carrying out of an offence referred to in Article 1 of this Convention, in the territory of or against a national of that Party;

b. when the offence was directed towards or resulted in the carrying out of an offence referred to in Article 1 of this Convention, against a State or government facility of that Party abroad, including diplomatic or consular premises of that Party;

c. when the offence was directed towards or resulted in an offence referred to in Article 1 of this Convention, committed in an attempt to compel that Party to do or abstain from doing any act;

d. when the offence is committed by a stateless person who has his or her habitual residence in the territory of that Party;

e. when the offence is committed on board an aircraft which is operated by the Government of that Party.

3. Each Party shall take such measures as may be necessary to establish its jurisdiction over the offences set forth in this Convention in the case where the alleged offender is present in its territory and it does not extradite him or her to a Party whose jurisdiction is based on a rule of jurisdiction existing equally in the law of the requested Party.

4. This Convention does not exclude any criminal jurisdiction exercised in accordance with national law.

5. When more than one Party claims jurisdiction over an alleged offence set forth in this Convention, the Parties involved shall, where appropriate, consult with a view to determining the most appropriate jurisdiction for prosecution.

Article 15—Duty to Investigate

1. Upon receiving information that a person who has committed or who is alleged to have committed an offence set forth in this Convention may be present in its territory, the Party concerned shall take such measures as may be necessary under its domestic law to investigate the facts contained in the information.

2. Upon being satisfied that the circumstances so warrant, the Party in whose territory the offender or alleged offender is present shall take the appropriate measures under its domestic law so as to ensure that person's presence for the purpose of prosecution or extradition.

3. Any person in respect of whom the measures referred to in paragraph 2 are being taken shall be entitled to:

a. communicate without delay with the nearest appropriate representative of the State of which that person is a national or which is otherwise entitled to protect that person's rights or, if that person is a stateless person, the State in the territory of which that person habitually resides;

b. be visited by a representative of that State;

c. be informed of that person's rights under subparagraphs a. and b.

4. The rights referred to in paragraph 3 shall be exercised in conformity with the laws and regulations of the Party in the territory of which the offender or alleged offender is present, subject to the provision that the said laws and regulations must enable full effect to be given to the purposes for which the rights accorded under paragraph 3 are intended.

5. The provisions of paragraphs 3 and 4 shall be without prejudice to the right of any Party having a claim of jurisdiction in accordance with Article 14, paragraphs 1.c and 2.d to invite the International Committee of the Red Cross to communicate with and visit the alleged offender.

[. . .]

Article 17—International Co-operation in Criminal Matters

1. Parties shall afford one another the greatest measure of assistance in connection with criminal investigations or criminal or extradition proceedings in respect of the offences set forth in Articles 5 to 7 and 9 of this Convention, including assistance in obtaining evidence in their possession necessary for the proceedings.

2. Parties shall carry out their obligations under paragraph 1 in conformity with any treaties or other agreements on mutual legal assistance that may exist between them. In the absence of such treaties or agreements, Parties shall afford one another assistance in accordance with their domestic law.

3. Parties shall co-operate with each other to the fullest extent possible under relevant law, treaties, agreements and arrangements of the requested Party with respect to criminal investigations or proceedings in relation to the offences for which a legal entity may be held liable in accordance with Article 10 of this Convention in the requesting Party.

4. Each Party may give consideration to establishing additional mechanisms to share with other Parties information or evidence needed to establish criminal, civil or administrative liability pursuant to Article 10.

Article 18—Extradite or Prosecute

1. The Party in the territory of which the alleged offender is present shall, when it has jurisdiction in accordance with Article 14, if it does not extradite that person, be obliged, without exception whatsoever and whether or not the offence was committed in its territory, to submit the case without undue delay to its competent authorities for the purpose of prosecution, through proceedings in accordance with the laws of that Party. Those authorities shall take their decision in the same manner as in the case of any other offence of a serious nature under the law of that Party.

2. Whenever a Party is permitted under its domestic law to extradite or otherwise surrender one of its nationals only upon the condition that the person will be returned to that Party to serve the sentence imposed as a result of the trial or proceeding for which the extradition or surrender of the person was sought, and this Party and the Party seeking the extradition of the person agree with this option and other terms they may deem appropriate, such a conditional extradition or surrender shall be sufficient to discharge the obligation set forth in paragraph 1.

Article 19—Extradition

1. The offences set forth in Articles 5 to 7 and 9 of this Convention shall be deemed to be included as extraditable offences in any extradition treaty existing between any of the Parties before the entry into force of this Convention. Parties undertake to include such offences as extraditable offences in every extradition treaty to be subsequently concluded between them.

2. When a Party which makes extradition conditional on the existence of a treaty receives a request for extradition from another Party with which it has no extradition treaty, the requested Party may, if it so decides, consider this Convention as a legal basis for extradition in respect of the offences set forth in Articles 5 to 7 and 9 of this Convention. Extradition shall be subject to the other conditions provided by the law of the requested Party.

3. Parties which do not make extradition conditional on the existence of a treaty shall recognise the offences set forth in Articles 5 to 7 and 9 of this Convention as extraditable offences between themselves, subject to the conditions provided by the law of the requested Party.

4. Where necessary, the offences set forth in Articles 5 to 7 and 9 of this Convention shall be treated, for the purposes of extradition between Parties, as if they had been committed not only in the place in which they occurred but also in the territory of the Parties that have established jurisdiction in accordance with Article 14.

5. The provisions of all extradition treaties and agreements concluded between Parties in respect of offences set forth in Articles 5 to 7 and 9 of this Convention shall be deemed to be modified as between Parties to the extent that they are incompatible with this Convention.

[. . .]

Article 23—Signature and Entry into Force
1. This Convention shall be open for signature by the member States of the Council of Europe, the European Community and by non-member States which have participated in its elaboration.

2. This Convention is subject to ratification, acceptance or approval. Instruments of ratification, acceptance or approval shall be deposited with the Secretary General of the Council of Europe.

3. This Convention shall enter into force on the first day of the month following the expiration of a period of three months after the date on which six Signatories, including at least four member States of the Council of Europe, have expressed their consent to be bound by the Convention in accordance with the provisions of paragraph 2.

4. In respect of any Signatory which subsequently expresses its consent to be bound by it, the Convention shall enter into force on the first day of the month following the expiration of a period of three months after the date of the expression of its consent to be bound by the Convention in accordance with the provisions of paragraph 2.

[. . .]

Article 25—Territorial Application
1. Any State or the European Community may, at the time of signature or when depositing its instrument of ratification, acceptance, approval or accession, specify the territory or territories to which this Convention shall apply.

2. Any Party may, at any later date, by a declaration addressed to the Secretary General of the Council of Europe, extend the application of this Convention to any other territory specified in the declaration. In respect of such territory the Convention shall enter into force on the first day of the month following the expiration of a period of three months after the date of receipt of the declaration by the Secretary General.

3. Any declaration made under the two preceding paragraphs may, in respect of any territory specified in such declaration, be withdrawn by a notification addressed to the Secretary General of the Council of Europe. The withdrawal shall become effective on the first day of the month following the expiration of a period of three months after the date of receipt of such notification by the Secretary General.

Article 26—Effects of the Convention
1. The present Convention supplements applicable multilateral or bilateral treaties or agreements between the Parties, including the provisions of the following Council of Europe treaties:

—European Convention on Extradition, opened for signature, in Paris, on 13 December 1957 (ETS No. 24);

—European Convention on Mutual Assistance in Criminal Matters, opened for signature, in Strasbourg, on 20 April 1959 (ETS No. 30);

—European Convention on the Suppression of Terrorism, opened for signature, in Strasbourg, on 27 January 1977 (ETS No. 90);

—Additional Protocol to the European Convention on Mutual Assistance in Criminal Matters, opened for signature in Strasbourg on 17 March 1978 (ETS No. 99);

—Second Additional Protocol to the European Convention on Mutual Assistance in Criminal Matters, opened for signature in Strasbourg on 8 November 2001 (ETS No. 182);

—Protocol amending the European Convention on the Suppression of Terrorism, opened for signature in Strasbourg on 15 May 2003 (ETS No. 190).

2. If two or more Parties have already concluded an agreement or treaty on the matters dealt with in this Convention or have otherwise established their relations on such matters, or should they in future do so, they shall also be entitled to apply that agreement or treaty or to regulate those relations accordingly. However, where Parties establish their relations in respect of the matters dealt with in the present Convention other than as regulated therein, they shall do so in a manner that is not inconsistent with the Convention's objectives and principles.

3. Parties which are members of the European Union shall, in their mutual relations, apply Community and European Union rules in so far as there are Community or European Union rules governing the particular subject concerned and applicable to the specific case, without prejudice to the object and purpose of the present Convention and without prejudice to its full application with other Parties.

4. Nothing in this Convention shall affect other rights, obligations and responsibilities of a Party and individuals under international law, including international humanitarian law.

5. The activities of armed forces during an armed conflict, as those terms are understood under international humanitarian law, which are governed by that law, are not governed by this Convention, and the activities undertaken by military forces of a Party in the exercise of their official duties, inasmuch as they are governed by other rules of international law, are not governed by this Convention.

Article 27—Amendments to the Convention
1. Amendments to this Convention may be proposed by any Party, the Committee of Ministers of the Council of Europe or the Consultation of the Parties.

2. Any proposal for amendment shall be communicated by the Secretary General of the Council of Europe to the Parties.

3. Moreover, any amendment proposed by a Party or the Committee of Ministers shall be communicated to the Consultation of the Parties, which shall submit to the Committee of Ministers its opinion on the proposed amendment.

4. The Committee of Ministers shall consider the proposed amendment and any opinion submitted by the Consultation of the Parties and may approve the amendment.

5. The text of any amendment approved by the Committee of Ministers in accordance with paragraph 4 shall be forwarded to the Parties for acceptance.

6. Any amendment approved in accordance with paragraph 4 shall come into force on the thirtieth day after all Parties have informed the Secretary General of their acceptance thereof.

Note by the Secretariat: See the Declaration formulated by the European Community and the Member States of the European Union upon the adoption of the Convention by the Committee of

Ministers of the Council of Europe, on 3 May 2005:

"The European Community/European Union and its Member States reaffirm that their objective in requesting the inclusion of a 'disconnection clause' is to take account of the institutional structure of the Union when acceding to international conventions, in particular in case of transfer of sovereign powers from the Member States to the Community.

This clause is not aimed at reducing the rights or increasing the obligations of a non-European Union Party vis-à-vis the European Community/European Union and its Member States, inasmuch as the latter are also parties to this Convention.

The disconnection clause is necessary for those parts of the Convention which fall within the competence of the Community/Union, in order to indicate that European Union Member States cannot invoke and apply the rights and obligations deriving from the Convention directly among themselves (or between themselves and the European Community/Union). This does not detract from the fact that the Convention applies fully between the European Community/European Union and its Member States on the one hand, and the other Parties to the Convention, on the other; the Community and the European Union Members States will be bound by the Convention and will apply it like any Party to the Convention, if necessary, through Community/Union legislation. They will thus guarantee the full respect of the Convention's provisions vis-à-vis non-European Union Parties."

Appendix

1. Convention for the Suppression of Unlawful Seizure of Aircraft, signed at The Hague on 16 December 1970;

2. Convention for the Suppression of Unlawful Acts Against the Safety of Civil Aviation, concluded at Montreal on 23 September 1971;

3. Convention on the Prevention and Punishment of Crimes Against Internationally Protected Persons, Including Diplomatic Agents, adopted in New York on 14 December 1973;

4. International Convention Against the Taking of Hostages, adopted in New York on 17 December 1979;

5. Convention on the Physical Protection of Nuclear Material, adopted in Vienna on 3 March 1980;

6. Protocol for the Suppression of Unlawful Acts of Violence at Airports Serving International Civil Aviation, done at Montreal on 24 February 1988;

7. Convention for the Suppression of Unlawful Acts Against the Safety of Maritime Navigation, done at Rome on 10 March 1988;

8. Protocol for the Suppression of Unlawful Acts Against the Safety of Fixed Platforms Located on the Continental Shelf, done at Rome on 10 March 1988;

9. International Convention for the Suppression of Terrorist Bombings, adopted in New York on 15 December 1997;

10. International Convention for the Suppression of the Financing of Terrorism, adopted in New York on 9 December 1999.

31.
Convention of the Organization of the Islamic Conference on Combating International Terrorism

The Organization of the Islamic Conference (OIC), having fifty-seven countries as members, was set up in 1969 to look into the problems facing the member nations. The term "Islam" (meaning submission) has been sullied due to various terrorist organizations committing crimes in the name of Islam. The OIC in its ministerial meeting in 1999 adopted a resolution stating that a peaceful religion has been vilified due to the illegal activities of a handful of Muslims. The OIC spelled out areas of cooperation in preventing various forms of terrorist crimes. It clearly stipulated in Article 2 (Part I) that certain crimes such as aggression against the head of the state or king, murder, robbery, and acts of sabotage would not be considered political crimes even if the motive was political. However, the convention in the same articles differentiated between unlawful terrorist acts and the struggle of people against foreign occupation, colonialism, and aggression.

Source
Organization of the Islamic Conference, http://www.oic-oci.org/english/convenion/terrorism_convention.htm.

The Member States of the Organization of the Islamic Conference,

Pursuant to the tenets of the tolerant Islamic Sharia which reject all forms of violence and terrorism, and in particular specially those based on extremism and call for protection of human rights, which provisions are paralleled by the principles and rules of international law founded on cooperation between peoples for the establishment of peace;

Abiding by the lofty, moral and religious principles particularly the provisions of the Islamic Sharia as well as the human heritage of the Islamic Ummah.

Adhering to the Charter of the Organization of the Islamic Conference, its objectives and principles aimed at creating an appropriate atmosphere to strengthen cooperation and understanding among Islamic States as well as relevant OIC resolutions;

Adhering to the principles of International Law and the United Nations Charter as well as all relevant UN resolutions on procedures aimed at eliminating international terrorism, and all other conventions and international instruments to which states acceding to this Convention are parties and which call, inter alia, for the observance of the sovereignty, stability, territorial, integrity, political independence and security of states, and non-intervention in their international affairs;

Proceeding from the rules of the Code of Conduct of the Organization of Islamic Conference for Combating International Terrorism;

Desiring to promote cooperation among them for combating terrorist crimes that threaten the security and stability of the Islamic States and endanger their vital interests;

Being committed to combating all forms and manifestations of terrorism and eliminating its objectives and causes which target the lives and properties of people;

Confirming the legitimacy of the right of peoples to struggle against foreign occupation and colonialist and racist regimes by all means, including armed struggle to liberate their territories and attain their rights to self-determination and independence in compliance with the purposes and principles of the Charter and resolutions of the United Nations;

Believing that terrorism constitutes a gross violation of human rights, in particular the right to freedom and security, as well as an obstacle to the free functioning of institutions and socio-economic development, as it aims at destabilizing States;

Convinced that terrorism cannot be justified in any way, and that it should therefore be unambiguously condemned in all its forms and manifestations, and all its actions, means and practices, whatever its origin, causes or purposes, including direct or indirect actions of States;

Recognizing the growing links between terrorism and organized crime, including illicit trafficking in arms, narcotics, human beings and money laundering;

Have agreed to conclude this Convention, calling on all Member States of the Organization of the Islamic Conference to accede to it.

Definition and General Provisions

Article 1

For the purposes of this Convention:

1. "Contracting State" or "Contracting Party" means every Member State in the Organization of the Islamic Conference that has ratified or adhered to this Convention and deposited its instruments of ratification or adherence with the General Secretariat of the Organization.

2. "Terrorism" means any act of violence or threat thereof notwithstanding its motives or intentions perpetrated to carry out an individual or collective criminal plan with the aim of terrorizing people or threatening to harm them or imperiling their lives, honor, freedoms, security or rights or exposing the environment or any facility or public or private property to hazards or occupying or seizing them, or endangering a national resource, or international facilities, or threatening the stability, territorial integrity, political unity or sovereignty of independent States.

3. "Terrorist Crime" means any crime executed, started or participated in to realize a terrorist objective in any of the Contracting States or against its nationals, assets or interests or foreign facilities and nationals residing in its territory punishable by its internal law.

4. Crimes stipulated in the following conventions are also considered terrorist crimes with the exception of those excluded by the legislations of Contracting States or those who have not ratified them:

   a) Convention on "Offences and Other Acts Committed on Board of Aircrafts" (Tokyo, 14.9.1963).

   b) Convention on "Suppression of Unlawful Seizure of Aircraft" (The Hague, 16.12.1970).

   c) Convention on "Suppression of Unlawful Acts against the Safety of Civil Aviation" signed at Montreal on 23.9.1971 and its Protocol (Montreal, 10.12.1984).

   d) Convention on the "Prevention and Punishment of Crimes against Persons Enjoying International Immunity, Including Diplomatic Agents" (New York, 14.12.1973).

   e) International Convention against the Taking of Hostages (New York, 1979).

   f) The United Nations Law of the Sea Convention of 1982 and its related provisions on piracy at sea.

   g) Convention on the "Physical Protection of Nuclear Material" (Vienna, 1979).

   h) Protocol for the Suppression of Unlawful Acts of Violence at Airports Serving International Civil Aviation-Supplementary to the Convention for the Suppression of Unlawful Acts Against the Safety of Civil Aviation (Montreal, 1988).

   i) Protocol for the Suppression of Unlawful Acts against the Safety of Fixed Platforms on the Continental Shelf (Rome, 1988).

   j) Convention for the Suppression of Unlawful Acts against the Safety of Maritime Navigation (Rome, 1988).

   k) International Convention for the Suppression of Terrorist Bombings (New York, 1997).

   l) Convention on the Marking of Plastic Explosives for the purposes of Detection (Montreal, 1991).

Article 2

a) Peoples struggle including armed struggle against foreign occupation, aggression, colonialism, and hegemony, aimed at liberation and self-determination in accordance with the principles of international law shall not be considered a terrorist crime.

b) None of the terrorist crimes mentioned in the previous article shall be considered political crimes.

c) In the implementation of the provisions of this Convention the following crimes shall not be considered political crimes even when politically motivated:

1. Aggression against kings and heads of state of Contracting States or against their spouses, their ascendants or descendants.
2. Aggression against crown princes or vice-presidents or deputy heads of government or ministers in any of the Contracting States.
3. Aggression against persons enjoying international immunity including Ambassadors and diplomats in Contracting States or in countries of accreditation.
4. Murder or robbery by force against individuals or authorities or means of transport and communications.
5. Acts of sabotage and destruction of public properties and properties geared for public services, even if belonging to another Contracting State.
6. Crimes of manufacturing, smuggling or possessing arms and ammunition or explosives or other materials prepared for committing terrorist crimes.

d) All forms of international crimes, including illegal trafficking in narcotics and human beings money laundering aimed at financing terrorist objectives shall be considered terrorist crimes.

Section II

Foundations of Islamic Cooperation for Combating Terrorism

Chapter I

In the Field of Security

Division I

Measures to Prevent and Combat Terrorist Crimes

Article 3
I. The Contracting States are committed not to execute, initiate or participate in any form in organizing or financing or committing or instigating or supporting terrorist acts whether directly or indirectly.

II. Committed to prevent and combat terrorist crimes in conformity with the provisions of this Convention and their respective domestic rules and regulations the contracting States shall see to:

(A) Preventive Measures:
1. Barring their territories from being used as an arena for planning, organizing, executing terrorist crimes or initiating or participating in these crimes in any form; including preventing the infiltration of terrorist elements or their gaining refuge or residence therein individually or collectively, or receiving hosting, training, arming, financing or extending any facilities to them.
2. Cooperating and coordinating with the rest of the Contracting States, particularly neighboring countries which suffer from similar or common terrorist crimes.
3. Developing and strengthening systems relating to detecting transportation, importing, exporting stockpiling, and using of weapons, ammunition and explosives as well as other means of aggression, killing and destruction in addition to strengthening trans-border and custom controls

in order to intercept their transfer from one Contracting State to another or to other States unless they are intended for specific legitimate purposes.

4. Developing and strengthening systems related to surveillance procedures, securing borders, and land, sea and air passages in order to prevent infiltration through them.

5. Strengthening systems for ensuring the safety and protection of personalities, vital installations and means of public transport.

6. Re-enforcing protection, security and safety of diplomatic and consular persons and missions; and regional and international organizations accredited in the Contracting State in accordance with the conventions and rules of international law which govern this subject.

7. Promoting security intelligence activities and coordinating them with the intelligence activities of each Contracting State pursuant to their respective intelligence policies, aimed at exposing the objectives of terrorist groups and organizations, thwarting their designs and revealing the extent of their danger to security and stability.

8. Establishing a data base by each Contracting State to collect and analyze data on terrorist elements, groups, movements and organizations and monitor developments of the phenomenon of terrorism and successful experiences in combating it. Moreover, the Contracting State shall update this information and exchange them with competent authorities in other Contracting States within the limits of the laws and regulations in every State.

9. To take all necessary measures to eliminate and prevent the establishment of webs supporting all kinds of terrorist crimes.

(B) Combating Measures:

1. Arresting perpetrators of terrorist's crimes and prosecuting them according to the national law or extraditing them in accordance with the provisions of this Convention or existing Conventions between the requesting and requested States.

2. Ensuring effective protection of persons working in the field of criminal justice as well as to witnesses and investigators.

3. Ensuring effective protection of information sources and witnesses on terrorist crimes.

4. Extending necessary assistance to victims of terrorism.

5. Establishing effective cooperation between the concerned organs in the contracting States and the citizens for combating terrorism including extending appropriate guarantees and appropriate incentives to encourage informing on terrorist acts and submitting information to help uncover them and cooperating in arresting the perpetrators.

Division II

Areas of Islamic Cooperation for Preventing and Combating Terrorist Crimes

Article 4

Contracting States shall cooperate among themselves to prevent and combat terrorist crimes in accordance with the respective laws and regulations of each State in the following areas:

First: Exchange of Information

1. Contracting States shall undertake to promote exchange of information among them as such regarding:

a) Activities and crimes committed by terrorist groups, their leaders, their elements, their headquarters, training, means and sources that provide finance and weapons, types of arms, ammunition and explosives utilized as well as other ways and means to attack, kill and destroy.

b) Means of communications and propaganda utilized by terrorist groups, how they act, movement of their leaders, their elements and their travel documents.

2. Contracting States shall expeditiously inform any other Contracting State regarding available

information about any terrorist crime perpetrated in its territory aimed at undermining the interests of that State or its nationals and to state the facts surrounding the crime in terms of its circumstances, criminals involved, victims, losses, devices and methods utilized to carry out the crime, without prejudicing investigation and inquiry requisites.

3. Contracting States shall exchange information with the other Parties to combat terrorist crimes and to inform the Contracting State or other States of all available information or data that could prevent terrorist crimes within its territory or against its nationals or residents or interests.

4. The Contracting States shall provide any other Contracting State with available information or data that will:

a) Assist in arresting those accused of committing a terrorist crime against the interests of that country or being implicated in such acts either by assistance, collusion, instigation, or financing.

b) Contribute to confiscating any arms, weapons, explosives, devices or funds spent or meant to be spent to commit a terrorist crime.

5. The Contracting States undertake to respect the confidentiality of information exchanged between them and shall refrain from passing it to any non-Contracting States or other parties without prior consent of the source country.

Second: Investigation

Each Contracting State pledges to promote cooperation with other contracting states and to extend assistance in the field of investigation procedures in terms of arresting escaped suspects or those convicted for terrorist crimes in accordance with the laws and regulations of each country.

Third: Exchange of Expertise

1. Contracting States shall cooperate with each other to undertake and exchange studies and researches on combating terrorist crimes as well as exchange of expertise in this field.

2. Contracting States shall cooperate within the scope of their capabilities to provide available technical assistance for preparing programs or holding joint training sessions with one or more Contracting State if the need arises for personnel required in the field of combating terrorism in order to improve their scientific and practical potential and upgrade their performance standards.

Fourth: Education and Information Field

The Contracting States shall cooperate in:

1. Promoting information activities and supporting the mass media in order to confront the vicious campaign against Islam, by projecting the true image of tolerance of Islam and exposing the designs and danger of terrorist groups against the stability and security of Islamic States.

2. Including the noble human values, which proscribe the practice of terrorism in the educational curricula of Contracting States.

3. Supporting efforts aimed at keeping abreast of the age by introducing an advanced Islamic thought based on ijtihad by which Islam is distinguished.

Chapter II

In the Judicial Field

Section I

Extraditing Criminals

Article 5

Contracting States shall undertake to extradite those indicted or convicted of terrorist crimes, requested for extradition by any of these countries in compliance with the rules and conditions stipulated in this Convention.

Article 6
Extradition shall not be permissible in the following cases:

1. If the Crime for which extradition is requested is deemed by the laws enforced in the requested Contracting State as one of a political nature and without prejudice to the provisions of Article 2. paragraphs 2 and 3 of this Convention for which extradition is requested.
2. If the Crime for which extradition is sought relates solely to a dereliction of military obligations.
3. If the Crime for which extradition is requested, was committed in the territory of the requested Contracting State, unless this crime has undermined the interests of the requesting Contracting State and its laws stipulate that the perpetrators of those crimes shall be prosecuted and punished providing that the requested country has not commenced investigation or trial.
4. If the Crime has been the subject of a final sentence which has the force of law in the requested Contracting State.
5. If the action at the time of the extradition request elapsed or the penalty prescribed in accordance with the law in the Contracting State requesting extradition.
6. Crimes committed outside the territory of the requesting Contracting State by a person who was not its national and the law of the requested Contracting State does not prosecute such a crime if perpetrated outside its territory by such a person.
7. If pardon was granted and included the perpetrators of these crimes in the requesting Contracting State.
8. If the legal system of the requested State does not permit extradition of its national, then it shall be obliged to prosecute whosoever commits a terrorist crime if the act is punishable in both States by a freedom restraining sentence for a minimum period of one year or more. The nationality of the person requested for extradition shall be determined according to the date of the crime taking into account the investigation undertaken in this respect by the requesting State.

Article 7
If the person requested for extradition is under investigation or trial for another crime in the requested State, his extradition shall be postponed until the investigation is disposed of or the trial is over and the punishment implemented. In this case, the requested State shall extradite him provisionally for investigation or trial on condition that he shall be returned to it before execution of the sentence issued in the requested State.

Article 8
For the purpose of extraditing crime perpetrators according to this Convention, the domestic legislations of Contracting States shall not have any bearing as to their differences with respect to the crime being classified as a felony or misdemeanor, nor as to the penalty prescribed for it.

Section II

Rogatory Commission

Article 9
Each Contracting State shall request from any other Contracting State to undertake in its territory rogatory action with respect to any judicial procedures concerning an action involving a terrorist crime and in particular:

1. To hear witnesses and testimonies taken as evidence.
2. To communicate legal documents.
3. To implement inquiry and detention procedures.
4. To undertake on the scene inspection and analyze evidence.
5. To obtain necessary evidence or documents or records or their certified copies.

Article 10

Each Contracting State shall implement rogatory commissions related to terrorist crimes and may reject the request for implementation with respect to the following cases.

1. If the crime for which the request is made, is the subject of a charge, investigation or trial in the country requested to implement rogatory commission.

2. If the implementation of the request prejudices the sovereignty or the security or public order of the country charged with this mission.

Article 11

The request for rogatory mission shall be implemented promptly in accordance with the provisions of the domestic laws of the requested State and which may postpone its implementation until its investigation and prosecution procedures are completed on the same subject or until the compelling reasons that called for postponement are removed. In this case the requesting State shall be informed of this postponement.

Article 12

The request for a rogatory commission related to a terrorist crime shall not be refused on the grounds of the rule of transaction confidentiality for banks and financial institutions. And in the implementation of the request the rules of the enforcing State are to be followed.

Article 13

The procedure, undertaken through rogatory commission in accordance with the provisions of this Convention, shall have the same legal effect as if it was brought before the competent authority in the State requesting rogatory commission. The results of its implementation shall only be utilized within the scope of the rogatory commission.

Section III

Judicial Cooperation

Article 14

Each Contracting State shall extend to the other contracting parties every possible assistance as may be necessary for investigation or trial proceedings related to terrorist crimes.

Article 15

If judicial competence accrues to one of the Contracting States for the prosecution of a subject accused of a terrorist crime, this State may request the country which hosts the suspect to prosecute him for this crime subject to the host country's consent and providing the crime is punishable in that country by a freedom restraining sentence for at least one year or by a more severe sanction. In such a case the requesting State shall pass all investigation documents and evidence related to the crime to the requested State.

Investigation or trial shall be conducted on the grounds of the case or cases brought by the requesting State against the accused in accordance with the legal provisions and procedures of the country holding the trial.

Article 16

The request for trial on the basis of para (1) of the previous article entails the suspension of procedures of prosecution, investigation and trial in the territory of the requesting State except those relating to the requisites of cooperation, assistance or rogatory commission sought by the State requested to hold the trial procedures.

Article 17

1. Procedures undertaken in either of the two States—the requesting State or the one where the trial is held—shall be subject to the law of the country where the procedure is executed and which shall have legal preeminence as may be stipulated in its legislation.

2. The requesting State shall not bring to trial or retrial the accused subject unless the requested State refuses to prosecute him.

3. In all cases the State requested to hold trial shall inform the requesting country of its action with respect to the request for trial and shall communicate to it the results of its investigations or trial proceedings.

Article 18

The State requested to hold trial may undertake all measures and procedures stipulated by its legislation regarding the accused both before and after the request for trial is received.

Section IV

Seized Assets and Proceeds of the Crime

Article 19

1. If the extradition of a subject is decided, the Contracting State shall hand over to the requesting State the assets and proceeds seized, used or related to the terrorist crime, found in the possession of the wanted subject or with a third party.

2. The material mentioned in the previous item shall be handed over even if the accused has not been extradited either due to his escape, death or any other reason after ensuring that these were connected with the terrorist crime.

3. The provisions contained in the two previous items shall not prejudice the rights of any of the Contracting States or bona fide from others with respect to the above-mentioned assets and proceeds.

Article 20

The State requested to hand over the assets and proceeds may undertake all necessary custodial measures and procedures for the implementation of its obligation. It may also retain them

provisionally if required for penal action implemented therein or hand them to the requesting State on condition that they shall be returned for the same purpose.

Section V

Exchange of Evidence

Article 21

A Contracting State shall see to it that the evidence and effects of any terrorist crime committed on its territory against another Contracting State are examined by its competent organs and may seek assistance to that end from any other Contracting State. Moreover, it shall take every necessary step to safeguard the evidence and proof of their legal relevance. It may communicate, if requested, the result to the country whose interest were targeted by the crime. The State or States which have assisted in this case shall not pass this information to others.

Part III

Mechanism for Implementing Cooperation

Chapter I

Extradition Procedures

Article 22

The exchange of extradition requests between Contracting States shall be Undertaken directly through diplomatic channels or through their Ministries of Justice or their substitute.

Article 23

A request for extradition shall be submitted in writing and shall include:

1. The original or an authenticated copy of the indictment, arrest order or any other instruments of identical weight issued in line with the condi-

tions stipulated in the requesting State's legislation.

2. A statement of the acts for which extradition is sought specifying the dates and places, where these acts were committed and their legal implications along with reference to the legal articles under which they fall as well as a copy of these articles.

3. Description, in as much detail as possible, of the subject wanted for extradition and any other information such as to determine his identity and nationality.

Article 24

1. The judicial authorities in the requesting State may approach the requested State by any channel of written communication and seek the preventive arrest of the wanted subject pending the arrival of the extradition request.

2. In this case the requested State may effect the preventive arrest of the wanted subject. However, if the request for extradition is not submitted together with the necessary documents listed in the above article, the subject whose extradition is sought may not be detained for more than thirty days as of the day of his arrest.

Article 25

The requesting State shall send a request together with the documents listed in Article 23 of this Convention. If the requested State accepts the request as valid, its competent authorities shall implement it in accordance with its legislation and shall promptly notify the requesting State of the action undertaken.

Article 26

1. In all cases stipulated in the two articles above, preventive detention shall not exceed sixty days after the date of arrest.

2. Temporary release may be effected during the period stipulated in the previous article and the requested State shall take appropriate measures to ensure that the wanted subject does not escape.

3. Release shall not prevent the re-arrest of the subject and his extradition if it was requested after his release.

Article 27

If the requested State requires additional clarification to ascertain the conditions stipulated in this chapter, it shall notify the requesting State thereof and fix a date for provision of such clarifications.

Article 28

If the requested State received a number of extradition requests from various countries related to the same or diverse acts, this State shall decide upon these requests bearing in mind the circumstances and in particular the possibility of subsequent extradition, date of receiving the requests, degree of the danger of the crime and where it was committed.

Chapter II

Measures for Rogatory Commissions

Article 29

Rogatory Commission requests must specify the following:

The competent authority that issued the request.

Subject of the request and its reason.

The identity and nationality of the person being the subject of the rogatory commission (as may be possible).

Information on the crime requiring rogatory commission, its legal definition and penalty inflicted on its perpetrators along with maximum available information on its circumstances in order to ensure the efficient implementation of the rogatory commission.

Article 30

1. The request for rogatory commission shall be forwarded by the Ministry of Justice in the requesting State to the Ministry of Justice in the requested State and returned in the same way.

2. In case of expediency, the request for rogatory commission shall be directly forwarded by the judicial authorities in the requesting State to the judicial authorities in the requested State. A copy of this rogatory commission shall also be sent at the same time to the Ministry of Justice in the requested State. The rogatory commission shall be returned together with the papers concerning its implementation in the way stipulated in the previous item.

3. The request for rogatory commission may be forwarded directly from the judicial authorities to the competent authority in the requested country. Answers may be sent directly through the said authority.

Article 31

Requests for rogatory commission and accompanying documents shall be signed or stamped with the seal of a competent authority or that authorized by it. These documents shall be exempted from all formal procedures that could be required by the legislation of the requested State.

Article 32

If the authority that received the request for rogatory commission was not competent enough to deal with it, it shall automatically transfer it to the competent authority in its country. If the request is forwarded directly the answer shall reach the requesting State in the same manner.

Article 33

Any refusal for rogatory commission shall be explained.

Chapter III

Measures for Protecting Witnesses and Experts

Article 34

If the requesting State deems that the appearance of the witness or expert before its judicial authorities is of special importance, reference thereto shall be made in its request. The request or summons shall include an approximate statement in terms of compensation, travel expenses, accommodation and commitment to make these payments. The requested State shall invite the witness or expert and inform the requesting State about his/her reply.

Article 35

1. No penalty nor coercive measure may be inflicted upon the witness or expert who does not comply with the summons even if the writ provides for such a penalty.

2. If the witness or expert arrives voluntarily to the territory of the requesting State, he shall be summoned according to the provisions of the internal legislation of this State.

Article 36

1. A witness or expert may not be subjected to trial, detained or have his freedom restricted in the territory of the requesting State, for acts or court rulings that preceded his departure for the requesting State, irrespective of his nationality, as long as his appearance before the judicial authorities of the said State is based on a summons.

2. No witness or expert, whatever his nationality, appearing before the judiciary of the State in question on the basis of a summons, may be prosecuted or detained or have his freedom restricted in any way on the requesting State's territory for other acts or court decisions not mentioned in the summons and predating his

departure from the State from which he is requested.

3. The immunity privileges stated in this Article shall become invalid if a witness or expert remains on the requesting State's territories for over thirty consecutive days despite his ability to return once his presence was no longer requested by the judiciary, or if he returns to the requesting State's territories after his departure.

Article 37

1. The requesting State shall undertake all necessary measures to ensure the protection of a witness or expert from publicity that could endanger him, his family or his property as a result of his testimony and in particular:

   a) To ensure confidentiality of the date and place of his arrival as well as the means involved.

   b) To ensure confidentiality of his accommodation, movements and locations where he may be found.

   c) To ensure confidentiality of the testimony and information given to the competent judicial authorities.

2. The requesting State shall provide necessary security required by the condition of the witness or expert and of his family, and circumstances of the case and types of expected risks.

Article 38

1. If the witness or expert who is summoned to the requesting State is imprisoned in the requested State, he shall be provisionally transferred to the location of the hearing at which he is to testify according to conditions and times determined by the requested State.

2. Transfer may be denied:

   a) If the witness or expert refuses.

   b) If his presence is necessary for undertaking criminal procedures in the territory of the requested State.

   c) If his transfer would prolong his imprisonment.

   d) If there are considerations militating against his transfer.

3. The transferred witness or expert shall remain in detention in the territory of the requesting State until he is repatriated to the requested state unless the latter requests his release.

32.
USA Patriot Act (Title III)

The Patriot Act came into existence after the devastating terrorist attacks of 11 September 2001. The act received presidential assent on 26 October 2001. This most comprehensive legislation, running 342 pages, drew criticism from civil liberty groups for infringing upon some of the fundamental rights of Americans. Some conservative groups criticized the act as giving unprecedented power to the government. Some of the important provisions of the Act are Title II, "Enhanced Surveillance Procedures"; Title III, "International Money Laundering Abatement and Anti-Terrorist Financing Act of 2001"; Title IV, "Protecting the Border"; and Title VIII, "Strengthening the Criminal Laws Against Terrorism." Title III of the act strengthened government control over financial transactions in domestic and international circles. The act increased the scope of earlier forfeiture laws, made record keeping more stringent, emphasized information-sharing requirements, and imposed new penalties. The functioning of the shell banks in the United States was restricted. The money remitters not complying with licensing as well as registration could be prosecuted easily as per the provisions of the act.

Source
Electronic Privacy Information Center,
http://www.epic.org/privacy/terrorism/hr3162.html.

Title III—International Money Laundering Abatement and Anti-Terrorist Financing Act of 2001

Sec. 301. Short Title

This title may be cited as the 'International Money Laundering Abatement and Financial Anti-Terrorism Act of 2001'.

Sec. 302. Findings and Purposes

(a) FINDINGS—The Congress finds that—

(1) money laundering, estimated by the International Monetary Fund to amount to between 2 and 5 percent of global gross domestic product, which is at least $600,000,000,000 annually, provides the financial fuel that permits transnational criminal enterprises to conduct and expand their operations to the detriment of the safety and security of American citizens;

(2) money laundering, and the defects in financial transparency on which money launderers rely, are critical to the financing of global terrorism and the provision of funds for terrorist attacks;

(3) money launderers subvert legitimate financial mechanisms and banking relationships by using them as protective covering for the movement of criminal proceeds and the financing of crime and terrorism, and, by so doing, can threaten the safety of United States citizens and undermine the integrity of United States financial institutions and of the global financial and trading systems upon which prosperity and growth depend;

(4) certain jurisdictions outside of the United States that offer 'offshore' banking and related facilities designed to provide anonymity, coupled with weak financial supervisory and enforcement regimes, provide essential tools to disguise ownership and movement of criminal funds, derived from, or used to commit, offenses ranging from narcotics trafficking, terrorism, arms smuggling, and trafficking in human beings, to financial frauds that prey on law-abiding citizens;

(5) transactions involving such offshore jurisdictions make it difficult for law enforcement officials and regulators to follow the trail of money earned by criminals, organized international criminal enterprises, and global terrorist organizations;

(6) correspondent banking facilities are one of the banking mechanisms susceptible in some circumstances to manipulation by foreign banks to permit the laundering of funds by hiding the identity of real parties in interest to financial transactions;

(7) private banking services can be susceptible to manipulation by money launderers, for example corrupt foreign government officials, particularly if those services include the creation of offshore accounts and facilities for large personal funds transfers to channel funds into accounts around the globe;

(8) United States anti-money laundering efforts are impeded by outmoded and inadequate statutory provisions that make investigations, prosecutions, and forfeitures more difficult, particularly in cases in which money laundering involves foreign persons, foreign banks, or foreign countries;

(9) the ability to mount effective counter-measures to international money launderers requires national, as well as bilateral and multilateral action, using tools specially designed for that effort; and

(10) the Basle Committee on Banking Regulation and Supervisory Practices and the Financial Action Task Force on Money Laundering, of both of which the United States is a member, have each adopted international anti-money laundering principles and recommendations.

(b) PURPOSES—The purposes of this title are—

(1) to increase the strength of United States measures to prevent, detect, and prosecute international money laundering and the financing of terrorism;

(2) to ensure that—

(A) banking transactions and financial relationships and the conduct of such transactions and relationships, do not contravene the purposes of subchapter II of chapter 53 of title 31, United States Code, section 21 of the Federal Deposit Insurance Act, or chapter 2 of title I of Public Law 91–508 (84 Stat. 1116), or facilitate the evasion of any such provision; and

(B) the purposes of such provisions of law continue to be fulfilled, and such provisions of law are effectively and efficiently administered;

(3) to strengthen the provisions put into place by the Money Laundering Control Act of 1986 (18 U.S.C. 981 note), especially with respect to crimes by non-United States nationals and foreign financial institutions;

(4) to provide a clear national mandate for subjecting to special scrutiny those foreign jurisdictions, financial institutions operating outside of the United States, and classes of international transactions or types of accounts that pose particular, identifiable opportunities for criminal abuse;

(5) to provide the Secretary of the Treasury (in this title referred to as the 'Secretary') with broad discretion, subject to the safeguards provided by the Administrative Procedure Act under title 5, United States Code, to take measures tailored to the particular money laundering problems presented by specific foreign jurisdictions, financial institutions operating outside of the United States, and classes of international transactions or types of accounts;

(6) to ensure that the employment of such measures by the Secretary permits appropriate opportunity for comment by affected financial institutions;

(7) to provide guidance to domestic financial institutions on particular foreign jurisdictions, financial institutions operating outside of the United States, and classes of international transactions that are of primary money laundering concern to the United States Government;

(8) to ensure that the forfeiture of any assets in connection with the anti-terrorist efforts of the United States permits for adequate challenge consistent with providing due process rights;

(9) to clarify the terms of the safe harbor from civil liability for filing suspicious activity reports;

(10) to strengthen the authority of the Secretary to issue and administer geographic targeting orders, and to clarify that violations of such orders or any other requirement imposed under the authority contained in chapter 2 of title I of Public Law 91–508 and subchapters II and III of chapter 53 of title 31, United States Code, may result in criminal and civil penalties;

(11) to ensure that all appropriate elements of the financial services industry are subject to appropriate requirements to report potential money laundering transactions to proper authorities, and that jurisdictional disputes do not hinder examination of compliance by financial institutions with relevant reporting requirements;

(12) to strengthen the ability of financial institutions to maintain the integrity of their employee population; and

(13) to strengthen measures to prevent the use of the United States financial system for personal gain by corrupt foreign officials and to facilitate the repatriation of any stolen assets to the citizens of countries to whom such assets belong.

Sec. 303. 4-Year Congressional Review; Expedited Consideration

(a) IN GENERAL—Effective on and after the first day of fiscal year 2005, the provisions of this title and the amendments made by this title shall terminate if the Congress enacts a joint resolution, the text after the resolving clause of which is as follows: 'That provisions of the International Money Laundering Abatement and Anti-Terrorist Financing Act of 2001, and the amendments made thereby, shall no longer have the force of law'.

(b) EXPEDITED CONSIDERATION—Any joint resolution submitted pursuant to this section should be considered by the Congress expeditiously. In particular, it shall be considered in the Senate in accordance with the provisions of section 601(b) of the International Security Assistance and Arms Control Act of 1976.

Subtitle A—International Counter Money Laundering and Related Measures

Sec. 311. Special Measures for Jurisdictions, Financial Institutions, or International

Transactions of Primary Money Laundering Concern

(a) IN GENERAL—Subchapter II of chapter 53 of title 31, United States Code, is amended by inserting after section 5318 the following new section:

'Sec. 5318A. Special measures for jurisdictions, financial institutions, or international transactions of primary money laundering concern'

(a) INTERNATIONAL COUNTER-MONEY LAUNDERING REQUIREMENTS—

'(1) IN GENERAL—The Secretary of the Treasury may require domestic financial institutions and domestic financial agencies to take 1 or more of the special measures described in subsection (b) if the Secretary finds that reasonable grounds exist for concluding that a jurisdiction outside of the United States, 1 or more financial institutions operating outside of the United States, 1 or more classes of transactions within, or involving, a jurisdiction outside of the United States, or 1 or more types of accounts is of primary money laundering concern, in accordance with subsection (c).

'(2) FORM OF REQUIREMENT—The special measures described in—

'(A) subsection (b) may be imposed in such sequence or combination as the Secretary shall determine;

'(B) paragraphs (1) through (4) of subsection (b) may be imposed by regulation, order, or otherwise as permitted by law; and

'(C) subsection (b)(5) may be imposed only by regulation.

'(3) DURATION OF ORDERS; RULEMAKING—Any order by which a special measure described in paragraphs (1) through (4) of subsection (b) is imposed (other than an order described in section 5326)—

'(A) shall be issued together with a notice of proposed rulemaking relating to the imposition of such special measure; and

'(B) may not remain in effect for more than 120 days, except pursuant to a rule promulgated on or before the end of the 120-day period beginning on the date of issuance of such order.

'(4) PROCESS FOR SELECTING SPECIAL MEASURES—In selecting which special measure or measures to take under this subsection, the Secretary of the Treasury—

'(A) shall consult with the Chairman of the Board of Governors of the Federal Reserve System, any other appropriate Federal banking agency, as defined in section 3 of the Federal Deposit Insurance Act, the Secretary of State, the Securities and Exchange Commission, the Commodity Futures Trading Commission, the National Credit Union Administration Board, and in the sole discretion of the Secretary, such other agencies and interested parties as the Secretary may find to be appropriate; and

'(B) shall consider—
'(i) whether similar action has been or is being taken by other nations or multilateral groups;
'(ii) whether the imposition of any particular special measure would create a significant competitive disadvantage, including any undue cost or burden associated with compliance, for financial institutions organized or licensed in the United States;
'(iii) the extent to which the action or the timing of the action would have a significant adverse systemic impact on the international payment, clearance, and settlement system, or on legitimate business activities involving the particular jurisdiction, institution, or class of transactions; and
'(iv) the effect of the action on United States national security and foreign policy.

'(5) NO LIMITATION ON OTHER AUTHORITY—This section shall not be construed as superseding or otherwise restricting any other authority granted to the Secretary, or to any other agency, by this subchapter or otherwise.

'(b) SPECIAL MEASURES—The special measures referred to in subsection (a), with respect to a jurisdiction outside of the United States, financial institution operating outside of the United States, class of transaction within, or involving, a jurisdiction outside of the United States, or 1 or more types of accounts are as follows:

'(1) RECORDKEEPING AND REPORTING OF CERTAIN FINANCIAL TRANSACTIONS—

'(A) IN GENERAL—The Secretary of the Treasury may require any domestic financial institution or domestic financial agency to maintain records, file reports, or both, concerning the aggregate amount of transactions, or concerning each transaction, with respect to a jurisdiction outside of the United States, 1 or more financial institutions operating outside of the United States, 1 or more classes of transactions within, or involving, a jurisdiction outside of the United States, or 1 or more types of accounts if the Secretary finds any such jurisdiction, institution, or class of transactions to be of primary money laundering concern.

'(B) FORM OF RECORDS AND REPORTS— Such records and reports shall be made and retained at such time, in such manner, and for such period of time, as the Secretary shall determine, and shall include such information as the Secretary may determine, including—

'(i) the identity and address of the participants in a transaction or relationship, including the identity of the originator of any funds transfer;

'(ii) the legal capacity in which a participant in any transaction is acting;

'(iii) the identity of the beneficial owner of the funds involved in any transaction, in accordance with such procedures as the Secretary determines to

be reasonable and practicable to obtain and retain the information; and

'(iv) a description of any transaction.

'(2) INFORMATION RELATING TO BENEFICIAL OWNERSHIP—In addition to any other requirement under any other provision of law, the Secretary may require any domestic financial institution or domestic financial agency to take such steps as the Secretary may determine to be reasonable and practicable to obtain and retain information concerning the beneficial ownership of any account opened or maintained in the United States by a foreign person (other than a foreign entity whose shares are subject to public reporting requirements or are listed and traded on a regulated exchange or trading market), or a representative of such a foreign person, that involves a jurisdiction outside of the United States, 1 or more financial institutions operating outside of the United States, 1 or more classes of transactions within, or involving, a jurisdiction outside of the United States, or 1 or more types of accounts if the Secretary finds any such jurisdiction, institution, or transaction or type of account to be of primary money laundering concern.

'(3) INFORMATION RELATING TO CERTAIN PAYABLE-THROUGH ACCOUNTS—If the Secretary finds a jurisdiction outside of the United States, 1 or more financial institutions operating outside of the United States, or 1 or more classes of transactions within, or involving, a jurisdiction outside of the United States to be of primary money laundering concern, the Secretary may require any domestic financial institution or domestic financial agency that opens or maintains a payable-through account in the United States for a foreign financial institution involving any such jurisdiction or any such financial institution operating outside of the United States, or a payable through account through which any such transaction may be conducted, as a condition of opening or maintaining such account—

'(A) to identify each customer (and representative of such customer) of such financial institution who is permitted to use, or whose transactions are routed through, such payable-through account; and

'(B) to obtain, with respect to each such customer (and each such representative), information that is substantially comparable to that which the depository institution obtains in the ordinary course of business with respect to its customers residing in the United States.

'(4) INFORMATION RELATING TO CERTAIN CORRESPONDENT ACCOUNTS—If the Secretary finds a jurisdiction outside of the United States, 1 or more financial institutions operating outside of the United States, or 1 or more classes of transactions within, or involving, a jurisdiction outside of the United States to be of primary money laundering concern, the Secretary may require any domestic financial institution or domestic financial agency that opens or maintains a correspondent account in the United States for a foreign financial institution involving any such jurisdiction or any such financial institution operating outside of the United States, or a correspondent account through which any such transaction may be conducted, as a condition of opening or maintaining such account—

'(A) to identify each customer (and representative of such customer) of any such financial institution who is permitted to use, or whose transactions are routed through, such correspondent account; and

'(B) to obtain, with respect to each such customer (and each such representative), information that is substantially comparable to that which the depository institution obtains in the ordinary course of business with respect to its customers residing in the United States.

'(5) PROHIBITIONS OR CONDITIONS ON OPENING OR MAINTAINING CERTAIN CORRESPONDENT OR PAYABLE-THROUGH ACCOUNTS—If the Secretary finds a jurisdiction outside of the United States, 1 or more financial institutions operating outside of the United States, or 1 or more classes of transactions within, or involving, a jurisdiction outside of the United States to be of primary money laundering concern, the Secretary, in consultation with the Secretary of State, the Attorney General, and the Chairman of the Board of Governors of the Federal Reserve System, may prohibit, or impose conditions upon, the opening or maintaining in the United States of a correspondent account or payable—through account by any domestic financial institution or domestic financial agency for or on behalf of a foreign banking institution, if such correspondent account or payable-through account involves any such jurisdiction or institution, or if any such transaction may be conducted through such correspondent account or payable-through account.

'(c) CONSULTATIONS AND INFORMATION TO BE CONSIDERED IN FINDING JURISDIC-TIONS, INSTITUTIONS, TYPES OF ACCOUNTS, OR TRANSACTIONS TO BE OF PRIMARY MONEY LAUNDERING CON-CERN—

'(1) IN GENERAL—In making a finding that reasonable grounds exist for concluding that a jurisdiction outside of the United States, 1 or more financial institutions operating outside of the United States, 1 or more classes of transactions within, or involving, a jurisdiction outside of the United States, or 1 or more types of accounts is of primary money laundering concern so as to authorize the Secretary of the Treasury to take 1 or more of the special measures described in subsection (b), the Secretary shall consult with the Secretary of State and the Attorney General.

'(2) ADDITIONAL CONSIDERATIONS—In making a finding described in paragraph (1), the Secretary shall consider in addition such information as the Secretary determines to be relevant, including the following potentially relevant factors:

'(A) JURISDICTIONAL FACTORS—In the case of a particular jurisdiction—

'(i) evidence that organized criminal groups, international terrorists, or both, have transacted business in that jurisdiction;

'(ii) the extent to which that jurisdiction or financial institutions operating in that jurisdiction offer bank secrecy or special regulatory advantages to nonresidents or nondomiciliaries of that jurisdiction;

'(iii) the substance and quality of administration of the bank supervisory and counter-money laundering laws of that jurisdiction;

'(iv) the relationship between the volume of financial transactions occurring in that jurisdiction and the size of the economy of the jurisdiction;

'(v) the extent to which that jurisdiction is characterized as an offshore banking or secrecy haven by credible international organizations or multilateral expert groups;

'(vi) whether the United States has a mutual legal assistance treaty with that jurisdiction, and the experience of United States law enforcement officials and regulatory officials in obtaining information about transactions originating in or routed through or to such jurisdiction; and

(vii) the extent to which that jurisdiction is characterized by high levels of official or institutional corruption.

'(B) INSTITUTIONAL FACTORS—In the case of a decision to apply 1 or more of the special measures described in subsection (b) only to a financial institution or institutions, or to a transaction or class of transactions, or to a type of account, or to all 3, within or involving a particular jurisdiction—

'(i) the extent to which such financial institutions, transactions, or types of accounts are used to facilitate or promote money laundering in or through the jurisdiction;

'(ii) the extent to which such institutions, transactions, or types of accounts are used for legitimate business purposes in the jurisdiction; and

'(iii) the extent to which such action is sufficient to ensure, with respect to transactions involving the jurisdiction and institutions operating in the jurisdiction, that the purposes of this subchapter continue to be fulfilled, and to guard against international money laundering and other financial crimes.

'(d) NOTIFICATION OF SPECIAL MEASURES INVOKED BY THE SECRETARY—Not later than 10 days after the date of any action taken by the Secretary of the Treasury under subsection (a)(1), the Secretary shall notify, in writing, the Committee on Financial Services of the House of Representatives and the Committee on Banking, Housing, and Urban Affairs of the Senate of any such action.

'(e) DEFINITIONS—Notwithstanding any other provision of this subchapter, for purposes of this section and subsections (i) and (j) of section 5318, the following definitions shall apply:

'(1) BANK DEFINITIONS—The following definitions shall apply with respect to a bank:

'(A) ACCOUNT—The term 'account'—

'(i) means a formal banking or business relationship established to provide regular services, dealings, and other financial transactions; and

'(ii) includes a demand deposit, savings deposit, or other transaction or asset account and a credit account or other extension of credit.

'(B) CORRESPONDENT ACCOUNT—The term 'correspondent account' means an account established to receive deposits from, make payments on behalf of a foreign financial institution, or handle other financial transactions related to such institution.

'(C) PAYABLE-THROUGH ACCOUNT—The term 'payable-through account' means an account, including a transaction account (as defined in section 19(b)(1)(C) of the Federal Reserve Act), opened at a depository institution by a foreign financial institution by means of which the foreign financial institution permits its customers to engage, either directly or through a subaccount, in banking activities usual in connection with the business of banking in the United States.

'(2) DEFINITIONS APPLICABLE TO INSTITUTIONS OTHER THAN BANKS—With respect to any financial institution other than a bank, the Secretary shall, after consultation with the appropriate Federal functional regulators (as defined in section 509 of the Gramm-Leach-Bliley Act), define by regulation the term 'account', and shall include within the meaning of that term, to the extent, if any, that the Secretary deems appropriate, arrangements similar to payable-through and correspondent accounts.

'(3) REGULATORY DEFINITION OF BENEFICIAL OWNERSHIP—The Secretary shall promulgate regulations defining beneficial ownership of an account for purposes of this section and subsections (i) and (j) of section 5318. Such regulations shall address issues related to an individual's authority to fund, direct, or manage the account (including, without limitation, the power to direct payments into or out of the account), and an individual's material interest in the income or corpus of the account, and shall ensure that the identification of individuals under this section does not extend to any individual whose beneficial interest in the income or corpus of the account is immaterial'.

'(4) OTHER TERMS—The Secretary may, by regulation, further define the terms in paragraphs (1), (2), and (3), and define other terms for the purposes of this section, as the Secretary deems appropriate'.

(b) CLERICAL AMENDMENT—The table of sections for subchapter II of chapter 53 of title 31, United States Code, is amended by inserting after the item relating to section 5318 the following new item:

'5318A. Special measures for jurisdictions, financial institutions, or international transactions of primary money laundering concern'.

[. . .]

Sec. 315. Inclusion of Foreign Corruption Offenses As Money Laundering Crimes
Section 1956(c) (7) of title 18, United States Code, is amended—

(1) in subparagraph (B)—
  (A) in clause (ii), by striking 'or destruction of property by means of explosive or fire' and inserting 'destruction of property by means of explosive or fire, or a crime of violence (as defined in section 16)';
  (B) in clause (iii), by striking '1978' and inserting '1978)'; and
  (C) by adding at the end the following:
    '(iv) bribery of a public official, or the misappropriation, theft, or embezzlement of public funds by or for the benefit of a public official;
    '(v) smuggling or export control violations involving—
      '(I) an item controlled on the United States Munitions List established under section 38 of the Arms Export Control Act (22 U.S.C. 2778); or
      '(II) an item controlled under regulations under the Export Administration Regulations (15 C.F.R. Parts 730–774); or
    '(vi) an offense with respect to which the United States would be obligated by a multilateral treaty, either to extradite the alleged offender or to submit the case for prosecution, if the offender were found within the territory of the United States;'; and
(2) in subparagraph (D)—
  (A) by inserting 'section 541 (relating to goods falsely classified),' before 'section 542';
  (B) by inserting 'section 922(1) (relating to the unlawful importation of firearms), section 924(n) (relating to firearms trafficking),' before 'section 956';
  (C) by inserting 'section 1030 (relating to computer fraud and abuse),' before '1032'; and

(D) by inserting 'any felony violation of the Foreign Agents Registration Act of 1938,' before 'or any felony violation of the Foreign Corrupt Practices Act'.

[. . .]

Sec. 318. *Laundering Money Through a Foreign Bank*

Section 1956(c) of title 18, United States Code, is amended by striking paragraph (6) and inserting the following:

'(6) the term 'financial institution' includes—

'(A) any financial institution, as defined in section 5312(a)(2) of title 31, United States Code, or the regulations promulgated thereunder; and

'(B) any foreign bank, as defined in section 1 of the International Banking Act of 1978 (12 U.S.C. 3101)'.

[. . .]

Sec. 320. *Proceeds of Foreign Crimes*

Section 981(a)(1)(B) of title 18, United States Code, is amended to read as follows:

'(B) Any property, real or personal, within the jurisdiction of the United States, constituting, derived from, or traceable to, any proceeds obtained directly or indirectly from an offense against a foreign nation, or any property used to facilitate such an offense, if the offense—

'(i) involves the manufacture, importation, sale, or distribution of a controlled substance (as that term is defined for purposes of the Controlled Substances Act), or any other conduct described in section 1956(c)(7)(B);

'(ii) would be punishable within the jurisdiction of the foreign nation by death or imprisonment for a term exceeding 1 year; and

'(iii) would be punishable under the laws of the United States by imprisonment for a term exceeding 1 year, if the act or activity constituting the offense had occurred within the jurisdiction of the United States'.

[. . .]

Sec. 329. *Criminal Penalties*

Any person who is an official or employee of any department, agency, bureau, office, commission, or other entity of the Federal Government, and any other person who is acting for or on behalf of any such entity, who, directly or indirectly, in connection with the administration of this title, corruptly demands, seeks, receives, accepts, or agrees to receive or accept anything of value personally or for any other person or entity in return for—

(1) being influenced in the performance of any official act;

(2) being influenced to commit or aid in the committing, or to collude in, or allow, any fraud, or make opportunity for the commission of any fraud, on the United States; or

(3) being induced to do or omit to do any act in violation of the official duty of such official or person, shall be fined in an amount not more than 3 times the monetary equivalent of the thing of value, or imprisoned for not more than 15 years, or both. A violation of this section shall be subject to chapter 227 of title 18, United States Code, and the provisions of the United States Sentencing Guidelines.

Sec. 330. *International Cooperation in Investigations of Money Laundering, Financial Crimes, and the Finances of Terrorist Groups*

(a) NEGOTIATIONS—It is the sense of the Congress that the President should direct the Secretary of State, the Attorney General, or the Secretary of the Treasury, as appropriate, and in consultation with the Board of Governors of the Federal Reserve System, to seek to enter into negotiations with the appropriate financial supervisory agencies and other officials of any foreign country the financial institutions of which do business with United States financial institutions or which may be utilized by any foreign terrorist organization (as designated under section 219 of the Immigration and Nationality Act), any person who is a member or representative of any such organization, or any person engaged in money laundering or financial or other crimes.

(b) PURPOSES OF NEGOTIATIONS—It is the sense of the Congress that, in carrying out any negotiations described in paragraph (1), the President should direct the Secretary of State, the Attorney General, or the Secretary of the Treasury, as appropriate, to seek to enter into and further cooperative efforts, voluntary information exchanges, the use of letters rogatory, mutual legal assistance treaties, and international agreements to—

(1) ensure that foreign banks and other financial institutions maintain adequate records of transaction and account information relating to any foreign terrorist organization (as designated under section 219 of the Immigration and Nationality Act), any person who is a member or representative of any such organization, or any person engaged in money laundering or financial or other crimes; and

(2) establish a mechanism whereby such records may be made available to United States law enforcement officials and domestic financial institution supervisors, when appropriate.

Subtitle B—Bank Secrecy Act Amendments and Related Improvements
[. . .]

Sec. 352. Anti-Money Laundering Programs
(a) IN GENERAL—Section 5318(h) of title 31, United States Code, is amended to read as follows:

'(h) ANTI-MONEY LAUNDERING PRO-
GRAMS—
'(1) IN GENERAL—In order to guard against money laundering through financial institutions, each financial institution shall establish anti-money laundering programs, including, at a minimum—
'(A) the development of internal policies, procedures, and controls;
'(B) the designation of a compliance officer;

'(C) an ongoing employee training program; and
'(D) an independent audit function to test programs.
'(2) REGULATIONS—The Secretary of the Treasury, after consultation with the appropriate Federal functional regulator (as defined in section 509 of the Gramm-Leach-Bliley Act), may prescribe minimum standards for programs established under paragraph (1), and may exempt from the application of those standards any financial institution that is not subject to the provisions of the rules contained in part 103 of title 31, of the Code of Federal Regulations, or any successor rule thereto, for so long as such financial institution is not subject to the provisions of such rules'.

(b) EFFECTIVE DATE—The amendment made by subsection (a) shall take effect at the end of the 180-day period beginning on the date of enactment of this Act.

(c) DATE OF APPLICATION OF REGULATIONS; FACTORS TO BE TAKEN INTO ACCOUNT—Before the end of the 180-day period beginning on the date of enactment of this Act, the Secretary shall prescribe regulations that consider the extent to which the requirements imposed under this section are commensurate with the size, location, and activities of the financial institutions to which such regulations apply.

Subtitle C—Currency Crimes and Protection

Sec. 5332. Bulk Cash Smuggling into or out of the United States
(a) CRIMINAL OFFENSE—

(1) IN GENERAL—Whoever, with the intent to evade a currency reporting requirement under section 5316, knowingly conceals more than $10,000 in currency or other monetary instruments on the person of such individual or in any conveyance, article of luggage, merchandise, or other container, and transports or transfers or attempts to transport or transfer such currency or

monetary instruments from a place within the United States to a place outside of the United States, or from a place outside the United States to a place within the United States, shall be guilty of a currency smuggling offense and subject to punishment pursuant to subsection (b).

'(2) CONCEALMENT ON PERSON—For purposes of this section, the concealment of currency on the person of any individual includes concealment in any article of clothing worn by the individual or in any luggage, backpack, or other container worn or carried by such individual.

'(b) PENALTY—

'(1) TERM OF IMPRISONMENT—A person convicted of a currency smuggling offense under subsection (a), or a conspiracy to commit such offense, shall be imprisoned for not more than 5 years.

'(2) FORFEITURE—In addition, the court, in imposing sentence under paragraph (1), shall order that the defendant forfeit to the United States, any property, real or personal, involved in the offense, and any property traceable to such property, subject to subsection (d) of this section.

'(3) PROCEDURE—The seizure, restraint, and forfeiture of property under this section shall be governed by section 413 of the Controlled Substances Act.

'(4) PERSONAL MONEY JUDGMENT—If the property subject to forfeiture under paragraph (2) is unavailable, and the defendant has insufficient substitute property that may be forfeited pursuant to section 413(p) of the Controlled Substances Act, the court shall enter a personal money judgment against the defendant for the amount that would be subject to forfeiture.

'(c) CIVIL FORFEITURE—

'(1) IN GENERAL—Any property involved in a violation of subsection (a), or a conspiracy to commit such violation, and any property traceable to such violation or conspiracy, may be seized and, subject to subsection (d) of this section, forfeited to the United States.

'(2) PROCEDURE—The seizure and forfeiture shall be governed by the procedures governing civil

forfeitures in money laundering cases pursuant to section 981(a)(1)(A) of title 18, United States Code.

'(3) TREATMENT OF CERTAIN PROPERTY AS INVOLVED IN THE OFFENSE—For purposes of this subsection and subsection (b), any currency or other monetary instrument that is concealed or intended to be concealed in violation of subsection (a) or a conspiracy to commit such violation, any article, container, or conveyance used, or intended to be used, to conceal or transport the currency or other monetary instrument, and any other property used, or intended to be used, to facilitate the offense, shall be considered property involved in the offense'.

33.
United Nations International Convention for the Suppression of the Financing of Terrorism

On 9 December 1999, the members of the United Nations signed a convention for combating the funding sources of terrorists. International cooperation was reiterated to prevent persons engaging in terrorist financing. The action of a person providing and collecting funds for terrorist activities will be treated as a criminal offense, and the member countries as per Article 5 should take appropriate measures. The offence is to be taken as an extraditable one.

Source
United Nations Treaty Collection,
http://untreaty.un.org/English/Terrorism/Conv12.pdf.

[. . .]

Article 1
For the purposes of this Convention:

1. "Funds" means assets of every kind, whether tangible or intangible, movable or immovable, however acquired, and legal documents or instruments in any form, including electronic or digital, evi-

dencing title to, or interest in, such assets, including, but not limited to, bank credits, travellers cheques, bank cheques, money orders, shares, securities, bonds, drafts, letters of credit.

2. "State or governmental facility" means any permanent or temporary facility or conveyance that is used or occupied by representatives of a State, members of Government, the legislature or the judiciary or by officials or employees of a State or any other public authority or entity or by employees or officials of an intergovernmental organization in connection with their official duties.

3. "Proceeds" means any funds derived from or obtained, directly or indirectly, through the commission of an offence set forth in article 2.

Article 2
1. Any person commits an offence within the meaning of this Convention if that person by any means, directly or indirectly, unlawfully and wilfully, provides or collects funds with the intention that they should be used or in the knowledge that they are to be used, in full or in part, in order to carry out:

(a) An act which constitutes an offence within the scope of and as defined in one of the treaties listed in the annex; or

(b) Any other act intended to cause death or serious bodily injury to a civilian, or to any other person not taking an active part in the hostilities in a situation of armed conflict, when the purpose of such act, by its nature or context, is to intimidate a population, or to compel a government or an international organization to do or to abstain from doing any act.

2. (a) On depositing its instrument of ratification, acceptance, approval or accession, a State Party which is not a party to a treaty listed in the annex may declare that, in the application of this Convention to the State Party, the treaty shall be deemed not to be included in the annex referred to in paragraph 1, subparagraph (a). The declaration shall cease to have effect as soon as the treaty enters into force for the State Party, which shall notify the depositary of this fact;

(b) When a State Party ceases to be a party to a treaty listed in the annex, it may make a declaration as provided for in this article, with respect to that treaty.

3. For an act to constitute an offence set forth in paragraph 1, it shall not be necessary that the funds were actually used to carry out an offence referred to in paragraph 1, subparagraphs (a) or (b).

4. Any person also commits an offence if that person attempts to commit an offence as set forth in paragraph 1 of this article.

5. Any person also commits an offence if that person:

(a) Participates as an accomplice in an offence as set forth in paragraph 1 or 4 of this article;

(b) Organizes or directs others to commit an offence as set forth in paragraph 1 or 4 of this article;

(c) Contributes to the commission of one or more offences as set forth in paragraphs 1 or 4 of this article by a group of persons acting with a common purpose. Such contribution shall be intentional and shall either:

(i) Be made with the aim of furthering the criminal activity or criminal purpose of the group, where such activity or purpose involves the commission of an offence as set forth in paragraph 1 of this article; or

(ii) Be made in the knowledge of the intention of the group to commit an offence as set forth in paragraph 1 of this article.

Article 3
This Convention shall not apply where the offence is committed within a single State, the alleged offender is a national of that State and is present in the territory of that State and no other State has a basis under article 7, paragraph 1, or article 7, paragraph 2, to exercise jurisdiction, except that

Primary Source Documents

the provisions of articles 12 to 18 shall, as appropriate, apply in those cases.

Article 4

Each State Party shall adopt such measures as may be necessary:

(a) To establish as criminal offences under its domestic law the offences set forth in article 2;

(b) To make those offences punishable by appropriate penalties which take into account the grave nature of the offences.

Article 5

1. Each State Party, in accordance with its domestic legal principles, shall take the necessary measures to enable a legal entity located in its territory or organized under its laws to be held liable when a person responsible for the management or control of that legal entity has, in that capacity, committed an offence set forth in article 2. Such liability may be criminal, civil or administrative.

2. Such liability is incurred without prejudice to the criminal liability of individuals having committed the offences.

3. Each State Party shall ensure, in particular, that legal entities liable in accordance with paragraph 1 above are subject to effective, proportionate and dissuasive criminal, civil or administrative sanctions. Such sanctions may include monetary sanctions.

Article 6

Each State Party shall adopt such measures as may be necessary, including, where appropriate, domestic legislation, to ensure that criminal acts within the scope of this Convention are under no circumstances justifiable by considerations of a political, philosophical, ideological, racial, ethnic, religious or other similar nature.

Article 7

1. Each State Party shall take such measures as may be necessary to establish its jurisdiction over the offences set forth in article 2 when:

(a) The offence is committed in the territory of that State;

(b) The offence is committed on board a vessel flying the flag of that State or an aircraft registered under the laws of that State at the time the offence is committed;

(c) The offence is committed by a national of that State.

2. A State Party may also establish its jurisdiction over any such offence when:

(a) The offence was directed towards or resulted in the carrying out of an offence referred to in article 2, paragraph 1, subparagraph (a) or (b), in the territory of or against a national of that State;

(b) The offence was directed towards or resulted in the carrying out of an offence referred to in article 2, paragraph 1, subparagraph (a) or (b), against a State or government facility of that State abroad, including diplomatic or consular premises of that State;

(c) The offence was directed towards or resulted in an offence referred to in article 2, paragraph 1, subparagraph (a) or (b), committed in an attempt to compel that State to do or abstain from doing any act;

(d) The offence is committed by a stateless person who has his or her habitual residence in the territory of that State;

(e) The offence is committed on board an aircraft which is operated by the Government of that State.

3. Upon ratifying, accepting, approving or acceding to this Convention, each State Party shall notify the Secretary-General of the United Nations of the jurisdiction it has established in accordance with paragraph 2. Should any change take place, the State Party concerned shall immediately notify the Secretary-General.

739

4. Each State Party shall likewise take such measures as may be necessary to establish its jurisdiction over the offences set forth in article 2 in cases where the alleged offender is present in its territory and it does not extradite that person to any of the States Parties that have established their jurisdiction in accordance with paragraphs 1 or 2.

5. When more than one State Party claims jurisdiction over the offences set forth in article 2, the relevant States Parties shall strive to coordinate their actions appropriately, in particular concerning the conditions for prosecution and the modalities for mutual legal assistance.

6. Without prejudice to the norms of general international law, this Convention does not exclude the exercise of any criminal jurisdiction established by a State Party in accordance with its domestic law.

Article 8
1. Each State Party shall take appropriate measures, in accordance with its domestic legal principles, for the identification, detection and freezing or seizure of any funds used or allocated for the purpose of committing the offences set forth in article 2 as well as the proceeds derived from such offences, for purposes of possible forfeiture.

2. Each State Party shall take appropriate measures, in accordance with its domestic legal principles, for the forfeiture of funds used or allocated for the purpose of committing the offences set forth in article 2 and the proceeds derived from such offences.

3. Each State Party concerned may give consideration to concluding agreements on the sharing with other States Parties, on a regular or case-by-case basis, of the funds derived from the forfeitures referred to in this article.

4. Each State Party shall consider establishing mechanisms whereby the funds derived from the forfeitures referred to in this article are utilized to compensate the victims of offences referred to in article 2, paragraph 1, subparagraph (a) or (b), or their families.

5. The provisions of this article shall be implemented without prejudice to the rights of third parties acting in good faith.

Article 9
1. Upon receiving information that a person who has committed or who is alleged to have committed an offence set forth in article 2 may be present in its territory, the State Party concerned shall take such measures as may be necessary under its domestic law to investigate the facts contained in the information.

2. Upon being satisfied that the circumstances so warrant, the State Party in whose territory the offender or alleged offender is present shall take the appropriate measures under its domestic law so as to ensure that person's presence for the purpose of prosecution or extradition.

3. Any person regarding whom the measures referred to in paragraph 2 are being taken shall be entitled to:

    (a) Communicate without delay with the nearest appropriate representative of the State of which that person is a national or which is otherwise entitled to protect that person's rights or, if that person is a stateless person, the State in the territory of which that person habitually resides;

    (b) Be visited by a representative of that State;

    (c) Be informed of that person's rights under subparagraphs (a) and (b).

4. The rights referred to in paragraph 3 shall be exercised in conformity with the laws and regulations of the State in the territory of which the offender or alleged offender is present, subject to

the provision that the said laws and regulations must enable full effect to be given to the purposes for which the rights accorded under paragraph 3 are intended.

5. The provisions of paragraphs 3 and 4 shall be without prejudice to the right of any State Party having a claim to jurisdiction in accordance with article 7, paragraph 1, subparagraph (b), or paragraph 2, subparagraph (b), to invite the International Committee of the Red Cross to communicate with and visit the alleged offender.

6. When a State Party, pursuant to the present article, has taken a person into custody, it shall immediately notify, directly or through the Secretary-General of the United Nations, the States Parties which have established jurisdiction in accordance with article 7, paragraph 1 or 2, and, if it considers it advisable, any other interested States Parties, of the fact that such person is in custody and of the circumstances which warrant that person's detention. The State which makes the investigation contemplated in paragraph 1 shall promptly inform the said States Parties of its findings and shall indicate whether it intends to exercise jurisdiction.

Article 10
1. The State Party in the territory of which the alleged offender is present shall, in cases to which article 7 applies, if it does not extradite that person, be obliged, without exception whatsoever and whether or not the offence was committed in its territory, to submit the case without undue delay to its competent authorities for the purpose of prosecution, through proceedings in accordance with the laws of that State. Those authorities shall take their decision in the same manner as in the case of any other offence of a grave nature under the law of that State.

2. Whenever a State Party is permitted under its domestic law to extradite or otherwise surrender one of its nationals only upon the condition that the person will be returned to that State to serve the sentence imposed as a result of the trial or proceeding for which the extradition or surrender of the person was sought, and this State and the State seeking the extradition of the person agree with this option and other terms they may deem appropriate, such a conditional extradition or surrender shall be sufficient to discharge the obligation set forth in paragraph 1.

Article 11
1. The offences set forth in article 2 shall be deemed to be included as extraditable offences in any extradition treaty existing between any of the States Parties before the entry into force of this Convention. States Parties undertake to include such offences as extraditable offences in every extradition treaty to be subsequently concluded between them.

2. When a State Party which makes extradition conditional on the existence of a treaty receives a request for extradition from another State Party with which it has no extradition treaty, the requested State Party may, at its option, consider this Convention as a legal basis for extradition in respect of the offences set forth in article 2. Extradition shall be subject to the other conditions provided by the law of the requested State.

3. States Parties which do not make extradition conditional on the existence of a treaty shall recognize the offences set forth in article 2 as extraditable offences between themselves, subject to the conditions provided by the law of the requested State.

4. If necessary, the offences set forth in article 2 shall be treated, for the purposes of extradition between States Parties, as if they had been committed not only in the place in which they occurred but also in the territory of the States that have established jurisdiction in accordance with article 7, paragraphs 1 and 2.

5. The provisions of all extradition treaties and arrangements between States Parties with regard to offences set forth in article 2 shall be deemed to be modified as between States Parties to the extent that they are incompatible with this Convention.

Article 12

1. States Parties shall afford one another the greatest measure of assistance in connection with criminal investigations or criminal or extradition proceedings in respect of the offences set forth in article 2, including assistance in obtaining evidence in their possession necessary for the proceedings.

2. States Parties may not refuse a request for mutual legal assistance on the ground of bank secrecy.

3. The requesting Party shall not transmit nor use information or evidence furnished by the requested Party for investigations, prosecutions or proceedings other than those stated in the request without the prior consent of the requested Party.

4. Each State Party may give consideration to establishing mechanisms to share with other States Parties information or evidence needed to establish criminal, civil or administrative liability pursuant to article 5.

5. States Parties shall carry out their obligations under paragraphs 1 and 2 in conformity with any treaties or other arrangements on mutual legal assistance or information exchange that may exist between them. In the absence of such treaties or arrangements, States Parties shall afford one another assistance in accordance with their domestic law.

Article 13

None of the offences set forth in article 2 shall be regarded, for the purposes of extradition or mutual legal assistance, as a fiscal offence. Accordingly, States Parties may not refuse a request for extradition or for mutual legal assistance on the sole ground that it concerns a fiscal offence.

Article 14

None of the offences set forth in article 2 shall be regarded for the purposes of extradition or mutual legal assistance as a political offence or as an offence connected with a political offence or as an offence inspired by political motives. Accordingly, a request for extradition or for mutual legal assistance based on such an offence may not be refused on the sole ground that it concerns a political offence or an offence connected with a political offence or an offence inspired by political motives.

Article 15

Nothing in this Convention shall be interpreted as imposing an obligation to extradite or to afford mutual legal assistance, if the requested State Party has substantial grounds for believing that the request for extradition for offences set forth in article 2 or for mutual legal assistance with respect to such offences has been made for the purpose of prosecuting or punishing a person on account of that person's race, religion, nationality, ethnic origin or political opinion or that compliance with the request would cause prejudice to that person's position for any of these reasons.

Article 16

1. A person who is being detained or is serving a sentence in the territory of one State Party whose presence in another State Party is requested for purposes of identification, testimony or otherwise providing assistance in obtaining evidence for the investigation or prosecution of offences set forth in article 2 may be transferred if the following conditions are met:

(a) The person freely gives his or her informed consent;

(b) The competent authorities of both States agree, subject to such conditions as those States may deem appropriate.

2. For the purposes of the present article:

(a) The State to which the person is transferred shall have the authority and obligation to keep the person transferred in custody, unless otherwise requested or authorized by the State from which the person was transferred;

(b) The State to which the person is transferred shall without delay implement its obligation to return the person to the custody of the State from which the person was transferred as agreed beforehand, or as otherwise agreed, by the competent authorities of both States;

(c) The State to which the person is transferred shall not require the State from which the person was transferred to initiate extradition proceedings for the return of the person;

(d) The person transferred shall receive credit for service of the sentence being served in the State from which he or she was transferred for time spent in the custody of the State to which he or she was transferred.

3. Unless the State Party from which a person is to be transferred in accordance with the present article so agrees, that person, whatever his or her nationality, shall not be prosecuted or detained or subjected to any other restriction of his or her personal liberty in the territory of the State to which that person is transferred in respect of acts or convictions anterior to his or her departure from the territory of the State from which such person was transferred.

Article 17

Any person who is taken into custody or regarding whom any other measures are taken or proceedings are carried out pursuant to this Convention shall be guaranteed fair treatment, including enjoyment of all rights and guarantees in conformity with the law of the State in the territory of which that person is present and applicable provisions of international law, including international human rights law.

Article 18

1. States Parties shall cooperate in the prevention of the offences set forth in article 2 by taking all practicable measures, *inter alia*, by adapting their domestic legislation, if necessary, to prevent and counter preparations in their respective territories for the commission of those offences within or outside their territories, including:

(a) Measures to prohibit in their territories illegal activities of persons and organizations that knowingly encourage, instigate, organize or engage in the commission of offences set forth in article 2;

(b) Measures requiring financial institutions and other professions involved in financial transactions to utilize the most efficient measures available for the identification of their usual or occasional customers, as well as customers in whose interest accounts are opened, and to pay special attention to unusual or suspicious transactions and report transactions suspected of stemming from a criminal activity. For this purpose, States Parties shall consider:

   (i) Adopting regulations prohibiting the opening of accounts the holders or beneficiaries of which are unidentified or unidentifiable, and measures to ensure that such institutions verify the identity of the real owners of such transactions;

   (ii) With respect to the identification of legal entities, requiring financial institutions, when necessary, to take measures to verify the legal existence and the structure of the customer by obtaining, either from a public register or from the customer or both, proof of incorporation, including information concerning the customer's name, legal form, address, directors and provisions regulating the power to bind the entity;

   (iii) Adopting regulations imposing on financial institutions the obligation to report promptly to the competent authorities all complex, unusual large transactions and unusual patterns of transactions, which have no apparent economic or obviously lawful purpose, without fear of assuming criminal or civil liability for breach of any restriction on disclosure of information if they report their suspicions in good faith;

(iv) Requiring financial institutions to maintain, for at least five years, all necessary records on transactions, both domestic or international.

2. States Parties shall further cooperate in the prevention of offences set forth in article 2 by considering:

(a) Measures for the supervision, including, for example, the licensing, of all money transmission agencies;

(b) Feasible measures to detect or monitor the physical cross-border transportation of cash and bearer negotiable instruments, subject to strict safeguards to ensure proper use of information and without impeding in any way the freedom of capital movements.

3. States Parties shall further cooperate in the prevention of the offences set forth in article 2 by exchanging accurate and verified information in accordance with their domestic law and coordinating administrative and other measures taken, as appropriate, to prevent the commission of offences set forth in article 2, in particular by:

(a) Establishing and maintaining channels of communication between their competent agencies and services to facilitate the secure and rapid exchange of information concerning all aspects of offences set forth in article 2;

(b) Cooperating with one another in conducting inquiries, with respect to the offences set forth in article 2, concerning:

(i) The identity, whereabouts and activities of persons in respect of whom reasonable suspicion exists that they are involved in such offences;

(ii) The movement of funds relating to the commission of such offences.

4. States Parties may exchange information through the International Criminal Police Organization (Interpol).

Article 19

The State Party where the alleged offender is prosecuted shall, in accordance with its domestic law or applicable procedures, communicate the final outcome of the proceedings to the Secretary-General of the United Nations, who shall transmit the information to the other States Parties.

Article 20

The States Parties shall carry out their obligations under this Convention in a manner consistent with the principles of sovereign equality and territorial integrity of States and that of non-intervention in the domestic affairs of other States.

Article 21

Nothing in this Convention shall affect other rights, obligations and responsibilities of States and individuals under international law, in particular the purposes of the Charter of the United Nations, international humanitarian law and other relevant conventions.

Article 22

Nothing in this Convention entitles a State Party to undertake in the territory of another State Party the exercise of jurisdiction or performance of functions which are exclusively reserved for the authorities of that other State Party by its domestic law.

Article 23

1. The annex may be amended by the addition of relevant treaties that:

(a) Are open to the participation of all States;

(b) Have entered into force;

(c) Have been ratified, accepted, approved or acceded to by at least twenty-two States Parties to the present Convention.

2. After the entry into force of this Convention, any State Party may propose such an amendment. Any proposal for an amendment shall be communicated to the depositary in written form. The depositary

shall notify proposals that meet the requirements of paragraph 1 to all States Parties and seek their views on whether the proposed amendment should be adopted.

3. The proposed amendment shall be deemed adopted unless one third of the States Parties object to it by a written notification not later than 180 days after its circulation.

4. The adopted amendment to the annex shall enter into force 30 days after the deposit of the twenty-second instrument of ratification, acceptance or approval of such amendment for all those States Parties having deposited such an instrument. For each State Party ratifying, accepting or approving the amendment after the deposit of the twenty-second instrument, the amendment shall enter into force on the thirtieth day after deposit by such State Party of its instrument of ratification, acceptance or approval.

Article 24
1. Any dispute between two or more States Parties concerning the interpretation or application of this Convention which cannot be settled through negotiation within a reasonable time shall, at the request of one of them, be submitted to arbitration. If, within six months from the date of the request for arbitration, the parties are unable to agree on the organization of the arbitration, any one of those parties may refer the dispute to the International Court of Justice, by application, in conformity with the Statute of the Court.

2. Each State may at the time of signature, ratification, acceptance or approval of this Convention or accession thereto declare that it does not consider itself bound by paragraph 1. The other States Parties shall not be bound by paragraph 1 with respect to any State Party which has made such a reservation.

3. Any State which has made a reservation in accordance with paragraph 2 may at any time

withdraw that reservation by notification to the Secretary-General of the United Nations.

34.

Protocol to Prevent, Suppress and Punish Trafficking in Persons, Especially Women and Children, Supplementing the United Nations Convention against Transnational Organized Crime

This protocol was adopted in 2000 and entered into force in 2003. It supplements the United Nations (UN) Convention against Transnational Organized Crime. As stated in Article 2, the primary purposes for enacting this international instrument are "to prevent and combat trafficking in persons, paying particular attention to women and children; to protect and assist the victims of such trafficking, with full respect for their human rights; and to promote cooperation among States Parties in order to meet those objectives." This document also calls for states to strengthen their borders, to cooperate with each other by exchanging information relative to criminal trafficking groups and travel documentation, and to adopt or strengthen relevant domestic legislation to prevent the unlawful trafficking in persons.

Source
United Nations Office on Drugs and Crime, http://www.unodc.org/pdf/crime/a_res_55/res5525e.pdf.

Preamble
The States Parties to this Protocol,

Declaring that effective action to prevent and combat trafficking in persons, especially women and children, requires a comprehensive international approach in the countries of origin, transit and destination that includes measures to prevent such trafficking, to punish the traffickers and to protect the victims of such trafficking, including by protecting their internationally recognized human rights,

Taking into account the fact that, despite the existence of a variety of international instruments containing rules and practical measures to combat the exploitation of persons, especially women and children, there is no universal instrument that addresses all aspects of trafficking in persons,

Concerned that, in the absence of such an instrument, persons who are vulnerable to trafficking will not be sufficiently protected,

Recalling General Assembly resolution 53/111 of 9 December 1998, in which the Assembly decided to establish an open-ended intergovernmental ad hoc committee for the purpose of elaborating a comprehensive international convention against transnational organized crime and of discussing the elaboration of, inter alia, an international instrument addressing trafficking in women and children,

Convinced that supplementing the United Nations Convention against Transnational Organized Crime with an international instrument for the prevention, suppression and punishment of trafficking in persons, especially women and children, will be useful in preventing and combating that crime,

Have agreed as follows:

I. General Provisions

Article 1

Relation with the United Nations Convention against Transnational Organized Crime
1. This Protocol supplements the United Nations Convention against Transnational Organized Crime. It shall be interpreted together with the Convention.

2. The provisions of the Convention shall apply, mutatis mutandis, to this Protocol unless otherwise provided herein.

3. The offences established in accordance with article 5 of this Protocol shall be regarded as offences established in accordance with the Convention.

Article 2

Statement of Purpose ·
The purposes of this Protocol are:

   (a) To prevent and combat trafficking in persons, paying particular attention to women and children;
   (b) To protect and assist the victims of such trafficking, with full respect for their human rights; and
   (c) To promote cooperation among States Parties in order to meet those objectives.

Article 3

Use of Terms
For the purposes of this Protocol:

   (a) "Trafficking in persons" shall mean the recruitment, transportation, transfer, harbouring or receipt of persons, by means of the threat or use of force or other forms of coercion, of abduction, of fraud, of deception, of the abuse of power or of a position of vulnerability or of the giving or receiving of payments or benefits to achieve the consent of a person having control over another person, for the purpose of exploitation. Exploitation shall include, at a minimum, the exploitation of the prostitution of others or other forms of sexual exploitation, forced labour or services, slavery or practices similar to slavery, servitude or the removal of organs;
   (b) The consent of a victim of trafficking in persons to the intended exploitation set forth in subparagraph (a) of this article shall be irrelevant where any of the means set forth in subparagraph (a) have been used;
   (c) The recruitment, transportation, transfer, harbouring or receipt of a child for the purpose of exploitation shall be considered "trafficking in

persons" even if this does not involve any of the means set forth in subparagraph (*a*) of this article;

(*d*) "Child" shall mean any person under eighteen years of age.

Article 4

Scope of Application

This Protocol shall apply, except as otherwise stated herein, to the prevention, investigation and prosecution of the offences established in accordance with article 5 of this Protocol, where those offences are transnational in nature and involve an organized criminal group, as well as to the protection of victims of such offences.

Article 5

Criminalization

1. Each State Party shall adopt such legislative and other measures as may be necessary to establish as criminal offences the conduct set forth in article 3 of this Protocol, when committed intentionally.

2. Each State Party shall also adopt such legislative and other measures as may be necessary to establish as criminal offences:

(*a*) Subject to the basic concepts of its legal system, attempting to commit an offence established in accordance with paragraph 1 of this article;

(*b*) Participating as an accomplice in an offence established in accordance with paragraph 1 of this article; and

(*c*) Organizing or directing other persons to commit an offence established in accordance with paragraph 1 of this article.

II. Protection of Victims of Trafficking in Persons

Article 6

Assistance to and Protection of Victims of Trafficking in Persons

1. In appropriate cases and to the extent possible under its domestic law, each State Party shall protect the privacy and identity of victims of trafficking in persons, including, inter alia, by making legal proceedings relating to such trafficking confidential.

2. Each State Party shall ensure that its domestic legal or administrative system contains measures that provide to victims of trafficking in persons, in appropriate cases:

(*a*) Information on relevant court and administrative proceedings;

(*b*) Assistance to enable their views and concerns to be presented and considered at appropriate stages of criminal proceedings against offenders, in a manner not prejudicial to the rights of the defence.

3. Each State Party shall consider implementing measures to provide for the physical, psychological and social recovery of victims of trafficking in persons, including, in appropriate cases, in cooperation with non-governmental organizations, other relevant organizations and other elements of civil society, and, in particular, the provision of:

(*a*) Appropriate housing;

(*b*) Counselling and information, in particular as regards their legal rights, in a language that the victims of trafficking in persons can understand;

(*c*) Medical, psychological and material assistance; and

(*d*) Employment, educational and training opportunities.

4. Each State Party shall take into account, in applying the provisions of this article, the age,

gender and special needs of victims of trafficking in persons, in particular the special needs of children, including appropriate housing, education and care.

5. Each State Party shall endeavour to provide for the physical safety of victims of trafficking in persons while they are within its territory.

6. Each State Party shall ensure that its domestic legal system contains measures that offer victims of trafficking in persons the possibility of obtaining compensation for damage suffered.

Article 7

Status of Victims of Trafficking in Persons in Receiving States
1. In addition to taking measures pursuant to article 6 of this Protocol, each State Party shall consider adopting legislative or other appropriate measures that permit victims of trafficking in persons to remain in its territory, temporarily or permanently, in appropriate cases.

2. In implementing the provision contained in paragraph 1 of this article, each State Party shall give appropriate consideration to humanitarian and compassionate factors.

Article 8

Repatriation of Victims of Trafficking in Persons
1. The State Party of which a victim of trafficking in persons is a national or in which the person had the right of permanent residence at the time of entry into the territory of the receiving State Party shall facilitate and accept, with due regard for the safety of that person, the return of that person without undue or unreasonable delay.

2. When a State Party returns a victim of trafficking in persons to a State Party of which that person is a national or in which he or she had, at the time of entry into the territory of the receiving State Party, the right of permanent residence, such return shall be with due regard for the safety of that person and for the status of any legal proceedings related to the fact that the person is a victim of trafficking and shall preferably be voluntary.

3. At the request of a receiving State Party, a requested State Party shall, without undue or unreasonable delay, verify whether a person who is a victim of trafficking in persons is its national or had the right of permanent residence in its territory at the time of entry into the territory of the receiving State Party.

4. In order to facilitate the return of a victim of trafficking in persons who is without proper documentation, the State Party of which that person is a national or in which he or she had the right of permanent residence at the time of entry into the territory of the receiving State Party shall agree to issue, at the request of the receiving State Party, such travel documents or other authorization as may be necessary to enable the person to travel to and re-enter its territory.

5. This article shall be without prejudice to any right afforded to victims of trafficking in persons by any domestic law of the receiving State Party.

6. This article shall be without prejudice to any applicable bilateral or multilateral agreement or arrangement that governs, in whole or in part, the return of victims of trafficking in persons.

III. Prevention, Cooperation and Other Measures

Article 9

Prevention of Trafficking in Persons
1. States Parties shall establish comprehensive policies, programmes and other measures:

  (a) To prevent and combat trafficking in persons; and
  (b) To protect victims of trafficking in persons, especially women and children, from revictimization.

2. States Parties shall endeavour to undertake measures such as research, information and mass media campaigns and social and economic initiatives to prevent and combat trafficking in persons.

3. Policies, programmes and other measures established in accordance with this article shall, as appropriate, include cooperation with non-governmental organizations, other relevant organizations and other elements of civil society.

4. States Parties shall take or strengthen measures, including through bilateral or multilateral cooperation, to alleviate the factors that make persons, especially women and children, vulnerable to trafficking, such as poverty, underdevelopment and lack of equal opportunity.

5. States Parties shall adopt or strengthen legislative or other measures, such as educational, social or cultural measures, including through bilateral and multilateral cooperation, to discourage the demand that fosters all forms of exploitation of persons, especially women and children, that leads to trafficking.

Article 10

Information Exchange and Training
1. Law enforcement, immigration or other relevant authorities of States Parties shall, as appropriate, cooperate with one another by exchanging information, in accordance with their domestic law, to enable them to determine:

(a) Whether individuals crossing or attempting to cross an international border with travel documents belonging to other persons or without travel documents are perpetrators or victims of trafficking in persons;
(b) The types of travel document that individuals have used or attempted to use to cross an international border for the purpose of trafficking in persons; and

(c) The means and methods used by organized criminal groups for the purpose of trafficking in persons, including the recruitment and transportation of victims, routes and links between and among individuals and groups engaged in such trafficking, and possible measures for detecting them.

2. States Parties shall provide or strengthen training for law enforcement, immigration and other relevant officials in the prevention of trafficking in persons. The training should focus on methods used in preventing such trafficking, prosecuting the traffickers and protecting the rights of the victims, including protecting the victims from the traffickers. The training should also take into account the need to consider human rights and child- and gender-sensitive issues and it should encourage cooperation with non-governmental organizations, other relevant organizations and other elements of civil society.

3. A State Party that receives information shall comply with any request by the State Party that transmitted the information that places restrictions on its use.

Article 11

Border Measures
1. Without prejudice to international commitments in relation to the free movement of people, States Parties shall strengthen, to the extent possible, such border controls as may be necessary to prevent and detect trafficking in persons.

2. Each State Party shall adopt legislative or other appropriate measures to prevent, to the extent possible, means of transport operated by commercial carriers from being used in the commission of offences established in accordance with article 5 of this Protocol.

3. Where appropriate, and without prejudice to applicable international conventions, such

measures shall include establishing the obligation of commercial carriers, including any transportation company or the owner or operator of any means of transport, to ascertain that all passengers are in possession of the travel documents required for entry into the receiving State.

4. Each State Party shall take the necessary measures, in accordance with its domestic law, to provide for sanctions in cases of violation of the obligation set forth in paragraph 3 of this article.

5. Each State Party shall consider taking measures that permit, in accordance with its domestic law, the denial of entry or revocation of visas of persons implicated in the commission of offences established in accordance with this Protocol.

6. Without prejudice to article 27 of the Convention, States Parties shall consider strengthening cooperation among border control agencies by, inter alia, establishing and maintaining direct channels of communication.

Article 12

Security and Control of Documents
Each State Party shall take such measures as may be necessary, within available means:

(*a*) To ensure that travel or identity documents issued by it are of such quality that they cannot easily be misused and cannot readily be falsified or unlawfully altered, replicated or issued; and

(*b*) To ensure the integrity and security of travel or identity documents issued by or on behalf of the State Party and to prevent their unlawful creation, issuance and use.

Article 13

Legitimacy and Validity of Documents
At the request of another State Party, a State Party shall, in accordance with its domestic law, verify within a reasonable time the legitimacy and validity of travel or identity documents issued or purported to have been issued in its name and suspected of being used for trafficking in persons.

IV. Final Provisions

Article 14

Saving Clause
1. Nothing in this Protocol shall affect the rights, obligations and responsibilities of States and individuals under international law, including international humanitarian law and international human rights law and, in particular, where applicable, the 1951 Convention and the 1967 Protocol relating to the Status of Refugees and the principle of non-refoulement as contained therein.

2. The measures set forth in this Protocol shall be interpreted and applied in a way that is not discriminatory to persons on the ground that they are victims of trafficking in persons. The interpretation and application of those measures shall be consistent with internationally recognized principles of non-discrimination.

Article 15

Settlement of Disputes
1. States Parties shall endeavour to settle disputes concerning the interpretation or application of this Protocol through negotiation.

2. Any dispute between two or more States Parties concerning the interpretation or application of this Protocol that cannot be settled through negotiation within a reasonable time shall, at the request of one of those States Parties, be submitted to arbitration. If, six months after the date of the request for arbitration, those States Parties are unable to agree on the organization of the arbitration, any one of those States Parties may refer the dispute to the International Court of Justice by request in accordance with the Statute of the Court.

3. Each State Party may, at the time of signature, ratification, acceptance or approval of or accession to this Protocol, declare that it does not consider itself bound by paragraph 2 of this article. The other States Parties shall not be bound by paragraph 2 of this article with respect to any State Party that has made such a reservation.

4. Any State Party that has made a reservation in accordance with paragraph 3 of this article may at any time withdraw that reservation by notification to the Secretary-General of the United Nations.

35.
Protocol against the Smuggling of Migrants by Land, Sea and Air, Supplementing the United Nations Convention against Transnational Organized Crime

This protocol entered into force in January 2004 and supplements the United Nations (UN) Convention against Transnational Organized Crime. As stated in Article 2, the primary purposes for enacting this international instrument are "to prevent and combat the smuggling of migrants, as well as to promote cooperation among States Parties to that end, while protecting the rights of smuggled migrants." This document calls for states to strengthen their borders and to cooperate with each other by exchanging information relative to criminal trafficking groups, transit and destination points and routes, and fraudulent travel documentation. Overall, this document establishes an international protocol to prevent the unlawful exploitation of migrants and establishes provisions for their humane treatment.

Source
United Nations Office on Drugs and Crime, http://www.unodc.org/pdf/crime/a_res_55/res5525e.pdf.

Preamble
The States Parties to this Protocol,

Declaring that effective action to prevent and combat the smuggling of migrants by land, sea and air requires a comprehensive international approach, including cooperation, the exchange of information and other appropriate measures, including socio-economic measures, at the national, regional and international levels,

Recalling General Assembly resolution 54/212 of 22 December 1999, in which the Assembly urged Member States and the United Nations system to strengthen international cooperation in the area of international migration and development in order to address the root causes of migration, especially those related to poverty, and to maximize the benefits of international migration to those concerned, and encouraged, where relevant, interregional, regional and subregional mechanisms to continue to address the question of migration and development,

Convinced of the need to provide migrants with humane treatment and full protection of their rights,

Taking into account the fact that, despite work undertaken in other international forums, there is no universal instrument that addresses all aspects of smuggling of migrants and other related issues,

Concerned at the significant increase in the activities of organized criminal groups in smuggling of migrants and other related criminal activities set forth in this Protocol, which bring great harm to the States concerned,

Also concerned that the smuggling of migrants can endanger the lives or security of the migrants involved,

Recalling General Assembly resolution 53/111 of 9 December 1998, in which the Assembly decided to establish an open-ended intergovernmental ad hoc committee for the purpose of elaborating a comprehensive international convention against transnational organized crime and of discussing the elaboration of, inter alia, an international instrument addressing illegal trafficking in and transporting of migrants, including by sea,

Convinced that supplementing the United Nations Convention against Transnational Organized Crime with an international instrument against the smuggling of migrants by land, sea and air will be useful in preventing and combating that crime,

Have agreed as follows:

I. General Provisions

Article 1

Relation with the United Nations Convention against Transnational Organized Crime
1. This Protocol supplements the United Nations Convention against Transnational Organized Crime. It shall be interpreted together with the Convention.

2. The provisions of the Convention shall apply, mutatis mutandis, to this Protocol unless otherwise provided herein.

3. The offences established in accordance with article 6 of this Protocol shall be regarded as offences established in accordance with the Convention.

Article 2

Statement of Purpose
The purpose of this Protocol is to prevent and combat the smuggling of migrants, as well as to promote cooperation among States Parties to that end, while protecting the rights of smuggled migrants.

Article 3

Use of Terms
For the purposes of this Protocol:

(*a*) "Smuggling of migrants" shall mean the procurement, in order to obtain, directly or indirectly, a financial or other material benefit, of the illegal entry of a person into a State Party of which the person is not a national or a permanent resident;

(*b*) "Illegal entry" shall mean crossing borders without complying with the necessary requirements for legal entry into the receiving State;

(*c*) "Fraudulent travel or identity document" shall mean any travel or identity document:

(i) That has been falsely made or altered in some material way by anyone other than a person or agency lawfully authorized to make or issue the travel or identity document on behalf of a State; or

(ii) That has been improperly issued or obtained through misrepresentation, corruption or duress or in any other unlawful manner; or

(iii) That is being used by a person other than the rightful holder;

(*d*) "Vessel" shall mean any type of water craft, including non-displacement craft and seaplanes, used or capable of being used as a means of transportation on water, except a warship, naval auxiliary or other vessel owned or operated by a Government and used, for the time being, only on government non-commercial service.

Article 4

Scope of Application
This Protocol shall apply, except as otherwise stated herein, to the prevention, investigation and prosecution of the offences established in accordance with article 6 of this Protocol, where the offences are transnational in nature and involve an organized criminal group, as well as to the protection of the rights of persons who have been the object of such offences.

Article 5

Criminal Liability of Migrants
Migrants shall not become liable to criminal prosecution under this Protocol for the fact of having been the object of conduct set forth in article 6 of this Protocol.

Article 6

Criminalization
1. Each State Party shall adopt such legislative and other measures as may be necessary to establish as criminal offences, when committed intentionally and in order to obtain, directly or indirectly, a financial or other material benefit:

   (a) The smuggling of migrants;
   (b) When committed for the purpose of enabling the smuggling of migrants:
      (i) Producing a fraudulent travel or identity document;
      (ii) Procuring, providing or possessing such a document;
   (c) Enabling a person who is not a national or a permanent resident to remain in the State concerned without complying with the necessary requirements for legally remaining in the State by the means mentioned in subparagraph (b) of this paragraph or any other illegal means.

2. Each State Party shall also adopt such legislative and other measures as may be necessary to establish as criminal offences:

   (a) Subject to the basic concepts of its legal system, attempting to commit an offence established in accordance with paragraph 1 of this article;
   (b) Participating as an accomplice in an offence established in accordance with paragraph 1 (a), (b) (i) or (c) of this article and, subject to the basic concepts of its legal system, participating as an accomplice in an offence established in accordance with paragraph 1 (b) (ii) of this article;

   (c) Organizing or directing other persons to commit an offence established in accordance with paragraph 1 of this article.

3. Each State Party shall adopt such legislative and other measures as may be necessary to establish as aggravating circumstances to the offences established in accordance with paragraph 1 (a), (b) (i) and (c) of this article and, subject to the basic concepts of its legal system, to the offences established in accordance with paragraph 2 (b) and (c) of this article, circumstances:

   (a) That endanger, or are likely to endanger, the lives or safety of the migrants concerned; or
   (b) That entail inhuman or degrading treatment, including for exploitation, of such migrants.

4. Nothing in this Protocol shall prevent a State Party from taking measures against a person whose conduct constitutes an offence under its domestic law.

II. Smuggling of Migrants by Sea

Article 7

Cooperation
States Parties shall cooperate to the fullest extent possible to prevent and suppress the smuggling of migrants by sea, in accordance with the international law of the sea.

Article 8

Measures against the Smuggling of Migrants by Sea
1. A State Party that has reasonable grounds to suspect that a vessel that is flying its flag or claiming its registry, that is without nationality or that, though flying a foreign flag or refusing to show a flag, is in reality of the nationality of the State Party concerned is engaged in the smuggling of migrants by sea may request the assistance of other States Parties in suppressing the use of the

vessel for that purpose. The States Parties so requested shall render such assistance to the extent possible within their means.

2. A State Party that has reasonable grounds to suspect that a vessel exercising freedom of navigation in accordance with international law and flying the flag or displaying the marks of registry of another State Party is engaged in the smuggling of migrants by sea may so notify the flag State, request confirmation of registry and, if confirmed, request authorization from the flag State to take appropriate measures with regard to that vessel. The flag State may authorize the requesting State, inter alia:

   (a) To board the vessel;
   (b) To search the vessel; and
   (c) If evidence is found that the vessel is engaged in the smuggling of migrants by sea, to take appropriate measures with respect to the vessel and persons and cargo on board, as authorized by the flag State.

3. A State Party that has taken any measure in accordance with paragraph 2 of this article shall promptly inform the flag State concerned of the results of that measure.

4. A State Party shall respond expeditiously to a request from another State Party to determine whether a vessel that is claiming its registry or flying its flag is entitled to do so and to a request for authorization made in accordance with paragraph 2 of this article.

5. A flag State may, consistent with article 7 of this Protocol, subject its authorization to conditions to be agreed by it and the requesting State, including conditions relating to responsibility and the extent of effective measures to be taken. A State Party shall take no additional measures without the express authorization of the flag State, except those necessary to relieve imminent danger to the lives of persons or those which derive from relevant bilateral or multilateral agreements.

6. Each State Party shall designate an authority or, where necessary, authorities to receive and respond to requests for assistance, for confirmation of registry or of the right of a vessel to fly its flag and for authorization to take appropriate measures. Such designation shall be notified through the Secretary-General to all other States Parties within one month of the designation.

7. A State Party that has reasonable grounds to suspect that a vessel is engaged in the smuggling of migrants by sea and is without nationality or may be assimilated to a vessel without nationality may board and search the vessel. If evidence confirming the suspicion is found, that State Party shall take appropriate measures in accordance with relevant domestic and international law.

Article 9

Safeguard Clauses
1. Where a State Party takes measures against a vessel in accordance with article 8 of this Protocol, it shall:

   (a) Ensure the safety and humane treatment of the persons on board;
   (b) Take due account of the need not to endanger the security of the vessel or its cargo;
   (c) Take due account of the need not to prejudice the commercial or legal interests of the flag State or any other interested State;
   (d) Ensure, within available means, that any measure taken with regard to the vessel is environmentally sound.

2. Where the grounds for measures taken pursuant to article 8 of this Protocol prove to be unfounded, the vessel shall be compensated for any loss or damage that may have been sustained, provided that the vessel has not committed any act justifying the measures taken.

3. Any measure taken, adopted or implemented in accordance with this chapter shall take due account of the need not to interfere with or to affect:

(a) The rights and obligations and the exercise of jurisdiction of coastal States in accordance with the international law of the sea; or

(b) The authority of the flag State to exercise jurisdiction and control in administrative, technical and social matters involving the vessel.

4. Any measure taken at sea pursuant to this chapter shall be carried out only by warships or military aircraft, or by other ships or aircraft clearly marked and identifiable as being on government service and authorized to that effect.

III. Prevention, Cooperation and Other Measures

Article 10

Information

1. Without prejudice to articles 27 and 28 of the Convention, States Parties, in particular those with common borders or located on routes along which migrants are smuggled, shall, for the purpose of achieving the objectives of this Protocol, exchange among themselves, consistent with their respective domestic legal and administrative systems, relevant information on matters such as:

(a) Embarkation and destination points, as well as routes, carriers and means of transportation, known to be or suspected of being used by an organized criminal group engaged in conduct set forth in article 6 of this Protocol;

(b) The identity and methods of organizations or organized criminal groups known to be or suspected of being engaged in conduct set forth in article 6 of this Protocol;

(c) The authenticity and proper form of travel documents issued by a State Party and the theft or related misuse of blank travel or identity documents;

(d) Means and methods of concealment and transportation of persons, the unlawful alteration, reproduction or acquisition or other misuse of travel or identity documents used in conduct set forth in article 6 of this Protocol and ways of detecting them;

(e) Legislative experiences and practices and measures to prevent and combat the conduct set forth in article 6 of this Protocol; and

(f) Scientific and technological information useful to law enforcement, so as to enhance each other's ability to prevent, detect and investigate the conduct set forth in article 6 of this Protocol and to prosecute those involved.

2. A State Party that receives information shall comply with any request by the State Party that transmitted the information that places restrictions on its use.

Article 11

Border Measures

1. Without prejudice to international commitments in relation to the free movement of people, States Parties shall strengthen, to the extent possible, such border controls as may be necessary to prevent and detect the smuggling of migrants.

2. Each State Party shall adopt legislative or other appropriate measures to prevent, to the extent possible, means of transport operated by commercial carriers from being used in the commission of the offence established in accordance with article 6, paragraph 1 (a), of this Protocol.

3. Where appropriate, and without prejudice to applicable international conventions, such measures shall include establishing the obligation of commercial carriers, including any transportation company or the owner or operator of any means of transport, to ascertain that all passengers are in possession of the travel

documents required for entry into the receiving State.

4. Each State Party shall take the necessary measures, in accordance with its domestic law, to provide for sanctions in cases of violation of the obligation set forth in paragraph 3 of this article.

5. Each State Party shall consider taking measures that permit, in accordance with its domestic law, the denial of entry or revocation of visas of persons implicated in the commission of offences established in accordance with this Protocol.

6. Without prejudice to article 27 of the Convention, States Parties shall consider strengthening cooperation among border control agencies by, inter alia, establishing and maintaining direct channels of communication.

Article 12

Security and Control of Documents
Each State Party shall take such measures as may be necessary, within available means:

(a) To ensure that travel or identity documents issued by it are of such quality that they cannot easily be misused and cannot readily be falsified or unlawfully altered, replicated or issued; and

(b) To ensure the integrity and security of travel or identity documents issued by or on behalf of the State Party and to prevent their unlawful creation, issuance and use.

Article 13

Legitimacy and Validity of Documents
At the request of another State Party, a State Party shall, in accordance with its domestic law, verify within a reasonable time the legitimacy and validity of travel or identity documents issued or purported to have been issued in its name and suspected of being used for purposes of conduct set forth in article 6 of this Protocol.

Article 14

Training and Technical Cooperation
1. States Parties shall provide or strengthen specialized training for immigration and other relevant officials in preventing the conduct set forth in article 6 of this Protocol and in the humane treatment of migrants who have been the object of such conduct, while respecting their rights as set forth in this Protocol.

2. States Parties shall cooperate with each other and with competent international organizations, non-governmental organizations, other relevant organizations and other elements of civil society as appropriate to ensure that there is adequate personnel training in their territories to prevent, combat and eradicate the conduct set forth in article 6 of this Protocol and to protect the rights of migrants who have been the object of such conduct. Such training shall include:

(a) Improving the security and quality of travel documents;

(b) Recognizing and detecting fraudulent travel or identity documents;

(c) Gathering criminal intelligence, relating in particular to the identification of organized criminal groups known to be or suspected of being engaged in conduct set forth in article 6 of this Protocol, the methods used to transport smuggled migrants, the misuse of travel or identity documents for purposes of conduct set forth in article 6 and the means of concealment used in the smuggling of migrants;

(d) Improving procedures for detecting smuggled persons at conventional and non-conventional points of entry and exit; and

(e) The humane treatment of migrants and the protection of their rights as set forth in this Protocol.

3. States Parties with relevant expertise shall consider providing technical assistance to States that are frequently countries of origin or transit for persons who have been the object of conduct set

forth in article 6 of this Protocol. States Parties shall make every effort to provide the necessary resources, such as vehicles, computer systems and document readers, to combat the conduct set forth in article 6.

Article 15

Other Prevention Measures
1. Each State Party shall take measures to ensure that it provides or strengthens information programmes to increase public awareness of the fact that the conduct set forth in article 6 of this Protocol is a criminal activity frequently perpetrated by organized criminal groups for profit and that it poses serious risks to the migrants concerned.

2. In accordance with article 31 of the Convention, States Parties shall cooperate in the field of public information for the purpose of preventing potential migrants from falling victim to organized criminal groups.

3. Each State Party shall promote or strengthen, as appropriate, development programmes and cooperation at the national, regional and international levels, taking into account the socio-economic realities of migration and paying special attention to economically and socially depressed areas, in order to combat the root socio-economic causes of the smuggling of migrants, such as poverty and underdevelopment.

Article 16

Protection and Assistance Measures
1. In implementing this Protocol, each State Party shall take, consistent with its obligations under international law, all appropriate measures, including legislation if necessary, to preserve and protect the rights of persons who have been the object of conduct set forth in article 6 of this Protocol as accorded under applicable international law, in particular the right to life and the right not to be subjected to torture or other cruel, inhuman or degrading treatment or punishment.

2. Each State Party shall take appropriate measures to afford migrants appropriate protection against violence that may be inflicted upon them, whether by individuals or groups, by reason of being the object of conduct set forth in article 6 of this Protocol.

3. Each State Party shall afford appropriate assistance to migrants whose lives or safety are endangered by reason of being the object of conduct set forth in article 6 of this Protocol.

4. In applying the provisions of this article, States Parties shall take into account the special needs of women and children.

5. In the case of the detention of a person who has been the object of conduct set forth in article 6 of this Protocol, each State Party shall comply with its obligations under the Vienna Convention on Consular Relations where applicable, including that of informing the person concerned without delay about the provisions concerning notification to and communication with consular officers.

Article 17

Agreements and Arrangements
States Parties shall consider the conclusion of bilateral or regional agreements or operational arrangements or understandings aimed at:

(a) Establishing the most appropriate and effective measures to prevent and combat the conduct set forth in article 6 of this Protocol; or
(b) Enhancing the provisions of this Protocol among themselves.

Article 18

Return of Smuggled Migrants

1. Each State Party agrees to facilitate and accept, without undue or unreasonable delay, the return of a person who has been the object of conduct set forth in article 6 of this Protocol and who is its national or who has the right of permanent residence in its territory at the time of return.

2. Each State Party shall consider the possibility of facilitating and accepting the return of a person who has been the object of conduct set forth in article 6 of this Protocol and who had the right of permanent residence in its territory at the time of entry into the receiving State in accordance with its domestic law.

3. At the request of the receiving State Party, a requested State Party shall, without undue or unreasonable delay, verify whether a person who has been the object of conduct set forth in article 6 of this Protocol is its national or has the right of permanent residence in its territory.

4. In order to facilitate the return of a person who has been the object of conduct set forth in article 6 of this Protocol and is without proper documentation, the State Party of which that person is a national or in which he or she has the right of permanent residence shall agree to issue, at the request of the receiving State Party, such travel documents or other authorization as may be necessary to enable the person to travel to and re-enter its territory.

5. Each State Party involved with the return of a person who has been the object of conduct set forth in article 6 of this Protocol shall take all appropriate measures to carry out the return in an orderly manner and with due regard for the safety and dignity of the person.

6. States Parties may cooperate with relevant international organizations in the implementation of this article.

7. This article shall be without prejudice to any right afforded to persons who have been the object of conduct set forth in article 6 of this Protocol by any domestic law of the receiving State Party.

8. This article shall not affect the obligations entered into under any other applicable treaty, bilateral or multilateral, or any other applicable operational agreement or arrangement that governs, in whole or in part, the return of persons who have been the object of conduct set forth in article 6 of this Protocol.

36.
Optional Protocol to the Convention on the Rights of the Child on the Sale of Children, Child Prostitution and Child Pornography

The exploitation of the world's children has been and continues to be a major international problem. The Optional Protocol to the Convention on the Rights of the Child on the Sale of Children, adopted on 25 May 2000 and entered into force on 18 January 2002, was developed specifically to protect children from sexual exploitation. It calls for all ratifying states to institute child protection laws relative to child prostitution, child pornography, and the selling of children for the purposes of forced labor or organ transfer.

Source
Interpol, http://www.unhchr.ch/html/menu2/6/crc/treaties/opsc.htm.

The States Parties to the present Protocol,

Considering that, in order further to achieve the purposes of the Convention on the Rights of the Child and the implementation of its provisions, especially articles 1, 11, 21, 32, 33, 34, 35 and 36, it would be appropriate to extend the measures that States Parties should undertake in order to guarantee the protection of the child from the sale of children, child prostitution and child pornography,

Considering also that the Convention on the Rights of the Child recognizes the right of the child to be protected from economic exploitation and from performing any work that is likely to be hazardous or to interfere with the child's education, or to be harmful to the child's health or physical, mental, spiritual, moral or social development,

Gravely concerned at the significant and increasing international traffic in children for the purpose of the sale of children, child prostitution and child pornography,

Deeply concerned at the widespread and continuing practice of sex tourism, to which children are especially vulnerable, as it directly promotes the sale of children, child prostitution and child pornography,

Recognizing that a number of particularly vulnerable groups, including girl children, are at greater risk of sexual exploitation and that girl children are disproportionately represented among the sexually exploited,

Concerned about the growing availability of child pornography on the Internet and other evolving technologies, and recalling the International Conference on Combating Child Pornography on the Internet, held in Vienna in 1999, in particular its conclusion calling for the worldwide criminalization of the production, distribution, exportation, transmission, importation, intentional possession and advertising of child pornography, and stressing the importance of closer cooperation and partnership between Governments and the Internet industry,

Believing that the elimination of the sale of children, child prostitution and child pornography will be facilitated by adopting a holistic approach, addressing the contributing factors, including underdevelopment, poverty, economic disparities, inequitable socio-economic structure, dysfunctioning families, lack of education, urban-rural migration, gender discrimination, irresponsible adult sexual behaviour, harmful traditional practices, armed conflicts and trafficking in children,

Believing also that efforts to raise public awareness are needed to reduce consumer demand for the sale of children, child prostitution and child pornography, and believing further in the importance of strengthening global partnership among all actors and of improving law enforcement at the national level,

Noting the provisions of international legal instruments relevant to the protection of children, including the Hague Convention on Protection of Children and Cooperation in Respect of Intercountry Adoption, the Hague Convention on the Civil Aspects of International Child Abduction, the Hague Convention on Jurisdiction, Applicable Law, Recognition, Enforcement and Cooperation in Respect of Parental Responsibility and Measures for the Protection of Children, and International Labour Organization Convention No. 182 on the Prohibition and Immediate Action for the Elimination of the Worst Forms of Child Labour,

Encouraged by the overwhelming support for the Convention on the Rights of the Child, demonstrating the widespread commitment that exists for the promotion and protection of the rights of the child,

Recognizing the importance of the implementation of the provisions of the Programme of Action for the Prevention of the Sale of Children, Child Prostitution and Child Pornography and the Declaration and Agenda for Action adopted at the

World Congress against Commercial Sexual Exploitation of Children, held in Stockholm from 27 to 31 August 1996, and the other relevant decisions and recommendations of pertinent international bodies,

Taking due account of the importance of the traditions and cultural values of each people for the protection and harmonious development of the child,

Have agreed as follows:

Article 1

States Parties shall prohibit the sale of children, child prostitution and child pornography as provided for by the present Protocol.

Article 2

For the purposes of the present Protocol:

(a) Sale of children means any act or transaction whereby a child is transferred by any person or group of persons to another for remuneration or any other consideration;

(b) Child prostitution means the use of a child in sexual activities for remuneration or any other form of consideration;

(c) Child pornography means any representation, by whatever means, of a child engaged in real or simulated explicit sexual activities or any representation of the sexual parts of a child for primarily sexual purposes.

Article 3

1. Each State Party shall ensure that, as a minimum, the following acts and activities are fully covered under its criminal or penal law, whether such offences are committed domestically or transnationally or on an individual or organized basis:

(a) In the context of sale of children as defined in article 2:

   (i) Offering, delivering or accepting, by whatever means, a child for the purpose of:

     a. Sexual exploitation of the child;

     b. Transfer of organs of the child for profit;

     c. Engagement of the child in forced labour;

   (ii) Improperly inducing consent, as an intermediary, for the adoption of a child in violation of applicable international legal instruments on adoption;

(b) Offering, obtaining, procuring or providing a child for child prostitution, as defined in article 2;

(c) Producing, distributing, disseminating, importing, exporting, offering, selling or possessing for the above purposes child pornography as defined in article 2.

2. Subject to the provisions of the national law of a State Party, the same shall apply to an attempt to commit any of the said acts and to complicity or participation in any of the said acts.

3. Each State Party shall make such offences punishable by appropriate penalties that take into account their grave nature.

4. Subject to the provisions of its national law, each State Party shall take measures, where appropriate, to establish the liability of legal persons for offences established in paragraph 1 of the present article. Subject to the legal principles of the State Party, such liability of legal persons may be criminal, civil or administrative.

5. States Parties shall take all appropriate legal and administrative measures to ensure that all persons involved in the adoption of a child act in conformity with applicable international legal instruments.

Article 4

1. Each State Party shall take such measures as may be necessary to establish its jurisdiction over the offences referred to in article 3, paragraph 1, when the offences are commited in its territory or on board a ship or aircraft registered in that State.

2. Each State Party may take such measures as may be necessary to establish its jurisdiction over the offences referred to in article 3, paragraph 1, in the following cases:

   (a) When the alleged offender is a national of that State or a person who has his habitual residence in its territory;

   (b) When the victim is a national of that State.

3. Each State Party shall also take such measures as may be necessary to establish its jurisdiction over the aforementioned offences when the alleged offender is present in its territory and it does not extradite him or her to another State Party on the ground that the offence has been committed by one of its nationals.

4. The present Protocol does not exclude any criminal jurisdiction exercised in accordance with internal law.

Article 5
1. The offences referred to in article 3, paragraph 1, shall be deemed to be included as extraditable offences in any extradition treaty existing between States Parties and shall be included as extraditable offences in every extradition treaty subsequently concluded between them, in accordance with the conditions set forth in such treaties.

2. If a State Party that makes extradition conditional on the existence of a treaty receives a request for extradition from another State Party with which it has no extradition treaty, it may consider the present Protocol to be a legal basis for extradition in respect of such offences. Extradition shall be subject to the conditions provided by the law of the requested State.

3. States Parties that do not make extradition conditional on the existence of a treaty shall recognize such offences as extraditable offences between themselves subject to the conditions provided by the law of the requested State.

4. Such offences shall be treated, for the purpose of extradition between States Parties, as if they had been committed not only in the place in which they occurred but also in the territories of the States required to establish their jurisdiction in accordance with article 4.

5. If an extradition request is made with respect to an offence described in article 3, paragraph 1, and the requested State Party does not or will not extradite on the basis of the nationality of the offender, that State shall take suitable measures to submit the case to its competent authorities for the purpose of prosecution.

Article 6
1. States Parties shall afford one another the greatest measure of assistance in connection with investigations or criminal or extradition proceedings brought in respect of the offences set forth in article 3, paragraph 1, including assistance in obtaining evidence at their disposal necessary for the proceedings.

2. States Parties shall carry out their obligations under paragraph 1 of the present article in conformity with any treaties or other arrangements on mutual legal assistance that may exist between them. In the absence of such treaties or arrangements, States Parties shall afford one another assistance in accordance with their domestic law.

Article 7
States Parties shall, subject to the provisions of their national law:

   (a) Take measures to provide for the seizure and confiscation, as appropriate, of:
      (i) Goods, such as materials, assets and other instrumentalities used to commit or facilitate offences under the present protocol;
      (ii) Proceeds derived from such offences;

(b) Execute requests from another State Party for seizure or confiscation of goods or proceeds referred to in subparagraph (a);

(c) Take measures aimed at closing, on a temporary or definitive basis, premises used to commit such offences.

Article 8

1. States Parties shall adopt appropriate measures to protect the rights and interests of child victims of the practices prohibited under the present Protocol at all stages of the criminal justice process, in particular by:

(a) Recognizing the vulnerability of child victims and adapting procedures to recognize their special needs, including their special needs as witnesses;

(b) Informing child victims of their rights, their role and the scope, timing and progress of the proceedings and of the disposition of their cases;

(c) Allowing the views, needs and concerns of child victims to be presented and considered in proceedings where their personal interests are affected, in a manner consistent with the procedural rules of national law;

(d) Providing appropriate support services to child victims throughout the legal process;

(e) Protecting, as appropriate, the privacy and identity of child victims and taking measures in accordance with national law to avoid the inappropriate dissemination of information that could lead to the identification of child victims;

(f) Providing, in appropriate cases, for the safety of child victims, as well as that of their families and witnesses on their behalf, from intimidation and retaliation;

(g) Avoiding unnecessary delay in the disposition of cases and the execution of orders or decrees granting compensation to child victims.

2. States Parties shall ensure that uncertainty as to the actual age of the victim shall not prevent the initiation of criminal investigations, including investigations aimed at establishing the age of the victim.

3. States Parties shall ensure that, in the treatment by the criminal justice system of children who are victims of the offences described in the present Protocol, the best interest of the child shall be a primary consideration.

4. States Parties shall take measures to ensure appropriate training, in particular legal and psychological training, for the persons who work with victims of the offences prohibited under the present Protocol.

5. States Parties shall, in appropriate cases, adopt measures in order to protect the safety and integrity of those persons and/or organizations involved in the prevention and/or protection and rehabilitation of victims of such offences.

6. Nothing in the present article shall be construed to be prejudicial to or inconsistent with the rights of the accused to a fair and impartial trial.

Article 9

1. States Parties shall adopt or strengthen, implement and disseminate laws, administrative measures, social policies and programmes to prevent the offences referred to in the present Protocol. Particular attention shall be given to protect children who are especially vulnerable to such practices.

2. States Parties shall promote awareness in the public at large, including children, through information by all appropriate means, education and training, about the preventive measures and harmful effects of the offences referred to in the present Protocol. In fulfilling their obligations under this article, States Parties shall encourage the participation of the community and, in particular, children and child victims, in such information and education and training programmes, including at the international level.

3. States Parties shall take all feasible measures with the aim of ensuring all appropriate assistance

to victims of such offences, including their full social reintegration and their full physical and psychological recovery.

4. States Parties shall ensure that all child victims of the offences described in the present Protocol have access to adequate procedures to seek, without discrimination, compensation for damages from those legally responsible.

5. States Parties shall take appropriate measures aimed at effectively prohibiting the production and dissemination of material advertising the offences described in the present Protocol.

Article 10
1. States Parties shall take all necessary steps to strengthen international cooperation by multilateral, regional and bilateral arrangements for the prevention, detection, investigation, prosecution and punishment of those responsible for acts involving the sale of children, child prostitution, child pornography and child sex tourism. States Parties shall also promote international cooperation and coordination between their authorities, national and international non-governmental organizations and international organizations.

2. States Parties shall promote international cooperation to assist child victims in their physical and psychological recovery, social reintegration and repatriation.

3. States Parties shall promote the strengthening of international cooperation in order to address the root causes, such as poverty and underdevelopment, contributing to the vulnerability of children to the sale of children, child prostitution, child pornography and child sex tourism.

4. States Parties in a position to do so shall provide financial, technical or other assistance through existing multilateral, regional, bilateral or other programmes.

Article 11
Nothing in the present Protocol shall affect any provisions that are more conducive to the realization of the rights of the child and that may be contained in:

    (a) The law of a State Party;
    (b) International law in force for that State.

Article 12
1. Each State Party shall, within two years following the entry into force of the present Protocol for that State Party, submit a report to the Committee on the Rights of the Child providing comprehensive information on the measures it has taken to implement the provisions of the Protocol.

2. Following the submission of the comprehensive report, each State Party shall include in the reports they submit to the Committee on the Rights of the Child, in accordance with article 44 of the Convention, any further information with respect to the implementation of the present Protocol. Other States Parties to the Protocol shall submit a report every five years.

3. The Committee on the Rights of the Child may request from States Parties further information relevant to the implementation of the present Protocol.

Article 13
1. The present Protocol is open for signature by any State that is a party to the Convention or has signed it.

2. The present Protocol is subject to ratification and is open to accession by any State that is a party to the Convention or has signed it. Instruments of ratification or accession shall be deposited with the Secretary-General of the United Nations.

Article 14
1. The present Protocol shall enter into force three months after the deposit of the tenth instrument of ratification or accession.

2. For each State ratifying the present Protocol or acceding to it after its entry into force, the Protocol shall enter into force one month after the date of the deposit of its own instrument of ratification or accession.

Article 15
1. Any State Party may denounce the present Protocol at any time by written notification to the Secretary-General of the United Nations, who shall thereafter inform the other States Parties to the Convention and all States that have signed the Convention. The denunciation shall take effect one year after the date of receipt of the notification by the Secretary-General.

2. Such a denunciation shall not have the effect of releasing the State Party from its obligations under the present Protocol in regard to any offence that occurs prior to the date on which the denunciation becomes effective. Nor shall such a denunciation prejudice in any way the continued consideration of any matter that is already under consideration by the Committee on the Rights of the Child prior to the date on which the denunciation becomes effective.

Article 16
1. Any State Party may propose an amendment and file it with the Secretary-General of the United Nations. The Secretary-General shall thereupon communicate the proposed amendment to States Parties with a request that they indicate whether they favour a conference of States Parties for the purpose of considering and voting upon the proposals. In the event that, within four months from the date of such communication, at least one third of the States Parties favour such a conference, the Secretary-General shall convene the conference under the auspices of the United

Nations. Any amendment adopted by a majority of States Parties present and voting at the conference shall be submitted to the General Assembly of the United Nations for approval.

2. An amendment adopted in accordance with paragraph 1 of the present article shall enter into force when it has been approved by the General Assembly and accepted by a two-thirds majority of States Parties.

3. When an amendment enters into force, it shall be binding on those States Parties that have accepted it, other States Parties still being bound by the provisions of the present Protocol and any earlier amendments they have accepted.

Article 17
1. The present Protocol, of which the Arabic, Chinese, English, French, Russian and Spanish texts are equally authentic, shall be deposited in the archives of the United Nations.

2. The Secretary-General of the United Nations shall transmit certified copies of the present Protocol to all States Parties to the Convention and all States that have signed the Convention.

37.
Council of Europe Convention on Action against Trafficking in Human Beings

Human trafficking is an important source of revenue for organized criminal groups in Europe. Human trafficking has no regard for the dignity of the person trafficked and violates his or her basic human rights. The Council of Europe has been proactive in its efforts to prevent the trafficking of human beings. The member countries of the Council of Europe called for combating human trafficking during its meeting in Warsaw, Poland, in May 2005 and sought international cooperation in the adoption of measures to eliminate it. As stated in Chapter II, Article

5, "Each Party shall take measures to establish or strengthen national co-ordination between the various bodies responsible for preventing and combating trafficking in human beings." Additionally, there would be specific measures to prevent the trafficking of children. Article 17 stipulates promotion of gender equality. Offenders are subject to monetary sanctions as well as imprisonment.

Source
Council of Europe, http://conventions.coe.int/Treaty/EN/Treaties/Html/197.htm.

Preamble
The member States of the Council of Europe and the other Signatories hereto,

Considering that the aim of the Council of Europe is to achieve a greater unity between its members;

Considering that trafficking in human beings constitutes a violation of human rights and an offence to the dignity and the integrity of the human being;

Considering that trafficking in human beings may result in slavery for victims;

Considering that respect for victims' rights, protection of victims and action to combat trafficking in human beings must be the paramount objectives;

Considering that all actions or initiatives against trafficking in human beings must be non-discriminatory, take gender equality into account as well as a child-rights approach;

Recalling the declarations by the Ministers for Foreign Affairs of the Member States at the 112th (14–15 May 2003) and the 114th (12–13 May 2004) Sessions of the Committee of Ministers calling for reinforced action by the Council of Europe on trafficking in human beings;

Bearing in mind the Convention for the Protection of Human Rights and Fundamental Freedoms (1950) and its protocols;

Bearing in mind the following recommendations of the Committee of Ministers to member states of the Council of Europe: Recommendation No. R (91) 11 on sexual exploitation, pornography and prostitution of, and trafficking in, children and young adults; Recommendation No. R (97) 13 concerning intimidation of witnesses and the rights of the defence; Recommendation No. R (2000) 11 on action against trafficking in human beings for the purpose of sexual exploitation and Recommendation Rec (2001) 16 on the protection of children against sexual exploitation; Recommendation Rec (2002) 5 on the protection of women against violence;

Bearing in mind the following recommendations of the Parliamentary Assembly of the Council of Europe: Recommendation 1325 (1997) on traffic in women and forced prostitution in Council of Europe member states; Recommendation 1450 (2000) on violence against women in Europe; Recommendation 1545 (2002) on a campaign against trafficking in women; Recommendation 1610 (2003) on migration connected with trafficking in women and prostitution; Recommendation 1611 (2003) on trafficking in organs in Europe; Recommendation 1663 (2004) Domestic slavery: servitude, au pairs and mail-order brides;

Bearing in mind the European Union Council Framework Decision of 19 July 2002 on combating trafficking in human beings the European Union Council Framework Decision of 15 March 2001 on the standing of victims in criminal proceedings and the European Union Council Directive of 29 April 2004 on the residence permit issued to third-country nationals who are victims of trafficking in human beings or who have been the subject of an action to facilitate illegal immigration, who cooperate with the competent authorities;

Taking due account of the United Nations Convention against Transnational Organized Crime and the Protocol thereto to Prevent, Suppress and Punish Trafficking in Persons, Especially Women and Children with a view to improving the protection which they afford and developing the standards established by them;

Taking due account of the other international legal instruments relevant in the field of action against trafficking in human beings;

Taking into account the need to prepare a comprehensive international legal instrument focusing on the human rights of victims of trafficking and setting up a specific monitoring mechanism,

Have agreed as follows:

Chapter I—Purposes, Scope, Non-discrimination Principle and Definitions

Article 1—Purposes of the Convention
1. The purposes of this Convention are:

   a. to prevent and combat trafficking in human beings, while guaranteeing gender equality
   b. to protect the human rights of the victims of trafficking, design a comprehensive framework for the protection and assistance of victims and witnesses, while guaranteeing gender equality, as well as to ensure effective investigation and prosecution;
   c. to promote international cooperation on action against trafficking in human beings.

2. In order to ensure effective implementation of its provisions by the Parties, this Convention sets up a specific monitoring mechanism.

Article 2—Scope
This Convention shall apply to all forms of trafficking in human beings, whether national or transnational, whether or not connected with organised crime.

Article 3—Non-discrimination Principle
The implementation of the provisions of this Convention by Parties, in particular the enjoyment of measures to protect and promote the rights of victims, shall be secured without discrimination on any ground such as sex, race, colour, language, religion, political or other opinion, national or social origin, association with a national minority, property, birth or other status.

Article 4—Definitions
For the purposes of this Convention:

   a. "Trafficking in human beings" shall mean the recruitment, transportation, transfer, harbouring or receipt of persons, by means of the threat or use of force or other forms of coercion, of abduction, of fraud, of deception, of the abuse of power or of a position of vulnerability or of the giving or receiving of payments or benefits to achieve the consent of a person having control over another person, for the purpose of exploitation. Exploitation shall include, at a minimum, the exploitation of the prostitution of others or other forms of sexual exploitation, forced labour or services, slavery or practices similar to slavery, servitude or the removal of organs;
   b. The consent of a victim of "trafficking in human beings" to the intended exploitation set forth in subparagraph (a) of this article shall be irrelevant where any of the means set forth in subparagraph (a) have been used;
   c. The recruitment, transportation, transfer, harbouring or receipt of a child for the purpose of exploitation shall be considered "trafficking in human beings" even if this does not involve any of the means set forth in subparagraph (a) of this article;
   d. "Child" shall mean any person under eighteen years of age;
   e. "Victim" shall mean any natural person who is subject to trafficking in human beings as defined in this article.

Chapter II—Prevention, Co-operation and Other Measures

Article 5—Prevention of Trafficking in Human Beings

1. Each Party shall take measures to establish or strengthen national co-ordination between the various bodies responsible for preventing and combating trafficking in human beings.

2. Each Party shall establish and/or strengthen effective policies and programmes to prevent trafficking in human beings, by such means as: research, information, awareness raising and education campaigns, social and economic initiatives and training programmes, in particular for persons vulnerable to trafficking and for professionals concerned with trafficking in human beings.

3. Each Party shall promote a Human Rights-based approach and shall use gender mainstreaming and a child-sensitive approach in the development, implementation and assessment of all the policies and programmes referred to in paragraph 2.

4. Each Party shall take appropriate measures, as may be necessary, to enable migration to take place legally, in particular through dissemination of accurate information by relevant offices, on the conditions enabling the legal entry in and stay on its territory.

5. Each Party shall take specific measures to reduce children's vulnerability to trafficking, notably by creating a protective environment for them.

6. Measures established in accordance with this article shall involve, where appropriate, non-governmental organisations, other relevant organisations and other elements of civil society committed to the prevention of trafficking in human beings and victim protection or assistance.

Article 6—Measures to Discourage the Demand

To discourage the demand that fosters all forms of exploitation of persons, especially women and children, that leads to trafficking, each Party shall adopt or strengthen legislative, administrative, educational, social, cultural or other measures including:

a. research on best practices, methods and strategies;
b. raising awareness of the responsibility and important role of media and civil society in identifying the demand as one of the root causes of trafficking in human beings;
c. target information campaigns involving, as appropriate, inter alia, public authorities and policy makers;
d. preventive measures, including educational programmes for boys and girls during their schooling, which stress the unacceptable nature of discrimination based on sex, and its disastrous consequences, the importance of gender equality and the dignity and integrity of every human being.

Article 7—Border Measures

1. Without prejudice to international commitments in relation to the free movement of persons, Parties shall strengthen, to the extent possible, such border controls as may be necessary to prevent and detect trafficking in human beings.

2. Each Party shall adopt legislative or other appropriate measures to prevent, to the extent possible, means of transport operated by commercial carriers from being used in the commission of offences established in accordance with this Convention.

3. Where appropriate, and without prejudice to applicable international conventions, such measures shall include establishing the obligation of commercial carriers, including any transportation company or the owner or operator of any means of transport, to ascertain that all passengers are in possession of the travel

documents required for entry into the receiving State.

4. Each Party shall take the necessary measures, in accordance with its internal law, to provide for sanctions in cases of violation of the obligation set forth in paragraph 3 of this article.

5. Each Party shall adopt such legislative or other measures as may be necessary to permit, in accordance with its internal law, the denial of entry or revocation of visas of persons implicated in the commission of offences established in accordance with this Convention.

6. Parties shall strengthen co-operation among border control agencies by, *inter alia,* establishing and maintaining direct channels of communication.

Article 8—Security and Control of Documents
Each Party shall adopt such measures as may be necessary:

   a. To ensure that travel or identity documents issued by it are of such quality that they cannot easily be misused and cannot readily be falsified or unlawfully altered, replicated or issued; and
   b. To ensure the integrity and security of travel or identity documents issued by or on behalf of the Party and to prevent their unlawful creation and issuance.

Article 9—Legitimacy and Validity of Documents
At the request of another Party, a Party shall, in accordance with its internal law, verify within a reasonable time the legitimacy and validity of travel or identity documents issued or purported to have been issued in its name and suspected of being used for trafficking in human beings.

Chapter III—Measures to Protect and Promote the Rights of Victims, Guaranteeing Gender Equality

Article 10—Identification of the Victims
1. Each Party shall provide its competent authorities with persons who are trained and qualified in preventing and combating trafficking in human beings, in identifying and helping victims, including children, and shall ensure that the different authorities collaborate with each other as well as with relevant support organisations, so that victims can be identified in a procedure duly taking into account the special situation of women and child victims and, in appropriate cases, issued with residence permits under the conditions provided for in Article 14 of the present Convention.

2. Each Party shall adopt such legislative or other measures as may be necessary to identify victims as appropriate in collaboration with other Parties and relevant support organisations. Each Party shall ensure that, if the competent authorities have reasonable grounds to believe that a person has been victim of trafficking in human beings, that person shall not be removed from its territory until the identification process as victim of an offence provided for in Article 18 of this Convention has been completed by the competent authorities and shall likewise ensure that that person receives the assistance provided for in Article 12, paragraphs 1 and 2.

3. When the age of the victim is uncertain and there are reasons to believe that the victim is a child, he or she shall be presumed to be a child and shall be accorded special protection measures pending verification of his/her age.

4. As soon as an unaccompanied child is identified as a victim, each Party shall:

a. provide for representation of the child by a legal guardian, organisation or authority which shall act in the best interests of that child;

b. take the necessary steps to establish his/her identity and nationality;

c. make every effort to locate his/her family when this is in the best interests of the child.

Article 11—Protection of Private Life

1. Each Party shall protect the private life and identity of victims. Personal data regarding them shall be stored and used in conformity with the conditions provided for by the Convention for the Protection of Individuals with regard to Automatic Processing of Personal Data (ETS No. 108).

2. Each Party shall adopt measures to ensure, in particular, that the identity, or details allowing the identification, of a child victim of trafficking are not made publicly known, through the media or by any other means, except, in exceptional circumstances, in order to facilitate the tracing of family members or otherwise secure the well-being and protection of the child.

3. Each Party shall consider adopting, in accordance with Article 10 of the Convention for the Protection of Human Rights and Fundamental Freedoms as interpreted by the European Court of Human Rights, measures aimed at encouraging the media to protect the private life and identity of victims through self-regulation or through regulatory or co-regulatory measures.

Article 12—Assistance to Victims

1. Each Party shall adopt such legislative or other measures as may be necessary to assist victims in their physical, psychological and social recovery. Such assistance shall include at least:

a. standards of living capable of ensuring their subsistence, through such measures as: appropriate and secure accommodation, psychological and material assistance;

b. access to emergency medical treatment;

c. translation and interpretation services, when appropriate;

d. counselling and information, in particular as regards their legal rights and the services available to them, in a language that they can understand;

e. assistance to enable their rights and interests to be presented and considered at appropriate stages of criminal proceedings against offenders;

f. access to education for children.

2. Each Party shall take due account of the victim's safety and protection needs.

3. In addition, each Party shall provide necessary medical or other assistance to victims lawfully resident within its territory who do not have adequate resources and need such help.

4. Each Party shall adopt the rules under which victims lawfully resident within its territory shall be authorised to have access to the labour market, to vocational training and education.

5. Each Party shall take measures, where appropriate and under the conditions provided for by its internal law, to co-operate with non-governmental organisations, other relevant organisations or other elements of civil society engaged in assistance to victims.

6. Each Party shall adopt such legislative or other measures as may be necessary to ensure that assistance to a victim is not made conditional on his or her willingness to act as a witness.

7. For the implementation of the provisions set out in this article, each Party shall ensure that services are provided on a consensual and informed basis, taking due account of the special needs of persons in a vulnerable position and the rights of children in terms of accommodation, education and appropriate health care.

Article 13—Recovery and Reflection Period

1. Each Party shall provide in its internal law a recovery and reflection period of at least 30 days, when there are reasonable grounds to believe that the person concerned is a victim. Such a period shall be sufficient for the person concerned to recover and escape the influence of traffickers and/or to take an informed decision on cooperating with the competent authorities. During this period it shall not be possible to enforce any expulsion order against him or her. This provision is without prejudice to the activities carried out by the competent authorities in all phases of the relevant national proceedings, and in particular when investigating and prosecuting the offences concerned. During this period, the Parties shall authorise the persons concerned to stay in their territory.

2. During this period, the persons referred to in paragraph 1 of this Article shall be entitled to the measures contained in Article 12, paragraphs 1 and 2.

3. The Parties are not bound to observe this period if grounds of public order prevent it or if it is found that victim status is being claimed improperly.

Article 14—Residence Permit

1. Each Party shall issue a renewable residence permit to victims, in one or other of the two following situations or in both:

   a. the competent authority considers that their stay is necessary owing to their personal situation;
   b. the competent authority considers that their stay is necessary for the purpose of their co-operation with the competent authorities in investigation or criminal proceedings.

2. The residence permit for child victims, when legally necessary, shall be issued in accordance with the best interests of the child and, where appropriate, renewed under the same conditions.

3. The non-renewal or withdrawal of a residence permit is subject to the conditions provided for by the internal law of the Party.

4. If a victim submits an application for another kind of residence permit, the Party concerned shall take into account that he or she holds, or has held, a residence permit in conformity with paragraph 1.

5. Having regard to the obligations of Parties to which Article 40 of this Convention refers, each Party shall ensure that granting of a permit according to this provision shall be without prejudice to the right to seek and enjoy asylum.

Article 15—Compensation and Legal Redress

1. Each Party shall ensure that victims have access, as from their first contact with the competent authorities, to information on relevant judicial and administrative proceedings in a language which they can understand.

2. Each Party shall provide, in its internal law, for the right to legal assistance and to free legal aid for victims under the conditions provided by its internal law.

3. Each Party shall provide, in its internal law, for the right of victims to compensation from the perpetrators.

4. Each Party shall adopt such legislative or other measures as may be necessary to guarantee compensation for victims in accordance with the conditions under its internal law, for instance through the establishment of a fund for victim compensation or measures or programmes aimed at social assistance and social integration of victims, which could be funded by the assets resulting from the application of measures provided in Article 23.

Article 16—Repatriation and Return of Victims

1. The Party of which a victim is a national or in which that person had the right of permanent residence at the time of entry into the territory of

the receiving Party shall, with due regard for his or her rights, safety and dignity, facilitate and accept, his or her return without undue or unreasonable delay.

2. When a Party returns a victim to another State, such return shall be with due regard for the rights, safety and dignity of that person and for the status of any legal proceedings related to the fact that the person is a victim, and shall preferably be voluntary.

3. At the request of a receiving Party, a requested Party shall verify whether a person is its national or had the right of permanent residence in its territory at the time of entry into the territory of the receiving Party.

4. In order to facilitate the return of a victim who is without proper documentation, the Party of which that person is a national or in which he or she had the right of permanent residence at the time of entry into the territory of the receiving Party shall agree to issue, at the request of the receiving Party, such travel documents or other authorisation as may be necessary to enable the person to travel to and re-enter its territory.

5. Each Party shall adopt such legislative or other measures as may be necessary to establish repatriation programmes, involving relevant national or international institutions and non governmental organisations. These programmes aim at avoiding re-victimisation. Each Party should make its best effort to favour the reintegration of victims into the society of the State of return, including reintegration into the education system and the labour market, in particular through the acquisition and improvement of their professional skills. With regard to children, these programmes should include enjoyment of the right to education and measures to secure adequate care or receipt by the family or appropriate care structures.

6. Each Party shall adopt such legislative or other measures as may be necessary to make available to victims, where appropriate in co-operation with any other Party concerned, contact information of structures that can assist them in the country where they are returned or repatriated, such as law enforcement offices, non-governmental organisations, legal professions able to provide counselling and social welfare agencies.

7. Child victims shall not be returned to a State, if there is indication, following a risk and security assessment, that such return would not be in the best interests of the child.

Article 17—Gender Equality
Each Party shall, in applying measures referred to in this chapter, aim to promote gender equality and use gender mainstreaming in the development, implementation and assessment of the measures.

Chapter IV—Substantive Criminal Law

Article 18—Criminalisation of Trafficking in Human Beings
Each Party shall adopt such legislative and other measures as may be necessary to establish as criminal offences the conduct contained in article 4 of this Convention, when committed intentionally.

Article 19—Criminalisation of the Use of Services of a Victim
Each Party shall consider adopting such legislative and other measures as may be necessary to establish as criminal offences under its internal law, the use of services which are the object of exploitation as referred to in Article 4 paragraph a of this Convention, with the knowledge that the person is a victim of trafficking in human beings.

Article 20—Criminalisation of Acts Relating to Travel or Identity Documents
Each Party shall adopt such legislative and other measures as may be necessary to establish as criminal offences the following conducts, when

committed intentionally and for the purpose of enabling the trafficking in human beings:

a. forging a travel or identity document;
b. procuring or providing such a document;
c. retaining, removing, concealing, damaging or destroying a travel or identity document of another person.

Article 21—Attempt and Aiding or Abetting
1. Each Party shall adopt such legislative and other measures as may be necessary to establish as criminal offences when committed intentionally, aiding or abetting the commission of any of the offences established in accordance with Articles 18 and 20 of the present Convention.

2. Each Party shall adopt such legislative and other measures as may be necessary to establish as criminal offences when committed intentionally, an attempt to commit the offences established in accordance with Articles 18 and 20, paragraph a, of this Convention.

Article 22—Corporate Liability
1. Each Party shall adopt such legislative and other measures as may be necessary to ensure that a legal person can be held liable for a criminal offence established in accordance with this Convention, committed for its benefit by any natural person, acting either individually or as part of an organ of the legal person, who has a leading position within the legal person, based on:

a. a power of representation of the legal person;
b. an authority to take decisions on behalf of the legal person;
c. an authority to exercise control within the legal person.

2. Apart from the cases already provided for in paragraph 1, each Party shall take the measures necessary to ensure that a legal person can be held liable where the lack of supervision or control by a natural person referred to in paragraph 1 has made possible the commission of a criminal offence

established in accordance with this Convention for the benefit of that legal person by a natural person acting under its authority.

3. Subject to the legal principles of the Party, the liability of a legal person may be criminal, civil or administrative.

4. Such liability shall be without prejudice to the criminal liability of the natural persons who have committed the offence.

Article 23—Sanctions and Measures
1. Each Party shall adopt such legislative and other measures as may be necessary to ensure that the criminal offences established in accordance with Articles 18 to 21 are punishable by effective, proportionate and dissuasive sanctions. These sanctions shall include, for criminal offences established in accordance with Article 18 when committed by natural persons, penalties involving deprivation of liberty which can give rise to extradition.

2. Each Party shall ensure that legal persons held liable in accordance with Article 22 shall be subject to effective, proportionate and dissuasive criminal or non-criminal sanctions or measures, including monetary sanctions.

3. Each Party shall adopt such legislative and other measures as may be necessary to enable it to confiscate or otherwise deprive the instrumentalities and proceeds of criminal offences established in accordance with Articles 18 and 20, paragraph a, of this Convention, or property the value of which corresponds to such proceeds.

4. Each Party shall adopt such legislative or other measures as may be necessary to enable the temporary or permanent closure of any establishment which was used to carry out trafficking in human beings, without prejudice to the rights of *bona fide* third parties or to deny the perpetrator, temporary or permanently, the

exercise of the activity in the course of which this offence was committed.

Article 24—Aggravating Circumstances
Each Party shall ensure that the following circumstances are regarded as aggravating circumstances in the determination of the penalty for offences established in accordance with Article 18 of this Convention:

a. the offence deliberately or by gross negligence endangered the life of the victim;
b. the offence was committed against a child;
c. the offence was committed by a public official in the performance of her/his duties;
d. the offence was committed within the framework of a criminal organisation.

Article 25—Previous Convictions
Each Party shall adopt such legislative and other measures providing for the possibility to take into account final sentences passed by another Party in relation to offences established in accordance with this Convention when determining the penalty.

Article 26—Non-punishment Provision
Each Party shall, in accordance with the basic principles of its legal system, provide for the possibility of not imposing penalties on victims for their involvement in unlawful activities, to the extent that they have been compelled to do so.

Chapter V—Investigation, Prosecution and Procedural Law

Article 27—Ex Parte and Ex Officio Applications
1. Each Party shall ensure that investigations into or prosecution of offences established in accordance with this Convention shall not be dependent upon the report or accusation made by a victim, at least when the offence was committed in whole or in part on its territory.

2. Each Party shall ensure that victims of an offence in the territory of a Party other than the one where they reside may make a complaint before the competent authorities of their State of residence. The competent authority to which the complaint is made, insofar as it does not itself have competence in this respect, shall transmit it without delay to the competent authority of the Party in the territory in which the offence was committed. The complaint shall be dealt with in accordance with the internal law of the Party in which the offence was committed.

3. Each Party shall ensure, by means of legislative or other measures, in accordance with the conditions provided for by its internal law, to any group, foundation, association or non-governmental organisations which aims at fighting trafficking in human beings or protection of human rights, the possibility to assist and/or support the victim with his or her consent during criminal proceedings concerning the offence established in accordance with Article 18 of this Convention.

Article 28—Protection of Victims, Witnesses and Collaborators with the Judicial Authorities
1. Each Party shall adopt such legislative or other measures as may be necessary to provide effective and appropriate protection from potential retaliation or intimidation in particular during and after investigation and prosecution of perpetrators, for:

a. Victims;
b. As appropriate, those who report the criminal offences established in accordance with Article 18 of this Convention or otherwise co-operate with the investigating or prosecuting authorities;
c. witnesses who give testimony concerning criminal offences established in accordance with Article 18 of this Convention;
d. when necessary, members of the family of persons referred to in subparagraphs a and c.

2. Each Party shall adopt such legislative or other measures as may be necessary to ensure and to offer various kinds of protection. This may include

physical protection, relocation, identity change and assistance in obtaining jobs.

3. A child victim shall be afforded special protection measures taking into account the best interests of the child.

4. Each Party shall adopt such legislative or other measures as may be necessary to provide, when necessary, appropriate protection from potential retaliation or intimidation in particular during and after investigation and prosecution of perpetrators, for members of groups, foundations, associations or non-governmental organisations which carry out the activities set out in Article 27, paragraph 3.

5. Each Party shall consider entering into agreements or arrangements with other States for the implementation of this article.

Article 29—Specialised Authorities and Co-ordinating Bodies
1. Each Party shall adopt such measures as may be necessary to ensure that persons or entities are specialised in the fight against trafficking and the protection of victims. Such persons or entities shall have the necessary independence in accordance with the fundamental principles of the legal system of the Party, in order for them to be able to carry out their functions effectively and free from any undue pressure. Such persons or the staffs of such entities shall have adequate training and financial resources for their tasks.

2. Each Party shall adopt such measures as may be necessary to ensure co-ordination of the policies and actions of their governments' departments and other public agencies against trafficking in human beings, where appropriate, through setting up co-ordinating bodies.

3. Each Party shall provide or strengthen training for relevant officials in the prevention of and fight against trafficking in human beings, including Human Rights training. The training may be agency-specific and shall, as appropriate, focus on: methods used in preventing such trafficking, prosecuting the traffickers and protecting the rights of the victims, including protecting the victims from the traffickers.

4. Each Party shall consider appointing National Rapporteurs or other mechanisms for monitoring the anti-trafficking activities of State institutions and the implementation of national legislation requirements.

Article 30—Court Proceedings
In accordance with the Convention for the Protection of Human Rights and Fundamental Freedoms, in particular Article 6, each Party shall adopt such legislative or other measures as may be necessary to ensure in the course of judicial proceedings:

   a. the protection of victims' private life and, where appropriate, identity;
   b. victims' safety and protection from intimidation, in accordance with the conditions under its internal law and, in the case of child victims, by taking special care of children's needs and ensuring their right to special protection measures.

Article 31—Jurisdiction
1. Each Party shall adopt such legislative and other measures as may be necessary to establish jurisdiction over any offence established in accordance with this Convention, when the offence is committed:

   a. in its territory; or
   b. on board a ship flying the flag of that Party; or
   c. on board an aircraft registered under the laws of that Party; or
   d. by one of its nationals or by a stateless person who has his or her habitual residence in its territory, if the offence is punishable under criminal law where it was committed or if the offence is committed outside the territorial jurisdiction of any State;
   e. against one of its nationals.

2. Each Party may, at the time of signature or when depositing its instrument of ratification, acceptance, approval or accession, by a declaration addressed to the Secretary General of the Council of Europe, declare that it reserves the right not to apply or to apply only in specific cases or conditions the jurisdiction rules laid down in paragraphs 1 (d) and (e) of this article or any part thereof.

3. Each Party shall adopt such measures as may be necessary to establish jurisdiction over the offences referred to in this Convention, in cases where an alleged offender is present in its territory and it does not extradite him/her to another Party, solely on the basis of his/her nationality, after a request for extradition.

4. When more than one Party claims jurisdiction over an alleged offence established in accordance with this Convention, the Parties involved shall, where appropriate, consult with a view to determining the most appropriate jurisdiction for prosecution.

5. Without prejudice to the general norms of international law, this Convention does not exclude any criminal jurisdiction exercised by a Party in accordance with internal law.

Chapter VI—International Co-operation and Co-operation with Civil Society

Article 32—General Principles and Measures for International Co-operation
The Parties shall co-operate with each other, in accordance with the provisions of this Convention, and through application of relevant applicable international and regional instruments, arrangements agreed on the basis of uniform or reciprocal legislation and internal laws, to the widest extent possible, for the purpose of:

  —preventing and combating trafficking in human beings;

  —protecting and providing assistance to victims;
  —investigations or proceedings concerning criminal offences established in accordance with this Convention.

Article 33—Measures relating to Endangered or Missing Persons
1. When a Party, on the basis of the information at its disposal has reasonable grounds to believe that the life, the freedom or the physical integrity of a person referred to in Article 28, paragraph 1, is in immediate danger on the territory of another Party, the Party that has the information shall, in such a case of emergency, transmit it without delay to the latter so as to take the appropriate protection measures.

2. The Parties to this Convention may consider reinforcing their co-operation in the search for missing people, in particular for missing children, if the information available leads them to believe that she/he is a victim of trafficking in human beings. To this end, the Parties may conclude bilateral or multilateral treaties with each other.

Article 34—Information
1. The requested Party shall promptly inform the requesting Party of the final result of the action taken under this chapter. The requested Party shall also promptly inform the requesting Party of any circumstances which render impossible the carrying out of the action sought or are likely to delay it significantly.

2. A Party may, within the limits of its internal law, without prior request, forward to another Party information obtained within the framework of its own investigations when it considers that the disclosure of such information might assist the receiving Party in initiating or carrying out investigations or proceedings concerning criminal offences established in accordance with this Convention or might lead to a request for co-operation by that Party under this chapter.

3. Prior to providing such information, the providing Party may request that it be kept confidential or used subject to conditions. If the receiving Party cannot comply with such request, it shall notify the providing Party, which shall then determine whether the information should nevertheless be provided. If the receiving Party accepts the information subject to the conditions, it shall be bound by them.

4. All information requested concerning Articles 13, 14 and 16, necessary to provide the rights conferred by these articles, shall be transmitted at the request of the Party concerned without delay with due respect to Article 11 of the present Convention.

Article 35—Co-operation with Civil Society
Each Party shall encourage state authorities and public officials, to co-operate with non-governmental organisations, other relevant organisations and members of civil society, in establishing strategic partnerships with the aim of achieving the purpose of this Convention.

Chapter VII—Monitoring Mechanism

Article 36—Group of Experts on Action against Trafficking in Human Beings
1. The Group of experts on action against trafficking in human beings (hereinafter referred to as "GRETA"), shall monitor the implementation of this Convention by the Parties.

2. GRETA shall be composed of a minimum of 10 members and a maximum of 15 members, taking into account a gender and geographical balance, as well as a multidisciplinary expertise. They shall be elected by the Committee of the Parties for a term of office of 4 years, renewable once, chosen from amongst nationals of the States Parties to this Convention.

3. The election of the members of GRETA shall be based on the following principles:

a. they shall be chosen from among persons of high moral character, known for their recognised competence in the fields of Human Rights, assistance and protection of victims and of action against trafficking in human beings or having professional experience in the areas covered by this Convention;
b. they shall sit in their individual capacity and shall be independent and impartial in the exercise of their functions and shall be available to carry out their duties in an effective manner;
c. no two members of GRETA may be nationals of the same State;
d. they should represent the main legal systems.

4. The election procedure of the members of GRETA shall be determined by the Committee of Ministers, after consulting with and obtaining the unanimous consent of the Parties to the Convention, within a period of one year following the entry into force of this Convention. GRETA shall adopt its own rules of procedure.

Article 37—Committee of the Parties
1. The Committee of the Parties shall be composed of the representatives on the Committee of Ministers of the Council of Europe of the member States Parties to the Convention and representatives of the Parties to the Convention, which are not members of the Council of Europe.

2. The Committee of the Parties shall be convened by the Secretary General of the Council of Europe. Its first meeting shall be held within a period of one year following the entry into force of this Convention in order to elect the members of GRETA. It shall subsequently meet whenever one-third of the Parties, the President of GRETA or the Secretary General so requests.

3. The Committee of the Parties shall adopt its own rules of procedure.

Article 38—Procedure

1. The evaluation procedure shall concern the Parties to the Convention and be divided in rounds, the length of which is determined by GRETA. At the beginning of each round GRETA shall select the specific provisions on which the evaluation procedure shall be based.

2. GRETA shall define the most appropriate means to carry out this evaluation. GRETA may in particular adopt a questionnaire for each evaluation round, which may serve as a basis for the evaluation of the implementation by the Parties of the present Convention. Such a questionnaire shall be addressed to all Parties. Parties shall respond to this questionnaire, as well as to any other request of information from GRETA.

3. GRETA may request information from civil society.

4. GRETA may subsidiarily organise, in co-operation with the national authorities and the "contact person" appointed by the latter, and, if necessary, with the assistance of independent national experts, country visits. During these visits, GRETA may be assisted by specialists in specific fields.

5. GRETA shall prepare a draft report containing its analysis concerning the implementation of the provisions on which the evaluation is based, as well as its suggestions and proposals concerning the way in which the Party concerned may deal with the problems which have been identified. The draft report shall be transmitted for comments to the Party which undergoes the evaluation. Its comments are taken into account by GRETA when establishing its report.

6. On this basis, GRETA shall adopt its report and conclusions concerning the measures taken by the Party concerned to implement the provisions of the present Convention. This report and conclusions shall be sent to the Party concerned and to the Committee of the Parties. The report and conclusions of GRETA shall be made public as from their adoption, together with eventual comments by the Party concerned.

7. Without prejudice to the procedure of paragraphs 1 to 6 of this article, the Committee of the Parties may adopt, on the basis of the report and conclusions of GRETA, recommendations addressed to this Party (a) concerning the measures to be taken to implement the conclusions of GRETA, if necessary setting a date for submitting information on their implementation, and (b) aiming at promoting co-operation with that Party for the proper implementation of the present Convention.

Chapter VIII—Relationship with Other International Instruments

Article 39—Relationship with the Protocol to Prevent, Suppress and Punish Trafficking in Persons, Especially Women and Children, Supplementing the United Nations Convention against Transnational Organised Crime
This Convention shall not affect the rights and obligations derived from the provisions of the Protocol to prevent, suppress and punish trafficking in persons, especially women and children, supplementing the United Nations Convention against transnational organised crime, and is intended to enhance the protection afforded by it and develop the standards contained therein.

Article 40—Relationship with Other International Instruments
1. This Convention shall not affect the rights and obligations derived from other international instruments to which Parties to the present Convention are Parties or shall become Parties and which contain provisions on matters governed by this Convention and which ensure greater protection and assistance for victims of trafficking.

2. The Parties to the Convention may conclude bilateral or multilateral agreements with one another on the matters dealt with in this Convention, for purposes of supplementing or strengthening its provisions or facilitating the application of the principles embodied in it.

3. Parties which are members of the European Union shall, in their mutual relations, apply Community and European Union rules in so far as there are Community or European Union rules governing the particular subject concerned and applicable to the specific case, without prejudice to the object and purpose of the present Convention and without prejudice to its full application with other Parties.

4. Nothing in this Convention shall affect the rights, obligations and responsibilities of States and individuals under international law, including international humanitarian law and international human rights law and, in particular, where applicable, the 1951 Convention and the 1967 Protocol relating to the Status of Refugees and the principle of *non-refoulement* as contained therein.

Chapter IX—Amendments to the Convention

Article 41—Amendments
1. Any proposal for an amendment to this Convention presented by a Party shall be communicated to the Secretary General of the Council of Europe and forwarded by him or her to the member States of the Council of Europe, any signatory, any State Party, the European Community, to any State invited to sign this Convention in accordance with the provisions of Article 42 and to any State invited to accede to this Convention in accordance with the provisions of Article 43.

2. Any amendment proposed by a Party shall be communicated to GRETA, which shall submit to the Committee of Ministers its opinion on that proposed amendment.

3. The Committee of Ministers shall consider the proposed amendment and the opinion submitted by GRETA and, following consultation of the Parties to this Convention and after obtaining their unanimous consent, may adopt the amendment.

4. The text of any amendment adopted by the Committee of Ministers in accordance with paragraph 3 of this article shall be forwarded to the Parties for acceptance.

5. Any amendment adopted in accordance with paragraph 3 of this article shall enter into force on the first day of the month following the expiration of a period of one month after the date on which all Parties have informed the Secretary General that they have accepted it.

Note by the Secretariat: See the Declaration formulated by the European Community and the Member States of the European Union upon the adoption of the Convention by the Committee of Ministers of the Council of Europe, on 3 May 2005:

"The European Community/European Union and its Member States reaffirm that their objective in requesting the inclusion of a 'disconnection clause' is to take account of the institutional structure of the Union when acceding to international conventions, in particular in case of transfer of sovereign powers from the Member States to the Community.

This clause is not aimed at reducing the rights or increasing the obligations of a non-European Union Party vis-à-vis the European Community/European Union and its Member States, inasmuch as the latter are also parties to this Convention.

The disconnection clause is necessary for those parts of the Convention which fall within the competence of the Community/Union, in order to indicate that European Union Member States cannot invoke and apply the rights and obligations deriving from the Convention directly among themselves (or between themselves and the European Community/Union). This does not detract from the fact that the Convention applies fully between the European Community/European Union and its Member States on the one hand, and the other Parties to the Convention, on the other; the Community and the European Union Members States will be bound by the Convention and will apply it like any Party to the Convention, if necessary, through Community/Union legislation. They will thus guarantee the full respect of the Convention's provisions vis-à-vis non-European Union Parties."

38.
Victims of Trafficking and Violence Protection Act of 2000

Human trafficking has become a lucrative business for organized crime. The United States has become determined to prevent and punish the perpetrators of this dastardly crime. The Victims of Trafficking and Violence Protection Act of 2000 was passed by the 106th Congress of the United States on 28 October 2000. This legislation was enacted to combat human trafficking. The act is broken down into three divisions. Division A, "Trafficking Victims Protection Act of 2000," establishes measures to prevent the trafficking of persons and to provide assistance to those victimized by this crime. Additionally, it sets forth prosecutorial measures to be taken against those involved in this activity. Section 111 addresses sanctions and penalties. The 108th Congress passed the Victims Protection Reauthorization Act of 2003 on 7 January 2003. The appropriated funds will continue to tackle the problem of human trafficking.

Source
U.S. Citizenship and Immigration Services, http://www.state.gov/documents/organization/10492.pdf.

Sec. 101. Short Title
This division may be cited as the 'Trafficking Victims Protection Act of 2000'.

Sec. 102. Purposes and Findings
(a) PURPOSES—The purposes of this division are to combat trafficking in persons, a contemporary manifestation of slavery whose victims are predominantly women and children, to ensure just and effective punishment of traffickers, and to protect their victims.

(b) FINDINGS—Congress finds that:

(1) As the 21st century begins, the degrading institution of slavery continues throughout the world. Trafficking in persons is a modern form of slavery, and it is the largest manifestation of slavery today. At least 700,000 persons annually, primarily women and children, are trafficked within or across international borders. Approximately 50,000 women and children are trafficked into the United States each year.

(2) Many of these persons are trafficked into the international sex trade, often by force, fraud, or coercion. The sex industry has rapidly expanded over the past several decades. It involves sexual exploitation of persons, predominantly women and girls, involving activities related to prostitution, pornography, sex tourism, and other commercial sexual services. The low status of women in many parts of the world has contributed to a burgeoning of the trafficking industry.

(3) Trafficking in persons is not limited to the sex industry. This growing transnational crime also includes forced labor and involves significant violations of labor, public health, and human rights standards worldwide.

(4) Traffickers primarily target women and girls, who are disproportionately affected by poverty, the lack of access to education, chronic unemployment, discrimination, and the lack of economic opportunities in countries of origin. Traffickers lure women and girls into their networks through false promises of decent working conditions at

relatively good pay as nannies, maids, dancers, factory workers, restaurant workers, sales clerks, or models. Traffickers also buy children from poor families and sell them into prostitution or into various types of forced or bonded labor.

(5) Traffickers often transport victims from their home communities to unfamiliar destinations, including foreign countries away from family and friends, religious institutions, and other sources of protection and support, leaving the victims defenseless and vulnerable.

(6) Victims are often forced through physical violence to engage in sex acts or perform slavery-like labor. Such force includes rape and other forms of sexual abuse, torture, starvation, imprisonment, threats, psychological abuse, and coercion.

(7) Traffickers often make representations to their victims that physical harm may occur to them or others should the victim escape or attempt to escape. Such representations can have the same coercive effects on victims as direct threats to inflict such harm.

(8) Trafficking in persons is increasingly perpetrated by organized, sophisticated criminal enterprises. Such trafficking is the fastest growing source of profits for organized criminal enterprises worldwide. Profits from the trafficking industry contribute to the expansion of organized crime in the United States and worldwide. Trafficking in persons is often aided by official corruption in countries of origin, transit, and destination, thereby threatening the rule of law.

(9) Trafficking includes all the elements of the crime of forcible rape when it involves the involuntary participation of another person in sex acts by means of fraud, force, or coercion.

(10) Trafficking also involves violations of other laws, including labor and immigration codes and laws against kidnapping, slavery, false imprisonment, assault, battery, pandering, fraud, and extortion.

(11) Trafficking exposes victims to serious health risks. Women and children trafficked in the sex industry are exposed to deadly diseases, including HIV and AIDS. Trafficking victims are sometimes worked or physically brutalized to death.

(12) Trafficking in persons substantially affects interstate and foreign commerce. Trafficking for such purposes as involuntary servitude, peonage, and other forms of forced labor has an impact on the nationwide employment network and labor market. Within the context of slavery, servitude, and labor or services which are obtained or maintained through coercive conduct that amounts to a condition of servitude, victims are subjected to a range of violations.

(13) Involuntary servitude statutes are intended to reach cases in which persons are held in a condition of servitude through nonviolent coercion. In United States v. Kozminski, 487 U.S. 931 (1988), the Supreme Court found that section 1584 of title 18, United States Code, should be narrowly interpreted, absent a definition of involuntary servitude by Congress. As a result, that section was interpreted to criminalize only servitude that is brought about through use or threatened use of physical or legal coercion, and to exclude other conduct that can have the same purpose and effect.

(14) Existing legislation and law enforcement in the United States and other countries are inadequate to deter trafficking and bring traffickers to justice, failing to reflect the gravity of the offenses involved. No comprehensive law exists in the United States that penalizes the range of offenses involved in the trafficking scheme. Instead, even the most brutal instances of trafficking in the sex industry are often punished under laws that also apply to lesser offenses, so that traffickers typically escape deserved punishment.

(15) In the United States, the seriousness of this crime and its components is not reflected in current sentencing guidelines, resulting in weak penalties for convicted traffickers.

(16) In some countries, enforcement against traffickers is also hindered by official indifference, by corruption, and sometimes even by official participation in trafficking.

(17) Existing laws often fail to protect victims of trafficking, and because victims are often illegal immigrants in the destination country, they are repeatedly punished more harshly than the traffickers themselves.

(18) Additionally, adequate services and facilities do not exist to meet victims' needs regarding health care, housing, education, and legal assistance, which safely reintegrate trafficking victims into their home countries.

(19) Victims of severe forms of trafficking should not be inappropriately incarcerated, fined, or otherwise penalized solely for unlawful acts committed as a direct result of being trafficked, such as using false documents, entering the country without documentation, or working without documentation.

(20) Because victims of trafficking are frequently unfamiliar with the laws, cultures, and languages of the countries into which they have been trafficked, because they are often subjected to coercion and intimidation including physical detention and debt bondage, and because they often fear retribution and forcible removal to countries in which they will face retribution or other hardship, these victims often find it difficult or impossible to report the crimes committed against them or to assist in the investigation and prosecution of such crimes.

(21) Trafficking of persons is an evil requiring concerted and vigorous action by countries of origin, transit or destination, and by international organizations.

(22) One of the founding documents of the United States, the Declaration of Independence, recognizes the inherent dignity and worth of all people. It states that all men are created equal and that they are endowed by their Creator with certain unalienable rights. The right to be free from slavery and involuntary servitude is among those unalienable rights. Acknowledging this fact, the United States outlawed slavery and involuntary servitude in 1865, recognizing them as evil institutions that must be abolished. Current practices of sexual slavery and trafficking of women

and children are similarly abhorrent to the principles upon which the United States was founded.

(23) The United States and the international community agree that trafficking in persons involves grave violations of human rights and is a matter of pressing international concern. The international community has repeatedly condemned slavery and involuntary servitude, violence against women, and other elements of trafficking, through declarations, treaties, and United Nations resolutions and reports, including the Universal Declaration of Human Rights; the 1956 Supplementary Convention on the Abolition of Slavery, the Slave Trade, and Institutions and Practices Similar to Slavery; the 1948 American Declaration on the Rights and Duties of Man; the 1957 Abolition of Forced Labor Convention; the International Covenant on Civil and Political Rights; the Convention Against Torture and Other Cruel, Inhuman or Degrading Treatment or Punishment; United Nations General Assembly Resolutions 50/167, 51/66, and 52/98; the Final Report of the World Congress against Sexual Exploitation of Children (Stockholm, 1996); the Fourth World Conference on Women (Beijing, 1995); and the 1991 Moscow Document of the Organization for Security and Cooperation in Europe.

(24) Trafficking in persons is a transnational crime with national implications. To deter international trafficking and bring its perpetrators to justice, nations including the United States must recognize that trafficking is a serious offense. This is done by prescribing appropriate punishment, giving priority to the prosecution of trafficking offenses, and protecting rather than punishing the victims of such offenses. The United States must work bilaterally and multilaterally to abolish the trafficking industry by taking steps to promote cooperation among countries linked together by international trafficking routes. The United States must also urge the international community to take strong action in multilateral fora to engage recalcitrant countries in serious

and sustained efforts to eliminate trafficking and protect trafficking victims.

Sec. 103. Definitions

In this division:

(1) APPROPRIATE CONGRESSIONAL COMMITTEES—The term 'appropriate congressional committees' means the Committee on Foreign Relations and the Committee on the Judiciary of the Senate and the Committee on International Relations and the Committee on the Judiciary of the House of Representatives.

(2) COERCION—The term 'coercion' means—

   (A) threats of serious harm to or physical restraint against any person;

   (B) any scheme, plan, or pattern intended to cause a person to believe that failure to perform an act would result in serious harm to or physical restraint against any person; or

   (C) the abuse or threatened abuse of the legal process.

(3) COMMERCIAL SEX ACT—The term 'commercial sex act' means any sex act on account of which anything of value is given to or received by any person.

(4) DEBT BONDAGE—The term 'debt bondage' means the status or condition of a debtor arising from a pledge by the debtor of his or her personal services or of those of a person under his or her control as a security for debt, if the value of those services as reasonably assessed is not applied toward the liquidation of the debt or the length and nature of those services are not respectively limited and defined.

(5) INVOLUNTARY SERVITUDE—The term 'involuntary servitude' includes a condition of servitude induced by means of—

   (A) any scheme, plan, or pattern intended to cause a person to believe that, if the person did not enter into or continue in such condition, that person or another person would suffer serious harm or physical restraint; or

   (B) the abuse or threatened abuse of the legal process.

(6) MINIMUM STANDARDS FOR THE ELIMINATION OF TRAFFICKING—The term 'minimum standards for the elimination of trafficking' means the standards set forth in section 108.

(7) NONHUMANITARIAN, NONTRADE-RELATED FOREIGN ASSISTANCE—The term 'nonhumanitarian, nontrade-related foreign assistance' means—

   (A) any assistance under the Foreign Assistance Act of 1961, other than—

      (i) assistance under chapter 4 of part II of that Act that is made available for any program, project, or activity eligible for assistance under chapter 1 of part I of that Act;

      (ii) assistance under chapter 8 of part I of that Act;

      (iii) any other narcotics-related assistance under part I of that Act or under chapter 4 or 5 part II of that Act, but any such assistance provided under this clause shall be subject to the prior notification procedures applicable to reprogrammings pursuant to section 634A of that Act;

      (iv) disaster relief assistance, including any assistance under chapter 9 of part I of that Act;

      (v) antiterrorism assistance under chapter 8 of part II of that Act;

      (vi) assistance for refugees;

      (vii) humanitarian and other development assistance in support of programs of nongovernmental organizations under chapters 1 and 10 of that Act;

      (viii) programs under title IV of chapter 2 of part I of that Act, relating to the Overseas Private Investment Corporation; and

      (ix) other programs involving trade-related or humanitarian assistance; and

   (B) sales, or financing on any terms, under the Arms Export Control Act, other than sales or financing provided for narcotics-related purposes following notification in accordance with the prior notification procedures applicable to reprogrammings pursuant to section 634A of the Foreign Assistance Act of 1961.

(8) SEVERE FORMS OF TRAFFICKING IN PERSONS—The term 'severe forms of trafficking in persons' means—

   (A) sex trafficking in which a commercial sex act is induced by force, fraud, or coercion, or in which the person induced to perform such act has not attained 18 years of age; or

(B) the recruitment, harboring, transportation, provision, or obtaining of a person for labor or services, through the use of force, fraud, or coercion for the purpose of subjection to involuntary servitude, peonage, debt bondage, or slavery.

(9) SEX TRAFFICKING—The term 'sex trafficking' means the recruitment, harboring, transportation, provision, or obtaining of a person for the purpose of a commercial sex act.

(10) STATE—The term 'State' means each of the several States of the United States, the District of Columbia, the Commonwealth of Puerto Rico, the United States Virgin Islands, Guam, American Samoa, the Commonwealth of the Northern Mariana Islands, and territories and possessions of the United States.

(11) TASK FORCE—The term 'Task Force' means the Interagency Task Force to Monitor and Combat Trafficking established under section 105.

(12) UNITED STATES—The term 'United States' means the fifty States of the United States, the District of Columbia, the Commonwealth of Puerto Rico, the Virgin Islands, American Samoa, Guam, the Commonwealth of the Northern Mariana Islands, and the territories and possessions of the United States.

(13) VICTIM OF A SEVERE FORM OF TRAFFICKING—The term 'victim of a severe form of trafficking' means a person subject to an act or practice described in paragraph (8).

(14) VICTIM OF TRAFFICKING—The term 'victim of trafficking' means a person subjected to an act or practice described in paragraph (8) or (9).

[. . .]

Sec. 105. Interagency Task Force to Monitor and Combat Trafficking
(a) ESTABLISHMENT—The President shall establish an Interagency Task Force to Monitor and Combat Trafficking.

(b) APPOINTMENT—The President shall appoint the members of the Task Force, which shall include the Secretary of State, the Administrator of the United States Agency for International Development, the Attorney General, the Secretary of Labor, the Secretary of Health and Human Services, the Director of Central Intelligence, and such other officials as may be designated by the President.

(c) CHAIRMAN—The Task Force shall be chaired by the Secretary of State.

(d) ACTIVITIES OF THE TASK FORCE—The Task Force shall carry out the following activities:

(1) Coordinate the implementation of this division.

(2) Measure and evaluate progress of the United States and other countries in the areas of trafficking prevention, protection, and assistance to victims of trafficking, and prosecution and enforcement against traffickers, including the role of public corruption in facilitating trafficking. The Task Force shall have primary responsibility for assisting the Secretary of State in the preparation of the reports described in section 110.

(3) Expand interagency procedures to collect and organize data, including significant research and resource information on domestic and international trafficking. Any data collection procedures established under this subsection shall respect the confidentiality of victims of trafficking.

(4) Engage in efforts to facilitate cooperation among countries of origin, transit, and destination. Such efforts shall aim to strengthen local and regional capacities to prevent trafficking, prosecute traffickers and assist trafficking victims, and shall include initiatives to enhance cooperative efforts between destination countries and countries of origin and assist in the appropriate reintegration of stateless victims of trafficking.

(5) Examine the role of the international 'sex tourism' industry in the trafficking of persons and in the sexual exploitation of women and children around the world.

(6) Engage in consultation and advocacy with governmental and nongovernmental organizations, among other entities, to advance the purposes of this division.

(e) SUPPORT FOR THE TASK FORCE—The Secretary of State is authorized to establish within the Department of State an Office to Monitor and Combat Trafficking, which shall provide assistance to the Task Force. Any such Office shall be headed by a Director. The Director shall have the primary responsibility for assisting the Secretary of State in carrying out the purposes of this division and may have additional responsibilities as determined by the Secretary. The Director shall consult with nongovernmental organizations and multilateral organizations, and with trafficking victims or other affected persons. The Director shall have the authority to take evidence in public hearings or by other means. The agencies represented on the Task Force are authorized to provide staff to the Office on a nonreimbursable basis.

Sec. 106. Prevention of Trafficking
(a) ECONOMIC ALTERNATIVES TO PREVENT AND DETER TRAFFICKING—The President shall establish and carry out international initiatives to enhance economic opportunity for potential victims of trafficking as a method to deter trafficking. Such initiatives may include—

(1) microcredit lending programs, training in business development, skills training, and job counseling;

(2) programs to promote women's participation in economic decisionmaking;

(3) programs to keep children, especially girls, in elementary and secondary schools, and to educate persons who have been victims of trafficking;

(4) development of educational curricula regarding the dangers of trafficking; and

(5) grants to nongovernmental organizations to accelerate and advance the political, economic, social, and educational roles and capacities of women in their countries.

(b) PUBLIC AWARENESS AND INFORMATION—The President, acting through the Secretary of Labor, the Secretary of Health and Human Services, the Attorney General, and the Secretary of State, shall establish and carry out programs to increase public awareness, particularly among potential victims of trafficking, of the dangers of trafficking and the protections that are available for victims of trafficking.

(c) CONSULTATION REQUIREMENT—The President shall consult with appropriate nongovernmental organizations with respect to the establishment and conduct of initiatives described in subsections (a) and (b).

Sec. 107. Protection and Assistance for Victims of Trafficking
(a) Assistance for Victims in Other Countries—

(1) IN GENERAL—The Secretary of State and the Administrator of the United States Agency for International Development, in consultation with appropriate nongovernmental organizations, shall establish and carry out programs and initiatives in foreign countries to assist in the safe integration, reintegration, or resettlement, as appropriate, of victims of trafficking. Such programs and initiatives shall be designed to meet the appropriate assistance needs of such persons and their children, as identified by the Task Force.

(2) ADDITIONAL REQUIREMENT—In establishing and conducting programs and initiatives described in paragraph (1), the Secretary of State and the Administrator of the United States Agency for International Development shall take all appropriate steps to enhance cooperative efforts among foreign countries, including countries of origin of victims of trafficking, to assist in the integration, reintegration, or resettlement, as appropriate, of victims of trafficking, including stateless victims.

(b) Victims in the United States—
(1) ASSISTANCE—

(A) ELIGIBILITY FOR BENEFITS AND SERVICES—Notwithstanding title IV of the Personal Responsibility and Work Opportunity Reconciliation Act of 1996, an alien who is a victim of a severe form of trafficking in persons shall be eligible for benefits and services under any Federal or State program or activity funded or administered by any official or agency described in subparagraph (B) to the same extent as an alien who is admitted to the United States as a refugee under section 207 of the Immigration and Nationality Act.

(B) REQUIREMENT TO EXPAND BENEFITS AND SERVICES—Subject to subparagraph (C) and, in the case of nonentitlement programs, to the availability of appropriations, the Secretary of Health and Human Services, the Secretary of Labor, the Board of Directors of the Legal Services Corporation, and the heads of other Federal agencies shall expand benefits and services to victims of severe forms of trafficking in persons in the United States, without regard to the immigration status of such victims.

(C) DEFINITION OF VICTIM OF A SEVERE FORM OF TRAFFICKING IN PERSONS—For the purposes of this paragraph, the term 'victim of a severe form of trafficking in persons' means only a person—
   (i) who has been subjected to an act or practice described in section 103(8) as in effect on the date of the enactment of this Act; and
   (ii) (I) who has not attained 18 years of age; or (II) who is the subject of a certification under subparagraph (E).

(D) ANNUAL REPORT—Not later than December 31 of each year, the Secretary of Health and Human Services, in consultation with the Secretary of Labor, the Board of Directors of the Legal Services Corporation, and the heads of other appropriate Federal agencies shall submit a report, which includes information on the number of persons who received benefits or other services under this paragraph in connection with programs or activities funded or administered by such agencies or officials during the preceding fiscal year, to the Committee on Ways and Means, the Committee on International Relations, and the Committee on the Judiciary of the House of Representatives and the Committee on Finance, the Committee on Foreign Relations, and the Committee on the Judiciary of the Senate.

(E) CERTIFICATION—
   (i) IN GENERAL—Subject to clause (ii), the certification referred to in subparagraph (C) is a certification by the Secretary of Health and Human Services, after consultation with the Attorney General, that the person referred to in subparagraph (C)(ii)(II)—(I) is willing to assist in every reasonable way in the investigation and prosecution of severe forms of trafficking in persons; and (II)(aa) has made a bona fide application for a visa under section 101(a)(15)(T) of the Immigration and Nationality Act, as added by subsection (e), that has not been denied; or (bb) is a person whose continued presence in the United States the Attorney General is ensuring in order to effectuate prosecution of traffickers in persons.
   (ii) PERIOD OF EFFECTIVENESS—A certification referred to in subparagraph (C), with respect to a person described in clause (i)(II)(bb), shall be effective only for so long as the Attorney General determines that the continued presence of such person is necessary to effectuate prosecution of traffickers in persons.
   (iii) INVESTIGATION AND PROSECUTION DEFINED—For the purpose of a certification under this subparagraph, the term 'investigation and prosecution' includes—(I) identification of a person or persons who have committed severe forms of trafficking in persons; (II) location and apprehension of such persons; and (III) testimony at proceedings against such persons.

(2) GRANTS—
   (A) IN GENERAL—Subject to the availability of appropriations, the Attorney General may make grants to States, Indian tribes, units of local government, and nonprofit, nongovernmental victims' service organizations to develop, expand, or strengthen victim service programs for victims of trafficking.

(B) ALLOCATION OF GRANT FUNDS—Of amounts made available for grants under this paragraph, there shall be set aside—
  (i) three percent for research, evaluation, and statistics;
  (ii) two percent for training and technical assistance; and
  (iii) one percent for management and administration.

(C) LIMITATION ON FEDERAL SHARE—The Federal share of a grant made under this paragraph may not exceed 75 percent of the total costs of the projects described in the application submitted.

(c) TRAFFICKING VICTIM REGULATIONS—Not later than 180 days after the date of the enactment of this Act, the Attorney General and the Secretary of State shall promulgate regulations for law enforcement personnel, immigration officials, and Department of State officials to implement the following:

(1) PROTECTIONS WHILE IN CUSTODY—Victims of severe forms of trafficking, while in the custody of the Federal Government and to the extent practicable, shall—

(A) not be detained in facilities inappropriate to their status as crime victims;

(B) receive necessary medical care and other assistance; and

(C) be provided protection if a victim's safety is at risk or if there is danger of additional harm by recapture of the victim by a trafficker, including—
  (i) taking measures to protect trafficked persons and their family members from intimidation and threats of reprisals and reprisals from traffickers and their associates; and
  (ii) ensuring that the names and identifying information of trafficked persons and their family members are not disclosed to the public.

(2) ACCESS TO INFORMATION—Victims of severe forms of trafficking shall have access to information about their rights and translation services.

(3) AUTHORITY TO PERMIT CONTINUED PRESENCE IN THE UNITED STATES—Federal law enforcement officials may permit an alien individual's continued presence in the United States, if after an assessment, it is determined that such individual is a victim of a severe form of trafficking and a potential witness to such trafficking, in order to effectuate prosecution of those responsible, and such officials in investigating and prosecuting traffickers shall protect the safety of trafficking victims, including taking measures to protect trafficked persons and their family members from intimidation, threats of reprisals, and reprisals from traffickers and their associates.

(4) TRAINING OF GOVERNMENT PERSONNEL—Appropriate personnel of the Department of State and the Department of Justice shall be trained in identifying victims of severe forms of trafficking and providing for the protection of such victims.

(d) CONSTRUCTION—Nothing in subsection (c) shall be construed as creating any private cause of action against the United States or its officers or employees.

(e) PROTECTION FROM REMOVAL FOR CERTAIN CRIME VICTIMS—

(1) IN GENERAL—Section 101(a)(15) of the Immigration and Nationality Act (8 U.S.C. 1101(a)(15)) is amended—

(A) by striking 'or' at the end of subparagraph (R);

(B) by striking the period at the end of subparagraph (S) and inserting '; or'; and

(C) by adding at the end the following new subparagraph:
'(T)(i) subject to section 214(n), an alien who the Attorney General determines—'(I) is or has been a victim of a severe form of trafficking in persons, as defined in section 103 of the Trafficking Victims Protection Act of 2000, '(II) is physically present in the United States, American Samoa, or the Commonwealth of the Northern Mariana Islands, or at a port of entry thereto, on account of such trafficking, '(III)(aa) has complied with any reasonable

request for assistance in the investigation or prosecution of acts of trafficking, or '(bb) has not attained 15 years of age, and '(IV) the alien would suffer extreme hardship involving unusual and severe harm upon removal; and '(ii) if the Attorney General considers it necessary to avoid extreme hardship—'(I) in the case of an alien described in clause (i) who is under 21 years of age, the spouse, children, and parents of such alien; and '(II) in the case of an alien described in clause (i) who is 21 years of age or older, the spouse and children of such alien, if accompanying, or following to join, the alien described in clause (i)'.

(2) CONDITIONS OF NONIMMIGRANT STATUS—Section 214 of the Immigration and Nationality Act (8 U.S.C. 1184) is amended—

(A) by redesignating the subsection (l) added by section 625(a) of the Illegal Immigration Reform and Immigrant Responsibility Act of 1996 (Public Law 104–208; 110 Stat. 3009–1820) as subsection (m); and

(B) by adding at the end the following:
'(n)(1) No alien shall be eligible for admission to the United States under section 101(a)(15)(T) if there is substantial reason to believe that the alien has committed an act of a severe form of trafficking in persons (as defined in section 103 of the Trafficking Victims Protection Act of 2000).
'(2) The total number of aliens who may be issued visas or otherwise provided nonimmigrant status during any fiscal year under section 101(a)(15)(T) may not exceed 5,000.
'(3) The numerical limitation of paragraph (2) shall only apply to principal aliens and not to the spouses, sons, daughters, or parents of such aliens'.

(3) WAIVER OF GROUNDS FOR INELIGIBILITY FOR ADMISSION—Section 212(d) of the Immigration and Nationality Act (8 U.S.C. 1182(d)) is amended by adding at the end the following:
'(13)(A) The Attorney General shall determine whether a ground for inadmissibility exists with respect to a nonimmigrant described in section 101(a)(15)(T).
'(B) In addition to any other waiver that may be available under this section, in the case of a nonimmigrant described in section 101(a)(15)(T), if the Attorney

General considers it to be in the national interest to do so, the Attorney General, in the Attorney General's discretion, may waive the application of—'(i) paragraphs (1) and (4) of subsection (a); and '(ii) any other provision of such subsection (excluding paragraphs (3), (10)(C), and (10)(E)) if the activities rendering the alien inadmissible under the provision were caused by, or were incident to, the victimization described in section 101(a)(15)(T)(i)(I)'.

(4) DUTIES OF THE ATTORNEY GENERAL WITH RESPECT TO 'T' VISA NONIMMIGRANTS—Section 101 of the Immigration and Nationality Act (8 U.S.C. 1101) is amended by adding at the end the following new subsection:
'(i) With respect to each nonimmigrant alien described in subsection (a)(15)(T)(i)—
'(1) the Attorney General and other Government officials, where appropriate, shall provide the alien with a referral to a nongovernmental organization that would advise the alien regarding the alien's options while in the United States and the resources available to the alien; and
'(2) the Attorney General shall, during the period the alien is in lawful temporary resident status under that subsection, grant the alien authorization to engage in employment in the United States and provide the alien with an 'employment authorized' endorsement or other appropriate work permit'.

(5) STATUTORY CONSTRUCTION—Nothing in this section, or in the amendments made by this section, shall be construed as prohibiting the Attorney General from instituting removal proceedings under section 240 of the Immigration and Nationality Act (8 U.S.C. 1229a) against an alien admitted as a nonimmigrant under section 101(a)(15)(T)(i) of that Act, as added by subsection (e), for conduct committed after the alien's admission into the United States, or for conduct or a condition that was not disclosed to the Attorney General prior to the alien's admission as a nonimmigrant under such section 101(a)(15)(T)(i).

(f) ADJUSTMENT TO PERMANENT RESIDENT STATUS—Section 245 of such Act (8 U.S.C 1255) is amended by adding at the end the following new subsection:

'(l)(1) If, in the opinion of the Attorney General, a nonimmigrant admitted into the United States under section 101(a)(15)(T)(i)—

'(A) has been physically present in the United States for a continuous period of at least 3 years since the date of admission as a nonimmigrant under section 101(a)(15)(T)(i),

'(B) has, throughout such period, been a person of good moral character, and

'(C)(i) has, during such period, complied with any reasonable request for assistance in the investigation or prosecution of acts of trafficking, or

'(ii) the alien would suffer extreme hardship involving unusual and severe harm upon removal from the United States, the Attorney General may adjust the status of the alien (and any person admitted under that section as the spouse, parent, or child of the alien) to that of an alien lawfully admitted for permanent residence.

'(2) Paragraph (1) shall not apply to an alien admitted under section 101(a)(15)(T) who is inadmissible to the United States by reason of a ground that has not been waived under section 212, except that, if the Attorney General considers it to be in the national interest to do so, the Attorney General, in the Attorney General's discretion, may waive the application of—

'(A) paragraphs (1) and (4) of section 212(a); and

'(B) any other provision of such section (excluding paragraphs (3), (10)(C), and (10(E)), if the activities rendering the alien inadmissible under the provision were caused by, or were incident to, the victimization described in section 101(a)(15)(T)(i)(I).

'(2) An alien shall be considered to have failed to maintain continuous physical presence in the United States under paragraph (1)(A) if the alien has departed from the United States for any period in excess of 90 days or for any periods in the aggregate exceeding 180 days.

'(3)(A) The total number of aliens whose status may be adjusted under paragraph (1) during any fiscal year may not exceed 5,000.

'(B) The numerical limitation of subparagraph (A) shall only apply to principal aliens and not to the spouses, sons, daughters, or parents of such aliens.

'(4) Upon the approval of adjustment of status under paragraph (1), the Attorney General shall record the alien's lawful admission for permanent residence as of the date of such approval'.

(g) ANNUAL REPORTS—On or before October 31 of each year, the Attorney General shall submit a report to the appropriate congressional committees setting forth, with respect to the preceding fiscal year, the number, if any, of otherwise eligible applicants who did not receive visas under section 101(a)(15)(T) of the Immigration and Nationality Act, as added by subsection (e), or who were unable to adjust their status under section 245(l) of such Act, solely on account of the unavailability of visas due to a limitation imposed by section 214(n)(1) or 245(l)(4)(A) of such Act.

Sec. 108. Minimum Standards for the Elimination of Trafficking

(a) MINIMUM STANDARDS—For purposes of this division, the minimum standards for the elimination of trafficking applicable to the government of a country of origin, transit, or destination for a significant number of victims of severe forms of trafficking are the following:

(1) The government of the country should prohibit severe forms of trafficking in persons and punish acts of such trafficking.

(2) For the knowing commission of any act of sex trafficking involving force, fraud, coercion, or in which the victim of sex trafficking is a child incapable of giving meaningful consent, or of trafficking which includes rape or kidnapping or which causes a death, the government of the country should prescribe punishment commensurate with

that for grave crimes, such as forcible sexual assault.

(3) For the knowing commission of any act of a severe form of trafficking in persons, the government of the country should prescribe punishment that is sufficiently stringent to deter and that adequately reflects the heinous nature of the offense.

(4) The government of the country should make serious and sustained efforts to eliminate severe forms of trafficking in persons.

(b) CRITERIA—In determinations under subsection (a)(4), the following factors should be considered as indicia of serious and sustained efforts to eliminate severe forms of trafficking in persons:

(1) Whether the government of the country vigorously investigates and prosecutes acts of severe forms of trafficking in persons that take place wholly or partly within the territory of the country.

(2) Whether the government of the country protects victims of severe forms of trafficking in persons and encourages their assistance in the investigation and prosecution of such trafficking, including provisions for legal alternatives to their removal to countries in which they would face retribution or hardship, and ensures that victims are not inappropriately incarcerated, fined, or otherwise penalized solely for unlawful acts as a direct result of being trafficked.

(3) Whether the government of the country has adopted measures to prevent severe forms of trafficking in persons, such as measures to inform and educate the public, including potential victims, about the causes and consequences of severe forms of trafficking in persons.

(4) Whether the government of the country cooperates with other governments in the investigation and prosecution of severe forms of trafficking in persons.

(5) Whether the government of the country extradites persons charged with acts of severe forms of trafficking in persons on substantially the same terms and to substantially the same extent as persons charged with other serious crimes (or, to the extent such extradition would be inconsistent with the laws of such country or with international agreements to which the country is a party, whether the government is taking all appropriate measures to modify or replace such laws and treaties so as to permit such extradition).

(6) Whether the government of the country monitors immigration and emigration patterns for evidence of severe forms of trafficking in persons and whether law enforcement agencies of the country respond to any such evidence in a manner that is consistent with the vigorous investigation and prosecution of acts of such trafficking, as well as with the protection of human rights of victims and the internationally recognized human right to leave any country, including one's own, and to return to one's own country.

(7) Whether the government of the country vigorously investigates and prosecutes public officials who participate in or facilitate severe forms of trafficking in persons, and takes all appropriate measures against officials who condone such trafficking.

[. . .]

Sec. 111. Actions against Significant Traffickers in Persons
(a) AUTHORITY TO SANCTION SIGNIFICANT TRAFFICKERS IN PERSONS—

(1) IN GENERAL—The President may exercise the authorities set forth in section 203 of the International Emergency Economic Powers Act (50 U.S.C. 1701) without regard to section 202 of that Act (50 U.S.C. 1701) in the case of any of the following persons:

(A) Any foreign person that plays a significant role in a severe form of trafficking in persons, directly or indirectly in the United States.

(B) Foreign persons that materially assist in, or provide financial or technological support for or to, or provide goods or services in support of, activities of a significant foreign trafficker in persons identified pursuant to subparagraph (A).

(C) Foreign persons that are owned, controlled, or directed by, or acting for or on behalf of, a significant foreign trafficker identified pursuant to subparagraph (A).

(2) PENALTIES—The penalties set forth in section 206 of the International Emergency Economic Powers Act (50 U.S.C. 1705) apply to violations of any license, order, or regulation issued under this section.

(b) REPORT TO CONGRESS ON IDENTIFICATION AND SANCTIONING OF SIGNIFICANT TRAFFICKERS IN PERSONS—

(1) IN GENERAL—Upon exercising the authority of subsection (a), the President shall report to the appropriate congressional committees—

(A) identifying publicly the foreign persons that the President determines are appropriate for sanctions pursuant to this section and the basis for such determination; and

(B) detailing publicly the sanctions imposed pursuant to this section.

(2) REMOVAL OF SANCTIONS—Upon suspending or terminating any action imposed under the authority of subsection (a), the President shall report to the committees described in paragraph (1) on such suspension or termination.

(3) SUBMISSION OF CLASSIFIED INFORMATION—Reports submitted under this subsection may include an annex with classified information regarding the basis for the determination made by the President under paragraph (1)(A).

(c) LAW ENFORCEMENT AND INTELLIGENCE ACTIVITIES NOT AFFECTED—Nothing in this section prohibits or otherwise limits the authorized law enforcement or intelligence activities of the United States, or the law enforcement activities of any State or subdivision thereof.

(d) EXCLUSION OF PERSONS WHO HAVE BENEFITED FROM ILLICIT ACTIVITIES OF

TRAFFICKERS IN PERSONS—Section 212(a)(2) of the Immigration and Nationality Act (8 U.S.C. 1182(a)(2)) is amended by inserting at the end the following new subparagraph:

'(H) SIGNIFICANT TRAFFICKERS IN PERSONS—

'(i) IN GENERAL—Any alien who is listed in a report submitted pursuant to section 111(b) of the Trafficking Victims Protection Act of 2000, or who the consular officer or the Attorney General knows or has reason to believe is or has been a knowing aider, abettor, assister, conspirator, or colluder with such a trafficker in severe forms of trafficking in persons, as defined in the section 103 of such Act, is inadmissible.

'(ii) BENEFICIARIES OF TRAFFICKING—Except as provided in clause (iii), any alien who the consular officer or the Attorney General knows or has reason to believe is the spouse, son, or daughter of an alien inadmissible under clause (i), has, within the previous 5 years, obtained any financial or other benefit from the illicit activity of that alien, and knew or reasonably should have known that the financial or other benefit was the product of such illicit activity, is inadmissible.

'(iii) EXCEPTION FOR CERTAIN SONS AND DAUGHTERS—Clause (ii) shall not apply to a son or daughter who was a child at the time he or she received the benefit described in such clause'.

(e) IMPLEMENTATION—

(1) DELEGATION OF AUTHORITY—The President may delegate any authority granted by this section, including the authority to designate foreign persons under paragraphs (1)(B) and (1)(C) of subsection (a).

(2) PROMULGATION OF RULES AND REGULATIONS—The head of any agency, including the Secretary of Treasury, is authorized to take such actions as may be necessary to carry out any authority delegated by the President pursuant to

paragraph (1), including promulgating rules and regulations.

(3) OPPORTUNITY FOR REVIEW—Such rules and regulations shall include procedures affording an opportunity for a person to be heard in an expeditious manner, either in person or through a representative, for the purpose of seeking changes to or termination of any determination, order, designation or other action associated with the exercise of the authority in subsection (a).

(f) DEFINITION OF FOREIGN PERSONS—In this section, the term 'foreign person' means any citizen or national of a foreign state or any entity not organized under the laws of the United States, including a foreign government official, but does not include a foreign state.

(g) CONSTRUCTION—Nothing in this section shall be construed as precluding judicial review of the exercise of the authority described in subsection (a).

Sec. 112. Strengthening Prosecution and Punishment of Traffickers
(a) TITLE 18 AMENDMENTS—Chapter 77 of title 18, United States Code, is amended—

(1) in each of sections 1581(a), 1583, and 1584—
   (A) by striking '10 years' and inserting '20 years'; and
   (B) by adding at the end the following: 'If death results from the violation of this section, or if the violation includes kidnapping or an attempt to kidnap, aggravated sexual abuse or the attempt to commit aggravated sexual abuse, or an attempt to kill, the defendant shall be fined under this title or imprisoned for any term of years or life, or both.'; (2) by inserting at the end the following: 'Sec. 1589. Forced labor

'Whoever knowingly provides or obtains the labor or services of a person—

'(1) by threats of serious harm to, or physical restraint against, that person or another person;

'(2) by means of any scheme, plan, or pattern intended to cause the person to believe that, if the person did not perform such labor or services, that person or another person would suffer serious harm or physical restraint; or

'(3) by means of the abuse or threatened abuse of law or the legal process, shall be fined under this title or imprisoned not more than 20 years, or both. If death results from the violation of this section, or if the violation includes kidnapping or an attempt to kidnap, aggravated sexual abuse or the attempt to commit aggravated sexual abuse, or an attempt to kill, the defendant shall be fined under this title or imprisoned for any term of years or life, or both.

'Sec. 1590. Trafficking with respect to peonage, slavery, involuntary servitude, or forced labor

'Whoever knowingly recruits, harbors, transports, provides, or obtains by any means, any person for labor or services in violation of this chapter shall be fined under this title or imprisoned not more than 20 years, or both. If death results from the violation of this section, or if the violation includes kidnapping or an attempt to kidnap, aggravated sexual abuse, or the attempt to commit aggravated sexual abuse, or an attempt to kill, the defendant shall be fined under this title or imprisoned for any term of years or life, or both.

'Sec. 1591. Sex trafficking of children or by force, fraud or coercion

'(a) Whoever knowingly—
   '(1) in or affecting interstate commerce, recruits, entices, harbors, transports, provides, or obtains by any means a person; or
   '(2) benefits, financially or by receiving anything of value, from participation in a venture which has engaged in an act described in violation of paragraph (1), knowing that force, fraud, or coercion

described in subsection (c)(2) will be used to cause the person to engage in a commercial sex act, or that the person has not attained the age of 18 years and will be caused to engage in a commercial sex act, shall be punished as provided in subsection (b).

'(b) The punishment for an offense under subsection (a) is—

'(1) if the offense was effected by force, fraud, or coercion or if the person transported had not attained the age of 14 years at the time of such offense, by a fine under this title or imprisonment for any term of years or for life, or both; or

'(2) if the offense was not so effected, and the person transported had attained the age of 14 years but had not attained the age of 18 years at the time of such offense, by a fine under this title or imprisonment for not more than 20 years, or both.

'(c) In this section:

'(1) The term 'commercial sex act' means any sex act, on account of which anything of value is given to or received by any person.

'(2) The term 'coercion' means—

'(A) threats of serious harm to or physical restraint against any person;

'(B) any scheme, plan, or pattern intended to cause a person to believe that failure to perform an act would result in serious harm to or physical restraint against any person; or

'(C) the abuse or threatened abuse of law or the legal process.

'(3) The term 'venture' means any group of two or more individuals associated in fact, whether or not a legal entity.

Index

Page ranges for main entries appear in boldface type.